The Praeger Handbook
of
Urban Education

THE PRAEGER HANDBOOK OF URBAN EDUCATION

Volume 2

Edited by Joe L. Kincheloe, kecia hayes,
Karel Rose, and Philip M. Anderson

GREENWOOD PRESS
Westport, Connecticut • London

Library of Congress Cataloging-in-Publication Data

The Praeger handbook of urban education / edited by Joe L. Kincheloe
. . . [et al.].
   p.   cm.
   Includes bibliographical references and index.
   ISBN 0–313–33324–6 (set : alk. paper) — ISBN 0–313–33511–7
(v. 1 : alk. paper) — ISBN 0–313–33512–5 (v. 2 : alk. paper)
   1. Education, Urban—United States—Handbooks, manuals, etc.
I. Kincheloe, Joe L. II. Title: Urban education.
LC5131.P7   2006
370.9173'2—dc22   2005031624

British Library Cataloguing in Publication Data is available.

Library of Congress Catalog Card Number: 2005031624
ISBN: 0–313–33324–6 (set)
      0–313–33511–7 (vol. 1)
      0–313–33512–5 (vol. 2)

First published in 2006

Greenwood Press, 88 Post Road West, Westport, CT 06881
An imprint of Greenwood Publishing Group, Inc.
www.greenwood.com

Printed in the United States of America

The paper used in this book complies with the
Permanent Paper Standard issued by the National
Information Standards Organization (Z39.48–1984).

10 9 8 7 6 5 4 3 2 1

Contents

Power and Urban Education

GLOBAL CAPITALISM AND URBAN EDUCATION

David Baronov

With the exception of the few remaining foreign-controlled lands such as Iraq and Puerto Rico, virtually all public education programs around the world are shaped by decisions taken at the national, state, and local levels. The role of global capitalism in shaping urban education is, therefore, perhaps not immediately evident. Indeed, global capitalism alone provides us with a far from complete understanding of urban education in the United States today. At best, it describes a set of compelling circumstances to which national, state, and local decision makers must respond. Ultimately, the state of urban education is the product of an ongoing political process in which various stakeholders consult, petition, and/or protest before the appropriate public officials. As such, it is largely the case that local decisions and activism continue to shape urban education. At the same time, the forces of global capitalism establish important limitations regarding the options available to those who set urban education policy in the United States.

THE NATURE OF CONTEMPORARY GLOBAL CAPITALISM

"Globalization" has emerged as the watchword of the new millennium. There is a common belief that we are today experiencing greater movement across the globe (by people, ideas, diseases, etc.) and greater articulation between far-flung social and economic processes (Chinese prison labor and Wal-Mart shoppers in Fargo, North Dakota). This points, internationally, to a growing economic interdependence. Globalization represents the most visible face of global capitalism. Its ideological and material forms advance the interests of global capitalism and, therefore, the term globalization can provide a useful shorthand when discussing the contemporary period of global capitalism. Two major developments have set the pace for this current era of globalization.

On the one hand, with the end of Cold War, the United States rose to a position of unchallenged global prominence, achieving hegemonic influence in the financial, industrial, and military realms. This permits the establishment of neoliberal policies and institutions that promote global trade and investment, such as the World Trade Organization, and allows U.S. officials to undermine those initiatives deemed counter to their interests, such as the Kyoto Agreement on global warming. On the other hand, the current era of globalization is associated with a series of advances in technology, communication, and transportation that have dramatically reduced the costs of locating production overseas and facilitated international financial transactions. This constitutes the technical and material infrastructure that undergirds a web of interlocking networks, which integrate disparate social and economic activities from around the world.

Thus, at the most general level, globalization refers to a set of policy decisions referred to as neoliberalism and a set of economic and material forces, such as technological innovation. In combination, these neoliberal policies and economic and material forces have unleashed an extraordinary transformation of people's lives around the world. Given the range of popular interpretations, it is helpful to try to capture some key features of globalization that mark it as a historically unique, contemporary phenomenon. The current era of globalization is characterized by five developments within global capitalism:

- Greater global trade
- Greater foreign direct investment by multinational corporations
- Greater economic regionalism
- Greater integration of international finance
- Greater role of "services" within global trade

Greater Global Trade

Beginning in the 1970s, there have been dramatic increases in global trade. The Japanese electronics industry and French automakers sought to enter U.S. markets, for instance, while U.S. farmers moved to expand agricultural exports. Most trade agreements at this time involved bilateral arrangements between individual nations or small groups of nations. The groundwork was being prepared, however, for the larger trade pacts of the 1990s. Global agreements (the World Trade Organization) and regional agreements (NAFTA, MERCOSUR) created international net-

works of global trade that have exponentially expanded the movement of goods and services around the world.[1]

The result of greater global trade has been multifaceted. On the one hand, the world has witnessed increasing economic interdependence between nations and between regions. Today, the industrial policies of one nation can have far-reaching consequences for other nations next door or halfway around the world. At the same time, this expanded contact between wealthy and poor nations has led to an increasing influence of Western culture in non-Western societies. Movies, music, and fast food are major exports from wealthy nations to poor.[2] A sense of despair and resentment by many has resulted—with the attacks on the Pentagon and the World Trade Center representing the most extreme manifestations. Lastly, increased global migration has followed from greater global trade. Along with the movement of goods and services, people have been on the move. This mass movement of humanity has primarily flowed from poor nations to wealthy nations in search of jobs and opportunities.[3]

Greater Foreign Direct Investment by Multinational Corporations

By the mid-1980s, the phenomenon of foreign direct investment was reaching new heights. Multinational corporations sought to move offshore and set up production and distribution plants across the globe. Today, multinational corporations—such as IBM, Nestlé, and Renault—have moved production facilities to low-wage nations in an effort to produce goods more cheaply. China, for example, has been a major winner in this move by corporations to directly invest in poorer nations for the production of goods (and increasingly services) that will primarily be sold to consumers in wealthy nations. The workforce in wealthy countries can scarcely compete with the cost of Chinese prison labor.

Greater foreign investment has resulted in dwindling employment prospects and decreasing unionization in the wealthy nations alongside deteriorating environmental conditions and labor rights in poor nations. The deindustrialization of the traditional heartland of manufacturing in many wealthy nations over the past decades has been accompanied by a patchwork of production plants (export production zones) in poor nations.[4] The movement of industrial jobs from the northeast region of the United States to cheap assembly plants along the Mexican/U.S. border is an example. This signals the so-called "race to the bottom" in which poor nations compete with one another to provide favorable investment conditions, such as low pay, antiunion policies, and lax environmental standards.[5]

Greater Economic Regionalism

In light of global trade agreements, a greater economic regionalism has emerged. The Cold War inspired a number of strategic regional pacts that coordinated military assets and defense policies between nations. The new regional pacts emphasize economic cooperation. These regional agreements promote eliminating trade barriers (by lowering tariffs), stabilizing currency exchanges, and regulating the movement of people between nations.[6] Examples of such regional pacts are the European Community and NAFTA. These agreements are designed to bind nations as regional partners in a strategic alliance that purportedly strengthens each nation's bargaining power in the global economy more effectively than an individual nation could muster on its own. For example, the United States continues to nervously eye the European Community as it strengthens its alliance and builds its leverage vis-à-vis the United States.

The result of greater economic regionalism has been to place greater emphasis on a nation's geopolitical location on the world map as a factor in its development.

As a consequence, an unfortunate location can greatly impede a nation's participation in the global economy—as is the case for many African and Latin American nations. Regionalism also tends to pressure those nations with progressive environmental or labor laws to come into conformity with others in the geographic alliance.[7] It is argued by many, as a consequence, that state actors have less and less influence in setting national policy.[8] This is why many who oppose aspects of globalization focus their protest on regional and global meetings (such as meetings of the European Union or the World Economic Forum), replacing past strategies that targeted national capitols.

Greater Integration of International Finance

International finance is a complex and highly profitable arena for wealthy global investors. The major activities associated with international finance are foreign exchange trading and foreign investment. Foreign exchange trading involves the buying and selling of national currencies. This is a highly speculative venture in which investors attempt to anticipate fluctuations in the value of different nations' currencies. Foreign investment involves the effort of wealthy individuals and companies to find profitable investment opportunities around the world. Advances in communication technology have greatly facilitated the rapid movement of such investments, allowing instantaneous shifts of enormous sums, at times, with highly damaging effect.[9] Driving this rapid growth within international finance are trade agreements that deregulate national financial markets alongside the expansion of assets held in mutual funds and pension funds in the 1990s (especially in the U.S.) in search of greater profit.

A result of the greater integration of international finance has been to radically accelerate the movement of investors' money around the world. Consequently, the impact of these investments, as seen in the 1997 Asian Crisis, has been significantly enhanced.[10] Given the degree of financial speculation in international currencies and other high-risk investment instruments, financial markets have grown increasingly volatile and are marked by considerable instability. Investors' interests in short-term profit do not coincide with a company's interest in building long-term value. As a result, investor speculative activity rather than publicly debated priorities or national industrial policies, tend to shape economic development patterns.[11] The power of the financial marketplace over democratic institutions is a very real concern.

Greater Role of "Services" within Global Trade

One of the most important developments within the global economy over the past decade has been the increasing role of services as a commodity in global trade. The category of services represents a wide-ranging set of activities that support economic transactions and productive activities. This includes everything from the work of a bank vice president to that of a filing clerk. Traditionally, activities tied to services have been the most difficult tasks to move overseas. Given modern communication and computer technologies, many routine service tasks, such as data entry, medical billing, customer services via telephone, and computer programming, have been increasingly relocated to low-wage nations.[12] Typically, the only service jobs remaining in wealthy nations are those requiring direct contact with the customer—such as retail sales, restaurant work, or auto repair. These jobs typically do not pay well.

The result of this greater role of services within global trade has been a major shift of routine service activities from high-wage wealthy nations to low-wage poor nations. Just as those workers from wealthy nations who lost jobs due to deindustrialization were being retrained for service industry jobs, those jobs have been increasingly outsourced to poor nations. The service jobs that remain in the wealthy nations are generally in high-paying occupations (lawyers, professors, financial consultants) or low-paying occupations (hospital orderlies, K–12 educators, fast-food workers), with a dwindling middle stratum.[13] The service jobs that go to poor nations carry the same threat as manufacturing jobs of further relocation if the host nation does not maintain conditions that are favorable to investors. As with foreign direct investment, the greater role of services within global trade primarily provides flexibility for investors to increase their profits by chasing after the cheapest labor force available within the global economy, pitting one poor nation against another.

URBAN REALITIES IN THE ERA OF GLOBALIZATION

Over the past thirty years, these forces of globalization have radically reshaped the entire socioeconomic topography of the United States. In this period, the gap between the wealthy and the poor has widened. Ethnic/racial segregation has increased and tens of thousands of manufacturing jobs have left the United States, while the remaining living-wage jobs have migrated from cities to the suburbs. Today, growing populations of disenfranchised and impoverished ethnic/racial minorities find themselves concentrated in large urban areas. The impact of these trends on cities in the United States has been profound and points to major challenges regarding policy options for those striving to improve urban education. Of particular concern are three developments stemming from globalization with direct consequences for urban education policy:

- Global migration from rural to urban areas and from poor to wealthy nations
- Transformation of the U.S. economy (alongside deindustrialization)
- Social and economic polarization within the United States.

Global Migration from Rural to Urban Areas and from Poor to Wealthy Nations

The processes of globalization have contributed to two major migration patterns. First, there has been a massive movement of people from rural to urban areas. As a result, growing rings of poverty and despair have surrounded major cities of the world, such as São Paulo, Bombay, and Johannesburg.[14] Today, great masses of displaced agricultural communities have taken refuge in urban centers teeming with shantytowns. Second, the movement of people from poor to wealthy nations has continued at a strong pace.[15] The dream of a better life remains a potent motivator among the world's poor. As a result, those who can, migrate from poor to wealthy nations. Invariably, the world's poor must take the lowest paying and least desirable jobs when they arrive. This entails either seasonal agricultural work, which tends to keep workers constantly on the move or, more typically, low-wage jobs in the urban-based service industry.

Given this pattern, most immigrants in the United States tend to disproportionately settle in urban areas and, consequently, urban school systems are increasingly asked to assist students both with their academic needs as well as their cultural adjustment to U.S. society. In addition, given the proximity of the United States to Latin America and due to changes in U.S. immigration policy in 1965, Latino/-a and Asian immigrants are especially prominent among these newcomers. While contributing to an exciting and vibrant multicultural learning environment, additional resources and time are required to meet bilingual needs and to facilitate adjustment.

Beyond differences tied to ethnicity and language, however, a large number of urban immigrant families represent displaced agrarian families. Thus, many students' families operate within the cultural norms of a rural household. Often the parents have little or no formal education and there is little in their backgrounds to orient either the students or their parents regarding the expectations and norms of the U.S. educational system—such as study habits or peer interaction. Compounding these cultural issues, many of these students reside in areas of significant poverty, which often requires both parents to work double shifts.

Transformation of the U.S. Economy

One of the central roles for any K–12 educational system is to prepare students to be responsible citizens and productive members of society. This entails, in part, developing a skilled workforce for the national economy.[16] However, given the pace of U.S. deindustrialization over the past few decades, and the accompanying occupational shifts, it is no longer clear what skills to emphasize or even what social role education plays in contemporary society. For example, preparing a workforce for the future was much easier during an era of onerous yet steady manufacturing jobs when employers' fortunes were tied to local community development. In light of the expanded role of low-wage, unstable jobs in the U.S. economy, it is difficult to tell students that working hard in school will reliably result in a set of employable skills and abilities.[17] The reality is that, as part of a global workforce, a student's future is one of uncertainty and change.

The urban/suburban divide is further exacerbated by these developments. The movement of wealthy whites from urban areas to the outer suburbs over the past few decades has accelerated the movement of jobs and resources away from the urban poor. Both the loss of urban manufacturing jobs along with the growth of exclusive, wealthy suburbs have hurt urban educational systems by shrinking the tax base and by moving living-wage jobs to the suburbs. As a result, the poorest of the poor remain concentrated in large urban school districts that feature a stark socioeconomic homogeneity and depleted and fragmented communities.[18]

This picture is further complicated by government policies designed to deter poor youth from illicit behavior in an era of great uncertainty and dismal job prospects. In 2002, the number of African Americans in prison exceeded 800,000. A labyrinth of anticrime measures targeting the urban poor—including curfews, three-strikes legislation, zero-tolerance drug laws, and anti-gang units with sweeping powers—are in force in urban areas across the country.[19] Urban educators must work with students whose daily lives involve interaction with punitive police tactics in their neighborhoods. The disruptive and dispiriting impact of these policies on students (and their families and friends) is a further obstacle for urban educators to overcome.

Social and Economic Polarization within the United States

The reason that urban education has fallen as a public priority is largely tied to the enormous gap between the wealthy and the poor in the United States. By the late 1990s, the poorest twenty percent of U.S. families had an average income of $14,620, while the wealthiest twenty percent of families had an average income ten times this amount, $145,990.[20] Today, the interests of the wealthy in the United States are tied more closely to the interests of the wealthy classes in other nations than to the interests of the poor in their own nation. Global trade and finance link their fortunes. One result of this wealth gap has been the concentration of the poor in large urban school districts. Thus, if the interests of the wealthy and the poor in

the United States do not coincide, it is not clear why, beyond philanthropy, the wealthy would have any concern for improving impoverished urban schools. Increasingly, the world of the wealthy and the world of the poor are separate and decidedly unequal.[21]

Along with the increasing gap between the wealthy and poor there has been an increasing segregation of U.S. ethnic/racial minorities. Ethnic/racial segregation in the United States today is of historic proportions.[22] Meanwhile, ethnic/racial minorities represent a majority (or plurality) of students in large urban educational systems across the country. The resource disparity between urban and suburban schools reflects this pattern. The predominantly white professional class has migrated to the suburbs, and a predictable shift of political power from urban machine politics to suburban soccer moms has accompanied them.[23] So long as their situation can be successfully sectioned off and kept from view, it is doubtful that non-minorities in the United States will act to improve urban schools.

URBAN EDUCATION IN THE CONTEXT OF GLOBAL CAPITALISM

It is impossible to provide any intelligible analysis of urban education absent an understanding of the profound social transformation across urban communities in light of global capitalism over the past three decades. The primary challenges presented by global capitalism for urban education today are:

- Increasing concentrations of poverty
- Hypersegregation of ethnic/racial minorities
- Disinvestment in urban areas and dwindling economic opportunities
- Repressive anticrime tactics directed at urban youth
- Concentration of political and economic power in the suburbs
- Educational aspirations of Asian and Latino/-a immigrant students with diverse cultural roots

The impact of globalization notwithstanding, an erroneous general consensus predominates among official U.S. policy makers that the major problems of urban education can be traced to any number of microlevel conditions—for instance, broken families, sexual promiscuity among teens, the drug epidemic, and teen violence. As a result, most urban education reforms downplay the influence of globalization and emphasize policies that address superficial, surface-level conditions. Ironically, these policies tend to be consistent with the same neoliberal, market-based solutions that provide the ideological underpinnings for globalization.

Pedro Noguera has written eloquently about this persistent gap between the chronic socioeconomic conditions confronting urban public schools and the inappropriate and inadequate policy responses.

Urban public schools frequently serve as important social welfare institutions. With meager resources, they attempt to address at least some of the nutritional and health needs of poor children. They do so because those charged with educating poor children generally recognize that it is impossible to serve their academic needs without simultaneously addressing their basic need for health and safety. For this reason, those who castigate and disparage urban public schools without offering viable solutions for improving or replacing them jeopardize the interests of those who depend on them ... Most of the popular educational reforms enacted by states and federal government (e.g., standards and accountability through high-stakes testing, charter schools, etc.) fail to address the severe social and economic conditions in urban areas that invariably affect the quality and character of public schools.[24]

Neoliberal Reforms

In the context of the current era of globalization, neoliberal policies represent efforts by governments to create a uniform global system for economic investment. Differences between nations' laws and policies are reduced. This has resulted in deregulating financial institutions, lowering tax rates, minimizing environmental standards, and eliminating labor laws. These neoliberal policies have their counterpart in policies designed to transform urban education. In fact, proponents of neoliberal education reforms argue that precisely because today we must compete in a competitive global environment, it is imperative, from the perspective of quality control, that we develop schools that produce students with a common and predictable set of skills and abilities. To gauge progress in this regard, it is vital that student learning be measurable. This requires standardized testing. It is further suggested that student learning outcomes can be made more consistent and uniform by developing homogeneous teaching practices and by demanding specific teacher certification requirements. Neoliberal ideologues advocate education reform in three areas.

- Standardized testing and curricula
- Teacher certification
- Focus on the three R's over extracurricular activities

Today, the movement for standardized student testing and standardized curricula is in full swing. The George W. Bush Administration's No Child Left Behind program is just one manifestation of this larger phenomenon.[25] The stated purpose of standardized testing is to create a measurable set of uniform criteria by which to compare students and schools, with the ultimate goal of minimizing differences in achievement.[26] A further benefit is greater control over each school's measures of success and its curricula. Today, testing students' retention and recitation of facts gleaned from rudimentary lesson plans is the primary measure of success. Alternative learning outcomes, such as creative problem solving, are less easily captured through standardized tests. Additionally, given the importance of these test scores for determining school rankings, whoever controls these tests controls the curricula to prepare for the test. The result is greater uniformity and standardization of the curricula. This goal of standardized learning outcomes is consistent with the aim of greater standardization and uniformity promoted by the stewards of global capitalism.

The current emphasis on teacher certification is a further example of a neoliberal policy advancing standardization through quality control measures. Teacher certification is held out as a method for guaranteeing minimal standards for teachers entering the classroom. The assumption is that the decline in urban school performance is tied, to a significant degree, to teacher incompetence. Certainly it is far simpler to rectify alleged teacher shortcomings than to directly address the rapidly deteriorating socioeconomic conditions that confront urban education today. The emphasis on teacher certification provides an opportunity to downplay the social environment as a factor explaining poorly performing schools as well as a venue for ensuring greater uniformity across the teaching pool.[27] This uniformity concerns both the knowledge of one's subject matter as well as teachers' values and attitudes. Fostering narrowly construed values and attitudes about the challenges of education facilitates efforts to downplay the role of globalization as a consideration within the learning process.

Alongside standardized testing and curricula and teacher certification, has been the perennial, national call for a return to the so-called three R's and an elimination of extracurricular activities.[28] The crude ideology that reduces K–12 education to a mere training ground for tomorrow's global workforce is most fully exposed by this emphasis on the "essentials" of education (reading, writing, math) rather than the "frills" such as art and music. Ironi-

cally, proponents of preparing a global workforce see no contradiction in cutting back on opportunities to study foreign languages, comparative religion, cultural anthropology, international politics, and so on. At the same time, those pushing for lesson plans that emphasize reading, writing, and math tend to prefer a rather narrow approach to these subjects that discourages creative problem solving and emphasizes rudimentary, rule-based understanding.[29] This further advances the agenda of generating standardized learning outcomes designed to produce students prepared to join a homogeneous and interchangeable global workforce.

Market-Based Reforms

Along with promoting neoliberal policies, advocates of globalization have actively championed the role of market-based solutions to social problems. Third World poverty and underdevelopment are attributed to government restrictions on free trade.[30] It is argued that creating free markets will lead to a more efficient allocation of resources, which will attract foreign investment and spur economic development. The magic of the competitive marketplace, it is argued, should replace government-directed social engineering in these poor countries. By analogy, many education reformers believe that the best solution to poorly performing urban schools is to introduce market-based reforms. Advocates of market-based solutions contend that once schools are forced to compete with one another, educational improvement will follow.[31] Magnet schools and privatization (charter schools, school voucher programs, outsourcing administrative services) are the primary examples of market-based reforms.

The basic purpose of magnet schools is to foster competition between schools within the public school system by developing a specialization in a particular academic field (math and science) or a pedagogical style ("open" classrooms).[32] A common criticism of magnet school programs is that they tend to marginalize those schools that are less successful within a district and that this disproportionately impacts students from the poorest areas. Roslyn Mickelson recounts developments in Charlotte's magnet school program in the early 1990s.

Soon after the [Charlotte school] district replaced its mandatory desegregation plan with a voluntary one built around choice among magnet schools, it became apparent to many parents and other citizens that there were gross inequalities in resources available in magnets, newer schools, and older schools primarily in the urban core. They noted that the magnet strategy for reform left many schools in dire need of attention and additional resources. In the view of some critics, these inequities exacerbated existing race and class disparities in opportunities to learn. People complained that the magnet program, rather than addressing educational inequality, was exacerbating it by draining funds that could be spent for all schools.[33]

The cornerstone of market-based urban school reform is privatization—the process whereby private corporations receive contracts to provide services traditionally delivered by government. In the field of urban education reform there are three primary forms of privatization: (1) Charter schools are privately established and administered schools supported with public funds. Proponents of charter schools argue that this structure permits greater freedom for school administrators to experiment with innovative approaches.[34] (2) School choice provides publicly funded vouchers for students to attend private schools. As with charter schools, it is argued that allowing students to choose between attending public or private school will pressure public schools to improve.[35] (3) Outsourcing the administration of schools to private companies involves hiring private firms—such as Education Alternative, Inc. or the Edison Project—to actually run an individual

school or potentially an entire school district. The rationale for outsourcing such services is that corporate leaders can bring efficiencies and best practices from the bottom-line world of business to public education.

The basic premise for each of these reforms is that the educational process is basically a commodity and that a school is, therefore, analogous to a company in the business of providing a service.[36] Teachers are service providers and students are their clients. It follows that, given their expertise in the field of effectively and efficiently providing services, businessmen and women should serve as the leaders for education reform. Because free markets and competition shape the guiding ideology of the U.S. business class, these are the strategies they emphasize for public school reform. Magnet schools, charter schools, school vouchers, and outsourcing are all designed to promote competition between schools and to spur innovation and improvement. This fits conveniently with the tenets of global capitalism, which advocate the broad privatization of traditional government functions so that the number of collective goods can be cut to a minimum.[37] Any restrictions on private enterprise (such as government-provided medical care) are considered obstacles to progress through free market competition. In this respect, public education systems represent a major target for the ideologues of globalization. If the superiority of privately run school systems can be demonstrated, this would mark a significant step in the dismantling of public education systems in the United States and around the world.

CONCLUSION

It remains the case that national, state, and local officials are most directly responsible for shaping urban education policy. At the same time, the forces of global capitalism today impose certain limitations on the options available to these officials. Greater global trade has increased economic interdependence internationally over the past few decades, as the movement of people, goods, and services has multiplied exponentially. The capacity of companies and industries to move production facilities to low-wage labor zones has created a fierce competition between wealthy and poor nations for these jobs. Regional trade agreements, such as NAFTA, have reduced trade barriers between nations and tied the interests of nations to others in their region. The deregulation of financial markets and currency exchanges has allowed investors to rapidly move their money and shift resources around the world at unprecedented rates. The ability to move service jobs to low-wage zones permits multinational corporations to realize significant profits and contributes to a race to the bottom among nations with low-wage zones.

These global changes have contributed to a host of growing challenges that face urban education today. The gap separating the wealthy and the poor has led to an increasing concentration of poverty, while ethnic/racial disparities have created a pattern of hypersegregation that gathers poor nonwhites in large urban areas ringed by wealthy, white suburbs. The expansion of suburbs alongside disinvestment in urban areas has left few viable economic opportunities for those remaining in cities. An array of repressive anticrime policies has been established to monitor and sanction the growing population of discouraged and marginalized urban youth. The concentration of political and economic power in the suburbs has reduced both the clout and the resources available to urban school districts. The contemporary pattern of U.S. immigration attracts many Asian and Latino/-a families to urban centers, where both their cultural adaptation as well as

their high educational aspirations must be accommodated.

The major policy responses to these challenges for urban education over the past two decades have typically emphasized neoliberal and market-based reforms. The neoliberal approach is consistent with the ideals of globalization that promote standardization and uniformity across all international transactions. Standardized testing and curricula, teacher certification requirements, and an emphasis on the three R's are all designed to enhance quality control within education and to create uniform student learning outcomes that produce students with a common set of interchangeable skills. Market-based reforms also reflect globalization's ideological influence. Fostering competition between schools (through magnet schools or school vouchers) and cultivating service-oriented, bottom-line, business practices (through privatization of school administration) are designed to improve urban education by pressuring schools to adopt the practices of others, while turning teachers into service providers and students into clients. The ultimate goal of neoliberal and market-based reforms is to transform urban public education into an efficient, privately managed, service-based industry with predictable and uniform student learning outcomes that generate homogenous, interchangeable students.

NOTES

1. NAFTA and MERCOSUR refer, respectively, to the North American Free Trade Agreement among Mexico, the United States, and Canada, and to *El Mercado Común del Sur* (The Common Market of the South) among Argentina, Brazil, Uruguay, and Paraguay; Gilpin, R. (2002). *Global political economy: Understanding the international economic order*. Princeton, NJ: Princeton University Press.

2. Abrahamson, M. (2004). *Global cities.* New York: Oxford University Press.

3. Sassen, S. (1988). *The mobility of labor and capital: A study in international investment and labor flow.* Cambridge: Cambridge University Press.

4. Falk, R. (1999). *Predatory capitalism: A critique.* Cambridge, UK: Polity Press.

5. Reich, R. (1991). *The work of nations: Capitalism in the 21st century.* New York: A.A. Knopf.

6. Mittleman, J. (2000). *The globalization syndrome: Transformation and resistance.* Princeton, NJ: Princeton University Press.

7. Mittleman (2000).

8. Kuttner, R. (2000). The role of governments in the global economy. In W. Hutton & A. Giddens (Eds.), *Global capitalism* (pp. 147–163). New York: The New Press.

9. Soros, G. (2000). The new global financial architecture. In W. Hutton & A. Giddens (Eds.), *Global capitalism* (pp. 86–93). New York: The New Press.

10. Falk (1999).

11. Gilpin (2002).

12. Sassen (1988); Braverman, H. (1975). *Labor and monopoly capital: The degradation of work in the 20th century.* New York: Monthly Review Press.

13. Reich (1999); Ray, C., & Mickelson, R. (1993). Restructured students for restructured work: The economy, school reform and noncollege-bound youth. *Sociology of Education, 66,* 1–23.

14. Falk (1999); Sassen (1988).

15. Falk (1999).

16. Bowles, S., & Gintis, H. (1976). *Schooling in capitalist America: Educational reform and the contradictions of economic life.* London: Routledge & K. Paul.

17. Wilson, J. (1996). *When work disappears: The world of the new urban poor.* New York: Random House; Anyon, J. (1997). *Ghetto schooling: A political economy of urban education reform.* New York: Teacher's College Press.

18. Kozol, J. (1991). *Savage inequalities: Children in America's schools.* New York: Crown Publishers; Massey, D., & Denton, N. (1993). *American apartheid: Segregation and the making of the underclass.* Cambridge, MA: Harvard University Press.

19. Wilson (1996).

20. Bernstein, J., Boushey, H., McNichol, E., & Zahradnik, R. (2002). *Pulling apart: A state-by-state analysis of income trends.* Washington, DC: Center on Budget and Policy Priorities.

21. Reich (1991).

22. Massey & Denton (1993); Fossey, R. (2003). School desegregation is over in the inner cities: What do we do now? In L. Mirón & E. St. John (Eds.), *Reinterpreting urban school reform: Have urban schools failed, or has the reform movement failed urban schools* (pp. 15–32). Albany, NY: SUNY Press.

23. Wilson (1996).

24. Noguera, P. (2003). *City schools and the American dream: Reclaiming the promise of public education* (p. 6). New York: Teachers College Press.

25. Mickelson, R. (2000). Corporations and classrooms: A critical examination of the business agenda for urban school reform. In K. McClafferty, C. Torres, & T. Mitchell (Eds.), *Challenges of urban education: Sociological perspectives for the next century* (pp. 127–174). Albany, NY: SUNY Press; Noguera (2003).

26. Noguera (2003).

27. Anyon (1997).

28. Firestone, W., Goertz, M., & Natriello, G. (1997). *From cashbox to classroom: The struggle for fiscal reform and educational change in New Jersey.* New York: Teachers College Press.

29. Firestone, Goertz, & Natriello (1997).

30. Abrahamson (2004).

31. Noguera (2003); Cookson, P. (1994). *School choice: The struggle for soul of American education.* New Haven: Yale University Press; Henig, J. (1994). *Rethinking school choice: Limits of the market metaphor.* Princeton, NJ: Princeton University Press; Rasell, E., & Rothstein, R. (1993). *School choice: Examining the evidence.* Washington DC: Economic Policy Institute.

32. Mickelson (2000).

33. Mickelson (2000), p. 134.

34. Rasell & Rothstein (1993).

35. Cookson (1994); Ridenour, C., & St. John, E. (2003). Private scholarships and school choice: Innovation or class reproduction. In L. Mirón & E. St. John (Eds.), *Reinterpreting urban school reform: Have urban schools failed, or has the reform movement failed urban schools* (pp. 177–208). Albany, NY: SUNY Press.

36. Henig (1994).

37. Kuttner, R. (1997). *Everything for sale: The virtues and limits of markets.* New York: Alfred Knopf; Falk (1999).

TOWARD AN ANTICOLONIAL EDUCATION

Mostafa Mouhie Eddine and Rebecca Sánchez

Under the green umbrella of capitalism, the West has been committing the worst atrocities known to humankind. From colonialism, slavery, genocide, and class and gender oppression, to appropriation, the West has been adamant about its agenda: profit. The education system, as a part of the colonial capitalist structure, perpetuates the hierarchical structure of oppression. The purpose of this piece is threefold. First, we will discuss capitalism and its colonial schema; second, we will accentuate the historical role of education in maintaining the colonial structures; and third, we will entertain the anticolonial discursive paradigm that banks on indigenous knowledge in order to create border-lands of resistance.

CAPITALISM AND COLONIALISM

Colonization begins with a forced entry; as in the conquest of the Americas and Algeria. After contact, the colonizing powers try zealously to undermine and sabotage the cultural values of the natives. These acts are performed by a minority, elite, ruling class that embodies the core: the spring of power. The core's position is further reinforced by racist ideologies that blame the natives for their own misery, savagery, and oppression. In this context, conquest is legitimized via "ridiculing" the "otherness" of the natives.[1]

The conqueror is driven by a capitalist agenda to acquire land, natural resources, cheap labor, and new markets. This is what Karl Marx described as primitive accumulation of capital.[2] Said magnifies the rapid rate at which Europe conquered the rest of the world in the following: "Consider that in 1800, Western powers claimed 55 percent but actually held approximately 35 percent of the earth's surface, and by 1878 the proportion was 67 percent, a rate of 83,000 square miles per year. By 1914, the annual rate has risen to an astonishing 240,000 square miles, and Europe held a grand total of roughly 85 percent of the earth as colonies, protectorates, dependencies, dominions, and commonwealths."[3]

In retrospect, the West needed raw material to support its growing economies. Africa, Asia, and the Americas were the fertile grounds for colonialism. In the United States, for example, the cotton industry thrived because the natives were displaced from their lands, and the slaves provided cheap labor in the South. The cotton industry accounted for 58 percent of the dollar value of all American exports.[4] The exploitations of the natives and the slaves were legitimized via the act of "othering."[5] The savage, the heathen, and the uncivilized needed the religious creeds, the values, and the language of the white master in order to be delivered from their own ignorance.

COLONIALISM IN THE UNITED STATES

The first Anglo-Saxon settlers in North America had developed a sense of cultural superiority during their conquest of Ireland. The English considered the Irish as savages whose salvation rested on assimilating to the Anglo way of life.[6] The feeling by the English and their belief in their own cultural superiority gave them *la carte blanche* to expropriate the lands of Native Americans, a source of raw material, and to enslave African Americans, a source of free labor. The Constitution of the United States further reinforced the superiority of the Anglo-Saxon. In fact, Benjamin Franklin, one of the Founding Fathers, argued that the English were the "principled body of white people" who should populate North America and that land, Native American lands, should be cleared for the principled race.[7] In addition, the Constitution, through the Naturalization Act of 1790, denied the right of citizenship to Native Americans because they were considered domestic foreigners.[8] African Americans, under the Constitution, were property whose job was to ensure that enough cotton was produced in order to keep the capitalist troglodytes up north happy.[9] In essence, the Declaration of Independence locked the natives, the slaves, and people of color to a "legalized" position of subordination. We will now analyze the role of education in maintaining colonialism.

EDUCATION AND ITS TREATMENT OF THE OTHER

The education system in the United States is colonialist in its nature, because it was built on Anglo-Saxon ideals. From its inception, the school system advocated Anglo-Saxon uniformity framed under a national culture, which excluded all the others, even the new European immigrants.[10] In the early period of the nineteenth century, for instance, Noah Webster, who is referred to as the Schoolmaster of the Americas, worked relentlessly to standardize an American version of the dictionary of the English language, an American version of the Bible, and an American spelling book.[11] Webster is one of the first American scholars who succeeded in his attempt to create a national Anglo-American culture, a norm which still beats at the heart of this country. The "culture of wars" at the university level is a lingering part of the debates about what national culture is and what type of knowledge is valued.[12]

It is vital to note that some pockets in the academia are succeeding in decentralizing the Anglo-Saxon core, which has reigned for the last 300 years. Levine in *The Opening of the American Mind* documents the culture of wars and shows the progress that has been gained throughout the last century at the university level.[13] The Anglo-Saxon canon is the colonial ideological force that excludes all the others. This exclusive canon will not reign for long though, as we are seeing a counter hegemonic discourse in the areas of women's studies, Chicana studies, African- American studies, and indigenous studies. The core of the Anglo culture is being challenged and the voices of the others are gaining strength. In order to engage in this further, the manner in which education has historically worked to maintain the colonial agenda of capitalism must be described.

The early settlers in the thirteen colonies were perplexed with how to deal with Native Americans. They could not kill them all. The answer to the "Indian problem" resulted in the mission of assimilation. It was the only way to salvage the natives' souls and deliver them from anguish.[14] In 1766, Samson Occom, an Anglican missionary, went to England to raise money to educate the Indians. His plea was received with much more consideration and sympathy in England than in the New World. He raised more than 11,000 pounds to later found Dartmouth College. Wheelock wrote,

I have turned out forty Indians who were good readers, writers, and instructed in the principles of Christian religion . . . Well behaved while with me . . . by contact with the vices of their tribes, not more than half preserved their characters unstained. The rest were sunk into as low, savage, and brutish way of living as they were before and many of the most promise have fallen lowest.[15]

The early attempts to assimilate the natives went in vain. One hundred years later, Lieutenant Richard Henry Pratt landed support from the community in Carlisle, Pennsylvania, and Congress to open up a boarding school whose motto was "to kill the Indian and save the man." Native children were taken from their nations and stripped from every element of their cultures. They were soaked and baptized in the new culture.[16] They could not speak their languages, and they were forced into domestication in accordance with Anglo-American values. The Carlisle Institute prepared Native American girls to become maids and servants. As for Native American boys, they were trained to fulfill menial jobs. Education for the natives meant assimilation and producing a class of obedient workers who filled the lower strata of the job market.[17] The outing system, a training program, helped native students to become apprenticed in positions of servitude. Education for the natives created a pool of a workforce that was exploited by capital greed.[18]

The Carlisle mission, along with the missions of other boarding schools, was not much different from the schools established for the free slaves. Contrary to popular beliefs, the slaves were very keen on obtaining education, even under the harshest conditions of slavery. Slaves were cruelly punished if caught reading and teaching others how to read. Anderson documented the history of black education in the South between 1860 and 1935.[19] He found that freed slaves started their own schools with little help from the government. The southern planters opposed and placed many obstacles to hinder the education of the freed slaves, yet they were unable to stop the freed slaves' desire and anguish for learning. Many African Americans believed that education would lead to true emancipation. Alas, the capitalist system had a different agenda for the freed slaves. Once again, under the green umbrella of profit, Southern and Northern whites supported the establishment of the Hampton and Tuskegee Institutes. These two schools focused on teaching manual labor and on producing a workforce that would satisfy the lower echelon of the job market. *Plessey v. Fergusson* (1896) cemented separation and made it legal. African Americans were institutionally denied access to equal education and were therefore rendered to the margins.

The Industrial Revolution, at the turn of the century, created a massive working class. Schools became an avenue through which the ideals of industrialism and Americanization were to be practiced. Immigrants and their children needed to be domesticated and apprenticed into the factory mentality. Schools were about what Peter McLaren and Henry Giroux call the avenues through which capitalist social relations and ideologies were reinforced.[20] In short, schools were a site of class reproduction. In his critique of modernism and postmodernism, Doll provides a historical litany that students were in fact objectified into automatons for the capitalist engines. "Our schools are in a sense, factories in which the raw material (children) is to be shaped and fashioned into products to meet the various demands of life."[21]

Education has always been a champion of the agendas of the elite classes. Schools are not only about reproducing colonialism, but also indoctrinate the oppressed into believing in the myths of meritocracy—a bourgeois idea that relegates the oppressed to the position of the periphery and shifts the blame to those who are exploited and oppressed.[22] In the case of the United States, the oppressed are further divided through the color lines and gender lines.[23] The capitalist system injected the white working class with psychological wages, indoctrinated them in the myth of meritocracy and in the allegory of education, separated them from the others, and displaced them when their skills were no longer needed. The working class, a marginal group along with the rest of the oppressed, is just another property, a by-product of colonialism.

Under the veil of profit, capitalism will go to bed with anybody. The bottom line is green. The mighty dollar is mightier than class, race, gender, sexuality, and ability. Sadly, we still fall prey to the politics of compartmentalization and separation. This form of disciplined pedagogy tends to essentialize a particular form of oppression at the expense of other forms of domination.[24] The anticolonial discursive calls into question the nature of power dynamics of oppression with a critical gaze without losing sight of the authority and the passion of experience.[25]

In these times of "post-," the passion and the authority of experience have become appropriated by capital. Now corporations such as Benetton are banking on human suffering throughout the world. Giroux in *Disturbing Pleasures* exposes the new commodity of capital: the consumption of social change.[26] Capital has caught up with the notion of fluidity and multiple subjectivities only to expose human affliction for the sake of manifold revenue. Under the multioppressive regime, race, gender, class, ability, and sexuality become multiple sites of profit. It is no longer customary to physically enslave and colonize; capital has found multiple ways to bank on the exotic other. Jonathan Rutherford as quoted in hooks, argues that

Paradoxically, capital has fallen in love with difference: advertisement thrives on selling us things that will enhance our uniqueness and individuality. It is no longer about keeping up with the Joneses; it's about being different from them. From world music to exotic holidays in Third World locations, ethnic TV dinners to Peruvian hats, cultural difference sells.[27]

Ironically, the exotic other still endures the savage inequalities and inequities of a school system that rewards property value over human principles. In New York, as described by Kozol, those who live in affluent neighborhoods (high property values) merit the right to a superior education.[28] The poor who live in the ghetto— the majority of this segment of the population being people of color—have no right to quality education. Race, class, and many forms of oppression do matter.[29]

ANTICOLONIAL INDIGENOUS KNOWLEDGE

The European conquest and colonization of much of the world was multifaceted and included but was not limited to forced labor, economic disruptions, genocide, and territorial appropriation. One of the most salient features of colonialism however, and the one of concern here, was the authoring of the colonized into Western narrative structures.[30] This form of narrative represents the colonial agenda. It is the formal narrative that becomes commonsensical, which is studied in school, and that society values.[31] In retrospect, official knowledge is the manifestation of the colonial structure that still insists on dominating most of the world.[32] At this juncture, however, we will call into presence the power of indigenous knowledge in creating liberatory borderlands that counter the Eurocentric view of the world. Such a knowledge base offers an alternative theoretical and pedagogical perspective that has the power to impact the oppressed and the marginalized in our schools.

The anticolonial discursive juxtaposes the situations of the oppressed through the power dynamics that are inherent to the colonial structures. It is pivotal to distinguish here between positivistic and deterministic dialogues that see colonial theory as locked in binaries and the fluidity of the anticolonial discursive.[33] The relationship between the center and the periphery, the colonizer and the colonized, the oppressor and the oppressed, are some of the examples of this positivist paradigm. In an attempt to move beyond this limiting scope, we choose to ascribe to the anticolonial discursive, not as a fixed theory, but as a theory in the making. It is fluid, hybrid, and contextual. This paradigm calls into question the power dynamics that subjugate and render the oppressed to the positions of subordination. Fluidity of the anticolonial discursive has to be understood under the guise of autonomy and the passion of experience.[34] There is nothing "post" about postcolonialism. Oppression is real, not fluid, yet individuals have the multiple subjectivities to combat the oppressive regime. One cannot ascribe to nihilism and despair. Racism, sexism, class oppression, heterosexism, and many forms of oppression are real and not imagined. Toni Morrison, for example, speaks eloquently to the symbolic worth of race: "Race has become metaphorical—a way of referring to distinguishing forces, events, classes, and expressions of social decay and economic division far more threatening to the body politic than biological 'race' ever was."[35] Race is woven in the very fabric of the United States.

As significant as race is, it has to be understood in relation to other forms of oppression. The anticolonial discursive looks at the dynamics of power structures with a critical gaze. Class, gender, and sexual orientation are looked at as sites of struggles, sites of marginality, and sites for possibilities to build alliances—a common zone of resistance.[36] In essence, common resistance alters the hegemonic discourse, by creating a third space,[37] a borderland— *una cultura Mestiza*—that transcends the boundaries of the Anglo-Saxon norms, and that plays by different rules.[38]

Borderlands are spaces in the margins inhabited by those who are the subjects of oppression, yet Anzaldua refuses to surrender and redefines the meaning of marginality.[39] Her story, along with the stories of other Chicanas and Chicanos, is transforming the peripheries and altering the colonial central structures of the United States. Along these lines, Delgado proposes that knowledge and reality are socially constructed, that indigenous knowledge provides members of a group with a catalyst for psychic self-preservation, and that exchanging knowledge helps people to overcome ethnocentrism.[40] In the case of the United States,

Eurocentrism is the discourse that needs to be overcome.

Marginality is a position defined by the center locking and determining the fate of the oppressed. This position robs individuals from their agencies. hooks redefined marginality:

Understanding marginality as a position and a place of resistance is crucial for oppressed, exploited, colonized people. If we only view the margin as a sign of marking despair, a deep nihilism penetrates in a destructive way the very ground of our being.[41]

Borderlands need to be expanded to accommodate the oppressed. Borderlands are created every day through alliance building, through counter storytelling, and through revitalizing the cultural, indigenous founts of knowledge.[42] Borderlands are about forming communities within the margins. Trueba speaks about resistance and defiance in the case of Latinos/as in facing discrimination, oppression, and exclusion: The common experience of oppression, rejection, and exclusion is redefined, reinterpreted, and used constructively to gain political power and collective recognition.[43] It is precisely the feelings of exclusion and oppression that create the need for developing the new ethnicities, a new kinship system, a new set of personal relationships, almost a new larger family where we can all protect each other.[44] Trueba's entreaty, in our perspective, is calling for the oppressed—the inhabitants of the borderlands—to dialogue, to form a system of affinity, and to form new sets of dialogical identities that redefine marginality and colonialism.

Anticolonial discursive is about the emancipatory process framed in the proclamation of the past, the present, and a vision for the future through conscious dialogue, alliance building, and through banking on indigenous knowledge. It is context bound and milieu specific. As importantly, decolonization is fluid and not fixed. Decolonization is not an intellectual act in the Western sense. It is a way of life through which the subject deprecates the forces of exploitation and subjugation, and claims the voices of the peasants, the working class, the natives, and all the displaced others. Decolonization is about denouncing the exploitative practices of the capitalist regime. At its nucleus is the disentanglement of the bourgeois class and its ideals. Decolonization is part of what Paulo Freire refers to as "*Conscientizacion.*"[45] Anticolonial education juxtaposes the realities of the oppressed and offers them a myriad of possibilities. This outcome can only be reached through conscious dialogue. It is with conscious love that we can begin to understand ourselves and our connectedness to the others. Neocolonialism is breathing under the protection of capitalism in our poor communities and in the so-called Third World countries. We, as loving and mindful human beings, need to decolonize our minds; decolonize our spaces; and form alliances to speak, to name, and to act. It is in this context that the colonized have a myriad of emancipatory possibilities that the colonizing other never envisioned. Along these lines, Paulo Freire speaks:

No matter where the oppressed are found, the act of love is commitment to their cause—the cause of liberation. And this commitment, because it is loving, is dialogical. As an act of bravery, love cannot be sentimental: as an act of freedom, it must not serve as a pretext for manipulation. It must generate other acts of freedom; otherwise, it is not love. Only by abolishing the situation of oppression is it possible to restore the love which that situation made impossible. If I do not love the world, if I do not love people I can not enter into dialogue.[46]

Armed with love, we dare to question that which separates the intellectual from the authentic and seeks to monopolize knowledge. We are humbly reminded that to engage in any kind of dialogue, one has to engage in the postdisciplinary "conversations" that strive to transform rather than conform.[47] Love is not sentimental. It is driven by an agenda to abolish oppression, to teach for emancipation, and to decolonize. Love for the human cause unites more than separates. It is the kind of love that flows in the midst of the harshest oppressive regimes to speak against atrocities and human sufferings. It is the kind of love that has no precincts regardless of where oppression exists. Love raises global consciousness. James Baldwin, an African-American freedom fighter and an intellectual who struggled to link his work to his world, dared to transcend the imposed colonial borders. He eloquently highlights and articulates global consciousness in the following:

Any real commitment to black freedom in this country will have the effect of reordering our priorities, and altering our commitments, so that, for horrendous examples, we would be supporting black freedom fighters in South Africa and Angola, and would not be allied with Portugal, would be closer to Cuba than we are to Spain, would be supporting Arab nations instead of Israel, and would never have felt compelled to follow the French into Southeast Asia.[48]

Anticolonial discursive encompasses teaching for freedom. This act of freedom is a way of life that sees education as instrumental to the cause of the oppressor, yet turns desolation into a flare that ignites and illuminates a path of resistance, a path of defiance, and a road that refuses to become a casualty of despondency. In the spirit of emancipation, Gordon Bennett describes his work in the following:

If I were to choose a single word to describe my art practice it would be the word question. If I were to choose a single word to describe my underlying drive it would be freedom. This should not be regarded as a heroic proclamation. Freedom is a practice. It is a way of thinking in other ways to those we have been accustomed to. Freedom is never assumed by laws and institutions that are intended to guarantee it. To be free is to be able to question the way the power is exercised, disputing claims to domination.[49]

NOTES

1. Said, E. (1993). *Culture and imperialism.* New York: Vantage Books. Said, E. (1979). *Orientalism.* New York: Vintage Book.

2. Miles, R. (1987). *Capitalism and unfree labor: Anomaly or necessity.* New York: Tavistock Publication.

3. Said, E. (1993), p. 8.

4. Takaki, R. (1993). *A different mirror: A history of multicultural America.* Boston: Little Brown and Company.

5. Said, E. (1979). *Orientalism.* New York: Vintage Books.

6. Takaki (1993).

7. Takaki (1993).

8. Takaki (1993).

9. King, J. (2000). *Race.* Mahwah, NJ: Lawrence Erlbaum Associates, Inc.

10. Takaki (1993); Macedo, D. (2002). The colonialism of the English-only movement. *Education Research, 29* (3), 15–24; Said (1993).

11. Spring, J. (2001). *Deculturalization and the struggle for equality.* New York: McGraw-Hill.

12. Levine, W. (1997). *The opening of the American mind.* Boston: Beacon Press.

13. Levine (1997).

14. Reyhner, J., & Eder, J. (1992). *A history of Indian education* (Jon Reyhner and Jeanne).

15. Reyhner & Eder (1992), p. 92.

16. Reyhner & Eder (1992).

17. Lomawaima, T. (1993). Domesticity in the federal Indian schools: The power of authority over mind and body. *American Ethnologist, 20* (2), 227–240.

18. Adams, W. (1995). *Education for extinction: American Indians and the boarding school experience.* Lawrence: University Press of Kansas.

19. Anderson, J. (1988). *The education of blacks in the South, 1860–1935.* Chapel Hill, NC: University of North Carolina Press.

20. Giroux, H. (1994). *Disturbing pleasures: Learning popular culture.* New York: Routledge.

21. Doll, W. (1993). *A postmodern perspective on curriculum.* New York: Teachers College Press, p. 47.

22. Freire, P. (1970). *Pedagogy of the oppressed.* New York: Continuum.

23. Du Bois, W. (1961). *The souls of black folk.* New York: Fawcett Publication, Inc. hooks, b. (1994). *Teaching to transgress.* New York: Routledge.

24. Dimitriadis, C. (2001). *Reading & teaching the postcolonial: From Baldwin to Basquiat and beyond.* New York: Teachers College Press.

25. hooks, b. (1994). *Teaching to transgress.* New York: Routledge.

26. Giroux (1994).

27. hooks (1994), p. 17.

28. Kozol, J. (1991). *Savage inequalities: Children in America's schools.* New York: Crown Publications.

29. hooks (1994); West, C. (1993). *Race matters.* Boston: Beacon Press.

30. Gutierrez, J. (2001). *Critical race narratives.* New York: New York University Press; Said (1993); Said (1979).

31. Wertsch, J. (1998). *Mind as action.* New York: Oxford.

32. Gutierrez (2001).

33. Alireza, D. (2001). The power of social theory: The anticolonial discursive framework. *Journal of Education Thought, 35* (3), 297–323.

34. hooks (1994).

35. Morrison, T. (1992). *Playing in the dark: Whiteness in the literacy imagination.* Cambridge, MA: Harvard University Press, p. 63.

36. Alireza (2001).

37. Pulido, L. (2001). To arrive is to begin: Benjamin Saenz's Carry Me Like Water and the Pilgrimage of Origin in the Borderlands. *STLC, 25* (1), 306–315.

38. Anzaldua, G. (1987). *Borderlands, the new mestiza = la frontera.* San Francisco: Spinsters/Aunt Lute.

39. Anzaldua (1987).

40. Delgado Bernal, B. (1998). Using a Chicana feminist epistemology in educational research. *Harvard Educational Review, 68* (4), 555–582.

41. hooks, b. (1990). *Yearning.* New York: Routledge, p. 150.

42. Moll, L., & Diaz, S. (1987). Change as the goal of education research. *Anthropology & Education Quarterly, 18* (4), 287–299.

43. Trueba, E. (1999). *Latinos unidos: From cultural diversity to politics of solidarity.* Lanham, MD: Rowman and Littlefield Publishers.

44. Trueba (1999).

45. Freire, P. (1996). *Pedagogy of hope.* New York: Continuum.

46. Dimitriadis (2001), pp. 70–71.

47. Dimitriadis (2001), p. 41.

48. Dimitriadis (2001), p. 34.

49. Dimitriadis (2001), p. 34.

EDUCATION IN A GLOBALIZED SOCIETY: OVER FIVE CENTURIES, THE COLONIAL STRUGGLE CONTINUES

Joseph Carroll-Miranda

AN INTRODUCTION TO THE INTRODUCTION

Urban cities like New York have unique characteristics that can be described as a *tecnópolis*.[1] Tecnópolises are the materialization of an urban-geographical segment of a technocratic society. As such, urban cities have the distinction that their economies and modes of production are seriously dependent on and mediated with information and communication technologies (ICT). The fusion of technology in all of the daily facets of the urban center's life creates a virtual cyborgzation of day-to-day praxis mediated via ICT.[2] In other words, information and communication technologies have historically restructured both the economy and internal dynamics of the urban center.[3] According to authors like Manuel Castells and Peter Hall, the tecnópolis condition is usually present in the urban centers of striving First World economies. New York City, known by many as the economic capital of the world, lives up to its name in this sense. The urban is transmutating into the techno-urban. In doing so, education becomes an institution that foments the constitution of the urban-techno subject. In other words, tecnópolis is the urban architecture of a Cyborg-State, and the cyborg condition reflects its citizen subjectivities. The cyborgzation of urban education policies, methodology, and curriculum is the main focus of this text.

In this general context, education has a similar fate. The urban scenarios of New York City's tecnópolis condition are rather mind-boggling. Not only are myriad cutting-edge policies, curricula, methodologies, and pedagogical praxes nurtured, produced, and given birth to within this global economy mecca, but they also become international standards of ideal education and international policy. The United Nations Educational, Scientific, and Cultural Organization (UNESCO) has a physical location in the tecnópolis of New York City. This organization plays a crucial role in the ways education policy is created, adopted, and implemented in developing countries. As such, the educational system of numerous countries will adopt the recommendations, suggestions, and expert knowledge produced within this international body.

Capitalist and modernist educational models have been the critique of the vast works of Paulo Freire, bell hooks, Stanley Aranowitz, Henry Giroux, Peter McLaren, Michael Apple, Joe Kincheloe, Shirley Steinberg, and Donaldo Macedo, as well as countless other critical pedagogues. Their works have given me a unique analytical perspective on the purpose of educational policy within urban centers in the United States and other parts of the world.

Interestingly enough, with an acquired critical pedagogue lens, UNESCO policies will become a center unit of analysis within this chapter. In addition, the type of education adopted internationally has the desired outcome of creating a myriad of tecnópolises worldwide. Better still, developing countries need to shift their traditional urban centers into cutting-edge tecnópolises, which ideally can function as peers in the global economy. To what extent this global tecnópolis phenomenon is truth or fallacy will be the task of the subsequent pages. Nonetheless, urban education tecnópolises such as New York City have the historical conjuncture of dictating international urban education policies, methodologies, curriculum, and models of pedagogy.

INTRODUCTION

Global capitalism, characterized by Antonio Negri and Michael Hardt as an empire,[4] has a specific agenda of expanding and consolidating its influence and dominion to the farthest corners of the world. Such characteristics of global capital are known by some as imperialism, neocolonialism, neoliberalism, hegemony, or just simply oppression and exploitation.[5] The empire uses various tactics ranging from military might to more "subtle" forms of domination via education and psychology.[6]

GLOBALIZATION AND NEOCOLONIALISM

Contemporary informatics makes the postmodern global order logistically workable just as modern technologies made modern states possible. Modern states, as well as modern science, the machine age, modern war and European Imperialism all developed simultaneously in a messy, bloody conversation and confrontation. This is all the more sobering when we realize that today we are in the midst of a similar conversation, as technoscience and politics make another staggering transition.

—*H. Gray and S. Mentor*[7]

The foregoing epigraph is an excellent pretext for the following discussion. Postmodern literature calls for the end of universalistic or grand narrative/meta-narrative overgeneralizing concepts.[8] As a result of our "postmodern" condition in the field of political economy, there is not a general consensus as to what globalization is. There is a common thread that refers to globalization as the extant transnational political and economical social order.[9] Other scholars ascribe to the belief that globalization is an ongoing historical process of over 500 years spearheaded by European westward, eastward, and southward expansions.[10] This European expansion constituted a colonial era where there was not a corner of the world that was not a victim of European colonialism and imperialism. Although particularly after World War II, there was a process of decolonization; many political, economical, and psychological influences and dependencies prevailed in these "liberated" colonies. In this context, globalization is an ongoing process of imperialism that materialized centuries of colonialism worldwide. Through time, colonialism metamorphosed into complex relationships of global networks that materialized the extant era of neocolonialism.[11] Postcolonial theory is an extreme fertile ground of theories that helps us to understand the myriad extant neocolonial relationships throughout the world. Via postcolonialism, scholars engage in a process of knowledge construction where the multiple influences, relationships, dynamics, and psyche characteristic of imperial and colonial conditions are perpetuated by ex-colonial states, policies, structures, and subjectivities.[12]

The understanding of neocolonial relationships is crucial to fully understand the social, political, cultural, and psychological effects of globalization. The abstract concept of globalization is perhaps even more significant than its rote definition. This chapter will focus on the following two main areas: (1) information and communication technologies (ITC) and flexible mode of production and (2) international structures and policies.

INFORMATION AND COMMUNICATION TECHNOLOGIES AND FLEXIBLE MODE OF PRODUCTION

In the context of "advanced" capitalism, like a retro virus, capitalism has the obligation to expand, self-perpetuate, or die. Capitalist expansion must consolidate its domain worldwide. Such consolidation is what Italian sociologist Toni Negri denominates as the empire. This empire materializes itself via the combination of the creation and dissemination of information and communication technologies, intertwined with centuries of bloody relationships of imperialism and colonialism that paved and continues to pave the way for the current social and political "stability" that guarantees this empire survives by any means.[13] The concept of empire will be used throughout this chapter to engulf the historical process of global capital and its pertinent political, economical, cultural, and psychological hegemonic projects of domination.

According to Spanish sociologist Manuel Castells, we live in the information age.[14] The information age is the extant sociohistorical reality in which our economies are mediated and interwoven with ICT. Information and communication technologies are defined as all those pieces of technologies that process, analyze, and host information (i.e., computers, routers, bridges, TCP/IP, servers, computers, UNIX, LINUX, etc.). In fact, according to Castells, information has become a commodity.[15] As such, wealth and surplus value are accumulated via the mode of information. This is why "advanced" capitalism is inherently mediated through ICTs. The means of production, nowadays, are dependent on both technology and information. Without ICTs, globalization would not be possible and the empire would be a sci-fi story instead of a reality.

Political economists concur that ICTs are the driving force that permitted the possibility of an ever increasingly fast global economical system.[16] The speeds of global capital transactions are only possible via ICTs. The vast networks of information interconnected via cellular, satellite, and microwave services permit what is called a flexible mode of production. Learning from the devastating effects of the overproduction crisis of 1929, capitalism avoids at all cost overproducing any product. In the context of globalization, corporations have adopted the policy of producing only what they can sell. For example, the Dell Computer Corporation does not make a computer unless it has already been sold. Dell production tactics are known as a flexible mode of production.[17] A flexible mode of production is characterized by multiple strategic geographical points of production integrated via information/communication technologies. For instance, Dell has multiple plants all over the world. In the different parts of the world, they produce different parts of a Dell computer. The casing could be built in China, the motherboards in Taiwan, and the transistors' parts in Mexico, while the administrative operations are conducted in the United States. Via information technologies, the U.S. administrative center coordinates the production of parts all over the world in such an integrated fashion that there is no overproduction of parts. This is what political economists call flexible mode of production. Dell does not produce computers for the 6.7-billion-world population. Doing so would be corporate suicide. Instead, they target the 500–800 million people worldwide who can afford to buy the products, and base their production on these more realistic numbers.

Another fundamental characteristic of ICTs and flexible mode of production is what Dickens refers to as time and space compression.[18] Time and space compression is the interwoven relationship between ICTs and flexible mode of production. In fact, flexible mode of production is economically viable due to time and space compression. The vast networks of ICTs create a historical phenomenon where notions of time and space are compressed.[19] Corporations can access and disseminate information vital to their success. Because of time and space compression, Dell Corporation can communicate, in various forms, to all of their assembly plants worldwide. At the stroke of a key, they can find out and decide how many parts need to be purchased, produced, and sold simultaneously. This is only possible through the materialization of vast networks of ICTs that are currently the lifeline of the information age and global capitalism.[20]

INTERNATIONAL STRUCTURES AND POLICIES

Toni Negri's empire is more than mere combinations of ICTs and economists' preference of a particular mode of production. The empire is a hybrid culmination of political, economical, cultural, and psychological historical processes. During and predominantly after World War II, there was a proliferation of international institutions. The United Nations (UN), International Monetary Fund (IMF), World Bank (WB), General Agreement of Trade and Tariffs (GATT), and North Atlantic Treaty Organization (NATO) were all created in less than a decade.[21] These organizations, among others, spearheaded the political and economical agenda of globalization. The creation of an international/transnational government and economical system became the agenda of all these international bodies, in their own particular way.

The WB, IMF, WTO, and GATT were and are the economical policy makers. The economic policies created by these international institutions benefit a transnational economical elite. The ways the policies are articulated creates a neocolonial condition known as economical dependency. The economic model of dependency has been the modus operandi for developing countries. The economical dependency model consists of multiple laws, structures, and policies that shape and mold a developing country's future. For instance, a developing country needs external investments, international loans, and a way to design a prosperous economy. To secure this financial backing, they need to both consult with and gain approval from the International Monetary Fund and the World Bank. The IMF and WB will give a developing country the resources and infrastructure it needs, as long as their recommendations are followed. So for example, if Ecuador needs the resources and infrastructure for better roads and transportation systems, both the IMF and WB will tell them where, how, and with what to build the roads. But if Ecuador wants to conserve its mountains and the IMF and WB believe it's cheaper and better to blow them up, Ecuador has to blow up the mountains to build the road. Also, if Ecuador wishes to stimulate the local economy by using Ecuadorian building material, but the IMF and WB believe they need to use U.S. or European construction material, they must submit to the IMF's and WB's will. The policies of economical development are geared and articulated to maintain a "subtle" dominance over countries that have been historically stripped of their wealth and resources via their colonial past.[22] Through the models of economical dependency, the colonies become neocolonies.

The emergence of the World Trade Organization and treaties such as the North American Free Trade Agreement (NAFTA), Asian Pacific Economic Cooperation (APEC), and *Mercado Común del Sur* (MERCOSUR), have accentuated the politics of economical dependencies. These international bodies articulate, implement, and materialize the way geographical regions will produce what is in function of the global economy. So, for instance, any country that wishes to enhance its agricultural industry is forced to submit itself to the will of these multiple international institutions. For instance, the northern African country of Somalia was the victim of an extreme famine that "needed" military intervention.[23] At the time, Somalia was undergoing some economical restructuring. Part of that restructuring affected its agricultural industry. Ironically, the country that was victim of a serious famine produced more than fifty percent of all the peanuts consumed by European countries.[24] As part of Somalia's strategy to insert itself in the global economy, it was forced to transform its agricultural industry into producing only peanuts. Lands that previously fed the Somalian people stopped producing multiple crops and had to just produce peanuts for exportation purposes only. All of this food is produced, but leaves the country.

Somalia is an extreme case, but multiple countries in Latin America, and all over the world, are instructed by the IMF, WB, WTO, and GATT to produce certain kinds of crops. For instance, Brazil provides soy and wood, Ecuador produces bananas, Ghana produces pineapple, China manufactures plastics, Haiti produces Disney paraphernalia and major league baseballs, Taiwan and Hong Kong produce electronic parts, and so on. The products that multiple countries produce are determined by the IMF, WB, WTO, GATT, NAFTA, APEC, MERCOSUR, and their respective treaties, models of economical development, funding, infrastructures, and policies.[25]

The empire's tactics of economic dependency models for developing countries are a continuation of colonial rule in postcolonial ways, materializing neocolonization worldwide. In the following sections, we will examine what globalization and the empire have to do with education and colonialism, postcolonialism, and neocolonialism.

THE U.N. DECADE OF LITERACY: A "SUBTLE" FORM OF NEOCOLONIALISM

A Sociohistorical Pretext

Toni Negri's empire is characterized by political economists as a point in human history where absolute poverty is at an unprecedented high.[26] Absolute poverty is the lack of even the most basic living conditions, which include at least one meal per day, a house or shelter in which to live, running water, electricity, and access to health care and education.[27] In the empire of the twenty-first century, the rich are getting richer and the poor are getting poorer. As you read this chapter, one percent of the world's population controls ninety percent of its wealth.[28] In times where there appears not to be enough wealth for everybody, conglomerates of elite capitalists have at least $1 trillion of speculative capital. This means there is a trillion dollars floating in ICT networks, waiting to be invested in a viable moneymaking scheme. The accumulation of wealth is such that if the conglomerate of elite capitalists wanted to invest in the enrichment of the human race, they could give $1,000 to each of the 6.7 billion inhabitants of the planet and still have billions of dollars left to invest in their moneymaking schemes. This accumulation of wealth and the heightening of poverty is truly a historical precedent never seen before.[29]

The empire needs to do something about these figures. It cannot maintain itself under such extreme conditions of global injustices. According to many scholars, a continuation of wealth accumulation without serious redistribution will cause an economical recession that will make the stock market crash look like a walk in the park. Multiple capitalist magnates, such as the Rockefellers, Carnegies, Bilderbergs, and Rothschilds, recognize this possibility. As such they have put time, money, and effort into creating some of the international institutions like the UN, WTO, WB, IMF, Council of Foreign Relations, and Trilateral Commission, among others.[30] In doing so, their economical empires perpetuate themselves. Furthermore, these international institutions are intertwined to create, disseminate, and implement models and policies of economic development, education, foreign aid, diplomatic treaties and negotiations, and humanitarian aid. In fact, it is the task of a division of the U.N.—the United Nations Educational, Cultural, and Scientific Organization (UNESCO)—to minimize and eliminate the reality of absolute poverty and deal with issues that greatly affect developing countries.

Education and Colonization

Historically, education has been a crucial tool to implement and perpetuate colonial and imperial relations of dominance.[31] According to Spring, education was the tool that, to a greater or lesser extent, "transformed" Native American culture to bring it into harmony with the emerging nation of the United States. Under the pretext of civilizing the savage natives, they dramatically altered their worldview from a collective one to a more individualistic one.[32] Furthermore, they instilled the importance and necessity of private property, using the land resources for purposes other than hunting, gathering, and performing religious ceremonies and pilgrimages to places that were considered sacred.[33] Education has been used in more "modern" times to "educate" the colonial natives about the virtues of liberal capitalist society. According to Carnoy, education has been used as a form of cultural imperialism. Educational programs in colonial and postcolonial India, Africa, and Latin America were the means to instill and guarantee that the capitalist system is perpetuated via a capitalist culture that will guarantee a capitalist society.[34] Values that are not in tune with the capitalist logic are deemed barbaric, uncivilized, and uneducated.[35] In the twenty-first century, Negri's empire is doing the same things. Under the guise of Gramcy's notion of hegemony, "modern" models and projects of global education are attempting to do the same thing.

Education for All

One of the few international institutions that has "aggressively" tried to deal with the issues and problems arising from global poverty is UNESCO. The lack of education, particularly literacy, is a big concern among developing and developed countries. For example, the U.N. published the *United Nations Literacy Decade: Education for All Plan of Action*, which states:

Literacy is not only an indispensable tool for lifelong education and learning but is also an essential requisite for citizenship and human and social development. The right of every individual to education, as recognized in the Universal Declaration of Human Rights, is strongly rooted in the right to literacy. Major efforts have been devoted to literacy over the last fifty years both through remedial and preventive measures.[36]

Under the agenda of the literacy decade, the U.N., via UNESCO, has the arduous task of eliminating illiteracy worldwide by 2012–2015. One of the sections of the *Literacy for All* document states,

Literacy for All has to address the literacy needs of the individual as well as the family, literacy in the workplace and in the community, as well as in society and in the nation, in tune with the goals of economic, social and cultural development of all people in all countries.[37]

As the reader can appreciate this quote, we can analyze how the literacy agenda has as a guiding light the global empire. According to the vision, literacy has to address the needs of illiterate populations worldwide "in tune with the goals of economic social and cultural development of all people in all countries."[38] In tune to what goals? Who defines them? What kind of development? Who dictates such development? Under the extant conditions of the empire, it appears to be the case that the transnational elite is the one doing all of the defining of both the pertinent goals and models of development. In other words, UNESCO's education for all is to summit the global illiterate population into the global economical, social, and cultural system of the empire. Although the literacy for all agenda is neither inherently good nor bad, and is paradoxically an undeniable necessity, the wording is highly problematic. The discourse, implicit within the wording, looks like, feels like, and tastes like neocolonial and cultural imperialist tactics to expand the empire's sphere of influence and domination.

The apparent definition of literacy is used rather loosely. In none of the U.N. documents reviewed was there a clear definition of literacy. They use literacy depending on their discursive needs. In the *Literacy for All* document, literacy is acquiring basic reading and writing skills. Paradoxically, the document suggests that the traditional definition of literacy is viewed as limited. For instance, "literacy policies and programs today require going beyond the limited view of literacy that has dominated in the past. Literacy for all requires a renewed vision of literacy."[39] Renewed visions of literacy include "updated" applications such as media literacy and information communication technology literacy, which can be broken down into computer literacy and network literacy, among others.[40] In this context, literacy, education, and ICT are interwoven in a broad international agenda of education in relation to global economy, politics, and culture.

ICTs, THE EMPIRE, AND NEOCOLONIZATION

In the rapidly changing world of today's knowledge society, with the progressive use of newer and innovative technological means of communication, literacy requirements continue to expand regularly. In order to survive in today's globalized world, it has become necessary for all people to learn new *literacies* and develop the ability to locate, evaluate, and effectively use information in multiple manners.[41]

—UNESCO

The empire has a concrete agenda to expand its influence and dominance worldwide. The implementation of the empire's agenda is disseminated via international institutions such as the U.N., WTO, WB, IMF, and treaties such as NAFTA, MERCOSUR, APEC, and GATT, among others. Informational and communications technologies, educational agendas of multiple literacies, and economic development are currently interwoven at both macroeconomic and microsocial levels. The macroeconomic structures of dependency combined with cultural imperialist education are consolidating the empire's reach to the farthest corners of the globe. The U.N.-implemented *Education for All* program is not necessarily interested in educating for the love of knowledge. In fact, it believes that the poorest and most underdeveloped countries do not have the capability to produce knowledge like First World countries can. The UNESCO general report of May 2001, states:

Poor countries—and poor people—differ from rich ones not only because they have less capital but also because they have less knowledge. Knowledge is often complex and costly to create and disseminate, and that is why much of it is created in industrialized countries. Developing countries can acquire knowledge from external sources as well as create their own. The success of the development experience in Asia relative to Africa and Latin America is due in part to the ability of East Asian countries to acquire and apply knowledge.[42]

According to the U.N. report, East Asia has been relatively more successful than Africa and Latin America because it has both acquired and applied knowledge that is relevant only within the context of global capital. The knowledge acquired and applied by East Asia goes hand in hand with the empire's neocolonial consolidation of power and dominance. If Africa and Latin America are not as successful, it is because either they do not acquire the proper knowledge or they apply it in the wrong ways. But who defines what is correct knowledge creation, acquisition, and proper application?

The U.N. report exposes that there are two kinds of knowledge: "(A) technical or 'know-how' knowledge; and (B) knowledge about attributes. Knowledge about attributes 'illuminates every economic transaction, revealing preferences, giving clarity to exchanges.'"[43] Furthermore, "the lack of such knowledge results in imperfect markets, the collapse of markets or, worse still, the absence of markets, all of which are detrimental to development and hurt the poor."[44]

In the empire context, certain forms of knowledge are privileged, particularly those in tune with global capital. For example,

Knowledge and information are incorporated into goods and services. Knowledge and information are sources of wealth creation and value added in their own right. As their amount and value increase, there is a proportionate decrease in the amount and value of other inputs such as labour, capital, materials etc. The concentration of knowledge and information-intensive industries in the industrialized countries contributes significantly to the development and technology gap between industrialized and developing countries.[45]

The impending necessity of creating knowledge and cultures that benefit and enrich global capital has propelled the United Nations to create an ICT task force. Similar to UNESCO's *Education for All* agenda, the ICT task force has the mandate to minimize and eliminate the global digital divide. According to the U.N.'s ICT task force document, they: "plan to use information and communications technologies to combat poverty."[46] Therefore, the ICT task force is looking for ways to create policies, educational programs, and efficient economic models. In their document, they state that there is a need to:

(a) forge strategic partnerships between the United Nations system, private industry, trusts and foundations, donor governments, program countries, and other relevant international actors; (b) develop innovative modalities for strengthening the ICT capacity of developing countries; (c) pool the experiences of both developed and developing countries in introducing and promoting ICT for development; and (d) mobilize resources supported by voluntary contributions.[47]

It is interesting to note that part of their partnerships with private sectors include information and communication magnates such as Cisco (they produce servers, hubs, bridges, and routers that serve as the nuts and bolts of the ICT networks) and Microsoft (a corporation that has an extant monopoly with software such as Office, Internet Explorer, Outlook, and Publisher, among others).[48]

The knowledge and information that are embedded within the vast ICT networks of global capital that are a source of accumulation of wealth will be considered as gold. Apparently this is the type of knowledge that needs to be taught via the *Education for All* and *Literacy Decade* programs of the United Nations. The development, creation, and dissemination of knowledge embedded within global capital are a form of neocolonization. Neocolonial dominance is asserted culturally and psychologically, via educational programs that legitimate certain knowledge as the only way for countries, citizens, communities, and individuals to insert themselves effectively in the global economy. Welcome to what George Bush, Sr., vehemently boasted of in his presidential term of 1988–92 as the New World Order.

FINAL THOUGHTS

Not everything the United Nation does is a form of neocolonization. The *Education for All* and *Literacy Decade* programs have been used as examples of instances where policies, construction of certain knowledges, legitimacy of certain knowledges, and the embedded nature of education and literacy with global capital, serve as instances of neocolonization. Neocolonization occurs when the education is only in relation to the global economy.

Some documents examined in this chapter (i.e., *Education for All*, *Literacy Decade*, and ICT task force) tie education agendas with neoliberal projects of economic, political, social, cultural, and psychological processes that facilitate the empire of global capital. The educational, literacy, and ICT programs serve as tools of neocolonization as long as they continue to privilege, validate, and legitimize knowledge in relation to global capital.

Historically, any geographical region that has defied the global capital empire has met stiff resistance and repression.[49] We have the current examples of both the Zapatistas in Mexico and the Ogoni in Nigeria. Both cultures have defied global capital. The Zapatistas are resisting being once again stripped from their land by oil companies and the Ogonis are both claiming their lands back and demanding reparations for serious environmental contamination due to oil extraction by Shell Oil Corporation. Both of them have suffered harsh repression in the forms of public executions, torture, and imprisonment, while simultaneously, any alternative non-economy-dependent model of economical development proposed has been systematically turned down.[50]

There is always reason for hope and empowerment. Global education programs and ICT dissemination have the potential to force the empire to reexamine its hegemonic ways.[51] The current macroeconomic structures are characterized by their policies of trickle-down economics. For instance, the fact that multiple anti-WTO manifestations have challenged the oppressive nature of such institutions at their meetings in Seattle; Washington, DC; Prague; and Cancun, to name a few, proves there is discontent among world citizens.[52] In the organization of such anti-WTO protests, ICTs were an integral organizational component.[53] In such context, extant neocolonial experiences and structures can be redefined in a global system of social justice.[54] The task falls upon those who are involved in the various programs of education, literacy, and ICT dissemination. If literacy is imparted within critical literacy models, education is based on practices of critical pedagogy geared toward emancipation, and ICT dissemination is nurtured to excel in its potential emancipatory possibilities, then we are faced with a conundrum of a global utopia. If, on the other hand, the current policies of economical, political, military, cultural, social, and psychological domination remain in place, then the global capital elite will continue to profit from their sophisticated structures, tactics, and policies of hegemonic neocolonization. In this gloomy social historical reality, educators, educational institutions, educational policies, and education advocates have the arduous task of becoming beacons of light in the struggle for education for all who ascribe to beliefs of social justice, solidarity, and emancipation as the driving force of all educational activity.[55]

NOTES

1. Castells, M., & Hall, P. (1994). *Las tecnópolis del mundo: La formación de los complejos industriales del siglo xxi*. Madrid: Alianza Editorial.

2. Hables, G. (Ed.). (1995). *The cyborg handbook*. New York & London: Routledge.

3. Castells, M. (1995). *La ciudad informacional: Tecnologías de la información, reestructuración económica y el proceso urbano-regional*. Madrid: Alianza Editorial.

4. Hardt, M., & Negri, A. (2000). *El imperio*. Madrid: Paidos y Sociedad 95.

5. Dickens, P. (1998). *The global shift: Transforming the world economy*. New York: The Guilford Press; Hoogvelt, A. (1998). *Globalization and the post-colonial world: The new political economy of the globe*. Baltimore: John Hopkins University Press; Horton, R. (1998). *Globalization and the nation state*. New York: St. Martin's Press; Carnoy, M. (1988). *Educación como imperialismo cultural*. Mexico: S.XXI; Klowby, J. (1997). *Inequity, power and development: The task of political sociology*. Atlantic Highlands, NJ: Humanities Press.

6. Hardt & Negri (2000).

7. Gray, H., & Mentor, S. (1995). The cyborg body politics: Version 1. In G. Hables (Ed.), *The cyborg handbook*. New York & London: Routledge.

8. Sarup, M. (1996). *Identity, culture and identity and the postmodern world.* Athens: The University of Georgia Press.

9. Dickens (1998); Horton (1998).

10. Klowby (1997); Robinson (1997), *Promoting poliarchy,* Atlantic Highlands, NJ: Humanities Press.

11. Hoogvelt, A. (1998). *Globalization and the post-colonial world: The new political economy of the globe.* Baltimore: John Hopkins University Press.

12. Ashcroft, B., Griffiths, G., & Tiffin, H. (1995). *Postcolonial study reader.* London: Routledge.

13. Hardt & Negri (2000).

14. Castells, M. (1998). *La era de la información: Economía, sociedad y cultura Vol. III fin del milenio.* Madrid: Alianza Editorial.

15. Castells, M. (2000). *The information age: Economy, society and culture: Vol. I. The rise of the network society.* Australia: Blackwell Publishing.

16. Please read the works of Dickens (1998); Klowby (1997); Horton (1998); and Castells (1998).

17. For a more detailed account on flexible mode of production, please look at Dickens (1998).

18. Dickens (1998).

19. Dickens (1998).

20. Castells (2000).

21. Hardt & Negri (2000).

22. Hoogvelt (1998).

23. Chomsky, N. (1998). *Deterring democracy.* New York: Hill and Wang.

24. Robinson (1997).

25. Stiglitz, J. (2003). *Globalization and its discontents.* New York: W.W. Norton.

26. Klowby (1997).

27. Klowby (1997).

28. Klowby (1997).

29. Klowby (1997).

30. Still, W. (1990). *New world order.* Lafayette, LA: Huntington House Publisher; Perloff, J. (1988). *The shadows of power: The council on foreign relations and the American decline.* Appleton, WI: Western Islands Publishers.

31. Carnoy, M. (1988). *La educación como imperialismo culutral.* S.XXI Mexico.

32. Spring, J. (2000). *Deculturalization and education.* New York: Houghton Mifflin.

33. Spring (2000).

34. Carnoy (1998).

35. Carnoy (1998).

36. UNESCO. (2002). *United Nations literacy decade: education for all: plan of action.* New York: United Nations Educational, Scientific and Cultural Organization.

37. UNESCO (2002).

38. UNESCO (2002).

39. UNESCO (2002).

40. Tyner, K. (1998). *Literacy in the digital world: Teaching and learning in the age of information.* Mahwah, NJ: Laurence Erlbaum Assoc.

41. UNESCO (2002).

42. UNESCO. (2001a). *The role of the United Nations in promoting development, particularly with respect to access to and transfer of knowledge and technology, especially information and communication technologies, inter alia, through partnerships with relevant stakeholders, including the private sector: Report of the Secretary General of the Economical and Social Council.* New York: United Nations Educational, Scientific and Cultural Organization.

43. UNESCO. (2001b). *Plan to use information & communications technologies to combat poverty.* New York: United Nations Educational, Scientific and Cultural Organization.

44. UNESCO (2001b).

45. UNESCO. (2001c). *Literacy for all: A United Nations literacy decade.* New York: United Nations Educational, Scientific and Cultural Organization.

46. UNESCO (2001b).

47. UNESCO (2001b).

48. UNESCO (2001b).

49. Blum, W. (1995). *Killing hope: U.S. military and CIA interventions since WW II.* Monroe, ME: Common Courage Press; Chomsky (1996).

50. Castells, M. (2004). *The information age: Economy, society and culture: Vol. II. The power of identity.* Australia: Blackwell Publishing; Stiglitz (2003).

51. Welton, N., & Wolf, L. (2002). *Global uprising: Confronting the tyrannies of the 21st century: Stories from a new generation of activists.* Canada: New Society Publishers; Castells (2004).

52. Welton & Wolf (2002); Castells (2004).

53. Vegh, S. (2003). Classifying forms of online activism: The case of cyberprotests against the world. In M. Mccaughey & M. Ayers (Eds.), *Cyberactivism: Online activism in theory and practice.* London: Routledge.

54. Welton, N., & Wolf, L. (2002).

55. See Freire, P. (1998). *Teachers as cultural workers: Letters to those who dare to teach.* New York: Westview Press; Freire, P. (1998). *Education for critical consciousness.* New York: Continuum Publishing Company; Freire, P. (1996).

Pedagogy of the oppressed. New York: Continuum Publishing Company; Aranowitz, S. (2001). *The last good job in America: Work and education in the global technoculture.* New York: Rowman & Littlefield Publishers, Inc.

UNIVERSITIES, REGIONAL POLICY, AND THE KNOWLEDGE ECONOMY

Michael A. Peters and Tim May

THE NEW ECONOMY?

In the West, educational policy has given way to talk of the knowledge economy under the sway of world policy organizations like the Organisation for Economic Co-operation and Development (OECD) and the World Bank. The terms "knowledge economy" and "knowledge capitalism" emerged in the mid-1990s to become national policy templates for many Western governments and developing economies. The government of the United Kingdom (U.K.), for example, has pronounced the end of the comprehensive school, based on a "one-size-fits-all" welfare state ideology, and signaled a shift to a fully consumer-driven system of public services in health and education, based on the market ideology of choice and diversity. This shift to the "social market" is underwritten and accompanied by an emphasis on national competitiveness within the global economy and the way in which the "new economy" demands new levels of flexible skilled knowledge workers. This chapter examines the discourse of the knowledge economy and education as an "industry of the future" that can promote regional development, with the attendant emphasis on public–private partnerships and the cultural reconstruction of city entrepreneurial cultures and clustering of knowledge capital activities.

Digitalization, speed, and compression are the forces at work that have transformed the global economy and now have begun to affect every aspect of knowledge production—its organization, storage, retrieval, and transmission. The knowledge economy has certainly arrived, although this does not mean the end of the business cycle, as many early advocates of the new economy maintained. But it does signal structural economic shifts and new sources of growth in some Western economies (e.g., U.S., Finland) that delivered both low unemployment and low inflation due to increased productivity. Although it is clear that investment in ICT (Information and Communications Technology) and ICT-driven productivity growth has led to a higher growth path, there is a risk of exaggerating the growth potential due to ICT investment alone. Yet as a recent OECD report put it:

It would be wrong to conclude that there was nothing exceptional about the recent U.S. experience, that the new economy was in fact a myth. Some of the arguments posited by new economy sceptics are of course true: the effect of ICT may be no greater than other important inventions of the past, like electricity generation and the internal combustion engine. Moreover, far greater productivity surges were recorded in previous decades, not least in the period before the 1970s.[1]

Nevertheless, the evidence suggests that something new is taking place in the structure of OECD economies. The report continues by maintaining that ICT has facilitated productivity-enhancing changes in the firm, in both new and traditional industries, but only when accompanied with greater skills and changes in the organisation of work. Consequently, policies that engage ICT, human capital, innovation and entrepreneurship in the growth process, alongside fundamental policies to control inflation and instil competition, while controlling public finances are likely to bear the most fruit over the longer term.[2]

Crucially, the report investigates and recommends a set of relationships and policies that harness ICT, human capital, innovation, and business creation, focusing on the wider diffusion of ICT and the role of education and training policies in meeting today's skill requirements.

Clearly, the Internet economy is becoming an integral part of the global economy, creating jobs, increasing productivity, and transforming companies and institutions. Employment in the Internet economy is growing faster than in the traditional economy. In the U.S. economy alone, the Internet generated an estimated $830 billion in revenues in 2000, which represented a 58 percent increase over 1989.[3] J. Bradford DeLong, former deputy assistant secretary for economic policy in the U.S. Department of the Treasury, depicts the "new economy," asserting it is both a knowledge and an innovation knowledge where clusters of innovation, based on new technologies and new business models, succeed each other. He maintains it is likely to continue for an extended time, and its consequences are pervasive. He provides an analytical overview of the digital economy, which conveys how different it is from the market economy of orthodox economics. He likens the digital economy to the enclosure of the common lands in early modern Britain, which paved the way for the agricultural and industrial revolutions. Digital commodities, he maintains, do not behave like standard goods and services of economic theory: They are nonrivalrous, barely excludable,

and not transparent. The store of music track is not diminished when one downloads a track from the Internet; it is difficult, if not impossible, to restrict distribution of goods that can be reproduced with no or little cost, and a consumer does not know how good software is before purchase or indeed how its successor versions will perform in the future.

It is important to recognize that the knowledge economy is both classical and new. Danny Quah of the London School of Economics indicates that the economic importance of knowledge can be found in examples where deployment of machines boosted economic performance such as in the Industrial Revolution. By contrast, he talks of the "weightless economy" "where the economic significance of knowledge achieves its greatest contemporary resonance" and suggests it comprises four main elements:

1. Information and communications technology (ICT), the Internet.
2. Intellectual assets: Not only patents and copyrights but also, more broadly, name brands, trademarks, advertising, financial and consulting services, and education.
3. Electronic libraries and databases: including new media, video entertainment, and broadcasting.
4. Biotechnology: carbon-based libraries and databases, pharmaceuticals.

Elsewhere he argues:

Digital goods are bitstrings, sequences of 0s and 1s, which have economic value. They are distinguished from other goods by five characteristics: digital goods are nonrival, infinitely expansible, discrete, aspatial, and recombinant.[4]

Quah has been influential in suggesting that knowledge concentrations spontaneously emerge in space, even when physical distance and transportation costs are irrelevant. The dynamics of spatial distributions manifest themselves in convergent clusters. This is an important feature, especially given the development of the economy first in Silicon Valley.

In *Getting the Measure of the New Economy*, Diane Coyle and Danny Quah note the 11 percent productivity gap between the U.K. and Germany, and the 45 percent productivity gap with the United States (1999 base year), while at the same time acknowledging the considerable impact of ICT on the economy.[5] They demonstrate on the basis of evidence from the United States that those businesses responding the quickest to ICT developments are driving forward the rest of the economy. At the same time, they maintain that technology takes time to filter through and set up the cascade effects that are evident in change organizational and business practices. They acknowledge that after the dotcom bubble burst, confidence in the new economy has waned, yet they remain optimistic about long-term technology-led economic growth based on the processing power of the microchip, which encompasses well-known developments like the Internet and developments in information and communications technologies with gene technology, nanotechnology, robotics, and advanced materials. They write:

Advocates of the notion of the new economy cited supporting factors uniquely combined in the U.S. economy, particularly minimal government, high levels of competition, encouragement of entrepreneurship, and access to venture capital. What gave the theory bite, though, was the vision that the widespread diffusion of technology had permanently changed the way economies had worked for the better.[6]

They also develop a set of indicators to measure the changes to the deep structure of the economy brought about by technology.

CLUSTERING EFFECTS OF NEW ICT-DRIVEN ECONOMY ACTIVITY

One of the most significant features of these economic changes is the way in which against expectations a sort of geographical clustering of new economic activity appears to have taken place. This clustering even applies to the boarder accounts of its development and spread. The Silicon Valley view of the e-conomy maintains that the center-periphery model with development spreading from the West Coast, south of Palo Alto, forced the development of a single international market that is dominated by U.S. multinationals. By contrast, the pluri-view suggests that Internet leading-edge use and e-commerce centers are beginning to emerge in Europe and Asia, and as new technologies emerge, along with different uses, business models, and legal frameworks, they will challenge the early dominance of U.S. policy and the international market. If there are different local configurations of market demand and distinct trajectories of development and separate national e-conomies, then they are most likely to emerge around fundamental empirical criteria such as distinct technologies and applications; locally differentiated market structures; different business models; perhaps, distinct structures of comparative advantage; and culturally different legal and policy frameworks.

The alleged aspatial character of digital goods seems to fly in the face of empirical evidence. Given their "weightlessness," digital goods are theorized to spread easily across the globe without favoring particular locations, yet empirical analysis reveals exactly the opposite—that the production of digital goods like other goods becomes geographically concentrated. In fact, as Quah argues, "the geographical clustering of computer software and digital media production, academic and commercial R & D, and financial services, among other digital goods, is likely tighter than for ordinary goods and services."[7] He argues further that the aspatiality of digital goods does not imply that space no longer matters; indeed, only transportation costs no longer matter, and others factors normally associated with geography take on a heightened importance.

He indicates that embodied human capital clusters geographically because communication of tacit knowledge is most efficient in close proximity. In other words, "synchronous face-to-face interactions matter for transmitting (nonbitstring) knowledge."[8] On this understanding, sometimes learning is considered the core of a theory of clustering, focusing on the existence, the internal organization, and boundaries of the cluster.[9]

The major theoretical question is, why has industry clustering reappeared in advanced economies when it had all but disappeared in the mid-twentieth century? Phillip Cooke suggests that the "knowledge economy" consists of fragments and runs against conventional economic analysis that assumes individualistic competition within an ordered economic equilibrium.[10] By contrast, with the knowledge economy he points to *disequilibrium* or economic and social imbalance, *collaborative* economic action as the basis of modern capitalism, and the *systemic* nature of strategic competitiveness of groups' actions based on consensus rather than individual opportunism. Against the status of the lonely Nietzschean heroic individual and entrepreneur characterized by Schumpeter, Cooke suggests the sources of innovation lie in networks of social relationships, that is, *knowledge networks*. He argues:

clusters are crucial to economic imbalance . . . they rest upon collaboration of a generally non-market-destroying type that is simply essential for modern economic organization, and . . . clusters have systemic organizational characteristics that go against much economic orthodoxy.[11]

Such an analysis then directly leads to an emphasis on "the geographical dimension of learning, knowledge transfer, collaboration and the exploitation of the spillovers." Cooke concurs with Quah that "proximity in a cluster offers the opportunity for tacit knowledge exchange or 'treacherous' learning that may be hindered in large firms by 'group think' and corporate culture."[12]

Government policy has changed to accent and foster the geographical cluster of new economic activity. It is clear that that Labour government sees the "knowledge-driven economy" as key to the U.K.'s competitive success. The strategy behind the adoption of this concept is to promote high-tech venture capital "clusters" in the regions. In part, the U.K. strategy is strongly influenced by Michael Porter's work on the role of clusters in forging U.S. innovativeness and competitiveness.[13] Regional development agencies (RDAs) in Britain are encouraged to develop "cluster" policies based on knowledge industries.

For instance, the *White Paper on Enterprise, Skills, and Innovation* (2001) emphasizes the role of universities in the regional development of clusters in the knowledge economy:

The role of our universities in the economy is crucial. They are powerful drivers of innovation and change in science and technology, the arts, humanities, design and other creative disciplines. They produce people with knowledge and skills; they generate new knowledge and import it from diverse sources; and they apply knowledge in a range of environments. They are also the seedbed for new industries, products and services and are at the hub of business networks and industrial clusters of the knowledge economy.[14]

The examples can be developed further. The U.K. Office of Sciences and Technology emphasizes the importance of "knowledge transfer."

Within a modern, knowledge-driven economy, knowledge transfer is about transferring good ideas, research results and skills between universities, other research organisations, business and the wider community to enable innovative new products and services to be developed.[15]

This kind of emphasis can be clearly seen in OST's Higher Education Innovation Fund (HEIF):

We have now established the Higher Education Innovation Fund (HEIF), which together with the existing Higher Education Reach Out to Business and the Community fund (HEROBC), is worth £140 million over three years, to further build on universities' potential to act as drivers of growth in the knowledge economy. HEIF provides special funding to enable HEIs to respond to the needs of business, through both the continuing development of capacity in universities to interact with business and the community (building on HEROBC), and large, strategic, collaborative projects to strengthen university-business partnerships.[16]

More broadly, the U.K. government's economic strategy can be seen as being based on investment in science, engineering, and technology. In the recent White Paper, *Investing in Innovation: A Strategy for Science, Engineering and Technology*, the focus is on the twin strategies of renewing the physical and human capital, which underpins research and investing in capacity to exploit the burgeoning opportunities of new science.[17] In this strategy, universities are encouraged to link with business to create value for the regional and national economy where Regional Development Agencies play an enhanced role in developing knowledge transfer programs.

The regional development role of knowledge industries has received increasing attention in the United States and by the European Union (EU). CEOs for Cities, for example, an organization that explores best practices in urban economic development and proposes new strategic frameworks on emerging trends, recently partnered with the Initiative for a Competitive Inner City (ICIC) to develop a national study of the impact of higher education on urban economies. The study introduces a strategic impact framework and features case studies and best practices in university partnerships, including studies of both Virginia Commonwealth University (VCU) in Richmond, and Columbia University in New York City. The report begins:

Unleashing the local economic development capacity of these institutions (colleges and universities) should be a national priority. While ambitious, it is an agenda that does not require massive new funding or heroic changes in day-to-day operations of colleges and universities, city government or community groups.[18]

The Lisbon European Council set the "bold and ambitious" ten-year goal of making the EU the most dynamic, competitive, sustainable knowledge-based economy in the world. Yet the transition to the knowledge-based economy has been slow, and there is now recognition that spending on higher education needs to be strengthened. The argument is made that the European ability to produce, diffuse, and use knowledge effectively relies heavily on its capacity to produce highly educated people for its firms to be engaged in a continuing process of innovation. Yet lifelong learning is still not a reality for most Europeans citizens. It is now recognized that the European innovation systems have not been successful in exploiting the new techno-economic paradigm rooted in information technology that is reflected in the European paradox of a strong science base but weak innovation performance. As Lundvall and Borras argue: "A major policy objective of innovation policy must be to contribute to the learning capability of firms, knowledge institutions and people and to promote innovation and adaptation."[19] They point to "human resource development, new forms of firm organisation, network formation, new role for knowledge intensive business services and for universities as the key elements in speeding up the catching-up within this paradigm." A new regional policy focusing increasingly on the role of universities and of higher education more generally, first recognized in the Bologne agreement, has begun to theorize these economic imperatives in new spatialized knowledge networks. The role of universities in regional development has gone beyond the study of technology transfer and direct employment effects of spin-off companies and the establishment of science parks to embrace the wider ethos of the enhancement of human and social capital within a region, including emphasis on student recruitment and regional placement policies, university professional development programs for local managers based on local research, the development of research networks that serve as a basis for embedding the local businesses in the global economy, and a more research- and information-sensitive negotiation of the local/global interface.

UNIVERSITIES: THE MANCHESTER KNOWLEDGE CAPITAL INITIATIVE

In the North West of the United Kingdom, this policy context is reflected in several recent developments. The North West Universities Association (NWUA) was formed in 1999 and works increasingly closely with the North West Development Agency (NWDA) and other regional partners. In 2001, the North West established England's first science council, bringing together representatives from industry, regional agencies, and the universities to lobby on behalf of the region and advise and launch the Regional Science Strategy.[20] This was subsequently published in 2002 and sets forward cluster-based actions in five priority areas (biotechnology, environmental technologies, chemicals, aerospace, and nuclear energy) to link universities better with industry and regional partners. The model is one of "excellence with relevance."

Many RDAs are now devolving the implementation of aspects of regional strategies to subregional bodies, recognizing that some issues are better tackled at a lower spatial scale. At the same time, local authorities are collaborating with neighbors and partners to "upscale" their cities and tackle joint issues through a cross-boundary approach. The movement also now includes health authorities, universities, LEAs, skills agencies, charities, and the police who are active in their own city-regional partnerships. In a number

of cases, the private sector is giving the lead to city-regional thinking, particularly in the arena of economic and planning policy.[21] In the Greater Manchester context, we see the development of the Greater Manchester subregional strategy, led by the Association of Greater Manchester Authorities (AGMA), launched on June 20, 2003. An essential element of this strategy focuses on enhancing the subregional core and building on the university assets concentrated therein.[22]

With this background in mind, the vision of Manchester: Knowledge Capital (KC) is

to create an internationally acclaimed "Knowledge Capital" within the Greater Manchester conurbation, which will position Manchester, branded as the Knowledge Capital, at the heart of the Knowledge Economy, significantly contributing to the economic growth of the nation and the North West region leading to a healthier city/region with a vibrant, safe and attractive environment in which to live, work and play, for people of all ages, social and cultural backgrounds.[23]

This initiative can be seen in the context of two major changes that are fundamentally reshaping our society, economy, and the institutions and practices of modern life: the development of the knowledge economy and changing notions of scale. These two factors have led to increasing attention being given to the role of universities in driving local and regional economies, reflected in a wealth of new policies being developed at international, national, regional, and subregional scales. These policies raise many challenges for universities and for their localities and a number of different responses, as international and national comparisons indicate. In this context, KC represents a much needed and valuable opportunity for the universities to position themselves at the heart of the city-region's response to the global knowledge economy.

From the forty interviews and documentary work conducted in the four universities (Manchester, MUU, Salford, and UMIST) with senior managers and those individuals who were considered key to successful implementation of KC, we can see the extent to which understandings remain aspirational at a variety of levels across the universities. Relatively speaking, the most well developed attempts at clarifying the meaning of KC are provided, not surprisingly, by those who are championing and driving the process for the universities. Overall, these are a small number of individuals in senior management positions. Here we see an explicit identification of a role; that is, creating the conditions that will enable its development. The role of senior managers is to create not only a vision, but also an infrastructure that will function without too much top-down planning to provide support and incentives.

Yet a clear aim of KC and one given by central government is that the universities should act in collaboration with each other and with other agencies for the benefit of the city-region. This was both implicit and explicit in many of the interviews. In particular, one senior manager spoke of a great strength of the city of Manchester being a "mutual trust between the key players." This is matched with the view of one senior manager in Manchester City Council who said that KC provided a context in which: "We construct the new HEI sector in such a way that it interfaces very effectively and coherently with a significantly wider world [than has been historically the case]." Many of these interviewees— while unpacking, or alternatively trying hard to populate, the notion of KC—also sought clarification as to its geographical focus. Some took it to concentrate on the North West of England, others Greater Manchester, some Manchester, but all with a degree of uncertainty. The idea of "capital" itself was also a source of ambiguity, with ideas of human capital and innovation mixing with those of cultural and physical capital and Manchester seeking to place itself more securely as

the "capital" of the North West. Importantly, what we see here are differences in aspiration and interpretation according to the remit of the individual interviewed. Those further up the hierarchy tended to be supportive of the idea in terms of its potential, while those with a concern for implementation and its implications for practice tended to be more uncertain. This belief came from an experience of so many "next big thing" initiatives that produced more work without tangible benefit. It also came from the institutional incentives that were available for engagement at different levels. As one interviewee put it, in relation to practices surrounding international research excellence (of which they were a part), KC should be about

achieving some sort of culture shift within the institution . . . the notion that you can only be taken seriously if you go to conferences in North America or Munich or whatever and that anything where you dirty your hands on things local, I mean, by definition is seen as trivial . . . the international and the local can readily co-exist together . . . [the University needs] levers to pull locally and to ensure that this might happen and all of the incentives and reward structures still tend to reinforce the argument.[24]

Incentivization and reward within the different institutions and how they relate to practice is clearly a major issue and one that has not been adequately considered in relation to the developmental potential of KC.

Two issues, in particular, then become important: (1) to develop the conditions that facilitate activities; and (2) for those activities to feed into KC in order that it moves from concept to action. What is required for this process is a set of practices that would populate the concept. As one person put it, it cannot just be about:

museums and office blocks and such like in the centre, but actually focus on regeneration through knowledge applied to entrepreneurial activities . . . that seems to me to be an excellent extension and the next stage after we've physically transformed the city into something worth living in . . . then we've got to jump start some entrepreneurial activity or it will be another Sheffield Centre for Popular Culture![25]

There were also differences between the institutions in terms of how they approach the potential of Knowledge Capital. Thus, those associated with UMIST/Victoria tended to see the development of KC as one of "added value." In other words, it was concerned with repackaging and exploiting existing opportunities for institutional benefit and that of the city as a whole, in terms of the location of the university and its relations with key stakeholders. This concerned the development of relations of mutuality with the city council and other organizations in providing a context and environment for attracting staff, finance, investment, and facilities to Manchester. It would also provide further evidence of an "innovative milieu" through the development of incubation facilities (for the exploitation of knowledge), infrastructure (physical and human), and other visible signs of activity (e.g., cultural in relation to art galleries, theatres, and museums). To this extent, the development of KC is part of the overall strategy of the "Project Unity" merger in seeking to counterbalance the "Golden Triangle" of Oxford, Cambridge, and London and become a "Harvard of the North" and part of an extended "Golden Diamond."

Such international aspirations should be seen against a change in recent years in which both institutions have moved a long way from being seen as "in" but not "of" the region. It was emphasized that the shift toward an internationally focused and renowned institution was not incompatible with a local and engaged focus, as it was a contributor to the "well-being" of an area. The development of Victoria as a world-class research university was illustrated by developments in biomedical research (a £40 million complex for biomedical research relates to what was described as a "biomedical corridor" in Oxford Road) and growing relationships between medical facilities, the National Health Service (NHS), pharmaceutical companies, and spin-out enterprises. Victoria's focus was in positioning itself as an international first-class, science-based research university able to attract the brightest students, leading-edge academics, and develop the facilities that match these aspirations to particular developments. The associations that exist between academics within Greater Manchester and the North West region temper the international dimension of activities in some departments (e.g., biomedical science and collaborative links with Liverpool). In addition, the level of activity may not directly relate to the locality, but that is not to suggest it does not have local implications. For instance, in terms of the opportunities presented by the merger for new centers of research excellence, this person spoke about a centre for climate change:

The atmospheric physicists know all about modelling of the climate and atmosphere etc, making connections with the earth sciences, setting up a more environmentally orientated physics and earth sciences school . . . the merger is an opportunity to reconfigure into these new knowledge lumps . . . so in that sense there's tremendous opportunity for rearranging some of the intellectual furniture, and I would have thought that presents opportunities for new research directions focused on spin off and entrepreneurial activities.[26]

Allowing such possibilities to flourish over time, as opposed to imposing a vision upon sets of practices, is precisely how some of the most advantageous developments may take place. In addition, while there are international aspirations, there are also different levels of engagement within Victoria and UMIST. Planning and Landscape and Architecture, for example, have worked on KC design projects and possess a long tradition of working with local communities in terms of outreach, widening participation, and issues associated with multiculturalism.

KC at MMU tended not to be seen as a repackaging of existing processes, but as a means of continually cultivating relationships between the university and the region around a number of strategic themes in which they were investing their energies and resources. These areas of activity were: Network for Enterprise; Innovation in Art and Design; Regeneration; Sport and Physical Activity; Clothing, Design and Technology; and Aviation, Transport and Environment.

KC was regarded as enhancing those areas of activity, as well as being transformative; in the process it brought greater recognition to the university in terms of its overall identity. This has been prevalent in terms of creativity and culture, for example, art, design, fashion, and sport. MMU was regarded as having a strong vocational base with a regional focus. The university possessed clear areas of research excellence (seven four-star departments and one five-star department in the latest research assessment exercise [RAE]), but was seen as having a focus on widening participation through outreach activities, through enterprise in local schools, through the large number of teachers who are trained in the institution, through continuing professional development, and via such initiatives as the Community Entrepreneurship Scheme. Problem solving and innovation with local businesses led in interviews to an emphasis upon practical engagement. For example, in terms of fashion, MMU deals with developments and ideas for clothes that sell at retail, not clothing that ranks as high fashion. Thinking about this emphasis in terms of seeking to welcome people into universities who wouldn't otherwise come in, this person noted in respect to the Manchester Fashion Network that there was an opportunity to enhance recognition through KC. Overall, it was viewed as an important means of providing coordination and coherence to a wide variety of activities that saw the university seeking to reach out to people who wouldn't normally engage with higher education.

This latter aspiration is shared with Salford in which one senior manager viewed KC as an "infrastructure of possibilities." Here academics and the institutions could form relationships of knowledge creation, production, and sharing for multiple beneficiaries. KC was an aspiration to create a structure within which people can move and be creative. There was also the sense generally that KC related to aspirations in terms of the mixed aims at Salford of teaching, research, and enterprise. The flow of knowledge and the movement of people within a defined area was key to this notion.

Salford was seen to have notable pockets of research excellence (e.g., in Information Systems, the Built Environment, European Studies and Urban Regeneration, Media, Art and Design, and Public Health, as well as in training in Professions Allied to Medicine). Its reputation in these areas was seen in terms of its distinctive strengths in addressing business, industrial, and commercial interests in, for example, the design and deployment of "enabling technologies" through working in partnership. This ethos was linked to the potential seen in KC. An emphasis was also placed on widening access and participation via a number of initiatives, with the aim of raising young people's aspirations. Mentoring was, for example, one program of work mentioned, while the relationship between skills and student was seen to be accommodated within Salford. Overall, therefore, KC was seen as enhancing existing agendas in teaching, enterprise, and research, all of which were driven by the idea of being an "engaged" university working in partnership with a variety of stakeholders.

All this takes place against a background of change in which understanding differences between institutions, as well as similarities among them, is required. At the launch of the Higher Education Funding Council for England's (HEFCE) draft strategic plan,[27] Sir Howard Newby was quoted as saying that individual universities "must build upon their own chosen areas of strength, and work in collaboration with other providers, so that the sector as a whole continues to deliver all that is required of it in the increasingly competitive global marketplace."

Complementarity, on the basis of an understanding of distinctiveness, was seen as crucial to the development of KC by all those interviewed. This is not to suggest there is no competition between the universities as they seek to differentiate their niche markets and convey a particular identity to an outside audience. That means recognizing the distinctive strengths of each institution.

In terms of further engagement and making the universities meaningful to citizens, a large number of deprived wards surround Manchester. As one person put it: "We have a huge mountain to climb in terms of raising the aspirations of local people . . . young people." Spatially speaking, this also relates to a tension between what is seen as the "urban core." KC might be very successful, for example, in attracting a larger pool of knowledge workers. Some of these may stay in the "center," but there are no schools and so where will they go if they have, or want children? In this sense, how will this community benefit those who already exist in areas such as East Manchester, Hulme, and Moss Side? How are these latter groups to benefit from KC?

New urban and regional education futures have recently become the basis for both the knowledge economy and also dreams of the renewal of the postindustrial city. This movement that depends upon a reconceptualization of regional development has the prospect of emphasizing the university as a local source of research, expertise, and innovation, and providing a knowledge base for local industries to thrive in the global economy. Perhaps,

more important, it holds the promise of rearticulating the links between the university and the communities it serves to enhance civic traditions and thickening democracy.

NOTES

1. OECD. (2001). *The new economy: Beyond the hype.* http://www.oecd.org/dataoecd/2/26/2380634.pdf.

2. Quah, D. (2001). *Economic growth: Measurement.* LSE Economics Department. Retrieved June 4, 2005, from http://econ.lse.ac.U.K./~dquah/p/0108iesbs.pdf.

3. See The Internet Economy Indicators at http://www.internetindicators.com/execsummry.html.

4. Quah, D. (2002). *Digital goods and the new economy.* Centre for Economic Performance, LSE. Retrieved September 3, 2004, from http://cep.lse.ac.U.K./pubs/download/dp0563.pdf.

5. Coyle, D., & Quah, D. (2002). *Getting the measure of the new economy.* http://www.theworkfoundation.com/pdf/New_Economy.pdf.

6. Coyle & Quah (2002).

7. Quah (2002).

8. Quah (2002).

9. Maskell, P. (2001). *Growth and territorial configuration of economic activity.* Retrieved September 3, 2004, from http://www.druid.dk/conferences/nw/paper1/maskell.pdf.

10. Cooke, P. (2002). *Knowledge economies: Clusters, learning and cooperative advantage.* London: Routledge.

11. Cooke (2002), p. 2.

12. Cooke (2002), p. 3.

13. Porter, M. (1999). *The microeconomic foundations of competitiveness and the role of clusters.* http://www.cit.ms/archive/gov_conf_2001/porter/exe_briefing.pdf.

14. *Opportunity for all in a world of change: A White Paper on Enterprise, Skills and Innovation.* http://www.dti.gov.U.K./opportunityforall/.

15. U.K. Office of Science and Technology (OST) on "Knowledge Transfer." http://www.ost.gov.U.K./enterprise/knowledge/index.htm.

16. OST on "Knowledge Transfer."

17. U.K. Office of Science and Technology (OST). (2002). *Investing in innovation: A strategy for*

science, engineering and technology. Available at www.ost.gov.uk/policy/science_strategy.pdf.

18. Joint Study by Initiative for a Competitive Inner City and CEOs for Cities (2002). *Leveraging colleges and universities for urban economic revitalization: An action agenda.* HYPERLINK "http://www.ceosforcities.org/research/2002/leveraging_colleges/"http://www.ceosforcities.org/research/2002/leveraging_colleges/.

19. Lundvall, B-A., & Borras, S. (1998). *Innovation policy in the globalising learning economy.* http://www.cordis.lu/tser/src/sumfinal.htm.

20. NWDA. (2002). *Science strategy England's northwest.* Warrington: North West Development Agency.

21. Centre for Sustainable Urban and Regional Futures (SURF). (2003). *Evaluating urban futures: Enhancing quality and improving effectiveness.* SURF: University of Salford. www.surf.salford.ac.U.K.

22. AGMA. (2002). http://www.agma.gov.U.K./agma/FinalVersionStrategy.pdf.

23. AGMA. (2002). http://www.manchester knowledge.com/knowledge.html.

24. Centre for Sustainable Urban and Regional Futures (SURF). (2003, May). *Knowledge capital from conception to action.* SURF: University of Salford.www.surf.salford.ac.U.K.

25. SURF (2003, May).

26. SURF (2003, May).

27. HEFCE's draft strategic plan (2003–08). http://www.hefce.ac.U.K./News/hefce/2003/stratplan.asp.

THE INDIVIDUAL VERSUS THE COLLECTIVE IN A TIME OF GLOBALIZATION: EDUCATIONAL IMPLICATIONS

Judith J. Slater

Institutions are produced as a response to and consequence of humanly produced perceptions of need. These perceptions are transformed into actions that are "taken for granted as reality by the ordinary members of society in the subjective meaningful conduct of their lives."[1] This real world and its enactment as action supercede the theoretical, and this plays out in a field that is collectively bargained for by rules that are internal and compromised as the situation warrants. Individuals navigate and persist in light of the collective nature of the institutions that they find themselves a part of. They balance their own perceptions with those of the collective even when they may be at odds with the prevailing notions and forms of acceptable behavior. Although individual behavior is situated within the context of the objective history of the collective, it is also influenced by the power and control of that society and by the relationships that society has with the rest of the world.

Globalization has confounded this perception of balance. It is no longer a question of the individual and the community, but the individual situated within a series of communities that are linked to global currents. This cumulative process of interacting and communication is greatly accelerated today and is evidenced by the interconnectedness of the world through finance, capital, and regulatory institutions. Historically periods of consolidation and innovation have been followed by reform of politics, society, and institutions that require restrictions in conflict with democratic ideals.[2] Today there are questions about universal freedom and equality of education in a globalized context. These questions are pressing as necessary conditions for human welfare and individual rights in globalized economies. The plethora of articles about globalization and its affects on people worldwide, on the economic and social, political, educational, and personal, point out that the movement today does not necessarily take into account human development. It is the larger collective that is paramount in decisions and individual voice and individual benefit is secondary. The future of human development and its sustainability is being shaped by conflicting trends of globalization and cultural and individual identity. Societies are evolving, transforming cultures, creating wealth, poverty, and innovation, and at the same time imposing and instilling loss of control and involvement for individuals.

An example of local response to this loss of control is the spiraling of rhetoric that escalates beyond reason, as when there is talk of war.[3] The parallel for education is the standards and accountability movement, whose stakes keep going up in the form of the rhetoric of competition and superiority worldwide. This is accompanied by threats of retaliation that move beyond reasonable expectations for success. There seems to be a snowball effect that there is too much invested in the rhetoric to stop, so more and more effort is expended in a process that is never profitable. Yet, further sanctions are put in place in the guise of compliance with an acceptable position of dogmatism. This is typical of hierarchical societies but less so of communal environments that might suggest to back off and wait so that the cost is not unrealistic to the goal unless judgment, conscious thinking, and mutual agreement are the means to achieve a solution to the problem.

The premise of this essay is that critical commentary is necessary at this time with regard to the effects of globalization on the individual and whether the practical effects of communal thinking locally, nationally, and globally can lead to enhancement of the moral and practical realities fostered upon education today. This premise that there be global consideration to this situation is clarified with what globalization is meant to signify unity and integration of purpose and goal seeking, but it has polarized rather than united.[4] It has dismantled a safety net enveloping the poor, as the regulatory system of protectionism has been taken apart in the name of promoting exports. In British Columbia, the lumberyards sit idle and the workers are jobless, as Japan stockpiled all the lumber it could in the past decade and now the one market has closed. Meanwhile, there has been a ripple effect on the economy, as the large proportion of lumber workers are unable to buy services offered by the rest of this fragile system. And this is in a developed nation! What of poor nations whose workers do not profit from globalization and are being left out of the loop? The most evident effect of globalization is the spikes and valleys that come from connecting economies of each country without placing control mechanisms from the state on the commerce.[5] Other examples exist such as the assemblage of parts of cars in Mexico without the transference of the technology to produce their own. Without technology transfer and the closing of markets to imports, little filters down to sustain growth and the poor remain an underclass that is unskilled.

[T]he poor suffer when America is the supermarket of the world, even at bargain prices. There is plenty of food for the world, and even many countries with severe malnutrition are food exporters. The problem is that people cannot afford it. Three-quarters of the world's poor are rural. If they are forced off their land by subsidized grain imports, they starve.[6]

The solution is import substitution, to close markets and develop domestic ability to produce their own products for the populace. Globalization needs to be a tool to provide food, health, housing, and education to those that need it for development.[7]

Education quantity in a global environment was thought to mean an investment in human capital that brought rewards to a population, and that there were real advantages to the accumulation of human capital by an individual. Today there is a view that educational payoff is to advance a skilled labor force to be competitive in a global market. Yet, variance in enrollment and quantity of education and its return seem more relevant than when the focus is on quality and real opportunity in terms of outcome. Therefore, questions of gender, race, and socioeconomic group impinge on the value of education to achieve economic advantage.[8]

Some call for a rethinking of relativistic morality in light of new interconnections requiring collaboration, networks, and global capitalistic intermingling that bring closer larger issues of poverty, war, famine, and disease.[9] One major role of education is to transmit the moral code to the population. But globalization issues question whether this can remain parochial. No longer can we turn our backs on poorer nations because now there is information and access. As in local communities, each life affects all others and all lives are now internationally created. This constrains us as well as offering opportunities to reexamine what it means to be connected to and respond to others. While this need has been responded to by crossboarder government collaboration in legal, policing, and military confabulations, it has had less of an effect on our parochial view of what it means to work together and to use education to create what Dewey refers to as community. Moral codes of conduct are part of the purposes of schooling, and the certainty of being governed legally in accordance with known rules (rules of law) is a mission of schools.[10] Yet, in light of globalization, government and the equilibrating mechanisms of the global market influence the applications as they affect education and the community. Globalization fragments

politics as it integrates markets. It also influences democratic practices by its enactment. A society of human freedom expects the certainty of being governed in accordance with known rules and laws. But industrialization led to a reduction of class conflict through the process of law. And what about a common rule of law applicable to all nations? It doesn't exist; therefore, rules are established that limit individual rights, and these rules may not be sustainable in the long run since the rules seem to benefit the few. The idea that communal norms will be established in this time of globalization that support the accumulation of human capital without more structural, hierarchical restrictions is unlikely.[11] Cooperative systems cannot evolve when there is lack of transparency in governance, established cultures, and lack of common rules of law and justice. Individuals follow the rules of law when it is in their best interests to do so. The conditions of doing so are that the other citizens do so as well. These conditions are not evident in this phase of globalization at any level of analysis.

How then is education made responsive to the global human context? How should the individual act in such a tenuous complex environment?

John Dewey notes that what is valued is temporal. What values guide acceptable behavior are tempered with other values when certain political, economic, or community mores are advanced as more correct at a particular moment in time.[12] All these influences are imbued with materialistic, or scientific (in pragmatist terms), conditions of usefulness at particular moments in history. It is not just situational; it is temporal in the sense that certain positions are perpetuated long after they have outlived their usefulness—or are they continued by the privileged to control the masses? Soros proposes, "Reality is affected by the beliefs of participants in the market."[13] The values are understood and accepted as a possibility of action, given certain circumstances and certain conditions that allow them to be acted upon.

What is judged best and how that judgment is made for a particular circumstance is based, we believe, on criteria. There are criteria for best skating routine at the Olympics, and opinions are formed by learned judgments, and the public accepts those opinions as truth. "Human beings have a yen for hierarchies; even if the most important aspects of our lives don't easily lend themselves to ranking, we feel compelled to try it anyway." Critics are "writers paid . . . to deliver scientifically unfalsifiable opinions."[14] Yet, the prize, the goal, is relativistic and relational, even though it is expected to be more definitive, like scores on a test, representing truth through the actions of the bearer. But real life in a complex world involves choices and those choices are made by individuals with a particular taste and point of view beyond the standard or code of behavior, beyond their actions, and ingrained in their beliefs and values, whether honorable or not. Although we rely on experts to give us expectations of behavior as it is supposed to be, it becomes a popular vote of morality that sets the standard. Critics, prize judges, and the marketplace are all involved in the celebration of those choices.

Questions of a priori theories about behavior are equally damaging. Dewey[15] says that tastes are not cultivated, that liking is liking, that enjoyment—in one's own life and in one's own decisions in action—cannot be regulated by having rules of conduct and morals delegated and mandated as rules and laws of behavior. We cannot rely on definite truth about behaviors, but instead upon the conditions of use at the moment in the real world. And we have the ability then to take action or not in each circumstance, as we make up our mind and influence others to do the same and to act in one way or another. Caleb Carr's book *The Lessons of Terror* cites Vattel's Law from the 1758 book, *The Law of Nations*, describing how to determine whether a war is just. The Law states that one needs to assess how the sides are fighting as well as what they are fighting for. "Just causes can be betrayed by unjust behavior on the battlefield, like killing civilians or prisoners or employing disproportionate force to attain an objective."[16] Good causes can be undermined by bad means, such as terrorism. The paradox is that you are more likely to win when both sides exercise restraint, when the battle is fought directly without the intervention of civilians. In *Killing Time*, Carr further notes that there is an inherent philosophical and ethical superiority of the United States termed moral exceptionalism.[17] It is the rationalization of action so you can live with yourself. Great crimes are committed in the name of moral exceptionalism in order to reach a position of unchallengeable power. When power is one sided, terror may pay off better. Power is the issue, and for our purposes the critical question is whose power makes the decisions of what behavior is moral and just. The strong must understand the weak and their subservient position to the conditions of the crisis. Restraint of those who hold the power is strength, according to Carr, and a precondition for victory.[18] The ideal is only useful if it fits into the reality of the moment. Sometimes less than the ideal is the best compromise for all concerned.

There is a further problem using old notions of behavior based on custom or institutional prescriptions concerning behavior. "[U]sing old standards to meet new conditions" without modification produces disruption in human life.[19] This is either fought back against as the old attitudes prevail, or they cause a change in orientation to what constitutes appropriate behavior. Hopefully, eventually these changes cause buy-ins to change beliefs and values that propel the behaviors in the environments under question. If not, we regulate and limit either the new or old behaviors until they conform to the ethic of behavior that has been adopted or perpetuated at the moment. Who regulates the transformation or the maintenance? Who has that responsibility in schools, in government, in economics, in global issues of access and control, that are guided by strict codes of conduct that are in turn promulgated as beliefs of indoctrination?

Rather, common interest, that of forsaking one's own interest for that of others, giving up our chance to be the only winner for the good of another winning, is the best position.[20] An example is that of the lottery to enter the country. The more people who apply to be part of the pool, the less of a chance the individual has to win a spot. Cooperation implies that fewer people apply, even precisely a maximum according to the number of openings, so that all get in this time. Subsequently, if this is done each time, it ensures entrance for everyone. Rather, there is competition to take advantage of opportunities, almost by chance, as individualistic interests are served at the expense of the community best interests.

What motivates human thinking that causes this decision making to be so individualistic at the expense of community? Can cooperation develop in a world where everyone is governed by his or her own self-interest?[21] Traits needed for cooperation include the following: niceness (never initiating competition), forgiveness (returning to cooperation after a lapse into individualistic behavior), provocability (if the opponent competes, react to the opponent and retaliate), and transparency (let the opponent know that you will give back what they give, which can lengthen the goal-seeking behavior of each).

For liberal democracy to work in a time of globalization and to sustain the liberal ideal in civic life, sustainable public investment in education is needed to facilitate and foster cultural diversity and responsible citizenry. This promotes the public good if coupled with mutual respect among citizens, mutual trust that the state acts in ways that are legitimized as necessary and not merely imposition of interests that do not share the public trust, and transparency in the actions of the state to make available the information necessary to make wise decisions. Of course, there is little to show that these three conditions are being met. There is a modicum of civic participation, and information disclosure is mired in opacity and disclosed only under threat of reprisal by other government agencies (such as the recent disclosures of pre-September 11 events by the government). The resulting culture is infused with a form of international taste in products, worldview, materialism, and virtual interchanges of commodity consciousness.[22] Capital flows are nontraditionally moved as are the trade in knowledge and information across borderless economies. To navigate the new waters of this boundaryless realm, there have to be civil minimums demanded from government. There has to be an unregulated flow of information that is free and does not coincide with civil interests and economic support of government. People are the first order, not economics or politics or long-term solutions, but individual accessibility and entrepreneurial advantage. There is little concern for the nation and for ideology as pragmatic self-interest holds sway.

Personal rights, through the vehicle of human rights, means a new normative framework for those who fall outside of the traditional national citizenship categories. This undermines the traditional notion of citizenship and civic training as a requirement for participation in political and social life.[23] This means that new processes must be established that can transform social action for economics, politics, and education. For education, Torres cites higher use fees, privatization, decentralization, and problems in quality as challenges faced by this new focus on personal rights, and that mass schooling as it is being transformed is only responding to the development of the cultural framework existing today, as it has in the past. Schooling is the

ceremonial induction into modern society, as an extended initiation rite that symbolically transforms unformed children into enhanced individuals authorized to participate in the modern economy, polity, and society, and it does so by definition.[24]

The state is therefore the modernizer as it reasserts itself and modernizes with current legitimization (material, capital, and technical know-how). It does this to externally survive in the globalization process. It faces problems when those signals are in conflict with the communities it serves.

Modern school reform has taken on social, political, and economic capital, and the rhetoric fueling the practices are driven by declining competitiveness in a global economy. His argument is that this type of reform is completely ahistorical, as evidenced by each new wave repeating the criticism, and the solutions, of old. The problem is that the residue of school reform remains as new ideas are implemented, layering on each other so that success and failure are murky in terms of cause and effect. Yet, economic utility driving schools is the effect of the global perspective of competition, and failure to enact real change comes as a result of "economic reality, not educational reasoning and moral principle."[25]

Where then does the individual fit in this global scheme? In an analysis of citizenship, at the first level are notions of identity and right; second is politics of identity, multiculturalism, and emerging membership in the community is multiple and spans boundaries of state, nation, and locality with the ensuing demands of association at each level; third is the internationalization of democracy worldwide and the system of attainment that is separate from that of nations and states.[26] In all, territorial boundaries are no longer relevant to the discussion, as societies are defined by multiple connections and networks that are political, social, economic entities that are evolving constantly.

If education is viewed under the notion of instrumental rationality (a Weberian notion of purposeful instrumental action), then there are certain expectations of behavior that can be predicted for the success of an individual or organization's goal. There are empirical predictions made to rational behaviors, and control of expectation is purposely formulated based on evidence and truthfulness,[27] but this does not take into account real-life situations and pragmatic determinations that are not transparent in origin. There is instability between democracy and capitalism, and the expectations of schools to strengthen society. This is not realistic or rational in a globalized world where the nature of democracy is changing. And this is the Deweyan promise—that democracy will change and be altered by circumstance as the community changes. But, if there is persistence in doing business the way it has always been done, then successful mediation between the individual and the collective, using education as a vehicle to provide knowledge and skills to facilitate that gap, will not be fulfilled.

In moving toward cooperation, Von Neumann's principle of rationality holds that you have to know the opponent can be as smart as you are and that each wants to profit as much as possible and that each will play the bargaining game optimally.[28] But you can't play without full information because you can't prepare for the negotiation without full disclosure. Such is the Weberian notion of rationality of values (which is a philosophic question) and rationality of means or method of decision making.[29] This is a pragmatic position that each person will promote his or her own pure interest depending on how advantageous the game is, and there is the assumption that the opponent does likewise. The rationality leads to diverse strategies. One's fate is bound to the other person's while each pursues his or her own future. Mutual defection creates a common optimum. Each person is forced to figure out the subjective value of a situation, and since there is no absolute correct decision, and complex choices affect the whole physical psyche, a lot of what goes on is intuitive based on feedback from participating.

EQUILIBRIUM

John Nash developed game theory and the notion of equilibrium. Starting with the accepted position of Adam Smith, the way people interact with each other was thought to be controlled by an invisible hand, by unseen forces that guided them as they do in competitive markets creating a natural equilibrium of price and value in capitalistic environments.[30] Nash proved this false by positing the theory of equilibrium to explain how, through compromise, many players sharing or hiding information can form coalitions and act the way ordinary people do in negotiations. Personal interest and gain are fundamental forces of such negotiation, and an individual's actions are of worth and matter. It is not a divine force, but just people interacting in space, distance, time, and relationships; therefore, behavior is not predictable. Attempts at systematizing and regulating what is not about to be regulated is relevant to our discussion, because the enactment of behaviors is a human interaction that exists as a thought in time and space and cannot precisely be described. Instead we can only enumerate the restriction we place on the behaviors that do not comply with the construct. On the one hand, we try to provide order in the messiness of life in relationships and in beliefs and values that form our identity. On the other hand, we get frustrated because it is hard to systematize and be

certain about that which is chaotic. That is the problem of transmission of morals or values in education that would prepare for global participation.

For Nash, selfish competitors create order from a competitive struggle, and selfish self-interest results in the most people losing. The classic example is the Prisoner's Dilemma. Two men are arrested as suspects in a major crime, but they arrest them for a minor one. They are separated and interrogated. They are given a choice: to confess the major crime and implicate the other, or to remain silent. If both remain silent, each gets one year in prison for the minor crime. If one confesses and the other does not, the other gets five years and the confessor is set free. If both confess, each prisoner gets three years. If both parties pursue their own interests, the outcome is far worse than if they both cooperate. The cooperative option here is for both to remain silent, while the noncompetitive option is to confess and both will be worse off. The dilemma is all about cooperation and the necessity and frequent near-impossibility of acting only in your own self-interest. The noncooperative strategy is competition whereas cooperation means that you give something up.

Because there are potential mutual gains, Nash's outcome results from an unspecified process of negotiation or strategizing by individual bargainers each acting in his or her own interests. The cooperative solution cuts through the details, so it is useful for predictive purposes about how people will act in the future.[31] Within schools we deal with the present rather than negotiate for positions in the future. We concentrate on the playing of the game to win, rather than to position ourselves for a less conflictual future. The current strategies used in schools set up winners and losers, restrictive positions that require enforcing punitive measures over and over again if the rules of conduct are broken. There is no resolution, only tacit collusion to change behaviors.

For Nash, everyone has to learn to play better, form coalitions, see what others do, and determine what is best for all. This is true especially in a time of globalization.

Decisions about behavior are strategic reactions to lived variables. Equilibrium is reached when each individual's behavior results in a similar reaction by all others. The best response of all players is to create equilibrium in accordance with each other and their community. You have to understand what is at stake and that if you persist only in your position the community will not respond as a collective. This strategy used in social conflict situations produces results that are consistent preferences represented by their utility and allows behaviors to become predictable over time. The rules of the game for the equilibrium, or strategies and player preferences of individuals and of institutions, exhibit four elements that can be used to analyze all situations of social conflict and cooperation. First, participants jointly determine the outcome in which each tries to obtain the outcome most favorable to them. Second, you have to know the other's position and have complete information about their preferences and possible strategies. Third, the players must be rational and base their actions on rational theory. This is important and part of the reason you cannot negotiate with irrational terrorists. Fourth, if not one player can profit, the best response is to do nothing. Bargaining is important because it leads to a unique solution that has each individual determining what it is worth to be able to participate in the bargaining. Behaviors are the result of open lines of communication, reduction of fixed threats of win-lose strategies, and being able to view the situation from the other person's perspective. Dogmatic demands and threats do not work to produce stability over time. Equilibrium is reached only from that which is negotiated as uncertainty of outcome is reduced. This process of equilibrium striving can be a gauge to determine the level of cooperation that will be achieved as a result of the negotiation. The robustness of the solution is its durability and utility long term, because it is an outcome of a social process of working together to form solutions and predictions of future behavior.[32] Thus, the individual forsakes their own interest for the good of the collective if they are better off than they would be in their present circumstance. No one gets exactly what they want as an optimum, but the compromise position, that of equilibrium, benefits all in ways that the community is better off.

SOLUTION SEEKING

Here is the position I would like to offer. To come to terms with a global communal ethic means to get people to give up their own faith in their personal capacity and capability to see the other's point of view. To persist in the behaviors that mimic others, to have faith that others will act in ways consistent with our own beliefs or values, will not occur unless we understand the other person's beliefs and values, unless we persist in finding creative solutions while understanding the human sensibility to take in cues for what is real and what is perceived, and we can then choose to accommodate or not.[33] Behaviors are choice driven, pragmatic, and based on their perceptions. It is personal or socially inspired, selfish or self-serving, or aimed toward Kant's Other, but it is theirs alone. A shared humanity and socially constructed authenticity is the best offering to understand the other. Personal authenticity is not enough since it requires confirmation from outside and exists only in relationship to others. Instead, there is a compromise solution, an equilibrium that is situational and appropriate for the moment that can be reached through compromise.

Our response to globalization and our response to terrorism are tied to identity formation. Responses are products of a collective point of view and interpretation of the other. Of course, we can transfer causes and make them our own, but the socially constructed reality of the habitus of everyday life limits the possibilities for action,[34] because the status of culture serves to censor information received and limits our ability to determine the truth. Goodness is imperfect, subject to exaggeration and abuse, but it is a reality that is strived for, but personally interpreted and acted upon.[35] Collective belief can be in the unbelievable, as in the Arthur Miller play *The Crucible*,[36] when evidence is rejected because of a purposeful falsity that feeds on faith. False beliefs, embedded socially constructed ones, are the hardest to change, especially if they are not true today but were true in the past. It is our job as curriculum workers to point out the falsities of theory and practice and to find strength in positions that are less dogmatic but yet respond to the global realities of our times. Civic education's effects are debatable in imparting to American students proper attitudes and dispositions concerning tolerance or love of country. Although the responsibility for civic education is delegated to public schooling, it is ineffective at best, especially in uncertain times as when there is threat of war and when civic education is focused on patriotism (as led to such exclusionary and restrictive behavior as the internment of Americans of Japanese ancestry after the bombing of Pearl Harbor and restrictions on teaching the German language in schools in 1917). The problem Murphy discloses is not in the content but in the ability of teaching attitudes,[37] which is best acquired, according to Dewey and others, through active participation in public life, by actively participating in the decision-making process and in the pursuit of knowledge to make informed decisions. Murphy suggests instead that we teach academic or intellectual virtues in the pursuit of truth rather than separate instruction in civic virtues. It must be grounded in the reality of the moment, in the pragmatic facts that drive decisions made to participate in a collective process that maximizes the use of that information for the benefit of the community. Those decisions must be tied to real efforts of participation and praxis so that the collective is better off in practice than it was before.

I am suggesting an awareness that there need not always be winners and losers in the negotiation of the behaviors that we find acceptable and appropriate, and that the compromise benefits everyone when rationally constructed and honestly played out. There are spirals in the relativistic game of community behaviors. At the core are the personal values and beliefs we have about ourselves. The next level outward is the environment and community in which we live. The level after that is the politically defined nationhood that we are a part of, and finally there is the realm of global relativism. As you move outward in the spiral, beliefs become more abstract. Inner-spiral choices are based on our identification and beliefs and values as individual interpretations of rules and restrictions. But outer-level beliefs are abstract representations that have less well-defined behavioral norms. They represent abstracts such as freedom, democracy, nationalism, truth, and beauty, issues of life, community, place, and time. These abstracts are increasingly interconnected in the global village. They represent orientations and choices made based on personal beliefs and identifications. If decisions to act are based on an understanding and empathy for the other's point of view, they can lead to authentic actions that are best for the larger international community.

In an age where there are potentially conflicts between individual, national, and international interests, globalization plays an important part in successfully reducing tensions by connecting people and places in environments that are peaceful and tolerant and solution seeking. Although education is a major factor in aiding this process of skill acquisition and resource utility, it also serves as a breeding ground for the preparation for economic independence for each participating region. Education is not able to find solutions alone without changes in practices that advance the notions of world citizenry and mutual problem solving that are beyond practices of domination and exploitation. Achieving equilibrium in changing times is hard work and needs to be shared by all agencies that participate in the game.

Curriculum workers are faced with the task of making sense of the translation of these, and we work in the "in-between,"[38] which makes our burden more difficult. That in-between represents the real work to be done in this area. The in-between for community occurs between the rule makers and the students, between the nation and the school systems, and between this nation and others who share a common interest and a common fate. It is the nebulous area that can influence the idea of belonging to a larger community and to the world. To benefit from that desired position, the students have to internalize a state of being where their core beliefs and values have an inclination to be associated with and connected to the larger community. They have to gain strategies and skills to keep them playing the game of community for them to achieve an internally housed sense that they want to belong. To maximize the potential of the association, cooperative equilibrium is the means. Selfish behaviors must be seen as destructive to the chance of building this community and it is only by recognizing this that culture moves forward.

NOTES

1. Berger, P., & Luckman, T. (1967). *The social construction of reality: A treatise in the sociology of knowledge.* New York: Random House.

2. Sirageldin, I. (2002). *Sustainable human development in the twenty-first century: An evolutionary perspective.* Unpublished position paper.

3. Merő, L. (1998). *Moral calculations: Game theory, logic, and human frailty.* New York: Springer-Verlag.

4. Rosenberg, T. (2002, August 18). The free trade fix. *New York Times Magazine,* pp. 28–33, 50, and 74–75.

5. Rosenberg (2002), p. 31.

6. Rosenberg (2002), p. 50.

7. Rosenberg (2002), p. 75.

8. Sirageldin (2002).

9. Sassen, S. (2002, January 18). Globalization after September 11. *The Chronicle of Higher Education,* pp. B11–B12.

10. Sirageldin (2002).

11. Sirageldin (2002).

12. Dewey, J. (1929/1960). *The quest for certainty.* New York: Capricorn Books.

13. Gottlieb, A. (2002, March 3). Who wants to be a millionaire? *New York Times Book Review,* p. 11.

14. Miller, L. (2002, February 4). Who's to judge? *New York Times Magazine,* pp. 9–10.

15. Dewey (1929/1960).

16. Ignatieff, M. (2002, February 17). Barbarians at the gates. *New York Times Book Review,* p. 8.

17. Carr, C. (2000). *Killing time.* New York: Warner Books.

18. Ignatieff, Barbarians at the gates.

19. Dewey (1929/1960), p. 273.

20. Merő (1998).

21. Merő (1998).

22. Torres, C. (2002). Globalization, education, and citizenship: Solidarity versus markets? *American Educational Research Journal, 39* (2), 363–378.

23. Torres (2002).

24. Torres (2002).

25. Goodlad, J. (2002). Kudzu, rabbits, and school reform. *Phi Delta Kappan, 84* (1), 16–23.

26. Torres (2002).

27. Torres (2002).

28. Merő (1998).

29. Merő (1998).

30. Rockmore, D. (2002, January 25). Exploiting a beautiful mind. *The Chronicle of Higher Education,* pp. B18–B19.

31. Dixit, A. *John Nash—Founder of modern game theory.* Retrieved January 25, 2000, from: www.princeton.edu/~dixitak/home/nashenco.pdf.

32. van Damme, E. *John Nash and the analysis of rational behavior.* Retrieved January 25, 2000, from: www.kub.nl/~few5/center/staff/vdamme/nashap.pdf.

33. Ruddick, L. (2001, November 23). The near enemy of the humanities is professionalism. *The Chronicle of Higher Education,* pp. B7–B9.

34. Bourdieu, P. (1993). *The field of cultural production.* New York: Columbia University Press.

35. Merullo, R. (2002, September 13). A skeptical appreciation of the value of goodness. *The Chronicle of Higher Education,* p. B20.

36. Miller, A. (1995). The crucible. In C. Bigsby (Ed.), *The portable Arthur Miller* (pp. 132–258). New York: Penguin Books.

37. Murphy, J. (2002, September 15). Good students and good citizens. *The New York Times,* p. WK15.

38. Arendt, H. (1958). *The human condition.* Chicago: University of Chicago Press.

SCHOOL FINANCE IN URBAN AMERICA

Lynne A. Weikart

A sea change in financing our schools is under way. It follows the changes in education itself: standards-based reform, accountability, and marketization. As these momentous movements shape our schools, so too are the ways we finance our schools changing—from the traditional local property tax to far greater state support and increased private funding.

The study of school finance focuses on how public schools are funded to educate 48 million students in the United States and examines the degrees of equity and adequacy in that funding. As an increasing number of states adopt standards based education reform that seeks to thrust students to greater achievement levels, school and district officials face many challenges in order to meet these standards. Clearly, in order to meet states' standards, sufficient resources must be provided to all schools. On average, school districts receive funding from three major sources: federal (7%), state (50%) and locality (43%). Because the states are providing half of all funding, it is unrealistic to think that the demand for higher standards will be met unless states provide adequate funding.

URBAN PROBLEM

Our cities have a large proportion of public school students. Over 31 percent of all students attend school in 226 large school districts among the 16,000 school districts in America. This translates into 31 percent of all students being educated in just 1.5 percent of school districts.[1]

Financing schools in our cities is particularly challenging because the school population is so needy. Eligibility for the free or reduced-price lunch program provides a proxy measure of low-income family status.

The hundred largest school districts had a disproportionate percentage of students eligible for the free and reduced-price lunch program relative to all public school districts. Among schools that reported free and reduced-price lunch eligibility, 54 percent of students in the 100 largest school districts were eligible, compared with 40 percent of students in all districts.[2] The Council of the Great City Schools, which tracks 62 of the largest cities, found that 70 percent of the students qualified for free or reduced-price lunch eligibility.[3]

There is another type of neediness. Students who speak a language other than

English are more costly to educate. Nationwide 10.4 percent of the U.S. population is foreign-born, which is the highest percentage since 1930, and the proportion in cities is 16 percent.[4] In cities an average of 21 percent of the students are English language learners compared with the national average of approximately 5 percent. The percentage can be as high as 58 percent in Miami-Dade County.[5]

An excellent tool for measuring neediness is the *Targeting Index* for state funding of major city school districts across the country. "This index shows the degree to which each urban school district receives state funding commensurate with that city's share of the state's poor school children."[6] The higher the index, the better the funding relative to poverty. The average for all 61 major cities was .62. In other words, these cities received about 62 percent of the state funding "they would otherwise acquire if the State distributed all of its K-12 education revenues on the basis of poverty alone."[7] New York City's target index was .54, similar to Baltimore, Chicago, and Cleveland.

The cities confront higher standards at a time when they can least afford to meet such standards. Urban district and school officials create and implement urban educational policy within a very difficult environment—less spending than the average spending in the country. In 2000, current expenditures per pupil were $6,911 in the United States and jurisdications, higher than the $6,000 in the 100 largest school districts.[8]

The last decade has witnessed greater investment in the cities, although the size of the city is a determining factor. In constant dollars, total expenditures (including capital) over time rose 25 percent from 1991–92 to 2000–01, from $6,950 to $8,500, but the patterns differ based on the size of city. The highest total expenditures were in big cities ($9,450) and in the urban fringes of large cities ($9,150). "Expenditures per student in midsize cities ($8,580) and in rural areas ($8,420) were below average, while those in urban fringes of midsize cities ($7,900), small towns ($7,700), and large towns ($7,530) were the lowest."[9] Of course, much of this relates to the variations in costs of living in different parts of the country. However, enrollment grew much faster in the urban fringes of large cities—over 115 percent—far greater than the 12 percent in large cities and 21.7 percent in midsize cities.[10] Families continued to settle in the suburbs.

Cities faced particular challenges because their tax base had been so eroded by the middle-class flight to the suburbs, leaving the cities with fewer resources to educate the poorest students. As minorities have entered urban school systems, whites have left. As schools struggle with increased educational standards, city school students have become increasingly minority. The Council of the Great City Schools is a coalition of 62 of the nation's largest urban public school systems. In these 62 cities 15.0 percent of the nation's public school students were enrolled in school year 2001–2002. More significantly, "76.9 percent of students in the Great City Schools in 2001–2002 were African American, Hispanic, Asian American or other students of color, compared with about 37.9 percent nationwide."[11]

Students in urban schools score lower in both math and reading tests than state and national averages. How much lower depends on the city, the state, and the test.[12] Urban schools face difficult problems, although that does not mean they are any less efficient than other schools. Studies demonstrate that urban schools spend proportionately less on administration and employ fewer administrative staff relative to teachers than either suburban or rural schools. Urban school systems actually devote a smaller share of current expenditures to administration, almost 15 percent less than rural districts.[13] It is not reassuring that schools with higher percentages of poor and minority students in the inner cities experience more teacher absenteeism.[14]

These trends did not happen overnight.

In the years between 1910 and 1970, more than 6.5 million African Americans migrated to urban areas. In 1990, approximately 83 percent of the African-American population lived in metropolitan centers . . . As a result, 40 percent of all African Americans are concentrated in only 11 central cities.[15]

Race and ethnicity cannot be ignored when discussing the financing of urban schools. This trend of African-American flight to the cities continues, but has changed directions in the last ten years; African Americans are moving back to the South but to the cities.

The South scored net gains of black migrants from all three of the other regions of the U.S. during the late 1990s, reversing a 35-year trend. Southern metropolitan areas, particularly Atlanta, led the way in attracting black migrants in the late 1990s. In contrast, the major metropolitan areas of New York, Chicago, Los Angeles, and San Francisco experienced the greatest out-migration of blacks during the same period.[16]

This massive movement out of the cities would not have been possible without federal policies such as tax deductions for homeowners. "[F]ederal sponsorship of secondary mortgage markets, and also the mortgage guarantee programs operated by the Federal Housing Administration subsidized and protected the suburbs."[17] Add to that the federal policy of massive highway construction, and it is understandable how suburbs and their schools flourished after World War II. Schools in the suburbs, regardless of racial makeup, often have more resources, and students score higher on achievement tests.[18] For example, in the largest urban system in the country, New York City, the 1997–98 per pupil expenditure was $8,171 while the surrounding suburbs had far higher expenditures, $12,467 in Nassau and $12,749 in Westchester.[19] However, sub-urbs are not immune to problems. Myron Orfield has pointed out that 40 percent of the suburbs are at risk fiscally.[20]

HISTORY OF FINANCING SCHOOLS

In America's early history, towns and counties used local property taxes to support their local schools. Many states required towns to do so. Gradually, in the late nineteenth and early twentieth centuries, a system of common schooling was fashioned throughout the country with the states providing some subsidies.[21] The major source of revenue remained the property tax. This dependence upon property tax meant that some school districts received a vast amount of financial support because their location was a wealthier suburb. Other school districts were not so lucky: Their towns and suburbs were poor, and they could not provide adequate funding.

When hard times hit beginning in the 1930s, city services were left to decay. And with the dependency upon the property tax, the schools suffered. Business leaders fought any tax increases. The decline in financing urban schools began in the 1930s. An interesting example is Newark, New Jersey, where spending for schools decreased beginning in the 1930s. By the 1960s, with more African Americans moving into the city and whites moving to the suburbs, financial support further eroded.[22]

The second stage of school finance began in 1970 when John Coons and Stephen Sugarman at Northwestern University Law School wrote *Private Wealth and Public Schools*, and argued for wealth neutrality; that is, given the Equal Protection Clause of the Constitution, states should not allow district spending to be related to district wealth.[23] Wealth neutrality grew out of the widespread belief in equal educational opportunity. It is no surprise that these ideas began to flourish during the civil rights struggle of the 1960s. During this time, Arthur Wise, a graduate student at the University of Chicago, wrote his dissertation on applying equal protection theory to school finance. A year later, in 1977, California courts in *Serrano v. Priest* agreed with Wise and Coons and held that the California education finance system violated the Equal Protection Clause. California relied too heavily on local property taxes, which were by definition inequitable across the state. The consequence of such a practice meant that the wealthy suburbs had highly financed schools while the inner cities were poorly financed.

Two years later in *San Antonio Independent School District v. Rodriguez*, the U.S. Supreme Court in 1973 ruled that the federal government was not responsible for education; rather, it was a state responsibility. That was the beginning. There were many court cases in many states all struggling over the issue of equity in resource allocation. Many of the attorneys and analysts involved in these court cases had been trained in universities that had received funding from James Kelly at the Ford Foundation. The Foundation had set out to force the states to deal with educational inequities. As of 1999, 43 out of 50 states "had faced legal challenges in state court alleging that the school finance system violated the state constitution's education and/or equal protection clauses; 20 states lost these challenges and were ordered to reform the education finance system."[24] These reforms often concentrated upon spending equity and wealth neutrality.

Equity can have many meanings. Berne and Stiefel (1984) summarized several concepts of equity and alternative ways to measure them.[25] Their major distinctions were horizontal and vertical equity. Horizontal equity specifies that "equally situated children should be treated equally."[26] Many court cases used horizontal equity when considering inputs because this is by definition equal opportunity. Vertical equity also came into prominence; that is, "differently situated children should be treated differently."[27]

Vertical equity is an appealing concept because it takes into consideration differences among pupils and also outcomes. Title 1 of the No Child Left Behind Act (NCLB) is based on vertical equity. Although there is basic agreement that some children may need more resources, there remains little agreement about how to measure this.

What has been the result of thirty years of court cases based upon equity of resources? Most studies agree that wealthy districts continue to spend more per pupil on education than poor districts. However, has there at least been improvement in spending equity or wealth neutrality? Studies differ. One proclaimed that court ordered reform resulted in "fundamentally restructuring school finance and generating more equitable distribution of resources."[28] However, in a more recent study, Hoxby argued "equalization efforts have often left poor districts worse off than before."[29] In general, thirty years of school finance reform has been disappointing.

California is an excellent example of the limits of emphasizing equity. The decision in *Serrano v. Priest* in 1977 was successful in achieving greater spending parity among California school districts.

While equally distributed, California education revenues became enmeshed in a downward spiral of defense department cutbacks and other economic setbacks . . . The outcome was ever lower per pupil spending levels relative to the national averages.[30]

There was greater equity, but less spending regardless of location—city, suburb, small town, or rural area.

Metzler explained Hoxby's findings through an examination of state funding approaches. He maintained that the "distribution of education resources is primarily a function of the distribution of political power in the state."[31] Such a distribution is usually an "inequitable equilibrium" which, regardless of court decisions, will eventually return to its state of inequitable equilibrium.

According to Metzler, the solution was really a political one: "If we were truly interested in a permanent shift of resources to a more equitable one, we would change the political equilibrium that exists in most states or rely on courts to impose solutions on resistant legislatures."[32]

CURRENT STRUGGLES

As school finance reformers confronted thirty years of mixed results in attempting to obtain equity, the reformers began to grapple with increased educational standards. Such a demand meant that the reformers could use the movement toward standards-based education reform as a path to gaining increased resources for underfunded schools. Hence, we arrive at adequacy, a third stage of educational finance. As the country has shifted toward standards-based education reform, the policy debate has shifted from a concern for equity in educational resources to ensuring that students have adequate resources to enable them to attain the higher educational standards.

Adequacy refers to "the cost and implementation structure needed to reach high minimum levels of student achievement in low-income schools."[33] The definition of adequacy begins with the idea of adequate performance by students. How much and what kinds of resources are needed to obtain that adequate performance? And that is an answer only the courts can provide. There have been a series of court cases based upon adequacy of resources rather than equity of resources. Several states—Alabama, Mississippi, New Hampshire, North Carolina, Ohio, Vermont, Wyoming, and New York—are examining practical definitions of adequacy for their education finance systems. In these discussions, adequacy is "increasingly being defined by the outcomes produced by school inputs, not by the inputs alone."[34] In essence, if students are not reaching expected standards, students are most likely attending schools with insufficient resources.

To determine adequate funding levels, policy judgments must be made about the level of attainment for students and the resource levels required for schools to succeed in their students' attaining the required levels.[35] *Pauley v. Kelley* (1979), heard in the West Virginia Supreme Court, was one of the earliest adequacy cases. The court listed a series of competencies that each child should obtain, and the legislature had to fund schools that could develop these capacities. The competencies delineated by the court were literacy, basic mathematics, knowledge of government, knowledge of the student's environment, work-training and advanced academic training, recreation, creative arts, and ethics.[36] Other court cases were similar.

Using adequacy as the measure of educational resources was established as a distinct theory in school finance litigation in 1989 when the Kentucky Supreme Court found that "the entire Kentucky system of education violated the mandates of the state constitution, and ordered the state to overhaul the entire system of education to bring it into compliance."[37] The Court emphasized how little funding the state provided for education. Adequacy became a powerful tool to force states to increase funds to schools. Using theories of adequacy rather than equity has made a difference. The plaintiffs have won about two-thirds of litigation based on adequacy; whereas plaintiffs have won only one-third of the cases based on equity.[38]

Pursuing adequacy rather than equity has changed the rules. Pursuing equity in school finance formulas does not necessarily lead to greater state control. But adequacy almost always increases state participation in the life of schools since it is the state that sets the standards of attainment. Similarly, pursuing equity does not focus attention on outcomes, just the inputs of resources. Adequacy focuses attention on the outcomes, particularly low performance of students. In addition, local control will suffer under adequacy since the individual schools and their districts are now being held to state standards. Adequacy of resources is now widely used in the state courts, and only time will tell the outcome. Clearly, the emphasis upon adequacy has meant more centralization of decision-making at the state level.

In the recent past, state policymakers were in the enviable position of being able to simultaneously increase education spending and cut taxes. From 1996 to 2001, per-student expenditures for K–12 education increased by $1,741, more than 30.6 percent. This increase was 13.6 percent above inflation (or $773 per student). That ended in 2001 with the nationwide recession. In March, 2001, the National Conference of State Legislatures (NCSL) reported that 19 states had either made cuts in their FY01 budgets or were on the verge of doing so.[39] Of the states making cuts, only one—Alabama—was forced to make actual cuts in education spending. In fact, most states were looking at education spending increases for FY02, albeit at a slower rate than in previous years.[40] All of this changed with the terrorist attacks on September 11, 2001. Significant slow-downs in spending at the state and local level have occurred. Certainly the current fiscal downturn in the states has meant that the states cut back significantly in spending in general and for education. It remains unclear how long this downturn will continue and how deep it will be.

CHALLENGES IN FINANCING URBAN SCHOOLS

The first challenge in financing urban schools is that the emphasis on adequacy of resources combined with the demand for higher educational standards has resulted in closer examination at the school level rather than the district level. Although much as been written about equity and adequacy of funding school districts, little has been written about the equity and adequacy resource issues of individual schools within a district. Research on ways districts allocate funds to the schools is miniscule. As pressures mount on students to achieve higher standards, pressures on how school officials allocate their dollars to ensure that students succeed dramatically expand. The research in how schools are financed and how schools allocate dollars has just begun. A common assumption is that in order for students to meet increased educational standards, the schools must have a better understanding of how their dollars are spent than schools currently have in a traditional top down system.[41]

A few cities—namely, Victoria, Australia, and Edmonton, Canada, and cities countrywide in England—have implemented school-based financing systems. A good example is Edmonton, where the assumption has been made that schools are in a much better position to decide how to allocate dollars.[42] States within the United States are not as interested in school-based finance or budgeting. The movement is curtailed by the demand of district officials for uniform policies that drastically reduces any decision-making at the school level. Providing more decision-making to school officials is hard to realize in the United States where states are heavily involved in dictating educational standards, curriculum, and accountability systems, and districts, under these increased pressures, dictate to the local schools.

The issue of equity and adequacy of resources within the districts has been examined at the state level, but not comparatively across the country. (See the work of the Education Finance Research Consortium in New York and the Public Policy Institute of California.)

The second challenge is to understand the impact of race and ethnicity upon the cities' schools. In cities, school district officials have moved toward centralization: New York, Chicago, and Los Angeles all have strong superintendents who seek to dictate ways schools will organize themselves and spend their dollars. Part of this centralization can be traced to minority children being the majorities in urban school districts. As whites retreated to the suburbs, minority children were left in the cities. The attempts to integrate the schools ended when it was clear that not enough white students existed for purposes of integration. Parents in suburban and more white districts have enormous say about their schools, not so the cities.

The only path toward integration would be a regional plan, and the Supreme Court's refusal to back metropolitan busing ended that.[43] There is an enormous task at hand: improving city schools, which have fewer resources and poorer students than the surrounding suburbs. The racial exclusivity of the suburbs is a reality that is difficult to overcome.

The third challenge is citizens' unwillingness to support further taxation. Since the local property tax is the most significant source of revenue for local schools, the success of that tax lies in the hands of the voting public in those school districts. In the case of California, voters agreed to freeze the property tax resulting in heavy cuts across school districts. Across the nation, voters can say no to school budgets by voting no on property tax increases.

With globalization, cities face increased competition in attracting corporations. The result is that corporations are demanding tax relief (tax abatements) to remain in the cities or to bring new business to the cities. For example, business tax relief has cost the Toledo School District about $13.7 million a year, which is about 14 percent of its revenues.[44] Illinois estimated that school districts' share of property tax from corporations had decreased from 50 to 44 percent in the last decade.[45] This decrease in educational tax bases comes at a time when states play a more central role in education.

Court cases have made local schools more dependent upon state fiscal support. In the case of several states (Ohio, New Hampshire, and Wyoming) where the low-wealth school districts won their legal challenges, it has meant a switch from local property taxes to a statewide tax structure.[46] Other states (Maryland and Oregon, for example) have tried to move to an adequacy-based funding formula without the pressure of being sued. The increasing shift to a more state-controlled school funding system has put further pressure on ever-shrinking state budgets. As the states play a larger financial role, they also play a greater regulatory and governance role. The extreme is Philadelphia School District, which was taken over by the state in December, 2001, for its poor performance. Pennsylvania, ranking significantly below the state average in financing education, moved immediately toward privatization of Philadelphia's public schools.

This is the fourth challenge—how to deal with the disinvestment in public education and the concomitant marketization of education, which may have dramatic effect on funding for public education. The conceptual framework supporting marketization is that competition inherent in market-based systems will result in greater efficiency and higher achievement with little or no increase in cost.[47] Such a movement is intertwined with capitalist globalization.

The movement toward private schools has been going on for some time. Many whites deserted public schools in the south after the Supreme Court decision of *Brown v. Board of Education* because whites fled the threat of integration and set up their own white schools. Concomitant with that movement was another movement—the fundamentalist Christians setting up their own schools. Once the whites abandoned the schools, funding for the minority students remaining behind was sharply curtailed. Now the abandonment of the public schools has moved to the North.

Both vouchers and charter schools encourage students to leave the traditional public schools. This includes the most ambitious black and Hispanic families.

Charter schools are usually publicly funded. However, charter schools almost always receive funding from the local public school district, which results in the public schools receiving fewer funds. By 2000, more than 1,400 charter schools were operating in 27 states and were educating more than 200,000 students, which is almost 1 percent of the school population. In Arizona, 4 percent of the students are enrolled in charter schools.[48] It is difficult to predict the future of charter schools; however, they have grown quickly, and low-income parents have responded positively to the idea of school choice.

The first state-funded voucher program established for disadvantaged students was in Milwaukee, Wisconsin, in 1989. It then spread to Cleveland, Ohio, and Florida, which became the first state to enact a statewide voucher program in 1999. Given the legal issues around the use of public funds for religious purposes, it is unclear how successful voucher programs will be.

CONCLUSION

It is too soon to say what impact adequacy will have on urban schools. An emerging trend is that state courts—when dealing with issues of adequacy of educational resources—are ordering legislatures to fix the problem, and that more court cases are being won by the plaintiffs. In Kentucky this order included revamping the entire system, and the Kentucky court's action has had a ripple effect across the country. Adequacy will bring the states to center stage. More state involvement need not result in urban investment. States could define adequacy as the bare minimum and invest even less in our urban schools. Yet, by the late 1990s, the states increased their investment. Throughout the country, the states' share of resources outpaced the funding provide on the local level.[49]

As the states increase their investment, the tax structure for education can shift from the property tax, a local stable tax, to state taxes, such as sales and income taxes, which are not as stable. This could indeed create problems for schools in general and urban schools in particular. Wealthier suburbs could resolve any financial issues leaving urban school systems to face declining state revenues. It is too soon to tell the results of the most recent turn in litigation.

NOTES

1. Fuhrman, S. (2004). *Urban educational challenges: Is reform the answer?* Retrieved June 15, 2005, from http://www.urbanedjournal. org/archive/Issue%201/FeatureArticles/article0004. html.

2. National Center of Educational Statistics. (2002a). *The Condition of education 2002.* Retrieved June 16, 2005, from http://nces.ed.gov/programs/coe/2002/section1/indicator03. asp.

3. Council of the Great City Schools. (2000). *Adequate state financing of urban schools: An analysis of state funding of the NYC public schools.* Washington, DC: Author.

4. Ellen, I., O'Regan, K., Schwartz, A., & Stiefel. L. (2001). *Immigrant children and urban schools: Evidence from NYC on segregation and its consequences for schooling.* (Working Paper #2001-20). New York: Robert F. Wagner Graduate School of Public Service, New York University.

5. Council of the Great City Schools (2000).

6. Council of the Great City Schools (2000).

7. Council of the Great City Schools (2000).

8. National Center of Educational Statistics. (2002b). Characteristics of the 100 largest public elementary and secondary school districts 2001–2002. Retrieved June 16, 2005, from http://nces.ed.gov/pubs2003/100_largest/discussion. asp#4.

9. National Center of Educational Statistics. (2004). *The Condition of education 2004. Public elementary and secondary education, indicator 25.* Retrieved June 15, 2005, from http://nces.ed. gov/programs/coe/2004/pdf/35_2004.pdf.

10. National Center of Educational Statistics. (2004).

11. Council of the Great City Schools. (2004, March). *Beating the odds IV: A city-by-city analysis of student performance and achievement gap on state*

assessments, results from 2002–2003 school year. Retrieved June 16, 2005, from http://www.cgcs.org/reports/beat_the_oddsIV.html.

12. Fuhrman (2004).

13. Ballou, D. (1998). *The condition of urban school finance: Efficient resource allocation in urban schools.* Retrieved June 16, 2005, from http://nces.ed.gov/pubs98/finance/98217-4.asp.

14. Ballou (1998).

15. Henig, J., Hula, R., Orr, M., & Pedescleaux, D. (1999). *The color of school reform: Race, politics, and the challenge of urban education.* Princeton, NJ: Princeton University Press.

16. Frey, W. (2004, May). The new great migration: Black Americans' return to the South, 1965–2000. Retrieved from http://www.brookings.edu/urban/publications/20040524_frey.htm.

17. Katznelson, I., & Weir, M. (1985). *Schooling for all: Class, race, and the decline of the democratic ideal* (p. 217). New York: Basic Books.

18. Guerrier, M. (2004). *High-need African-American and Latino students doing better in suburban districts* (p. 6). New York: Educational Priorities Panel.

19. Council of the Great City Schools (2004).

20. Orfield. M. (2002). *American metropolitics: The new suburban reality.* Washington, DC: The Brookings Institution.

21. Guthrie, J., & Rothstein, R. (2001). A new millennium and a likely new era of education finance. In S. Chaikind & W. Fowler (Eds.). *Education finance in the new millennium, American Education Finance Association 2001 Yearbook* (p. 100). Larchmont, NY: Eye on Education.

22. Anyon. J. (1997). *Ghetto schooling: A political economy of urban education reform.* New York: Teachers College Press.

23. Coons, J., & Sugarman, S. (1970). *Private wealth and public schools.* Boston, MA: Harvard University Press.

24. Metzler, J. (2003). Studies in judicial remedies and public engagement. In *Inequitable equilibrium: School finance in the United States* (p. 5). New York: Campaign for Fiscal Equity.

25. Berne, R., & Stiefel, L. (1984). *The measurement of equity in school finance.* Baltimore: John Hopkins University Press.

26. Berne, R., & Stiefel, L. (1999). Concepts of school finance equity: 1970 to the present. In H. Ladd, R. Chalk, & J. Hansen (Eds.), *Equity and adequacy in school finance* (p. 19). Washington, DC: National Academy Press.

27. Berne & Stiefel (1999), p. 20.

28. Evans, W., Murray, S., & Schwab, R. (1999). The impact of court-mandated school finance reform. In H. Ladd, R. Chalk, and J. Hansen (Eds.), *Equity and adequacy in education finance: Issues and perspectives* (p. 72). Washington, DC: National Academy Press.

29. Hoxby, C. (2001). All school finance equalizations are not created equal. *Quarterly Journal of Economics*, 1189–1190.

30. DeMoss, K., & Wong, K. (2004). *Money, politics, and law: Intersections & conflicts in the provision of educational opportunity* (2004 Yearbook of the American Education Finance Association, p. 5). Larchmont, NY: Eye on Education.

31. Metzler (2003), p. 5.

32. Metzler (2003), p. 46.

33. Clune, W. (2005). Available at http://www.wcer.wisc.edu/people/pi.php?sid=105.

34. Guthrie, J., & Rothstein, R. (2000). Enabling adequacy to achieve reality. In H. Ladd, R. Chalk & J. Hansen (Eds.), *Equity, and adequacy in Education Finance: Issues and Perspectives* (p. 215). Washington, DC: National Academy Press.

35. Guthrie & Rothstein (2001), p. 104.

36. Guthrie & Rothstein (2001), p. 105.

37. Minorini, P., & Sugarman, S. (1999). Educational adequacy and the courts. In H. Ladd, R. Chalk & J. Hansen (Eds.), *Equity, and adequacy in Education Finance: Issues and Perspectives* (p. 195). Washington, DC: National Academy Press.

38. Education Commission of the States. 2004. Retrieved from http://www.ecs.org/ecsmain.asp?page=/html/issues.asp.

39. National Conference of State Legislatures (2001). Web site.

40. Education Commission of the States (2004). Retrieved June 17, 2005, from http://www.ecs.org/ecsmain.asp?page=/html/issues.asp.

41. Goertz, M., & Odden, A. American Educational Finance Association. (1999). *School-based financing* (p. 159). Thousand Oaks, CA: Corwin Press.

42. Caldwell, B., & Spinks, J. (1992). *Leading the self-managed school.* London: Falmer Press.

43. Katznelson & Weir (1985), p. 206.

44. Tomsho. R. (2001, July 18). Public interests: In Toledo, a tension between school funds and business breaks—Hefty tax abatements keep firms in town but drain education coffers, too—Moldy walls, aging boilers. *Wall Street Journal*, p. A1.

45. Tomsho (2001).

46. Education Commission of the States (2004).

47. Rossmiller, R. (2001). Funding in the new millennium. In S. Chaikind & W. Fowler (Eds.), *Education finance in the new millennium, American Education Finance Association 2001 Yearbook* (p. 12). Larchmont, NY: Eye on Education.

48. Rossmiller (2001), p. 29.

49. Fowler, W. Jr., and Chaikind, S. (2001). Conclusion. In S. Chaikind & W. Fowler (Eds.), *Education finance in the new millennium, American Education Finance Association 2001 Yearbook* (p. 193). Larchmont, NY: Eye on Education.

Language and Urban Education

EVALUATING PROGRAMS FOR ENGLISH LANGUAGE LEARNERS: POSSIBILITIES FOR BILITERACY IN URBAN SCHOOL DISTRICTS IN CALIFORNIA

Karen Cadiero-Kaplan and Alberto M. Ochoa

By 2030, English Language Learners (ELLs) will represent 70 percent of the total student population in the United States.[1] This is becoming a reality in the urban communities of Southern California, as these areas account for more than 57 percent of the ELL enrollment in the state.[2] An analysis of demographic characteristics of California K–12 students indicates that since 1985, there has been an increase of more than 100 percent in the number of ELLs.[3] Presently, there are more than 1.6 million students whose first language is not English. It is estimated that these numbers will increase to 3 million students by 2010, with more than 80 percent of students coming from Spanish-speaking backgrounds and attending schools in urban areas.[4]

At the same time that the K–12 student population is growing more linguistically diverse, present policy and programming in schools is marginalizing students whose first language is not English. In large part this occurs by failing to nurture each student's native language and culture as part of their educational development;[5] doing so would require a commitment toward equity and excellence for ethnolinguistically diverse students. To incorporate such values, schools must have a pluralistic vision—one inclusive of language and culture, where high-quality educational materials are available to all, and where human and financial resources are utilized to promote academic achievement and high biliteracy standards (i.e., attainment of academic proficiency in two languages) for all students, with authentic accountability systems across all levels. This requires a public policy commitment to high-quality education that includes community responsibility as a part of the process.[6]

This chapter will highlight two urban school districts committed to a multilingual pluralistic vision for schools. We will articulate the self-evaluation process that administrators, teachers, parents, and university professors engaged in to determine each district's potential to work toward equity and excellence in programming for ethnolinguistically diverse students.

In the process of engaging such ideals, we also recognize that schools are stratified institutions. As such, they provide education programs that can be depicted as "high-status," where knowledge yields social and economic control for its members, or "low-status," where education relegates students to a second-class citizenship both within the K–12 public school system and in the larger society.[7] Further, we acknowledge that urban schools approach bilingual programming in one of two ways: either through a compensatory or high-quality education model. According to Brisk, a *compensatory education* policy focuses on the choice of language, where the policy makers determine which language of instruction will be utilized.[8] Within this model the overriding goal of education is to "teach students English as quickly as possible."[9] Because "English is viewed as the only means for acquisition of knowledge, students' fluency in English is the essential condition to receiving an education."[10] This latter view is most prevalent today in many urban schools. Conversely, a *high-quality education* model focuses on a student's right to a good education with the goal being "to educate students to their highest potential" where English is only a part of the educational goal. In a high-quality model, "bilingual learners access knowledge not only through English but through their native languages."[11] Within this model there is a recognition and value for the varied cultural experiences and knowledge of students, goals the two districts we work with have as part of their mission statements.

EVALUATION FOCUS

The challenge for urban schools serving large numbers of ELLs is to have strategies to evaluate their language and academic programs. These strategies, which we will outline, have the potential to raise the status of the academic success of urban students through high-quality educational models that value the language and cul-

ture of ELLs. The questions driving these projects were:

- What are the present services being provided to ELLs in the La Vista Elementary (LVESD) and Dulce Union High (DUHSD) School Districts to support biliteracy development?
- What instructional services are in place in the LVESD and DUHSD that have the potential to develop biliteracy competence?

An action research approach was used in the examination of these two questions, involving a team from each school district and guided by an observational instrument designed to collect data on eight program components.

This chapter focuses on the process utilized by the LVESD and DUHSD in the evaluation of their programs for ELLs, on what they learned, and on next steps. In this section we provide background data and definitions regarding bilingual programming, district demographics, and the politics and pedagogy that spurred the project, along with key research regarding policy and programming issues.

Defining Bilingual Education

Because the focus of this project is bilingual education, it is important to note the varying models and goals of bilingual education. The first model considered, the *early-exit transitional bilingual program*, is the most common, where children are taught in their native language in addition to English, with the goal of mainstreaming students into an English-only curriculum within two to three years without further native language instruction. Second, *maintenance bilingual* or *late-exit* programs help students maintain and preserve their native language as they acquire English. They are taught in both languages, from four to six years, with the goal of acquiring English (L2) and the ability to maintain fluency in their native or primary language (L1) in the process.[12] Third are *developmental* or *enrichment bilingual* programs, where academic proficiency in both the student's primary language and English is the goal. This occurs in dual-language immersion models, where both non-English speakers and monolingual English speakers participate in learning both social and academic language in two languages simultaneously for a period of at least six years; the goal of these programs is full biliteracy. For this project, biliteracy is defined as the development of academic proficiency in the primary language (L1), simultaneous with the development of language and academic proficiency in English (L2), resulting in academic biliteracy in both the L1 and L2 by the fifth and sixth-grade levels. Academic proficiency is ongoing at the junior and high school levels, enabling students to take rigorous biliteracy courses under the core requirements for entry into the California university system. Research indicates that success with bilingual education occurs when language minority children use their native or heritage language in the school as a medium of instruction. The overriding goal of such programs is the development of full bilingualism, linguistically and academically.[13] All of these models were present to some degree in the LVES and DUHS districts; also key are the bilingual teachers, who work most directly with this population.

Bilingual teachers are linguistically and academically proficient in English and another language. In the case of the schools addressed in our context, the language is Spanish. In addition, these teachers are trained to teach core subject areas (i.e., science and math) in both English and Spanish, and are trained in teaching English language development (ELD) with the ability to implement bilingual teaching strategies to address the linguistic, cultural, and academic development of ELLs.[14]

Student Population: Demographics and National Achievement Trends

The participating school districts currently have 40 elementary schools and 27 middle and high schools. By 2004, LVESD had become the largest urban elementary school district in California, serving more than 25,000 students, including 8,890 ELL students. The DUHSD district comprises of eight middle schools, two junior high schools, ten senior high schools, and seven adult education programs. The high school district serves more than 38,000 students, including approximately 9,400 ELL students (or 25%), with the majority having Spanish as their first language. The district demographic data in Table 2 indicate the top four language populations for the both districts from 1997 to 2002, with Spanish speakers making up the majority of students receiving services for ELD and bilingual education, with an average increase of 448 students per year at the high school level; these data are similar for the elementary district.

Academic rigor in California urban schools is lacking for ethnically and linguistically diverse students. In 1997, Latino/-a students represented 7.5 percent of Advanced Placement (AP) math students and 6.7 percent of AP science students, whereas 8.2 percent of AP math students and 8.5 percent of AP science students were black. In the same year, white students represented 72.4 percent of AP math students and 72.8 percent of AP science students.[15]

The National Center for Education Statistics (NCES 2001) reports on the status of dropouts from 1972 to 1999 of 16- to 24-year-olds by race and ethnicity across the country. In 1999, Latino/-a and Hispanic students accounted for 37.7 percent of all dropouts. This is reflected in Table 3, Dropout Rates by Race and Ethnicity, which presents a persistent and disproportional dropout rate for Latino/-a and Hispanic students, the majority population both of these urban school districts serve.

Since the early 1970s the percentage of underachieving Latino/-a and low-income students has changed very little. It has been found that more than 75 percent of

Table 2.
LVESD- and DUHSD-Wide Language Census 1997–2002 Comparison

School District	1997	1998	1999	2000	2001	2002
LCESD LEP Population by Native Language	**7067**	**7327**	**7409**	**7718**	**8438**	**8898**
Spanish	6505	6794	6918	7240	7851	8251
Philippino	133	125	77	75	122	174
Japanese	131	115	135	140	127	138
Korean	128	113	117	121	165	121
DUHSD LEP Population by Native Language	**6349**	**6975**	**7288**	**7773**	**7699**	**9925**
Spanish	5858	6459	6821	7227	7499	9437
Philippino	240	254	247	243	222	249
Japanese	71	65	57	64	54	42
Korean	30	37	32	50	66	55

Source: CBEDS R-30 DATA Quest Language Census 1997–2002.

Table 3.
Dropout Rates by Race and Ethnicity

Year	Total Rate for All Groups	White	Black/African American	Latino/-a Hispanic
1972	14.6	12.3	21.3	34.3
1975	13.9	11.4	22.9	29.2
1978	14.2	11.9	20.2	33.3
1981	13.9	11.4	18.4	33.2
1984	13.1	11.0	15.5	29.8
1987	12.7	10.4	14.1	28.6
1990	12.1	9.0	13.2	32.4
1993	11.0	7.9	13.6	27.5
1996	11.1	7.3	13.0	29.4
1999	11.2	7.3	12.6	28.6

Source: National Center for Educational Statistics. (2001). The condition of education 2001. Washington, DC: U.S. Department of Education, Table 23-1.

Latino students are generally under-achieving by the third grade[16] and the achievement gap remains constant in middle and high school. In addition, there is an absence of data and accountability for assessing and developing the skills of these students to provide them access to the core curriculum and courses that yield access to the systems of higher education. The absence of a systemic school accountability process to determine instructional and school program effectiveness allows schools to perpetuate educational expectations that justify low achievement and student disempowerment,[17] which are concerns for LVESD and DUHSD.

Policy Context

Due to the demographics, achievement trends, and language needs of the student populations these districts serve, they along with us had a strong interest in evaluating their educational programming for ELLs after the passage of California's Proposition 227, which abruptly changed the way bilingual programs were maintained; that is, rather than the "default option" for the education of ELLs in the schools being a bilingual program, the "conventional option" for these students became structured English immersion (SEI), a program lasting normally one year in which students are taught "overwhelmingly" in English.[18] This language policy is subtractive, or compensatory, in nature because the goal is to have students speak English as rapidly as possible without native language instructional support or development.[19] Thus, Proposition 227 shifted the responsibility of bilingual instruction from schools providing such instruction based on their existing programs to parents having to request a bilingual program as an alternative to SEI. This program model contradicts key research findings on second language acquisition that indicate, first, it takes six to seven years to fully acquire a second language, and second, students best acquire English when they are fluent in reading and writing in the their L1 and maintain support for L1 as they acquire and learn English in appropriate bilingual programs or programs that provide L1 support in literacy with a combination of English as a second language (ESL) and English language development (ELD) classes, and sheltered or specially designed academic instruction in English (SDAIE) classes for contextualized content area instruction in English.[20]

So, although Proposition 227 was intended to restrict schools' offerings of bilingual programming, with the support of parents and school communities, it is possible for urban schools to provide language-rich and academically rigorous programs that promote biliteracy.

EVALUATION PROCESSES

In both the LVESD and the DUHSD, we worked with a team of concerned administrators, teachers, and parents to plan the approach to undertake each district's program curriculum audit, named the Post-Proposition 227 Curriculum Audit. The evaluation project began with LVESD in August, 2000, and followed with DUHSD in August, 2001. Both curriculum audits utilized the same model and processes described below. It is important to note that the LVESD first approached us, and what was supposed to be a one-year evaluation/audit continued for two years. During the first year of the LVESD, project administrators from the DUHSD approached and invited us to work with them for the same purpose; since the LVESD is a feeder district to the DUHSD, it also served to inform articulation across districts. Thus, both evaluation projects were initiated by concerned stakeholders from the school districts, with the shared purpose of assessing how well they were achieving the goals of their district's vision or mission statement. The mission statements share the goals of developing

- Students who are high-achieving innovative thinkers
- Learning that is connected to the student's culture and experiences
- Multiliterate students with multicultural perspectives
- Strength in diversity
- Student-based decision making
- Parental voice
- Learning linked to the world outside the classroom

These goals support the bilingual policy of both urban districts with an aim to provide equitable academic experiences for students who have a home language other than English and to implement flexible, student-centered courses of study that prepare students for the global, multilingual society of the twenty-first century.

Methodology

For each district, the curriculum audit process was conducted over a one-year period, beginning in August and ending in July of the following year. This process was conducted twice for the LVESD and once for the DUHSD because of the level of funding available.

Due to the impact of Proposition 227, other districts with bilingual programs across the state were also concerned and so audits began to be conducted at both state and local levels. However, this project was unlike other Post-227 reviews, in that rather than going in from the outside as "researchers" or "policy makers" looking in on programs, we started from inside, the districts and schools worked collaboratively with key stakeholders.[21] This was not a mandated process but rather, a proactive review to assess strengths and needs in serving ELL students. As outside consultants, we worked with each district's curriculum audit team, made up of at least ten members, including school principals, the bilingual director, and concerned teachers and parents. The audit teams met to formulate the research processes, instruments, and procedures. School site visits were scheduled and teachers surveyed at the selected school sites. The main procedures outlined in Table 4, Curriculum Audit Process, reflect the procedure each district went through.

School Identification

It was apparent at the outset that it would not be possible to evaluate all schools in either district, given the limited resources both financial and human. As a result, of the 37 schools in the LVESD, 12 schools were visited during the first year of the audit and 11 in the second year. For DUHSD, 8 schools of the 27 in the district were selected for site vis-

its during spring of 2002. The criteria used to determine which schools were to be included were socioeconomic status (SES), number of ELL students, and feeder school patterns both across districts and within the DUHSD. The schools were selected based on low to high enrollment of ELLs, low to high SES; in addition, middle/junior high schools were selected based on their respective feeder high schools. The researchers along with each district's curriculum audit committee visited each school site for two days. During each visit the team observed classrooms, met with students, teachers, parents, and the school advisory team for bilingual and ELD services. The number of committee members to visit any one school site ranged from at least four to no more than eight and always included a university researcher, administrator, teacher, and parent participant.

Instruments, Field Testing, and Data Gathering

The data gathered provide an overview of trends in how these school districts addressed the educational needs of ELL students across a continuum of eight key areas of educational programming: Program Approaches, Value for Learners, Expectations for Learners, Instructional Goals, Literacy Orientation, Resources, Accountability and Assessment, Parent Involvement/Engagement.

These eight dimensions of programming are derived from the research literature on policy and programming of ELLs,[22] and were used to develop an observational instrument that was utilized by the visiting team to collect data.

- *Program Design and Approaches.* This dimension examined the multiple programs presently utilized or engaged to service ELLs within classrooms and schools.
- *Value for Learners.* This area examined views of ELLs in relation to school policy and program and by concerned stakeholders (i.e., teachers, administrators, parents, and students).

Table 4.
Curriculum Audit Process

Task	Purpose	Outcome	Timeline
Establish process for curriculum audit design and school coordination	Involve district bilingual committee and coordinate with schools' schedules and school staff; develop review process	Design, plan, and establish process for post-227 curriculum audit with rubrics and timelines	August–October
Design post-227 curriculum audit study approach	Curriculum 227 audit committee meetings to conceptualize focus	Committee discussion of design, conceptualization, and formulation of study approach	November
Review existing school data	Identify schools with low and high critical mass of students and existing ELL academic trends	Identification of schools, school profiles by ELL student, and academic achievement trends in selected academic areas	December
Identify schools to be visited	Calendar of schools to be visited in academic year	Set appointment dates and send letters to sites as to purpose of visit	January
Adaptation and field test of instrument/rubrics	Identify eight areas of curriculum audit and operationalize each area	Adaptation and field testing of instrument for data collection & analysis	February–March
School visits	Visit school sites—two days by team of 5 to 8 members including parents, teachers, administrator	Observations, interviews, teacher surveys, and data collection by school, N = 23 elementary N = 8 secondary	March–April
Analysis of data	Identify patterns based on services, approaches, and depth of services to ELL children	Findings reviewed by committee for reporting to district administration & school board; development of school profiles using observations, interviews, and data on each of the selected schools	May & June
Report of findings to school board	Findings of service, approaches, depth of services to ELL children Reviewed by committee for report to district administration school board	Report on findings based on services, approaches, depth of services to ELL students	July

- *Expectations for Learners.* This area identified and examined the expectations of students as defined by the stakeholders, policy, and programs.
- *Instructional Goals.* This area identified and examined the goal of instruction and learning, along with expectations related to academic development in L1 and L2.
- *Literacy Orientation.* This area examined the type of literacy promoted among stakeholders. Areas examined included the value that is placed on literacy and recognition for various forms of literacy and language learning.
- *Curriculum Resources.* This area examined the financial and human resources allocated or dedicated to programming and curricula for ELLs.

- *Instructional Accountability and Assessment.* This area examined the accountability of not only student achievement and success, but program implementation and fiscal allocation of resources.
- *Parent Involvement and Engagement.* This area identified and examined how parents are valued and involved in school activities and degree of collaboration between home and school.

To validate the eight constructs of the evaluation, the instrument was field tested in two comparable schools not involved in the study. Observations of each of the eight areas were collected at the two school sites visited, data analyzed and discussed, and a rubric was developed to assess the level of evidence and consistency across sites.

The rubric, with a rating scale of 1 to 5, was used to identify the perceptions of the visiting team in each of the eight areas of observation.[23] A score of 5 indicated that the team found exceptional evidence and consistency with regard to the area under observation (e.g., Program Design and Approaches). A score of 1 indicated that the team found low evidence and consistency. For each of the eight dimensions, the visiting team identified guiding questions to operationalize its findings. (For example, relative to the Program Design and Approaches dimension, it was inquired of ELD academic staff, "Are the particular teachers who are assigned to teach the most knowledgeable and experienced?")

The data gathering per school site consisted of a minimum of one set of two-day visits. Before each school site visit, the visiting team was provided with data and characteristics of the school and how the school acknowledged and recognized ELL students as part of the school community. The visits yielded many notes and observations. At the end of each two-day visit, members of the respective committees met to discuss their individual ratings. Consensus was derived for each rating across the eight dimensions. Notes were recorded; for each rating, a report was drafted and

sent to the school site and each committee member for their input. The input was incorporated into the data and the final school site report was shared.

School site interviews involved the school principal and members of the leadership team. These interviews focused on understanding the organizational climate of the school and on the type of programs and services to ELLs. Interviews with parents and teachers took the form of focus groups, each group consisting of three to ten participants. The focus of teacher and parent interviews consisted of ascertaining the intensity and consistency of services to ELLs with regard to school expectations, program design, curriculum materials, literacy development, professional development, and school support. Parent interviews focused on their access to information, involvement with the school site, and type and quality of parental engagement. Notes from all interviews and focus groups were taken and summarized, then correlated with observations, surveys, and school data in reporting the findings.[24]

OVERALL FINDINGS AND RECOMMENDATIONS

The following is a synthesis of the results derived from the observational and survey data collected from both school districts. These results reflect the trends the committee identified across the 23 elementary schools and 8 middle and high schools. Along with the findings in each area are general recommendations that are aligned with the eight components of schooling assessed. Any significant differences between the LVESD and DUHSD are noted where they might have differed.

Program Design and Approaches

Across all the schools, it was found that at least adequate ELD programming was offered and provided to ELLs. However, all the school programs for ELLs varied from structured English immersion (SEI) to early and late exit bilingual transitional models.

In addition, both elementary and secondary schools that did not have a clearly articulated bilingual or ELD program did not provide the necessary academic rigor to ELL students to assure their academic development. Although all schools visited met legal ELL compliance under the guidelines of Proposition 227, the majority of schools did not offer a comprehensive academic or cognitively demanding curriculum to ELLs that promotes biliteracy. There were of course exceptions to this, as there were several elementary schools with late exit or dual language immersion programs that ran counter to this finding and did provide key examples of programming that fostered academic literacy in both Spanish and English.

To address these concerns we recommended greater academic rigor in ELD and across school programs. As a result of these recommendations both districts have begun to reassess the rigor of their ELD and academic programming. For example, DUHSD approved the granting of a high school biliteracy diploma that meets the standards set by the district for college entrance. To date, more than 100 students in the district have received this honor.

Value for Learners

It was found that all school sites articulated a value for and understanding of biliteracy for all of their students. It was noted that the majority of administrators, teachers, and staff value their students' language and culture as resources and assets, but many schools did not demonstrate the value as an academic outcome. It was recommended that the schools and district make it a priority to promote and articulate an agenda that makes clear the value of biliteracy to lifelong social, economic, and educational goals. In addition, a biliteracy agenda and policy for DUHSD needs to be articulated so all schools have the opportunity to establish additive biliteracy programs.

Expectations for Learners

In this area, all school sites focused on high achievement in reading and math for their students. However, the expectation for the majority of ELLs, especially at the 4th- to 12th-grade levels, is to transition to English. Therefore, although all schools are working and demonstrating educational processes that align state standards with school curriculum, the curriculum alignment for ELLs in many bilingual and most SEI settings was not evident. To address this concern it was recommended that schools continue to increase the academic rigor of ELLs and programs by establishing a cognitively demanding curriculum, one that promotes academic status equalization for their ELL students and fosters expectations for high achievement in reading and math in Spanish and English.

Instructional Goals

It was agreed that all school sites had teachers with knowledge of SDAIE instructional strategies. Yet, evidence of SDAIE strategies being utilized across classrooms and programs was inconsistent. At the elementary schools the quality of ELD and the use of ELD standards were found to be lacking consistency and intensity. At the middle- and high-school levels, there was inconsistent articulation of ELD and/or bilingual programs as an academic department. This addresses the need to value the professional rigor of ELD and bilingual programs as equal to other academic departments. For example, at some school sites ELD was part of the English department, whereas at others it was part of a content-specific academic department.

Literacy Orientation

The overall literacy orientation of the majority of 4th- to 12th-grade levels was English reading and writing. For example, most school sites had more than one English literacy intervention program. At the elementary level they included Project RESULTS, GLAD, use of accelerated reading programs and phonics in English, WriteSource, Open Court, and INTO English. At the middle-high school sites they included Accelerated Reader, Project WRITE, Corrective Reading, and several other commercial programs. Although these are important components, native language development or Spanish interventions were nonexistent or limited to no more than one or two programs. This sets up a priority on developing English readers and writers, rather than developing biliterate individuals.

Our recommendations are for more programs that focus on academic rigor in L1 and L2 and to promote and implement more curriculum programs/interventions that focus on Spanish literacy development.

Resources and Curriculum: L1 (Spanish) and L2 (English)

When examining resources for curriculum in L1 and English, it was found that the school sites had varying qualities of L1 textbooks and resources for academic development (e.g., computer software and reference materials). The quantity and quality of L1 materials varied from high to low in the schools. In this area, most school sites lacked quality curriculum subject matter resources in L1. For English, all school sites have and use district-recommended ELD curriculum texts and resources; all school sites provided quality curriculum subject matter resources in English that match the basic college requirements, but lacked the same resources in Spanish.

It was recommended that the district provide greater equity in the quantity and quality of L1 textbooks and resources for the academic development and support of ELL students' access to and comprehension of core subject matter. At a minimum, the district should provide for the acquisition of L1 books and reference resources in all school libraries.

Resources: Professional Development

It was determined that teachers at all school sites have received ongoing and appropriate support for ELD professional development. However, the teacher focus groups and survey data indicated that a significant number of teachers were not aware of how bilingual students were placed. At the same time, most teachers agreed that for ELLs the degree of proficiency in both their L1 and English is positively related to academic achievement. Positively, we found that school sites provided time and space for department meetings; we recommended this time as an opportunity for dialogue and articulation of ELL placement and services.

Both districts agreed to continue to provide training for teachers in the use of SDAIE strategies, as well as to develop the professional capacity of teachers to provide ELD and core curriculum instruction to ELL students.

Instructional and Fiscal Accountability and Assessment

It was observed that K–6 and 7–8 school sites had weak articulation across programs, and although grades 7–8 and 9–12 school sites had stronger academic articulation, it was generally perceived as not strong across districts. The use of multiple measures was evident with a strong focus on standardized tests including the SAT-9 (Stanford Academic Test), STAR (Standardized Testing and Reporting), and CAHSEE (California High School Exit Exam), all of which serve as strong academic indicators in English. In some instances, a Spanish equivalent to the SAT-9, the SABE (Spanish Assessment of Basic Education), was utilized as a measure for Spanish-literate students. In terms of ELD, all schools utilized the state-mandated CELDT exam (California English Language Development Test). This assessment, along with other classroom authentic assessments, determines a student's level of English proficiency and placement. Although all assessment measures provided rich data on student progress and achievement, schools lacked a consistent systematic way of utilizing the data for informing instructional processes and program articulation.

To ensure greater equity in assessment for ELL students, we recommended the need for districts to promote and monitor all assessment systems, including classroom-based assessment measures and outcomes. In addition, schools should take more time to develop K–6, 7–8, and 9–12 curriculum articulation. It is imperative that urban school communities implement accountability systems that address the prevention of early underachievement and provide its youth with the core curriculum that prepares them for a multilingual world that is based on an information economy. In the area of fiscal accountability, school data indicated adequate evidence of necessary resources that need to be more adequately allocated to service ELL students.

Parent Involvement

All schools visited provided minimal to adequate support services to Latino/-a parents and students. All school sites had parent committees that discussed ELL issues and held meetings from two to eight times a year. Parents had access to information across all sites, but the quality and accuracy of information provided varied. It was observed that all school sites were searching for ways to better connect with the parent community in general.

Parent involvement was the lowest rated area of these projects. Schools, for the most part, did not provide parents with the depth and insights as to what is necessary for their children to have access to a rigorous curriculum. We recommend ongoing training for parents on home-school collaboration, including supporting processes in educating parents on how to navigate the school system.

Research on parent involvement speaks to the importance of their inclusion in the school community to raise student achievement, however, as this study found few schools actively involve parents.[25] To truly involve parents in the school community, parent activities and practices need to match the culture and schedules of parents, not the school system.

CONCLUSIONS AND IMPLICATIONS

The results of these curriculum audits provide insights as to what is possible when stakeholders and researchers focus on examining urban school practices that align with core goals and concepts of the mission and policies districts set forth. The findings of these curriculum audits address more generally the educational crisis of our ELL students who are negotiating two languages and two cultures. The ELL student population presently faces many obstacles to achieve educational equity and excellence. The findings revealed that although the school district has the capacity, including credentialed personnel, value, and intent to provide pedagogically sound programs to ELLs, schools services lacked the educational consistency and academic rigor to provide equal educational access. Although Spanish/English biliteracy programs in both school districts is a goal, it is not a reality. No school allocated more than 5 percent of its courses to an academic biliteracy approach. Although both LVESD and DUHSD had adequate and consistent ELD programs, few schools incorporated ELD and academic instruction in the primary language toward a viable academic biliteracy program.

This project suggests that four major policies need to be implemented at the elementary to high school levels to shift the paradigm from remediation, or compensatory, to one of quality or academic empowerment with a goal of access to higher education for ethnolinguistically diverse students. First, action research curriculum audits need to be instituted involving all stakeholder groups in the school district in order to be informed about the quality, consistency, and depth of educational practice being provided to ELLs. Second, there is a need for a *language policy* that is supportive of additive language programs that have multiliteracy as an educational outcome and world standard for all students. Third, there must be *accountability* of school programs and services that ensures equal opportunity to the core curriculum and uses multiple measures to assess the language and academic development for our nations ethnolinguistically diverse students. Last, there must be high academic standards that promote biliteracy, including courses that are rigorous and aligned to the core curriculum necessary for access to our nations college and university systems. Thus, if we truly believe in equal educational opportunity, it is imperative that educators begin preparing our ELL learners for fundamental biliteracy communication, along with computational and problem-solving skills that are necessary to have access to higher education and the world of work in the informational and technological society of the twenty-first century.

Our present global economy calls for multiliteracy standards, not monolingualism. To achieve this goal, the findings of this type of action research curriculum audit will need to be duplicated in other urban schools. This approach, however, requires researchers, educators, and policy makers to examine the wide variety of urban settings that are made up of ethnolinguistic communities that bring more than seventy languages and cultures to our schools every day. The rich diversity of languages they bring should not be viewed as deficits or obstacles to be diminished, denied, or overcome, but as national treasures, assets to be nurtured and developed to their highest potential. We must work toward the status equalization of languages in not just schools, but also in the nation, for biliteracy can only enrich cross-cultural understanding for our children, their families, and our world.

NOTES

1. Garcia, E. (2001). *Hispanic education in the United States: Raices y alas*. New York: Rowan & Littlefield.

2. California Consortium for Teacher Development. (1997). *Teacher education and credentialing for student diversity: The case in California*. Santa Cruz: University of California, Santa Cruz.

3. California Basic Educational Data Systems (CBEDS). (2001). Sacramento, CA: California Department of Education. An annual collection of basic student and staff data; including student enrollment, numbers of graduates and dropouts, course enrollment figures, and enrollment in alternative, gifted, and talented education. Retrieved from http://www.cde.ca.gov/ds/sd/cb/.

4. U.S. Department of Commerce. (2000, March). *Current population survey: The Hispanic population in the United States, population characteristics*. Washington, DC: U.S. Bureau of the Census.

5. Tollefson, J. (2000). Policy and ideology in the spread of English. In J. Hall & W. Eggington (Eds.), *The sociopolitics of English language teaching*. Buffalo, New York: Multilingual Matters.

6. Kozol, J. (1991). *Savage inequalities: Children in America's schools*. New York: Harper Perennial; Macedo, D., & Bartolome, L. (1999). *Dancing with bigotry*. New York: St. Martin's Press; McCaleb, S. (1994). *Building communities of learners: A collaboration among teachers, students, families, and community*. New York: St. Martin's Press.

7. Barrera, M. (1988). *Beyond Aztlan: Ethnic autonomy in comparative perspective*. Notre Dame, IN: University of Notre Dame Press; Darder, A. (1995). *Culture and difference: Critical perspectives*. Westport, CT: Bergin & Garvey; Espinosa, R., & Ochoa, A. (1992). *The educational attainment of California youth: A public equity crisis*. San Diego, CA: San Diego State University; Kitchen, D. (1990). *Educational tracking*. Unpublished. San Diego State University, San Diego, CA, and Claremont Graduate School, Claremont, CA; Oakes, J. (1985). *Keeping track: How schools structure inequality*. New Haven, CT: Yale University Press; Ochoa, A. (1995). Language policy and social implica-

tions for addressing the bicultural immigrant experience in the United States. In A. Darder (Ed.), *Culture and difference: Critical perspectives.* Westport, CT: Bergin & Garvey.

8. Brisk, M. (1998). *Bilingual education: From compensatory to quality schooling.* Mahwah, NJ: Lawrence Erlbaum Associates.

9. Brisk (1998).

10. Brisk (1998), p. xviii.

11. Brisk (1998), p. xix.

12. Baker, C. (2001). *Foundations of bilingual education and bilingualism.* Clevedon Avon, England: Multilingual Matters.

13. Baker (2001).

14. Baker (2001).

15. Latino Educational Summit. (2001). *Educational summit report 2003.* San Diego, CA: San Diego County Office of Education.

16. Garcia (2001); Orfield, G., & Yun, J. (1999). *Resegregation in American schools.* The Civil Rights Project. Boston, MA: Harvard University.

17. Espinosa & Ochoa (1992).

18. Kerper-Mora, J. *Proposition 227's second anniversary: Triumph or travesty?* Retrieved December, 2000, from: http://coe.sdsu.edu/people/jmora/Prop227/227YearTwo.htm.

19. Baker (2001).

20. Baker (2001); Cummins, J. (1994). Primary language instruction and the education of language minority students. In C. Leyba (Ed.), *Schooling and language minority students: A theoretical framework* (pp. 3–49). Los Angeles, CA: Evaluation Dissemination and Assessment Center, California State University, Los Angeles.

21. Elliot, J. (1991). *Action research for educational change.* Philadelphia: Open University Press; Noffke, S., & Stevenson, R. (Eds.). (1995). *Educational action research: Becoming practically critical.* New York: Teachers College Columbia.

22. Cummins (1994); August, D., & Hakuta, K. (Eds.). (1997). *Improving schooling for language minority children: Research agenda.* Washington, DC: National Academy Press; Kelly, U. (1997). *Schooling desire: Literacy, cultural politics, and pedagogy.* New York: Routledge.

23. Ochoa, A., & Cadiero-Kaplan, K. (2004). Towards promoting biliteracy and academic achievement: Educational programs for high school Latino English language learners. *The High School Journal, 87* (3), 27–43.

24. Ochoa & Cadiero-Kaplan (2004).

25. Nuñez, R. (1994). *Schools, parent,s and empowerment: An ethnographic study of Mexican-American-origin parents' participation in their children's education.* Unpublished doctoral dissertation, San Diego State University, San Diego, CA and Claremont Graduate School, Claremont, CA; Olivos, E. (2003). *Dialectical tensions, contradictions, and resistance: A study of the relationship between Latino parents and the public school system within a socioeconomic structure of dominance.* Unpublished doctoral dissertation, San Diego State University, San Diego, CA and Claremont Graduate School, Claremont, CA.

BILINGUAL-BICULTURAL LITERACY PEDAGOGIES AND THE POLITICS OF PROJECT HEAD START

Ronald L. Mize, Silverio Haro, Claudia Huiza, Anthony Navarrete, Patricia Rivas-McCrae, and Alfonso Rodriguez

San Diego, the seventh largest metropolitan city in the United States according to the 2000 U.S. Census, is home to a population that is becoming increasingly immigrant and nonwhite. Although whites currently constitute 55 percent of the population (the only major metropolitan city in California that has retained a majority-majority population in spite of the statewide trend toward majority-minority status), Latinos/-as comprise more than one-fourth of the total population (27%).[1] According to the San Diego Unified School District, school-aged children are now majority-minority and overwhelmingly Latino/-a—41 percent, compared to the second largest group, whites, who constitute 26 percent.[2] By the end of this decade, it is expected that Latinos/-as will constitute the outright majority of students in the city. The San Diego economy is increasingly bimodal, a city of haves and have-nots. Even though the city is on the U.S.-Mexico border, the lived experiences of Latinos/-as do not necessarily benefit from a proximity to Mexico. Latinos/-as are at the bottom of every social, economic, health, and education indicator of well-being.

Project Head Start, initiated as one facet of the 1960s War on Poverty, is the last-standing poverty relief program in the face of what is often deemed by scholars as the current War on the Poor.[3] It was initially introduced in San Diego to serve the economically disadvantaged from African-American inner-city neighborhoods and Mexican-American *barrios*. Yet, Project Head Start in San Diego has attempted to respond to the changing demographics of the city. This entry is based upon data collected from a training program funded, under the auspices of a Hispanic Serving Higher Education Institution partnership grant, by the Administration on Children, Youth, and Families and administered at California State University–San Marcos. An exploration of our cultural pedagogy training program is based on the testimony of the Head Start teachers who began the first early childhood classrooms in San Diego to the recent inductees into the *kulturkampf* (culture wars) of contemporary urban San Diego. In particular, the training program we administered assisted teachers in developing and in many ways legitimating pedagogical practices that focus on early literacy efforts for bilingual/bicultural students. We introduce mural making by introducing Head Start teachers to the muralists of Chicano Park, Mexican and Chicano musical styles by local musicians, culturally relevant bilingual children's literature, Chicano history, Chicano and Mexican culture, and many other aspects in the hope of bridging the home culture/school culture divide that places so many Latino/-a

students at a serious disadvantage at such an early age.

This project, highly aware of the cultural politics of promoting a positive view of Chicano/-a culture, is situated in the larger political forces that attempt to impede its full actualization. On one front, the overall conservative attack on education[4] has found a new federal target for elimination as witnessed by the current attempts at dismantling Head Start at the highest levels. On another but closely related front, the attack on bilingual education in the aftermath of California Proposition 227 has led to the influx of English-only immersion programs while seriously undercutting the mission of Head Start aimed at educating preschool children in both their home language and English. As racialized minorities take on a numerical majority in urban San Diego, it is the aim of this chapter to both detail the current attacks on immigrants, language rights, and cultural pluralism, as well as document the substantial progress made by Latina *soldaderas-maestras* (soldier-teachers) who succeed in imparting culturally relevant and linguistically appropriate knowledge formation to early learners.

After a delineation of the social demographics that relate to the San Diego Head Start population, a historical periodization of Head Start will show how the federal program has had to alter its aims, missions, and directions to ensure continued funding. A brief discussion of the neoconservative attack on education programs such as Head Start will be coupled with the California propositions that have directly impacted the Latino/-a population in San Diego. Our training program on bicultural/bilingual cultural competencies will demonstrate how we view our work, and the work of Head Start teachers in San Diego, as attempts at stemming the tide of anti-Latino/-a, anti-immigrant activities. These attempts will be demonstrated through the examples of various teachers, center directors, family social workers, and parents associated with Head Start.

THE SOCIODEMOGRAPHICS OF URBAN SAN DIEGO

Nationwide, Latinos/-as are the fastest growing group at a rate of 9.8 percent in the past two years. Estimates published on the *USA Today* Census Web site project the Latino/-a population to exceed 114 million by 2060—a figure that represents nearly 40 percent of the current U.S. total population.[5] In California, Latinos/-as are the largest minority group in the state (a nationwide trend as well) and according to the 2000 Census comprise 32.4 percent of the population. If demographic trends continue, the Latino/-a population will be the largest single group in the state within the next few decades.

Even though whites constitute 60 percent of the total California state population, in the major cities, they constitute less than one-half of the population. In Los Angeles; San Francisco; Orange County; and larger cities in the Central and Imperial Valleys such as Fresno, Modesto, Sacramento, Brawley, and El Centro, whites do not constitute the majority of the population. San Diego is the last major California city that is still majority-majority, but current Asian and Latino/-a growth rates demonstrate that by the end of the decade, San Diego, too, will join the ranks of majority-minority cities.

In addition to ethnic and racial stratification, San Diego also demonstrates many of the features of a bimodal class structure (an erasure of the middle class and a metropolis that is increasingly divided between the haves and have-nots). In San Diego, the increasingly bimodal class structure is evidenced with a median per capita personal income (MSA) in 2001 of $33,883 for Latinos/-as (compared to whites' median income of $65,000). With a median home sale price of $230,000, the ability to achieve a comfortable standard of living is restricted to those at the top ranks of the income spectrum. Statewide, the Latino/-a population has the highest rate of those living in poverty (more than 20%) and children constitute 42 percent of the state's poor. In San Diego, the current population has 82,509 children under the age of 5. This represents 7 percent of the total population and all children represent 27 percent of total population.[6] The vast majority of those children are nonwhite and/or immigrant.

Data from the San Diego Unified School District (which covers the city of San Diego) show that Latinos/-as constitute 41 percent of the student population and, by the end of the decade, will constitute more than 50 percent of the student base. The second largest group, whites, only constitutes 26 percent of the total student population. If one looks at the entire county of San Diego, one will find that whites and Latinos/-as constitute an equal percentage of students (both at 39.8%). Nearly 60 percent of San Diego Unified students qualify for free or reduced school lunches.

Other educational and health and indicators show Latinos/-as are consistently ranked at the bottom of nearly all well-being measures. Native Americans and African Americans tend to drop out of San Diego high schools at the highest rate, but Latinos/-as also drop out at a rate much higher than the overall average, ranking third in terms of most dropouts. In standardized examinations, Latinos/-as in San Diego rank drastically lower then all other groups in percentage of scores at or above the 50th national percentile rank in reading on the Stanford-9 Test. From 1998 to 2000, only 24 percent of San Diego Latino/-a third-graders scored at or above the national ranking whereas overall, 50 percent of all students and 70 percent of white students scored at or above the national average. Latinos/-as had the highest rate of teenage pregnancy in San Diego County at a rate of 64.4 per 1,000 females age 15–17. Latino/-a children ranked last in terms of percentage covered by any form of health insurance. One-fourth of all Latino/-a children go without health coverage in San Diego. Coupling these statistics with the highest rates of poverty and lowest median income, Latinos/-as are finding themselves at the bottom of the socioeconomic ladder and suffering the consequences. Considering the fact that poverty is concentrated within the youngest age groups, one of the few resources still available to poor Latino/-a children is Head Start.

A BRIEF HISTORY OF HEAD START

Head Start was designed as a poverty relief measure enacted among the War on Poverty policies of the Lyndon Baines Johnson administration. Aimed at preschool-aged children, Head Start is a means-tested program designed to address poverty, particularly in racialized communities, in both urban and rural locales. Head Start was enacted in 1963 to ensure low-income students would be given not just a fair start, but a head start, in a pre-K comprehensive program that included academic, social, nutritional, health, and family support services. President Johnson, in his speech, "To Fulfill These Rights," encapsulates the rationale for Head Start and other antipoverty programs. He stated:

You do not take a person who, for years, has been hobbled by chains and liberate him, bring him up to the starting line of a race and then say, 'You are free to compete with all the others,' and still justly believe that you have been completely fair. Thus it is not enough just to open the gates of opportunity. All our citizens must have the ability to walk through those gates.[7]

So in many ways, Head Start became the first line of attack in the War on Poverty. Yet, Project Head Start was hampered from the beginning by two interrelated factors: (1) a reliance upon the deficit model of education as defining black cul-

ture, and (2) the overall racist climate of the day. Sociologist Stephen Steinberg has noted that the remainder of Johnson's speech was based on Daniel Patrick Moynihan's delineation of the cultural deficit model and many of the programs derived from this liberal approach assumed that cultural and familial deficiencies had to be overcome before economic and racial equality could be attained.[8] Historical sociologist Jill Quadagno has demonstrated in *The Color of Welfare* how the measures within the War on Poverty amounted to half-hearted attempts at remedying socioeconomic inequalities due to the prevalence of racism in shaping the political debate.[9]

The first phase of Project Head Start was the "community empowerment" phase (1965–80) that sought to bypass state and local governments in the funding process and provide federal funds directly to community action groups that served the underserved populations of the United States. Many Southern politicians viewed this as a federal government attempt at instituting programs and providing funding for poor African Americans to thwart their locally controlled systems of racial segregation and unequal access to public services. But the origins of Head Start in predominately Latino/-a areas such as the Southwest meant that this national program with a black-white binary focus would be regionalized and localized to the communities in which it would be deployed. Most of the scholarly literature on Head Start tends to be focused on race as a black-white issue, but Head Start is beginning to acknowledge the relevance of Latinos/-as and Native Americans as a crucial component of Project Head Start. At the national level, this bureaucratic recognition has certainly come before a full scholarly awareness of the special issues that Latino/-a children face in their social, emotional, linguistic, and cognitive development.

As Head Start at the federal level moved away from community empowerment and thus many community action groups became much more bureaucratized, the issue of cultural awareness was supplanted by calls for "school readiness." This second phase, which really defined Head Start in the 1990s but can trace its origins throughout the 1980s as well, came precisely at the time when Head Start was becoming much more diverse in its student base. It was a time also marked by the beginning of the outright dismantlement of the safety net and minimal welfare state that developed out of the New Deal and Great Society programs. The outright war on the poor that began with the Reagan administration required Head Start to redesign itself into a politically salient language and focus. School readiness became the vehicle for keeping Head Start off the chopping block. Given this confluence of factors, it probably was no surprise that when the Department of Health and Human Services implemented the Head Start Family and Child Experiences Survey in 2000, it reported program weakness in the area of cultural awareness for 75 percent of the national Head Start–surveyed sites.

The current phase of "accountability" is in some ways a logical extension of school readiness and the implicitly anticommunity empowerment aspect of a narrow focus on academics rather than a whole child approach. The current political situation of neoconservatism means that Project Head Start will be even further underfunded and greater cultural awareness will be replaced by "universal" early literacy programs that assume one language, one culture, one ethnicity. Amid the current debates about the Bush administration lying to secure a free pass to declare war on Iraq, the FCC deregulation debacle, corporate fraud scandals, the constitutional amendment to "protect marriage," and cutting funds from Temporary Assistance for Needy Families (TANF) to support a "marriage enrichment program," a person would most likely have

missed a very quietly "debated" reauthorization bill (HR 2210) that passed 217 to 216 just after 1 AM EST on Friday, July 25, 2003. Yet the reauthorization bill, approved by the House over the objection of 11 Republicans voting with the Democrats (with two Democrats not voting), might have led to the complete dismantlement of Head Start, if the bill had made it through the Senate.

The Senate never called the bill for a vote, and Head Start has been operating without a reauthorization act through the time of writing. In September 2005, the House approved H.R. 2123, the School Readiness Act, without block grants and with temporary suspension of the National Reporting System. Chipping away at the foundation of Head Start, rather than fully dismantling it, seems to be the current strategy in Congress. Recently introduced in Head Start legislation are language that emphasizes English proficiency for LEP students, more coordination with LEAs (public school districts), and greater autonomy for religious organizations to make employment decisions based on religious principles (seen by some as discrimination on the basis of religion). At the time of writing, the Senate has not set a date to vote on its version of the School Readiness Act.

The initial reason that Head Start bypassed state governments to fund community action programs (including nonprofit religious organizations) was because states had historically denied services to their poor, particularly their minority poor. Head Start was created specifically to bypass racist and segregationist Southern states that would ensure that funds targeted to help poor children out of poverty would never find their way into aggrieved communities. The Bush administration-sponsored bill is in fact pushing to turn back the clock 40 years in how Head Start is funded. The Title 2 provision would allow eight state governments to apply for the block-granting of

Head Start (i.e., allow funds to be controlled and disbursed by the states, not directly by the federal government to local governments).

But the larger issue is the impetus in Head Start reauthorization for an even larger bureaucratic shift that will most likely take away that which is most effective. The Bush plan calls for moving Head Start out of the Department of Health and Human Services (DHHS) and into the Department of Education. The call is a result of forcing Head Start into a school-readiness model. Rather than treating Head Start children from the "whole child" approach, the exclusive focus will be on early literacy and some mathematical awareness (i.e., academic preparation). Much of what constitutes Head Start as a provider of comprehensive family services will be reduced to pre-K academic preparation.

Currently, the DHHS Web site has published a research report on how Head Start is "failing," with suggestions for "improving Head Start."[10] Not coincidentally, every deficiency cited fits perfectly with each recommendation in the Bush plan for Head Start. The report, titled "Strengthening Head Start: What the Evidence Shows," relies upon carefully selected case studies and measures to support the rationale for the creation of the report: "The President's Plan will strengthen Head Start and enable coordination of early childhood systems" (actual title of report Section VI). With the results preordained, the report consists of evidence that supports the Bush plan for universal literacy pedagogical approaches (all children learn one way via one language—English—and the one "American" culture as defined by cultural conservatives such as William J. Bennett and Lynne Cheney).

CONSERVATIVE ATTACK ON EDUCATION

Apple has very aptly elucidated the current conservative attack on U.S. educa-

tion.[11] Whether it be a call for school vouchers and homeschooling, the imposition of state or federal standards on educational outcomes, right-wing religious assaults on curricula, or the aim of turning education into vocational-technical training for business, Apple identifies each group within the conservative restoration that is attempting to control the educational process according to its goals and ideologies. His delineation of the right-wing agenda articulates with the Bush plan for Head Start—the emphasis on outcomes based on federal mandates for testing, the notion that early literacy equals English-only literacy, one universal pedagogical method for English language acquisition, and holding teachers accountable while ignoring the fact that Head Start has not been fully funded for more than 20 years. In fact, more children qualify for Head Start than can be accepted by centers, and the pay for most Head Start teaching staff with dependents is so low, they qualify for Head Start.

These restrictive measures are compounded in states like California that have publicly expressed particularly anti-immigrant and anti-Latino/-a stances. The voter initiatives in recent California elections certainly attest to the racialized climate of urban education. California Proposition 63 in 1986 was designed to make English the "official language of the state." It was followed by Proposition 227 in 1998, the so-called Save Our Children initiative, which required the placement of "limited English proficiency" students in English-only classrooms (so-called immersion programs) after one year of English as a second language (ESL) instruction. Coupling these propositions with those that deny public services to immigrants (Proposition 187) and ending affirmative action in state hiring and school admittance decisions (Proposition 209), cultural critic George Lipsitz calls "California in the 1990s the human rights equivalent of Mississippi in the 1960s."[12] Within Head Start guidelines, it quite clearly states that students are to be taught in their home language as well as English. The architects of Head Start realized quite early what researchers on bilingual education are now coming to realize as a social fact— non-English speaking students learn English better when their home language skills are enhanced concomitantly.

BILINGUAL/BICULTURAL EARLY LITERACY TRAINING

Recent research on bilingual education can be viewed in some ways as an attempt at transcending a political debate steeped in an ideological debate on assimilation versus cultural pluralism into a vehicle for understanding how language acquisition impacts learning. In our training program with Head Start teachers, we introduce several popular myths about language diversity and the best data available on why bilingual-bicultural pedagogical approaches tend to best facilitate learning for initial non-English speakers.[13] The four major popular myths we discuss are (1) the predominance of English is threatened, (2) English literacy is the only literacy that matters, (3) English illiteracy is high because language minorities do not want to learn English, and (4) the best way to promote English literacy is through English-only instruction.

To counter the myth that the predominance of English is under attack, we cite that according to Census data, in 1990 only 13.8 percent of the population spoke a language other than English. Whereas in 1910, 23 percent of the U.S. population age 10 and older did not speak English. We show how the United States has always been a multilingual nation from its inception. We discuss the early role of the German language in many Midwestern states and the fact that the original California State Constitution was in English and Spanish and provisions were made in that Constitution to make the state's official documents available in both languages.

To counter the second myth that English literacy is the only literacy worth knowing, we refer to research conducted on cohorts of students in San Diego Unified School District.[14] Portes and Rumbaut find that among Latino/-a and Asian students, those most likely to score highly on predictors of high school success were those with bilingual abilities. As expected, limited English proficiency students were likely to drop out and have lower grade point averages (GPAs), but students with English-only proficiency were more likely to drop out and have lower GPAs than their bilingual counterparts. All too often, literacy itself is often assumed to be the same as English literacy. Current Head Start documents on early literacy have universally subscribed to this fallacy. It is also assumed that lack of English literacy is seen as being a sign of low intelligence. Yet, we find in the current global labor market that bilingual and multilingual abilities have become highly marketable job skills.

The third myth is that English illiteracy is high because language minorities are not eager to learn English. On the day that California Proposition 63 passed, more than 40,000 adults were on waiting lists for ESL classes in Los Angeles alone. During our extensive work with Head Start teachers and parents over the past four years, the single most requested adult education program was English instruction courses of study.

Finally, the myth that the best way to promote English literacy is through English-only programs has been countered by recent research that finds that second language learners benefit from the continued development of their first language. In Feliciano's Census-based study of Asians and Latino/-as, she finds:

bilingual students are less likely to drop out than English-only speakers, students in bilingual households are less likely to drop out than those in English-dominant or English-limited households, and students in immigrant households are less likely to drop out than those in nonimmigrant households. These findings suggest that those who enjoy the greatest educational success are not those who have abandoned their ethnic cultures and are most acculturated. Rather, bicultural youths who can draw resources from both the immigrant community and mainstream society are best situated to enjoy educational success.[15]

As we move toward a multilingual world, we challenge Head Start teachers in San Diego to recognize the difference between literacy and English literacy, stress attitudes and curricula that support positive examples of biculturalism as well as bilingualism, encourage staff development in the areas of cultural proficiencies necessary for the local pre-K population, and emphasize the benefits of multilingual knowledge for all children.

HEAD START AND LATINO/-A EMPOWERMENT

In the face of this political maelstrom are Head Start families, teachers, directors, and family social workers who are creating genuine and long-lasting changes for Latino/-a children. In San Diego County, approximately 56 percent of Head Start enrollees are Latino/-a. Overall, when Head Start programs work well in reaching their Latino/-a clientele, they hold minicelebrations for *Cinco de Mayo*, Mexican Independence Day (*16 de Septiembre*), and *El Dia de los Muertos;* make art projects for Mother's Day; and seek parental input in deciding other events to celebrate. Some teachers complain that they cannot celebrate the *Dias de los Santos* because of the strictly enforced separation between church and state. Other teachers find ways to incorporate holy days of significance to Mexican culture into their curriculum in creative ways. Through the illustration of a few Latino/-a Head Start parents, teachers and family social workers, their positive impact can be evidenced.

When we initially started our research with Latino/-a families, we found that generally they wanted to go unnoticed, will go out of their way to not disturb or even call attention to themselves, and reluctantly will speak to any stranger who approaches them. Even though our research group is Latino/-a and bilingual/bicultural, rarely did Head Start parents give information about themselves unless we described ourselves as affiliated with Head Start. From this, we posit that Head Start has made an important headway into their people's lives, by first of all posing no obvious threat to them.

We found that, for the most part, parents are interested in their children's education and they tend to their children as much as their budget will allow. The families we have worked with, who are currently struggling with their undocumented status, are extremely hard workers and ingenious at finding ways of honestly making a living. One such parent, Don Francisco, has a seven-year-old child who was, at the time we met him, in his last months of the Head Start program. He formerly worked in the fields, but hurt his back, so he was unemployed and had to devise a way to make ends meet. He rents a room in a house with at least two other families and now drives a van picking up people from home and taking them to their *mandado* (grocery shopping) or work. He clears about $800 to $1000 per month and with this he supports his partner and his son. He has a case pending due to the nature of his injury at the job.

Head Start teachers often get the help of Head Start parents, as part of the program is for the parents to donate time and spend time with the children in the classroom. The families we interviewed rarely have any type of health insurance, and they generally do not visit a doctor until they are extremely ill, because they cannot afford it. They will take their family across the border to Tijuana, if at all possible, or to an herbalist before tapping into Medicaid or community health clinics.[16] These impediments on life chances make the efforts and triumphs of individual teachers in Head Start all that more powerful.

Ms. Evelia Alcaraz[17] is certainly the mainstay and memory of Head Start in San Diego. Although she makes her classrooms accessible and open to all, her passing on and celebration of Mexican culture is the hallmark of her center. The only female originator of San Diego's renowned Taco Shop Poets, Ms. Evelia has raised her children, some of her grandchildren, and thousands of Head Start children while working as a teacher and center director for San Diego Head Start since the first program was introduced to the city in 1965.

Ms. Marie Alianza is newer to Head Start, but her dedication to Head Start families is evidenced by her working with a Sudanese family in an exclusively Mexican Head Start center. Her goal is not only to make the family feel welcome, but find ways to express Sudanese culture to all of the children. In some ways, she is ensuring a lesson learned from the early days of Head Start in San Diego. When Latinos/-as were the numerical minority in several Head Start centers, some African-American teachers made sure that families would feel welcomed and their cultural and linguistic traits would be fostered as a community project.

This notion of Head Start as a community of helpers is demonstrated in the efforts of three family social workers–(FSWs)—Toni Marquez, Connie Valdez, and Dora Hernandez—who arranged for an undocumented family to move into one of their homes in San Diego while an FSW moved her entire family to their second home in Tijuana. Families cannot qualify for Head Start if they cannot prove a permanent place of residence and because this family was living in a hotel, this was the sacrifice made to ensure high-quality Head Start for children, regardless of their parents' citizenship status.

CONCLUSION

There are certain structural features of Head Start that facilitate empowerment. Parental involvement and authoritative decision making by parent councils, the presence of community action organizations even through all the changes, the requirement that children be taught in their home language, and a commitment to promote from within make Head Start an organization with a potential for alleviating poverty. The barriers are many and most employees of Head Start, if they have children, often qualify for Head Start themselves. But it is most often the teachers and staff, those who unfortunately often go unnamed and unrecognized, who commit themselves and their children to the Project and make Head Start the positive force for social change in the lives of Latino/-as and poor folks, in general, particularly in urban San Diego.

Specific Head Start centers have been able to create an entire, fully enveloping environment that both affirms cultural expression and provides a high-quality standard of living. Two public housing projects, El Mercado Apartments in Barrio Logan and San Marcos III Head Start and city housing project, aim at reaching Mexican immigrants in the central city and migrant/seasonal farm workers in North County of San Diego, respectively. Located adjacent to Chicano Park, Mercado Head Start is the community center of a unique housing project that relies on traditional Mexican architecture and colors to bring a vibrant feeling to the most economically depressed community in San Diego. The public space of Chicano Park makes for a wonderfully integrated fusion of culture, art, and living for its low-income residents. In our training programs, we work with Chicano Park muralist Mario Torero throughout San Diego to help Head Start teachers think about including mural making and their local communities into their curricula. The San Marcos Head Start, operated by the Mexican-American Anti-Poverty Advisory Committee (MAAC), a Chicano advocacy group, represents a partnership with the city of San Marcos to provide high-quality housing and Head Start facilities in a community that is not particularly receptive to the needs of its Latino/-a farm worker residents. Both centers understand that childhood development does not exist in a vacuum, and that proper housing, nutrition, medicine, bridging to kindergarten, economic options outside of seasonal and temporary employment, and adult education (from ESL and job training to higher education preparation)—all in a culturally relevant and affirming environment—make Head Start work in the manner it was intended (to improve life chances by attending to the whole needs of pre-K children by addressing both their individual and environmental disadvantages). Bridging the homeschool culture divide will never be a one-sided process that requires a serious state commitment (from the local to national) to again put the whole needs of the child at the forefront of socially relevant programs.

NOTES

Funding for this research and training comes from the Department of Health and Human Services, Administration on Children, Youth and Families (Grant 90-YP-0003) to California State University San Marcos (CSUSM). Ronald L. Mize, PhD, main Principal Investigator and Assistant Professor, Department of Development Sociology and Latino Studies Program, Cornell University; Silverio Haro, Co-Principal Investigator CSUSM; Claudia Huiza, CPhil, University of California San Diego; Anthony Navarrete, CPhil, University of California San Diego; Patricia Rivas-McCrae, CSUSM; Alfonso Rodriguez, PhD, In-Kind Co-Principal Investigator and Director of Training, Research, and Evaluation, Neighborhood House Association Head Start Program of San Diego County. Dr. Rodriguez has been involved in research and training in Head Start for the past 24 years. Please direct all inquiries to Ronald L. Mize, Department of Development Sociology, Warren Hall, Cornell University, Ithaca, NY 14853-7801; phone (607) 255-2024; e-mail: rlm65@cornell.edu.

1. San Diego Association of Governments (SANDAG). Demographics and Other Data. Retrieved November 20, 2005, from http://www.sandag.org/resources/demographics_and_other_data/demographics/census/pdfs/profiles_may02.pdf.

2. San Diego Unified School District (SDUSD). Ed-Data Profiles and Reports 2004 Data. Retrieved November 20, 2005, from http://www.ed-data.k12.ca.us/.

3. Ehrenreich, B. (2002). *Nickeled and dimed: On (not) getting by in America.* New York: Metropolitan Books; Gans, H. (1996). *The war against the poor: The underclass and anti-poverty policy.* New York: Basic Books; Sidel, R. (1998). *Keeping women and children last: America's war on the poor.* New York: Penguin Books.

4. Apple, M. (2000). *Official knowledge: Democratic education in a conservative age* (2nd ed.). New York: Routledge; Apple, M. (2001). *Educating the "right way": Markets, standards, God, and inequality.* New York: Routledge.

5. *USA Today.* Census 2000 Website. Retrieved November 20, 2005, from http://www.usatoday.com/news/nation/census/front.htm.

6. SANDAG. SANDAG Data Warehouse. Retrieved November 20, 2005, from http://www.sandag.org.

7. Steinberg, S. (1997). The liberal retreat from race during the post-civil rights era. In W. Lubiano (Ed.), *The house that race built: Black Americans, U.S. terrain* (pp. 13–47). New York: Pantheon Books.

8. Steinberg (1997).

9. Quadagno, J. (1994). *The color of welfare: How racism undermined the war on poverty.* New York: Oxford University Press.

10. U.S. Department of Health and Human Services (DHHS). Official Web site of Head Start Bureau. Retrieved November 20, 2005, from http://www.acf.hhs.gov/programs/hsb/; DHHS, Strengthening Head Start: What the evidence shows. Retrieved November 20, 2005, from http://aspe.hhs.gov/hsp/Strengthen HeadStart03/index.htm.

11. Apple (2000); Apple (2001).

12. Lipsitz, G. (1998). *The possessive investment in whiteness: How white people profit from identity politics* (p. xviii). Philadelphia: Temple University Press.

13. Crawford, J. (2000). At war with diversity: U.S. language policy in an age of anxiety. *Bilingual education and bilingualism* (Vol. 25). New

York: Multilingual Matters; Feliciano, C. (2001). The benefits of biculturalism: Exposure to immigrant culture and dropping out of school among Asian and Latino/-a youths. *Social Science Quarterly, 82* (4), 865–879; Krashen, S. (1997). *Under attack: The case against bilingual education.* New York: Language Education Association; Krashen, S. (1999). *Condemned without a trial: Bogus arguments against bilingual education.* New York: Heinemann; Portes, A., & Rumbaut, R. (1996). *Immigrant America.* Berkeley: University of California Press; Tse, L. (2001). *Why don't they learn English: Separating fact from fallacy in the U.S. language debate.* Language and Literacy Series. New York: Teachers College Press; Valdes, G. (2001). Learning and not learning English: Latino/-a students in American schools. *Multicultural Education* (Vol. 9). New York: Teachers College Press.

14. Portes & Rumbaut (1996), pp. 201–207.

15. Feliciano (2001).

16. Specific data can be found in Seid, M., Castañeda, D., Mize, R., Zivkovic, M., & Varni, J. (2003). Crossing the border for health care: Access and primary care characteristics for young children of Latino/-a farm workers along the U.S.-Mexico border. *Ambulatory Pediatrics, 3* (3), 121–130.

17. Head Start teacher profiles can also be found in Mize, R., Haro, S., Huiza, C., Navarrete, A., Rivas-McCrae, P., & Rodriguez, A. (Publication forthcoming March, 2006). Latinas and Project Head Start. In V. Ruiz & V. Sanchez Korrol (Eds.), *Latinas in the United States: A historical encyclopedia.* Bloomington: University of Indiana Press.

Cultural Studies and Urban Education

HOLLYWOOD'S DEPICTION OF URBAN SCHOOLS: DOCUMENTARY OR FICTION?

Amanda M. Rudolph

Nearly everyone in America has seen a fictionalized representation of the nation's public school system. Schools, teachers, and students are represented in movies, plays, situation comedies, TV dramas, commercials, books, and music. In any entertainment genre one can find a fictional depiction of students, teachers, or schools. As Americans are bombarded with these images, their impressions and ideas of urban schools and schools in general are shaped and molded. For the Mid-western stay-at-home mom, her only exposure to urbanicity may be through these types of experiences. It is important for educators to look at the representations of schools and analyze the messages that are being sent to the American population.

Fictional representations of schools and students are abundant. For this chapter, only representations of urban schools will be addressed. And to narrow down the field to a manageable topic, only dramatic films will be discussed. The school film genre encompasses dramas, thrillers, comedic spoofs,

dark comedies, and many more. Interestingly, it is the drama that repeatedly depicts urban students and schools. James Trier, faculty member at University of North Carolina at Chapel Hill, suggests that, in contrast to urban school movies, movies about suburban students tend to be comedies such as *Ferris Bueller's Day Off* and *American Pie*.[1] Hollywood has repeatedly produced and distributed dramatic films that portray urban schools: *Stand and Deliver, Lean on Me, Dangerous Minds*, and *187*. Evidently, there is something about the dramatic urban school movie formula that leads to successful films. The popularity and continued production of such films raises the following several questions:

1. Why are these movies so successful?
2. What messages or ideas are these movies conveying to viewers?
3. What are the implications of such messages for educators?

This chapter will address these issues and offer suggestions for educators.

Bulman's research on school-based films lists twenty films that depict urban schools.[2] Obviously all these films cannot be dealt with in great detail in this discussion. For the purposes of this chapter, three films will be used as examples of urban school movies: *Lean on Me*,[3] *Dangerous Minds*,[4] and *187*.[5] These films offer a diverse sample of the types of urban movies included on Bulman's list. An overview of the plot and story of the films will be provided. The discussion will then address the common characteristics of the films and will compare those to the actual demographics of urban schools. Finally, implications based on the comparisons will be explored for the general population and educators.

OVERVIEW OF EXAMPLE FILMS DEPICTING URBAN SCHOOLS

The three movies chosen as examples of films depicting urban schooling are *Lean on Me*, *Dangerous Minds*, and *187*. Each of these films contains similar representations of urban students and teachers; each film is also unique in its depiction of the school system. A brief synopsis of each film follows.

Lean on Me

Lean on Me tells the story of Joe Clark, a black educator in New Jersey, who is offered the job of principal in the worst school in the city of Paterson. The film begins with a background scene from 1967. Joe Clark is an engaging and enthusiastic but rogue teacher. His class is disrupted when a coworker enters and informs him that the union is meeting without them. Clark bursts into the meeting and learns that he has been transferred to another school as a condition to pay raises for the rest of the faculty. The film then cuts to the present, 1987, and East Side High School. The school is shown with excessive graffiti and trash in the halls. The majority of the students are

black and Hispanic. In these few minutes of film set to rap music, students are fighting each other, vandalizing the school, selling drugs, assaulting teachers, and carrying guns. The film then cuts to the mayor of the town talking with the superintendent about East Side's test scores. On last year's standardized test, East Side had a 38 percent pass rate. To avoid a takeover of the school by the state, this year's pass rate must be 75 percent. The person chosen for the job is Joe Clark, currently an elementary school principal. After much debate, Clark takes the job.

Joe Clark takes over East Side High School. On his first day, he reassigns teachers and expels 300 students who are drug dealers and problem students. Immediately his administration ignites controversy in the community. He continues to implement standards of zero tolerance and drastic measures such as locking the doors with chains so drug dealers cannot get into the school. Eventually, these tactics get him arrested but win over the students of the school. In the final scene of the movie, students have gathered to protest his arrest and possible dismissal by the school board. In the very last moment of the movie, the vice principal runs through the crowd with a letter for Clark; it is the news that East Side has a pass rate above 75 percent. Clark saved East Side High, the students, and his job.[6]

Dangerous Minds

In the opening scenes of *Dangerous Minds*, which are filmed in black and white and set to rap music, the audience sees a run-down neighborhood covered with graffiti and filled with black and Hispanic youths waiting for the bus. Around the children are drug dealers and homeless people. The students board the bus and as the bus approaches the school the film fades into color. At the school, veteran teacher Hal Griffith introduces Louanne Johnson to the school principal. Johnson is looking for a place to finish her student teaching and the vice principal hires her as a full-time teacher for the Academy class. The principal explains the Academy classes are filled with "special kids."[7] Johnson will start work the next day.

Johnson's first day in class ends with her leaving frustrated and ready to quit. The class full of Hispanic and black students hardly acknowledge her, and when they do, it is only to harass her. Her mentor Griffith tells her, "All you gotta' do is get their attention."[8] Overnight, Johnson reads several texts on discipline, including *Assertive Discipline* by Lee Canter, and laughs off the suggestions. The next day Johnson arrives at school dressed in jeans, boots, and a leather jacket. She begins class by writing, "I am a U.S. Marine" on the board and asks the students if they know karate. She succeeds in getting their attention. Her tactics are not ignored by the administration; the principal reprimands her for allowing fighting in class and demands she follow the established curriculum. She continues to engage the students by offering candy for correct answers, trips to theme parks for reading poetry, and dinner for research. The one student who will not participate, Emilio, finally connects to her after she breaks up a fight and gets personally involved with students by conducting home visits. A drug dealer threatens Emilio and Johnson brings him to her home to hide. During the night she convinces him to talk to the principal about the situation. In the morning, she learns the principal turned Emilio away because he did not knock on the door. Later, she is given the news of Emilio's murder. Overwhelmed by everything she has experienced this year, Johnson decides to quit. The students come together and convince her to stay. She has changed their lives for the better and hers as well.[9]

187

The beginning of *187* provides the background for the rest of the film. The opening of the film show a run-down Bronx high school filled with trash. Students are mostly Hispanic and black. In classrooms, students respond to teachers' questions with cursing and vulgarities. Trevor Garfield is a science teacher who seems to be reaching his students. During class, he opens a textbook to find "187" written along with his name on all the pages. He informs the principal that "187" is the police code for murder and he takes the graffiti as a serious threat since he has failed this particular student. The principal tells him not to worry. On the way back to class Garfield is stabbed several times by the student in the hall.

The film picks up 15 months later. Garfield has moved to Los Angeles and is working as a substitute teacher. The film shows the school at which Garfield will be working. The school has a police officer with a metal detector wand at the entrance. There is graffiti on the walls and desks. The entire school has chain link fence around it. Several classrooms are housed in portable buildings that do not have air conditioning. Garfield begins the day teaching and looks for chalk in the teacher's desk only to find a gun. Dave Childress, teacher, enters and informs Garfield he is in the wrong classroom and shows him the correct class. Garfield is taking over a pregnant teacher's class. The previous week the teacher was cornered by several young Hispanic males and in self-defense kicked one of the students. She is on leave pending an investigation of her assault on a student. The administration is scared of any type of lawsuit from any student. The same students, Benny and Cesar, threaten and bully Garfield as well as the computer teacher, Ellen Henry. Childress and Henry befriend Garfield. After Henry confides in Garfield about her fear of Benny, Benny disappears. During class, Garfield accuses Cesar of stealing his pocket watch. A few days later, Cesar is shot with a syringe of drugs and wakes up with his finger missing. Luckily, the finger is mailed to the hospital and reattached. Cesar is convinced Garfield is responsible and tells the police who are not convinced. Benny's body is found by the L.A. Police Department and Henry becomes suspicious of Garfield after finding rosary beads in Garfield's house that look like Benny's. Meanwhile, Garfield has been tutoring a young Hispanic girl, Rita, in the school library and once at his home. The school board becomes concerned with Garfield's behavior with the girl and decides not to ask him back next year in order to avoid any legal problems. Cesar rallies his friends and they break into Garfield's house to confront him. Garfield admits he killed Benny and cut off Cesar's finger. Inspired by the movie *Deer Hunter*, Cesar loads a gun with one bullet and spins the chamber. He insists Garfield shoot himself. Garfield pulls the trigger and nothing happens. Garfield and Cesar argue about machismo and fear. Garfield bullies Cesar into playing a dangerous game of Russian roulette. After several rounds and much arguing, Garfield screams he will take Cesar's turn because he is willing to die to show Cesar how stupid he is. He fires the gun, killing himself. Cesar is outraged and angry that he did not take his turn; he fires the gun, killing himself. The friends flee. The final scene of the movie shows Rita reading an essay at graduation about Garfield's positive influence on her life.[10]

It is interesting to note that *Lean on Me* and *Dangerous Minds* are advertised as being based on true events. *187* ends with an addendum that the movie was written by a teacher. All three films claim a connection to reality, but the Hollywood perspective also influences all three.

DISCUSSION OF COMMON CHARACTERISTICS IN FILMS

These films all share some common characteristics about the representations of urban schools and issues that are represented in the stories. These characteristics can be broken down into two main categories: demographic facts and Hollywood influences. The demographic facts can be compared to educational statistics to determine if the film representation of the schools is realistic. Hollywood influences are issues and ideas in the films that are enhanced or highlighted to create dramatic tension; these influences may or may not represent a realistic picture of schools.

Common Demographics Facts in Urban School Films

In the films *Lean on Me*, *Dangerous Minds*, and *187*, there are several commonalities based on demographics. According to Bulman, the urban student is characterized as being from "lower- and working-class homes" and "are often nonwhite."[11] He also states that these students are part of a violent school system and "behave poorly in the classroom, and express a great deal of frustration with the formal structure of the school."[12] Each film depicts these very concepts by portraying an urban high school with: a majority population of Hispanic and black students, a majority population of poor students, rundown and graffiti-covered buildings, and extreme violence.

Representation of Ethnicity

All three of the example films show urban schools with a student population comprised of almost exclusively Hispanic and black students. *Lean on Me* contains a scene that shows Clark addressing the entire student body. He asks the white students to stand and a small group rises. Clark states that these are his white kids and if they had anywhere else to go they would have already left the school.[13] In *Dangerous Minds*, Johnson's students are mainly Hispanic students with a few white and black students. Interestingly, all the student roles integral to the plot are Hispanic or black.[14] *187* depicts a high school almost completely Hispanic. Of the student characters, only one is white.[15] In 2000, 38.7 percent of the entire enrolled K–12 student population in America were minorities.[16] In another report, 36.7 percent of schools that enrolled 900 or more students reported a minority population of more than 75 percent of the total student population.[17] Overall, minority students make up almost 40 percent of the student population. According to the U.S. Department of Education, minorities may comprise the majority of the student population in *some* larger schools. By no means are all large schools solely composed of Hispanic and black students, as Hollywood films may lead the audience to believe.

Representation of Poverty

The three example films also show a great number of students as poor students. In *Lean on Me* and *187,* the students' homes are shown as run-down and crowded apartments and trailers.[18] In *Dangerous Minds*, Emilio tells Johnson that he fights because he is poor and from a broken home. In fact, he asks her if she hasn't "seen all the movies" implying that the films offer poverty and divorce as causes for violence.[19] The U.S. Department of Education reports that 15.8 percent of all students enrolled in an urban area school are considered to be living in poverty.[20] In a central city of a large metropolitan statistical area, 24.4 percent of students are living in poverty.[21] Up to one-fourth of a school population could be poor based on the statistics, but in the films of Hollywood the majority of the students are depicted as living in poverty.

Representation of Facilities

Of the three movies, *187* depicts the worst facilities for school buildings. The movie shows a school campus surrounded by chain link fences, classes meeting in portable buildings with no air conditioning, and graffiti and trash.[22] The facilities

in *Lean on Me* are not much better; the school is covered in graffiti and trash.[23] *Dangerous Minds* is set in a run-down older school.[24] According to the U.S. Department of Education, 45 percent of all central city schools have portable buildings compared to 44 percent in urban fringe/large towns and 29 percent in rural/small towns.[25] The percentage of schools with at least one building feature rated as less than adequate is 56 percent for central city, 44 percent for urban fringe/large town, and 52 percent for rural/small town schools.[26] Comparatively, higher percentages of central city schools report plans to make building improvements in the next two years.[27] Based on the statistics, it seems that most school systems in America are in need of updating and repairs. Interestingly, it is more urban schools that report initiating these repairs in the near future. The representation that schools are forced to use portable buildings may be accurate, but it is not a problem exclusive to urban schools.

Representation of Violence

All of the example movies contain extreme acts of violence. Both *Lean on Me* and *Dangerous Minds* include fights between students that are ended with teacher intervention.[28] *187* shows a student stabbing a teacher repeatedly with a large nail.[29] Also, all three movies show guns at school as well as some type of sexual harassment. The U.S. Department of Education reports that 17 percent of city schools reported serious violent crimes, with 5 percent reporting rape or other sexual battery and 10 percent reporting physical attacks or fights with weapons.[30] These percentages were higher than urban fringe (11%, 4%, and 6%), town (5%, 1%, and 3%), and rural (8%, 2%, and 5%) schools. The percentages of schools reporting less serious or nonviolent crimes were higher for the urban fringe and town schools than for the central city schools.[31]

Although the percentage of city schools reporting serious crimes is higher than the other types of schools, the percentage is still relatively low compared to the numerous representations of violence in urban school films.

Hollywood Influences in Urban School Films

Hollywood has added issues and ideas in the urban school films that make for a more dramatic film. Two major ideas are repeated in the urban school genre: the heroic individual teacher and the domineering bureaucratic administration. Each of these films centers on a single teacher who goes against the system to help his or her students. The films also show the administration as oppositional to the heroic teacher. These two concepts have an impact on the representations of urban schools.

Teacher as Hero

In *Lean on Me* and *Dangerous Minds*, the protagonist is an individual educator (teacher or principal) who fights the system as a lone revolutionist. Principal Joe Clark carries a bat to school and locks the children in while dominating and intimidating the faculty.[32] Johnson discards the canon of research on classroom management to implement her own token economy as she also disregards the developed curriculum for what she considers more engaging.[33] These representations of teachers are common in urban school films. In his research, Bulman discusses the idea of the individual reformationist.

This lone figure is able to ignore the cynicism of veteran teachers, escape the iron cage of the school bureaucracy, and speak directly to the hearts and minds of these troubled youth who are, by the end of the film, transformed from apathetic working-class and poor students into studious and sincere students with middle-class aspirations.[34] Bulman continues, saying that these teachers can succeed

without: teacher training, smaller class sizes, a supportive staff, strong leadership, parental participation, technological tools, corporate partnership, school restructuring, a higher salary, a longer school day, vouchers, or more financial resources. All they need to bring to the classroom is discipline, tough love, high expectations, and . . . common sense about individual achievement and personal responsibility.[35]

The idea that a single teacher can change a class is not troublesome; it is the idea that *only* an untrained or rogue educator can make those changes that is disconcerting. The message from Hollywood is clear. Educated and veteran teachers and educators are not successful in their jobs.

Administration as Antihero

In the three example films, the administration fails or hinders the progress of the teacher and/or principal. Principal Joe Clark is given edicts from the superintendent that undermine his decisions. Eventually, the school board questions his strategies as well.[36] In *Dangerous Minds*, Johnson is told to stick to the curriculum and is reprimanded for teaching karate. In a later scene, the principal asks Johnson if she took the students on a field trip as a reward for schoolwork. She replies that the trip to the theme park was a spontaneous decision and she paid for the students because she was so moved by the invitation.[37] She resorts to lying to the administration in order to continue her teaching practices. The most outlandish example of an inept administration is in *187*. Garfield tells his principal he has been mortally threatened and the principal says he will fine the student for writing in the textbook.[38] In his film research, Bulman also discusses the administration.

The teachers and staff are generally shown as uncaring, incompetent, and ineffective educators. These characters represent what many Americans believe to be typical of the urban public school "crisis"—a selfish, inept, wasteful, and uncaring bureaucracy. These are schools with no soul—just troubled students, failed educational methods, burned-out school personnel, too many arcane rules, and too much paperwork.[39] Obviously, the message is that the faculty and administration cannot work together to educate the urban student. The administrative bureaucracy has grown so large it has become completely ineffective.

All of these representations in the urban school film have an impact on the audiences of the movies. The representation of ethnicity, poverty, facilities, and violence color the way the public views urban schools. The Hollywood spin on the heroic teacher and the villainous administration will also influence the public's opinion of urban schools. And some of those audience members will be educators and administrators. What are they learning from these and other films?

IMPLICATIONS FOR THE AUDIENCE

The implications for the audiences of these films are wide ranging. First, the general public will view these movies and come away with skewed and dramatized ideas about the urban school. These ideas may shape the way the average citizen votes or supports legislation. Second, educators will see these films and their impressions of urban schools based on the films could impact their pedagogy and educational philosophy.

The General Public

As discussed earlier, the typical urban school film may not be an accurate representation of urban schools. The movies are usually dealing with Hispanic and black students from poverty level homes attending run-down and violent schools. The statistics reflect a somewhat tamer picture of the urban school. So what is the general audience member learning from these movies?

Unfortunately, the urban school movie helps to maintain the stereotypes of minority groups and the urban school. Bulman concludes his research, saying that by simplifying the many problems of urban public education and turning inner-city students and public-school teachers into caricatures of their respective social classes, Hollywood is doing nothing but reflecting middle-class anxiety about the problems of inner-city schools and the naive hope that such problems need not a substantial political commitment from all members of society, but merely the individual moral conversion of the poor students.[40] The movies offer a quick fix to many of society's issues. An individual teacher with enough courage and gumption can reduce school violence, drug use, apathy, and crime. If the general public buys into the fiction of the teacher-hero, the real problems of education will not be addressed.

The Future Educator

The implications for future educators are unique and interesting. It is an oversight to dismiss the urban school movie as insignificant in the preservice teacher's education. In the past few years I have watched many students use clips from these movies in lessons and presentations as examples of good teaching. I have also seen teacher educators ask for reviews of movies about education as assignments. The use of these movies in the curriculum can be an effective means for discussion; the danger is not to discuss the films critically. Trier reports that in his preservice teacher classes, students "admitted that their own images of inner city schools were probably derived from having watched such films."[41] If the preservice teacher is basing his or her ideas of urban education solely on these films, he or she is getting an inaccurate picture of urban education.

Teacher educators need to address the issues raised in the urban school film in a critical manner. Trier uses the "videocompi-lations" of school films to spark discussion about schools and schooling. His students made realistic evaluations of the films.[42]

Most students observed that all school films were unrealistic to some degree, and sometimes they were unrealistic in absurd ways, but students also explained that analyzing the discrepancies between the cinematic representation and their own experiences in schools was valuable and productive.[43] Even though the urban school film offers a fantastic representa-tion of schools and students, it also offers an opportunity to analyze and discuss those representations.

CONCLUSION

In conclusion, the urban school genre usually creates movies that are mostly unre-alistic representations of urban schools, urban teachers, and urban students. If our future educators and our teacher educators do not challenge these stereotypes, they will only be perpetuated. To address and solve the real issues of urban schools, it is necessary to discuss why Hollywood con-tinues to portray the urban school in such a way. The urban school film genre began in 1955 with *Blackboard Jungle* and shows no signs of disappearing anytime soon. For the sake of the urban student, these films must be viewed and discussed. Without knowing what Hollywood and the movie-going pub-lic perceive as the reality of the urban school, how can urban schools and teachers and students grow and improve?

NOTES

1. Toppo, G. (2003, April 24). A "cinematic smear" of school life. *USA Today*, p. 10D. Retrieved May 20, 2004, from the Academic Search Premier database, http://search.epnet. com/login.aspx?direct=true&db=aph&an= J0E110849704003.

2. Bulman, R. (2002). Teachers in the 'hood: Hollywood's middle-class fantasy. *The Urban Review, 34* (3), 251–276.

3. Avildsen, J. (Director). (1989). *Lean on me* [Motion picture]. United States: Warner Brothers.

4. Smith, J. (Director). (1995). *Dangerous minds* [Motion picture]. United States: Holly-wood Pictures.

5. Reynolds, K. (Director). (1997). *187* [Motion picture]. United States: Icon Production.

6. Avildsen (1989).

7. Smith (1995).

8. Smith (1995).

9. Smith (1995).

10. Reynolds (1997).

11. Bulman (2002), p. 257.

12. Bulman (2002), p. 257.

13. Avildsen (1989).

14. Smith (1995).

15. Reynolds (1997).

16. U.S. Department of Education. (2003). *The condition of education 2003* (NCES 2003-067). Washington, DC: U.S. Government Printing Office, p. 125.

17. U.S. Department of Education (2003), p. 150.

18. Avildsen (1989); Reynolds (1997).

19. Smith (1995).

20. U.S. Department of Education (2003), p. 97.

21. U.S. Department of Education (2003), p. 97.

22. Reynolds (1997).

23. Avildsen (1989).

24. Smith (1995).

25. U.S. Department of Education. (2002). *Digest of educational statistics 2002* (p. 126). Washington, DC: U.S. Government Printing Office. Retrieved May 30, 2004 from National Center for Educational Statistics Web Site: http://nces.ed.gov/programs/digest/d02.

26. U.S. Department of Education (2002), p. 126.

27. U.S. Department of Education (2002).

28. Avildsen (2003); Smith (1995).

29. Reynolds (1997).

30. U.S. Department of Education (2002), p. 168.

31. U.S. Department of Education (2002), p. 169.

32. Avildsen (2003).

33. Smith (1995).

34. Bulman (2002), p. 262.

35. Bulman (2002), p. 262.

36. Avildsen (1989).

37. Smith (1995).

38. Reynolds (1997).

39. Bulman (2002), p. 260–261.

40. Bulman (2002), p. 273–274.

41. Trier, J. (2001). The cinematic representation of the personal and professional lives of teach-ers. *Teacher Education Quarterly, 28* (3), 128.

42. Trier, J. (2003). School film "videocompilations" as pedagogical texts in preservice education. *Journal of Curriculum Theorizing, 19* (1), 125–147. Retrieved May 30, 2204 from First Search database, http://newfirstsearch.oclc.org/images/WSPL/wsppdf1/HTML/07253/AXT37/4FT.HTM.

43. Trier (2003), p. 10.

THE REVOLUTIONARY PRAXIS OF PUNKORE STREET PEDAGOGY

Joseph Carroll-Miranda and Curry Malott

Nearly everyone knows of Robin Hood, the hero of Sherwood Forest who stole from the rich to give to the poor. The story perseveres because it speaks to enduring conditions of inequality and injustice, and equally enduring fantasies of righteous rebellion. This myth of the social bandit is part of our cultural heritage.[1]

—*Eric Hobsbawm*

This chapter is about youth resistance, written from the old-school, bi-classed (working- and middle-), multiethnic, and multicultured perspectives of the authors—a west-coast SK8punk of British, German, and Irish descent, and a Puerto Rican undergrounder. While recognizing the importance of other subcultures (such as hip-hop for example), we focus on PunKore scenes—the multiple communities that evolve around punk, hard-core, and other forms of rockish underground culture. Our personal experience and knowledge of Punkore scenes span our twenty years' participation in them.

The arguments herein primarily deal with the progressive aspects of PunKore's specific street pedagogical practices (as we understand and know them) that have changed lives and rendered PunKore part of a potentially revolutionary force capable of dismantling the social relationships that lead to what Glenn Rikowski refers to as "the capitalization of humanity."[2] What follows is, first, a discussion of youth resistance as it relates to the capitalization of humanity. Next, we will outline what we think have been and continue to be the essence of the most revolutionary aspects of PunKore pedagogy. Finally, we will outline what the pedagogical practices of these PunKore scenes of human resistance mean for us in terms of our lived praxis.

EMERGENCE OF THE PUNKORE SCENE

Subcultures are cultural resistance. The question is where does this resistance lead?

—*S. Duncombe (Ed.)*
Cultural Resistance Reader

Michael Neary argues that "the Modern condition of 'youth' was invented in 1948, as part of the Employment and Training Act of 1948" in order to lure more young people into British training programs designed to produce a workforce conducive to the capitalist imperative.[3] According to Neary, "the status of youth does not refer to any young person, but is a status attributed to the young working class based entirely on their capacity to become the commodity of labor power: to exist as abstract labor."[4] Similar patterns abound in the United States, and throughout the capitalized world, as capitalist education seeks to instill in youth a commitment to capitalism, and a naturalized desire to sell one's labor power in the market for a wage, that is, to become capital.[5]

This drive to capitalize humanity, of course, is threatened and challenged by what Glenn Rikoski describes as "our capacity for reflexivity, to attain awareness of the existence and practical application of processes of the production of ourselves as labor-power."[6] It is therefore not surprising that there exists a long and continuing history of human resistance to the capitalization of humanity, that at its best is marked by a taking back of one's labor power to fight capital through the combined strategies of direct action in the workplace, as well as a refusal to work and live as capital, informed by the creation of oppositional, yet always complex and contradictory, cultural practices such as PunKore scenes.

The generations born in postwar Britain were largely disenfranchised by the status quo as jobs became less available, wages fell, and racism and other forms of divisiveness rose. Those postwar youth who understood that the extant government and economic system would never alleviate the human suffering engendered by capitalism, took their struggle to the streets through the creation of subcultures based on the refusal to participate in traditional society. As a result, countercultural manifestations have been informed by both progressive and reactionary motivations. Beginning in the 1950s and the 1960s, many progressive youth began to create their own culture.

It was within this context of working-class disempowerment and rising racism that the youth-based countercultures in Britain (and the U.S.) emerged. At their most radical and potentially revolutionary moments, the mods, Rude Boys, and skinheads challenged British society to guarantee what was promised and expected as a minimum of social stability and recognition by, among other things, fighting racism. At their worst, they terrorized

innocent people and strengthened capital by further limiting workers' ability to come together as exploited labor in struggle against the divisive tendencies of capital.

Urban street riots, depicted in the film *Quadrophenia* as an expression of youthful rage against government and the capitalist system, were common in the United Kingdom during the 1960s.[7] Hebdige expands on this general social discontent, arguing that "the MOD was determined to compensate for his relatively low position in the daytime status—stakes over which he had no control, by exercising complete dominion over his private estate—his appearance and choice of leisure pursuits."[8] Although a necessary first step and thus a place of departure, it is not enough to take control of one's leisure time. As many ethnographers of student resistance underscore, resistance does not tend to be motivated by concrete critiques of capital and social injustices in general, or by a conscious desire to work for social justice. Rather, resistance tends to be motivated by an intuitive, reflexive response to oppressive and dehumanizing educational and social systems and relationships.[9]

We concur with Hill et al. that the complete loss of faith in the system to live up to its democratic promises is what sparked the countercultures of the 1960s and 1970s, and paved the way for the late 1970s, early 1980s PunKore scenes.[10] For example, we could not commence to talk about punk or a hard-core scene if it were not for the influence of the United Kingdom's mods, Rude Boys, skinheads, and street punks.[11] The cultural and musical revolution that these countercultures sparked are being felt to this day.[12]

The skinhead counterculture, whose roots stem not from fascism, but from the Jamaica-based African Rude Boys, is a working-class youth phenomenon, which emerged in the United Kingdom in the late 1960s. As a counterculture, they challenged the industrial and postindustrial economic conditions of workers' exploitation, motivated by their general disenchantment with Britain's social and political order. George Marshall,[13] an original skin from the late '60s, in his book *Spirit of '69: A Skinhead Bible,* gives us an historical overview of how the skinhead counterculture emerged. Skinheads are a fusional metamorphosis of the mods and the Rude Boys.[14]

While the mods emerged as a predominantly white countercultural phenomenon of the early '60s, the Rude Boys, on the other hand, grew from Jamaican immigrants in southern neighborhoods such as Brixton. The Rude Boys were known as one of the roughest and toughest street cultures in the postwar United Kingdom.[15] The potentially revolutionary militancy of the Rude Boys influenced some in Britain's white working class to the extent that they started their own version, the skinheads, reflected by their passion to be tough enough to resist anything, while simultaneously enjoying the music of rock-steady, ska, and reggae. However, it is important to note that fascist skinheads rarely praise the African roots of their culture. In bands like Symarip, The Specials, and Madness, the interconnectivity between skinheads and the Rude Boy 2tone counterculture is reflected.[16] Within this scene are strong currents of racial harmony and of healing the hatred of racism predominating in those and these times. In fact, the precursors of reggae, rock steady, and ska are commonly referred to in PunKore scenes as "Skinhead Reggae."[17]

In its more progressive and potentially revolutionary countercultural moments, the skinheads produced a working-class culture of resistance, expressed in lyrics from "The Business," "The Oppressed," "Stiff Little Fingers," "Angelic Upstarts," "Sham 69," "The Blitz," "Cock Sparrow," and countless others. The skinhead music of the early to mid-'70s is referred to as "Oi,"[18] also known as "street punk" by others in the PunKore scene. Regardless of the name, Oi and street punk lyrics, both pro-

gressive and reactionary, continue to give us series of documented oral histories, experiences of street life, and beliefs shared by the working class, the lumpen proletariat, and even the middle class. For example, these 1978 lyrics from "Sham 69":

Hey little rich boy. Take a good look at me.
Hey little rich boy. Take a good look at me.
Why should I let it worry me?
I'll never believe you're better than me.

Although it is true that PunKore scenes (like other subcultures or cultures in general) can at times be sexist, racist, and homophobic and support the labor/capital relationship, these traits are not inherent within the scene. They are indicative of the larger society from which the scene emerged. Those in PunKore scenes, like everyone else in society, suffer at various levels of intensity from the counterrevolutionary illnesses of white supremacy, sexism, homophobia, and the idea that capitalism is humankind's only choice. The progressive role of the subculture is therefore to heal people while simultaneously creating the foundations for revolutionary change. For example, according to Kathleen Hanna,[19] lead singer of the popular underground street punk band Bikini Kill, self-healing can and does occur within PunKore scenes. In the Riot Grrrl Manifesto, a document informing the actions of an entire music-oriented, subcultural movement, Hanna states:

We hate capitalism in all forms and see our main goal as sharing information and staying alive, instead of making profits or being cool according to traditional standards . . . Because self-defeating behaviors (like fucking boys without condoms, drinking to excess, ignoring true-soul girlfriends, or belittling ourselves and other girls) would not be so easy if we lived in communities where we felt loved and wanted and valued.[20]

From this quote we see how one participant views the possibilities of a PunKore pedagogy as both the reality and the potential of a self-healing community. Through the self-healing praxis and street pedagogy, members of the PunKore scene engage in Freire's concept of *"conscientización."*[21] To facilitate and advance this discussion, we look to recent academic works on pedagogies of revolution.

THE TEMPORARY AUTONOMOUS ZONE (TAZ) AND REVOLUTIONARY PEDAGOGY OF PUNKORE SCENES

In fact I have deliberately refrained from defining the TAZ- I circle around the subject, firing off exploratory beams. In the end the TAZ is almost self-explanatory. If the phrase became current it would be understood without difficulty . . . understood in action.[22]

—*Hakim Bey*

Rikowski argues that Peter McLaren has been leading the struggle to rekindle the revolutionary potency of critical pedagogy by "reclaiming [it] for the urgent task of increasing our awareness of our social condition, as a first step in changing it."[23] What is more, McLaren stresses the point that awareness by itself is not sufficient. That is, what is needed is a commitment to social justice giving way to a transformation of consciousness to action.[24] As we will attempt to demonstrate below, McLaren's pedagogy of revolution can help not only to advance our PunKore pedagogies, but also shares common characteristics with the PunKore scenes' revolutionary pedagogy of the late '70s and early '80s and its continuing legacy of independent resistance.

However, youth countercultures have been co-opted, and thus need to be reclaimed and revitalized for the purpose of social justice. That is, the results of corporate advertisers and marketers taking out the social message of punk rock and turning it into a new style can currently be purchased and consumed in the form of clothing as well as watered-down music. Nevertheless, because of the independent

nature of progressive PunKore scenes, much of it has retained its potentially revolutionary aspects. An important difference of focus between the revolutionary pedagogy outlined by McLaren and the one outlined below is music, and its unique ability to mobilize people across space and time. The unique experience created through music is referred to by Hakim Bey as a temporary autonomous zone (TAZ), whether progressive or reactionary.[25] We will explain this phenomenon in subsequent paragraphs.

Echoing Bey's concept of the TAZ, Everyman and Jamison argue that the music generated by particular movements can inspire to action future generations who live under similar conditions.[26] The current popular underground group, the Dropkick Murphys, an Irish skinhead band out of Boston, for example, not only adorn their album sleeves with the anti-racist quotes of Martin Luther King, but have also done covers of labor songs from the Industrial Workers of the World (IWW). Their 1998 "Which Side Are You On?" and their 2003 cover of Woody Guthrie's "Gonna' Be a Blackout Tonight" are two examples. These songs exemplify the Murphys' message of working-class solidarity and struggle. In "Which Side Are You On?" the lyric, "My daddy was a miner, and I'm a miner's son, I'll stick with the union until every battle's won," is representative of the attention the Dropkick Murphys pay to forging bonds between PunKore rockers and members of the working class such as police officers and construction workers. On their 2002 "Live on St. Patrick's Day" album, lead singer Al Barr introduces a song about "good cops who don't abuse their power who are just protectin' our sorry asses because in the punk world everybody writes songs about hatin' cops, and some of 'em are fuckin' good shits, and they're here tonight. This one's called John Law." In this potentially revolutionary pedagogical performance, the Murphys led the struggle to create a space where working-class youth and working-class police officers could come together. This is reminiscent of how the IWW, with the tactic of music and slogan of "one big union" attempted to show the interconnectedness of the entire working class.

What does a PunKore revolutionary pedagogy look like? At its best, it is a pedagogy of community, of coming together to heal wounds and organize against oppression. It is a pedagogy of emotion, of venting one's frustration, and of expressing oneself through the rhythm of the music—but most important, it is a pedagogy of possibility, and a celebration of the collective creative potential realized through the discoveries made when engaged in a DIY (Do It Yourself) praxis in the midst of a TAZ. In 1991, Jesse—aka "J," of Operation Ivy—highlighted the potentialities of a revolutionary PunKore pedagogy as follows:

Music is an indirect force for change because it provides an anchor against human tragedy. In this sense, it works toward a reconciled world. It can also be the direct experience of change. At certain points during some shows, the reconciled world is already here, at least in that second, at that place. Operation Ivy was very lucky to have experienced this. Those seconds reveal that the momentum that drives a subculture is more important then any particular band. The momentum is made of all the people who stay interested, and keep their sense of urgency and hope.

Jesse's comments reflect the materialization of a progressive TAZ, spaces created out of, and for, collective struggle. These zones are the lifeline of what we consider to be the PunKore scene and the focus of the potentially revolutionary PunKore pedagogy. As "J" eloquently articulates, "at certain points during shows the reconciled world is already here at least in that second, at that place." This goes to the heart of Bey's notion of the TAZ.[27] It has been our experience that in PunKore scenes a mood, energy, feeling, emotion—hence, a reality—

is created. Many times, this temporarily created reality shows us that we can live, interact, and establish human relationships, tactics, and a DIY praxis that defies global-capitalist hegemony.

The PunKore scenes that create TAZs become the foundation from which a countercultural praxis emerges and counterhegemonic identities are formed. Defiant and revolutionary ideas and praxis become and are a way of life. As a Sk8terpunker and an undergrounder, we have experienced how the TAZ serves as a breeding ground for a revolutionary pedagogy defying oppressive conditions of both global capital and cultural/social relations. As veterans of the PunKore scenes we have seen a TAZ second expanding to minutes, minutes to hours, hours to days, days to weeks, weeks to months and sometimes months to years.

For example, in 1999 and 2000, the UNAM (National Autonomous University of México) was paralyzed in a student strike that lasted more than a year. The strike was a reaction to and protest of President Carlos Salinas de Gortari's neoliberal policies in all facets of Mexican life. Under direction of the World Bank and International Monetary Fund, Salinas was responsible for the privatization, deregulation, and liberalization of formally public institutions and corporations. This paved the way for adoption of the North American Free Trade Agreement, which has opened the economic floodgates of the U.S./Mexico border and allowed the wealth created by the Mexican working class to flow North, against gravity. As a result, Mexican poverty and suffering have skyrocketed.

During the strike, the image of punk anarchist Zapatistas was used to discredit the validity of the students' claims. Nevertheless, through the strike, UNAM students created a TAZ that evoked memories of the Paris communes and revolts of 1968. However, the UNAM students' turn-of-the-century uprising lasted much longer than had the protest of the summer of 1968. In this TAZ, UNAM students got a taste of communal freedom that, owing to its collective solidarity, lasted more than a year.

Music, arts, and theater were the soul of the UNAM students' struggle. Close to the one-year anniversary of the strike, the students reaffirmed their vows against neoliberalism and demanded free, high-quality education for all at a music festival that lasted more than one day. The internationally known revolutionary band, Rage Against the Machine, participated in a solidarity concert called "The Battle of Mexico City." Money raised at the concert was given to the striking students of UNAM.

The anecdote of the UNAM strike, among countless others, has been a source of inspiration that translates into aspirations of creating a liberating TAZ where oppressive relationships of global capital and social/cultural praxis are deconstructed, destroyed, altered and mutated into a different way of life freed from the constraints of the past. Experiencing and striving to forge the TAZ through our PunKore pedagogy of revolution has convinced us we can live in a different way. That is, through participating in the construction and maintenance of a TAZ were participants have the opportunity to simultaneously become aware of their social position and act to change it through an ethics of social justice.

In these spaces of resistance (progressive TAZs) constructed by the vibes, lyrical content, and overall message of the band(s) dominating a scene or particular show, and the consciousness and actions of the audience the acts attract, which, in most motivated cities, occur almost every night, participants are in a unique position to channel the constant flow of collective energy. Through the revolutionary, counterhegemonic PunKore pedagogy, despite the omnipresent existence of the counterrevolutionary, hegemonic pedagogy of the white supremacist, sexist, homophobic, glorifier of the working class PunKore,

this energy is converted into a social movement for social justice, thereby making strides in reconciling the internal contradictions of the counter-revolutionary. The counterrevolutionary PunKore participants' sexism and glorification of manual labor work against their own class interests and against the counterhegemonic potential of the scene.

In his reflections and analysis of "the scene," Steven Blush highlights the "messiness" of any democratic movement for social justice.[28] That is, because not every participant was motivated by the same drive against oppression, or haunted by the self-destruction of despair, it has continued to form and re-form around its internal contradictions responding to both larger social structures, and the participants society creates and is created by. As a result, potentially revolutionary PunKore scenes tend to not only transmit "thought-provoking lyrics," but are also backed up by a "fuck-you attitude." This combination, at its best, not only encourages deeper understandings of one's social position as it relates to larger social structures, but also challenges participants to take action as advocated by such critical pedagogues as McLaren.[29]

For example, in the late 1980s and early 1990s, lead singer Raybeez of the New York City hard-core group, Warzone, emerged as one of the main organizers protesting policies that created the gentrification of less affluent sectors of the city. Through live musical performances and squatting in buildings targeted for demolition, Raybeez and other activists achieved success in halting rent increases. Punks, skinheads, hard-core kids, and others in the PunKore scene took the streets in protest. However, owing to multiple factors related to the power of capital, and in the wake of Raybeez's death, over time, the rents did increase, and Warzone's mobilization was temporarily halted. These examples point to the power of music as a mobilizing force in the creation of a revolutionary pedagogy.

Like Guevara and Freire, revolutionary PunKore bands and "the scene" make the potentially revolutionary PunKore scene what it is, as demonstrated in the above quotes, and play important roles in constructing progressive TAZs. That is, the punkore scene, in its nascent days especially, served an important uniting function for those disaffected youth who were unaware of the existence of others like themselves.

PunKore scenes can also practice a pedagogy of hatred, by uncritically supporting their internalized ideas, values, and beliefs transmitted through the cultural institutions controlled by the ruling class such as the mass media, education, and the state. Sometimes PunKore scenes can teach sexism, racism, and homophobia, and can even support the labor-capital relation through the celebration of manual labor. We are neither glorifying nor demonizing the PunKore scene. We merely recognize its historic role, in a specific time and space—characterized as a TAZ—where revolution is created, planned, and lived in multiple facets of our day-to-day lives. For a full discussion of the hegemonic and counterhegemonic tendencies of punk rock, see Malott and Peña.[30] In the last section we will demonstrate how we live the PunKore pedagogy, described above, through our own praxis as SK8punk and undergrounder academics.

THE PRAXIS OF ONE SK8PUNK

I was a maintenance man, a line cook, I worked in the factories I went to school, I hated it, I got my Cs and Ds. We rode our skates, we smoked our weed, we chilled with the fuckin' jonesers . . . We used our punk rock skating, and built a fuckin' crew . . . The time is now, the place is here, what do you stand for? . . . Will we fuckin' buckle, under all this pressure? Or do we have the skills, to commit a radical gesture?

—*Curry Malott*

I sing these lyrics from my song, "Jonez Boyz," as an old-school, West Coast, SK8punk, and member of the band, Ajogún, in Las Cruces, New Mexico, situated in the U.S./Mexican borderlands, at PunKore shows at local underground music stores, parties, and clubs. Las Cruces is situated within a relatively small urban county of approximately 100,000 people, over thirty percent of whom live below the official poverty line.

My role is therefore to attempt to engage people, through my music, in conversations concerning our social situation. I draw on my own experiences and perspectives as examples and points of departure. Driving this point home and using the space not only in the songs, but also between the songs, the band members (including the co-lead vocalist and coauthor of this chapter) and I let the audience know about our various campaigns such as our Cop Watch activities. We accompany this with the distribution of fliers describing the rights people have in interactions with the police.

As a group that is part of the local progressive PunKore scene, we frequently play shows with out-of-town bands on tour. It is not uncommon for bands with similar political bent to express their joy at knowing of other bands engaged in fighting the good fight. Other bands and fans in general who like our vibe mention not only our music, but our lyrics as well. Perhaps it's because it's easier to express feelings about lyrics than about music that folks always mention how enthused they are that our lyrics—be they mine or the other singers,' and often transmitted in Spanish—have substance and generate debate.

Folks unfamiliar with the skateboard scene—a scene fused with punk rock in its most underground moments—assume that it is just another sport, the youthful pastime of "juveniles," and that I, a 32-year-old PhD, need to "grow up." Skateboarding, however, is not a mere "sport." It is a way of life, and true, die-hard skaters, those who are in it for "the duration," create progressive TAZs that can last a lifetime. This attitude does not, however, invoke a pedagogy of violence as much as it declares a pedagogy of "let me create my own reality and my own life, and I won't bother you." When I was in high school, my crew, the Jonez Boyz, through the creation of our own TAZ, hooked up with other crews, creating larger, better connected networks of solidarity. Through this pedagogy of love and brother- and sisterhood, and existing on the margins of society, ways of living, previously unlived, were formed. Our DIY pedagogy coupled with a praxis of communal living materialized through some of the skaters I used to ride with, including Marc "Red" Scott from Portland, Oregon, and Mark "Munk" Hubbard from Seattle, Washington.

These guys and their crews took the DIY philosophy to a level none of us ever thought possible through the construction of an anti-park skate park, "Burnside," in Portland, Oregon under the Burnside Bridge.[31] Red, whose father was a carpenter, and his crew started constructing banks under the Burnside Bridge in 1990 without permission from the city—they just went for it. In the 2003 documentary, *Northwest*, Red describes how he and his friends started building bowls and quarter-pipes out of cement under the Burnside Bridge, regardless of what anybody said.[32] Red describes how through this process they met "some allies along the way who said 'leave these guys alone, they're not hurting anybody.'" As a result, the city eventually granted them permission to keep what turned into the pirated Burnside Skate Park. Red and his crew learned to build world-class skate parks, and have since been commissioned to build city parks throughout the Northwest and all over the world.

Through his pedagogy, Munk humbly takes on not only the DIY philosophy of punk, but—despite his pro-skater status—is also open to working with anyone inter-ested in participating in the scene, which is similar to the pedagogy of Ché Guevara described by McLaren.[33] This potentially revolutionary pedagogy is in stark contrast to other professional skaters and park designers who practice a much more elitist pedagogy of exclusion, working with only those deemed sufficiently experienced and committed. Within Munk's SK8punk pedagogy, which I, myself, practice in the Southwest, a potentially revolutionary force exists with the potential to transform not only our immediate lives within the capitalist system, as many skaters have, but also to completely uproot and transform the labor-capital relation through a DIY pedagogy of community building, humility, and courage practiced on a large scale. What follows is the complementary pedagogical praxis of revolution emerging out of Puerto Rico.

THE PRAXIS OF ONE UNDERGROUNDER

The TAZ is like an uprising which does not engage directly with the State, a guerilla operation which liberates an area (of land, of time, of imagination) and then dissolves itself to reform elsewhere/elsewhen, before the State can crush it.[34]

—*Hakim Bey*

Born in the revolutionary struggle within Puerto Rico, I was introduced to a world where dreams were a concrete way of materializing revolutions. This belief was inculcated shortly but surely through the Latin American struggle folk songs of Aires Bucaneros, Roy Brown, Silvio Rodriguez, Pablo Milanes, Mercedes Sosa, Victor Jara, and Intillimani, among others. Through "Trova," a sense of pride, emancipation, self-determination, and sensibility to all forms of oppression became what are known as my pillars of an undergrounder subjectivity. I stress underground, for in her experience as a radical student in the 1960s, my mother and her comrades had to live a semiclandestine life. The FBI, CIA, and local government tactics of repression were a day-to-day reality that resulted in the political persecution, torture, and assassination of many in the struggle. Through the underground community and mutual solidarity, many managed to survive.

In my teen years I was introduced to the world of underground punk, hard–core, and OI musical scenes. Raw and aggressive music perfectly complemented my rage against the U.S. empire and its historic role in killing anything that came in its way of consolidating hegemonic control. It was in this progressive PunKore scene where I would discuss the nationalist and socialist movements of liberation for Puerto Rico. While drinking and hanging out, we aspired and plotted to create emancipatory TAZs through our multiple shows as a source of instigating, breeding, and materializing revolution. Shows of the PunKore scenes were instances where our revolutionary tendencies bloomed, for they had a fertile and concrete community, space, and time to grow in. For us, revolutionary TAZs were and are a way of life. We felt free so we became free.

Later I embarked upon higher education and brought my PunKore praxis with me. In fact, many of my friends in the PunKore scene were also students at the University of Puerto Rico. The PunKore scene was not only in the streets but in the university as well. There I got involved in multiple student movements that engaged in a Latin American style of revolutionary praxis. For us, the TAZ, created via the PunKore scene, was the lifeline of our revolution. It would have been practically impossible to mobilize thousands of students to paralyze the university without multiple musical concerts and rallies. TAZ, via music and theater, broke barriers of apathy facilitating the bloom of various movements against multiple forms of injustices. We dealt with all kinds of issues: imperialism, decolonization, capitalism, racism, homophobia, and xenophobia, among other forms of oppression.

As an undergrounder I've lived the phenomenon that any form of underground music creates a space where revolutionary tactics and life help materialize in counter cultures and counter hegemonic forces. For me it has been vital to any form of resistance against oppressive conditions. Music is the soul of the revolution without it I think its dead.

Music as a form of organizing is not inherently the property of the Latin American struggle. Here in the United States, it has been used on a constant basis throughout its history. Music massified and mobilized revolutions. Some of the most recent examples have been tours with Rage Against the Machine. Their tours they rallied the cause for clemency and immediate release of both Leonard Peltier and Mumia Abu-Jamal, while simultaneously shining light on the Zapatista struggle. Other musical groups such as Ozomatli are always to be found in Chicana/-o and borderland issues.

Music in an underground fashion was and is a key element in helping organize the massive mobilizations against the oppressive nature of the World Trade Organization and other transnational capitalist elite organizations in Seattle, Prague, and elsewhere. It is in this fashion that the authors of this chapter engage in consciously creating temporary autonomous zones of liberation where the praxis of the PunKore scenes' pedagogy helps create a community that addresses the eradication of oppression, however it may manifest itself.

Currently I work in multiple community efforts with my colleague, TAZ-mate, and coauthor of this chapter. From staffing literature tables, to free speech activism, Cop Watch, *migra* watch, the *Ni una Más* campaign to stop the assassination of *maquiladora* workers in Ciudad Juarez, to anti-war protests and theater of the oppressed workshops, we have been seriously involved in borderland politics and resistance. Our DIY TAZ-making praxis materialized in creating a PunKore band in the borderland scene known as Ajogún.

CONCLUSION

PunKore represents part of the world's working- and middle-class response to an increasingly unjust world. It represents one youth subculture out of many, which, if united with all countercultures beyond all boundaries, possesses a revolutionary potential capable of smashing the relationships that oppress us, and building new ones that allow us to develop our collective creative capacities in the humanization of not only the world, but our selves. Our vision of PunKore resonates particularly well with the pedagogies of previous revolutionary struggles. Translating into English some words of Ernesto Ché Guevara, our revolutionary TAZ-creating praxis strives to create a community and alternative way of life where we all "feel that indignation against any form of oppression against anyone in the world becomes and is the most beautiful quality of a revolutionary." We want to "be realists and do the impossible."

To all undergrounders worldwide who are creating TAZ/counterhegemonic communities, *hasta la victoria siempre*.

NOTES

This chapter is based on the article by Curry Malott and Joseph Carroll-Miranda, "PunKore Scenes as Revolutionary Street Pedagogy," published in *JCEPS* 1 (2) and located online at http://www.jceps.com/index.php?pageID=article&articleID=13.

1. Hobsbawm, E. (2002). Primitive rebels. In S. Duncombe (Ed.), *Cultural resistance reader.* London: Verso.

2. Rikowski, G. (2002). Education, capital, and the transhuman. In D. Hill, P. McLaren, and G. Rikowski (Eds.), *Marxism against post-*

modernism in educational theory. New York: Lexington Books.

3. Neary, M. (2002). Youth, training, and the politics of "cool." In D. Hill, P. McLaren, and G. Rikowski (Eds.), *Marxism against postmodernism in educational theory.* New York: Lexington Books.

4. Neary (2002).

5. McLaren, P. (2000). *Che Guevara, Paulo Freire, and the pedagogy of revolution.* New York: Rowman & Littlefield; McLaren, P. (2000). Reconsidering Marx in post-Marxist times: A requiem for postmodernism? *Educational Researcher,* 25–33; McLaren, P. & Farahmand-pur, R. (2002). Breaking signifying chains: A Marxist position on postmodernism. In D. Hill, P. McLaren, and G. Rikowski (Eds.), *Marxism against postmodernism in educational theory.* New York: Lexington Books; Ross, W. (2000). Diverting democracy: The curriculum standards movement and social studies education. In D. Hursh & W. Ross (Eds.), *Democratic social education: Social studies for social change.* New York: Falmer Press.

6. Rikowski (2002).

7. Hebdige, D. (2002). The meaning of MOD. In S. Duncombe. (Ed.), *Cultural resistance reader.* London: Verso.

8. Hebdige (2002).

9. Willis, P. (1977). *Learning to labour: How working-class kids get working-class jobs.* Westmead, England: Saxon House; MacLeod, J. (1987). *Ain't no makin' it: Leveled aspirations in a low-income neighborhood.* Boulder, CO: Westview; Weis, L. (1990). *Working-class without work: High school students in a deindustrializing economy.* New York: Routledge.

10. Hill, D., Sanders, M., & Hankin, T. (2002). Marxism, class analysis, and postmodernism. In D. Hill, P. McLaren, and G. Rikowski (Eds.), *Marxism against postmodernism in educational theory.* New York: Lexington Books.

11. Hobsbawm (2002); Hebdige (2002); Clarke, J. (2002). The skinheads and the magical recovery of community. In S. Duncombe. (Ed.), *Cultural resistance reader.* London: Verso.

12. Hanna, K. (2002). Interview in *Punk Planet.* In S. Duncombe (Ed.), *Cultural resistance reader.* London: Verso.

13. Marshall, G. (1991). *Spirit of '69: A skinhead Bible.* U.K.: STP Publishing.

14. Marshall (1991).

15. Marshall (1991).

16. Symarip (1991). *Skinhead Moonstomp*. Trojan Records, 10786-20564 [CD].

17. Marshall (1991).

18. Marshall (1991).

19. Hanna (2002).

20. Hanna (2002).

21. Freire, P. (1998). *Pedagogy of freedom*. Lanham, MD: Rowman & Littlefield.

22. Bey, H. (2002). TAZ: The temporary autonomous zone. In S. Duncombe (Ed.), *Cultural resistance reader*. London: Verso.

23. Rikowski (2002).

24. Rikowski (2002).

25. Bey (2002).

26. Eyerman, R. & Jamison, A. (1998). *Music and social movements: Mobilizing traditions in the twentieth century*. Cambridge, England: Cambridge University Press.

27. Bey (2002).

28. Blush, S. (2001). *American hardcore: A tribal history*. Los Angeles: Feral House.

29. McLaren, P. (2002). Marxist revolutionary praxis: A curriculum of transgression. *Journal of Critical Inquiry into Curriculum and Instruction*, 3 (3), 36–41.

30. Malott, C. & Peña, M. (in press). *Punk rocker's revolution: Pedagogy of gender, race, and class*. New York: Peter Lang.

31. Borden, L. (2001). *Skateboarding, space and the city: Architecture and the body*. New York: Berg.

32. Nichols, B., and Charnoski, R. (Producer and Director). (2003). *Northwest* [Film]. New York: Charnoski Productions and Flexifilm.

33. McLaren (2000).

34. Bey (2002).

CIVIL RIGHT, NOBLE CAUSE, AND TROJAN HORSE: NEWS PORTRAYALS OF VOUCHERS AND URBAN EDUCATION

Eric Haas

If you are an African-American child going to an urban school, a voucher will protect your right to a quality education. If Americans want to help improve the education of poor, inner-city students, then they should give them vouchers to go to the school of their choice. Government bureaucracies have caused urban school to be failures. Private business and the marketplace will make them excellent.

The sentences above are some of the latest language about urban education in the news. Linking vouchers with urban education continues the rhetoric that government is the problem, whereas private business and marketplace practices are the solution. Further combining vouchers and urban education with a civil right to education extends the reach of this rhetoric. Private business and the marketplace, once the opponent of civil rights, are now presented as their protector. This expansion of the logic of the education marketplace will likely have a profound effect on urban schools.

THE LANGUAGE OF EDUCATION POLICY IN THE NEWSPAPER MATTERS

How an urban education policy is framed—what parts of our identity, values, and hopes it evokes through the language used to promote it—determines in part how it is enacted or defeated. This chapter examines how proponents of vouchers are linking them with inner-city schools and civil rights to gain acceptance of pilot programs throughout the country. Understanding the assumptions, ambiguities, and contradictions of this language can give educators, researchers, and policy makers insight into the development of public opinion and policy on urban education.

The language examined is taken from newspaper articles that concern vouchers and urban schools. Newspaper articles are examined because the news media both reflect and shape the terms of education policy debates.[1] In other words, the manner in which vouchers and urban education are presented together in newspapers is evidence of how the relationship between the two is viewed by the news media, the policy advocates presented in the news articles, and the policy makers and the public who read them.[2]

THE IMPORTANCE OF POLICY LANGUAGE

Terms such as "urban education," "voucher," and "civil rights" do not have intrinsic, universal meanings. Instead, what they mean can differ by person and context and over time.[3] How "urban education," "voucher," and "civil rights" are understood depend on the language used to describe them, on past and current events, and on the knowledge, experience, and values of readers. For example, policy language that links the terms "vouchers" and "urban education" with civil rights will likely create a different meaning for those terms than language that links "vouchers" and "urban education" with religious freedom. The meanings of these collections of terms will also differ and change depending on past and current events that involve vouchers, urban education, and a host of other social happenings, including the success or failure of other voucher programs, higher or lower test scores in urban schools, legal gains or setbacks in affirmative action cases and, say, concerns about terrorists using vouchers to run anti-American schools. How much weight policy makers and the public attribute to any of these events often depends on the extent and character of their coverage in the news.[4]

The meaning of an urban education policy in a newspaper piece will also depend on who is reading it. The ideas, emotions, and experiences that a reader brings to the piece will interact with what the news piece states explicitly, what it leaves ambiguous, and what it leaves out.[5] A news piece that links vouchers and urban education may evoke feelings in some readers that this education policy will be a threat to stable, high-achieving schools. Adding language about the use of vouchers to protect the civil right to a quality education for urban students may ease tensions by evoking an egalitarian purpose.[6] Similarly, parents who think of marketplace exploitation when they read about voucher proposals may be more supportive when vouchers are presented as a means to protect the right to quality education set down in *Brown v. Board of Education*.[7]

To uncover the layers of possible meaning associated with linking vouchers, urban education, and civil rights, it is important to examine three aspects of the newspaper pieces: (1) the education policy language itself; (2) references to other language and ideas in the education policy language; and (3) the larger context of events that surround vouchers and urban education.[8] There is not sufficient space for an extensive analysis here; however, select examples of news articles are scrutinized for the link among vouchers, urban education, and civil rights. Specifically examined is how the right to quality education is perceived.

THE LANGUAGE ITSELF

Examining news pieces that report on vouchers and urban education demonstrates some patterns in how the two are linked. Proponents link them in two main ways. First, proponents emphasize quality education for urban students as a civil right, and advocate vouchers as the best means to meet the legal obligation to provide it. Second, they emphasize quality urban education as a moral imperative—but not a legal obligation—and vouchers as the best way to meet it. In the latter, providing vouchers to inner-city students is made equivalent to a noble cause. Both characterize the purpose and process of education in business language.

Newspaper articles also include voucher opponents who contend that vouchers are a Trojan horse. They will bring high promises, but they will deliver low-quality education that will eventually end public education. Newspaper articles generally reference voucher opponents to present the possible failures of voucher programs without offering alternative public school reforms. Thus, voucher opponents indirectly affirm the purpose and process of education in business terms. Examples of each of these presentations are examined below.

Vouchers as a Civil Right

Voucher proponents who link them with urban education present vouchers as a more effective way to protect the civil right to a quality education. They are, the proponents contend, better than the current government-managed urban public schools. As such, vouchers are presented as the best, and possibly only, means to fulfill the hard-won civil right to equal educational opportunity set forth in *Brown v. Board of Education*. This presentation of voucher programs follows a general pattern: (1) the terrible state of all urban schools is noted; (2) the failure of urban schools is linked to government bureaucracy or teachers unions; (3) the civil right to a quality education is evoked as the foundational impetus for reform; and (4) marketplace and business-oriented reforms are presented as the best or only way to protect this civil right.

An opinion piece written by Jeff Jacoby and published in the *Boston Globe* is a representative example. The premise of Jacoby's piece, titled "Vouchers and Equal Education," is that a marketplace reform is needed to achieve the educational quality called for in *Brown v. Board of Education*.[9] Jacoby's argument includes the four elements listed above.

The article states repeatedly that public schools are in terrible shape. For example, Jacoby states that overall public schools are "nothing to boast about" and that "few are crummier than the dreadful urban public schools."[10] He backs his conclusion with the chilling statistic, "the average black high school senior today is less competent in reading, math, and history than the average white eighth-grader."[11] Although some would argue that Jacoby's condemnation of urban education is overly simplistic and broad,[12] he presents them as well-accepted truths in no need of further support.[13]

Jacoby places the blame for the sad state of urban schools in two places: the government bureaucracy that manages them and the deficiencies of poor, black culture. He calls government management of public schools the "Soviet model" and a "monopoly . . . [that] wastes money, performs indifferently, and doesn't care much if its customers— American mothers and fathers—are satisfied."[14] Urban public schools, he asserts, are "inferior" because they are a "one-size-fits-all product of sclerotic government bureaucracies."[15] Jacoby also blames poor student performance on the bad culture of black families. Poor, black students would do better, he contends, if their families had higher expectations, worked harder, and watched less television. Again, Jacoby presents his condemnations as accepted truths, although others do disagree.[16]

Jacoby reminds the reader that *Brown v. Board of Education* held that the U.S. Constitution requires that all students must be given an equal opportunity to receive a quality education. Jacoby claims that, despite soaring per-pupil spending and the hiring of a large number of additional teachers, the promise of *Brown* "is still a mirage."[17] *Brown* set forth a legal mandate that the government management of public schools has not, and cannot, meet.

Jacoby's solution is the marketplace management of public schools in the form of vouchers.

By now it is obvious that spending even more money and hiring even more teachers isn't going to bring about the equality that *Brown* called for. Neither will shifting students around on the basis of skin color, as decades of forced busing certainly proved. So maybe it's time to try a really radical reform: choice. . . For two generations we have claimed that educational equality is a constitutional right. The way to finally make good on that claim is to offer a voucher of equal value to the parents of every child—letting the funding follow the student, no matter who runs the school. Putting power in the hands of parents is the real key to equality—and the key to excellence, too.[18]

Jacoby presents simplistic, and likely false, dichotomies that contrast effective and ineffective schools as equivalent to public versus marketplace management. One might agree with Jacoby that more money and more teachers alone will not bring about equal educational opportunity for urban students without reaching his conclusion that the only solution is vouchers. Other changes that would likely contribute to more effective urban schools, such as better, more affordable health care and a living wage for all U.S. citizens, including urban residents, are not discussed in Jacoby's article.[19]

In sum, Jacoby argues that the right to a quality education created by the U.S. Constitution and the Supreme Court can only be protected by private enterprise and market competition. Through the marketplace, competition alone will produce equality by making all schools excellent. Government bureaucracy, in contrast, can only produce educational haves and have-nots.

Other newspaper pieces similarly link vouchers, urban schools, and civil rights. For example, the *New York Times* published a news analysis of the George W. Bush Administration's plan to give vouchers to parents of students in "failing" Title I schools.[20] In this article, titled "Adding a Financial Threat to Familiar Promises on Education," the *New York Times* quotes William Taylor, now of a group called the Citizens' Commission on Civil Rights, who presents President Bush as a maverick who will use vouchers to protect the rights of disadvantaged minorities in the spirit of 1960s civil rights activism:

"But," he [William Taylor] added, "the whole history of civil rights enforcement has been that when the government shows it's serious, the recipients of government money will comply and the kids will get the services they need."

In seeking to flex the punitive muscle of federal education law—specifically the 36-year-old $8 billion Title I program, which aids the nation's poorest and lowest-achieving students—Mr. Bush is allying himself most closely with President Lyndon B. Johnson, who withheld money from Southern school districts that refused to embrace desegregation, said Mr. Taylor, the director of the United States Commission on Civil Rights in the Johnson Administration.[21]

According to Taylor, vouchers are the successor to the civil rights movement because they punish the government bureaucrats who refuse to offer quality education to the nation's poor.

The importance of this shift in language lies in its attempt to change the perception of the relationship between two contradictory forces in U.S. society: civil rights and private enterprise. For centuries, U.S. private businesses regularly violated the civil rights of people of color.[22] Only recently have the Civil Rights Act of 1964 and numerous protests limited (but not ended) discrimination by private businesses. More fundamental is the contention that education in a capitalist society is inherently discriminatory.[23] A capitalist marketplace operates through competition based on the threat and promise of differential accumulation. Under the logic of the education marketplace, a school would make itself more successful by the ability to develop within its students the knowledge and talent to give them an economic advantage over graduates of other schools.

Education policy language that links equal educational opportunity with marketplace competition becomes an Orwellian proposition: Hierarchy is equality.

One way to soften this contradiction is to present vouchers as a noble gesture rather than as the protector of a legal right. In this presentation of education policy, proponents present vouchers as a noble cause through which society can assist less fortunate students who attend urban schools. The structure of noble cause logic uses language similar to the four elements contained in the language of vouchers as a civil right.

Vouchers as a Noble Cause

One example of this noble cause language is a news analysis of the education policy debate in the *New York Times*, titled "Education Plan by Bush Shows New Consensus."[24] First, it states that urban schools are in a terrible state. Urban education is described as the "the plight of poor, minority children in inner-city schools" and as being inflicted with "plagues of illiteracy and high dropout rates."[25] Second, the problems of urban education are loosely attributed to "experimental curriculums and individual portfolios" as well as to "people with a direct interest in the status quo" and "the power of the teachers' unions."[26] Then, the solutions are drawn exclusively from the language of business and the marketplace: "competition, accountability and a focus on fundamentals" including vouchers.[27]

In noble cause language, compassion is the fundamental impetus for school reform and it is grounded in legislation, not the U.S. Constitution. Noble cause language shifts society's relationship to urban education from a legal obligation individually enforceable as a U.S. Constitutional right to a moral obligation that is compelling, but individually unenforceable, absent legislation. The difference is subtle, but significant. U.S. Constitutional rights are grounded in one's humanity and citizenship and are thus inalienable. These rights are the closest U.S. society has to unalterable human rights. Rights derived from legislation, on the other hand, are grounded in the will of the political majority. They are inherently impermanent and they change as the political majority modifies them over time. Thus, no legislation ever needs to be enacted or continued. Vouchers and other business-model changes are linked to a desire, but not a constitutional obligation, to assist the less fortunate that continues from President Johnson's Great Society legislation. The *New York Times* article includes this description of the history preceding the current federal voucher debate:

To be sure, the education debate has always emphasized the disadvantaged, particularly at the federal level. From the desegregation of schools in the 1950s to the Great Society programs of the 1960s, the bulk of federal attention and money has focused on the needy.[28]

The current push for federal education vouchers is presented as the latest descendent of the civil rights move\ment. Yet, by describing the students as "needy" rather than "entitled," this language shifts education away from a legal right and more toward neighborly assistance.

Continuing in this theme, the article links a better urban education and vouchers to the need for a more educated labor force, the desire for educational equity, and the altruistic push to "help":

With corporate leaders dissatisfied about the quality of the labor pool helping steer the discussion, talk from years past about experimental curriculums and individual portfolios has been overshadowed by a bottom-line approach stressing basic skills, tests and accountability—all aimed at the neediest students in impoverished urban districts.

"The whole discussion is an equity discussion," said Diane Ravitch, the education historian. "The tenor of the discussion is: Do charter schools help poor kids? Do vouchers help poor kids? Is state testing good or bad for poor kids? How can we design a system that increases equity?"[29]

This article equates equity with business and the marketplace in two ways. Business and the marketplace are both the management process and the primary goals of education. Quality education for all concerns making urban students more prepared for the workforce. The best way to achieve that is for schools to be managed like businesses. That the aim of urban education might also include contesting and transforming society and the workforce is not considered.[30]

The language of vouchers as a noble cause also softens some of the contradictions inherent in presenting them as a means to protect civil rights. While invoking the marketplace as the primary means of providing for the right to quality education, vouchers are also presented as help rather than as the only means to a quality education. The implication appears to be that they would only be implemented when they would be an improvement over government-run public schools. That this may be inherently impossible or unlikely is not addressed. Despite these likely contradictions, the mere expansion of voucher language to include urban education and civil rights has important policy implications.

REFERENCES TO BUSINESS LANGUAGE AND IDEAS

When voucher supporters present vouchers as a means to fulfill the promises of *Brown* and Title I,[31] they present a subtle but important shift in the relationship between individuals and society. Civil rights language that emerged out of the 1960s was based on the concept of entitlement to fundamental rights based on common humanity and shared citizenship.[32] This language placed a large responsibility on society to ensure a level playing field, even going so far as having the government, not just protect civil rights, but also take active steps to eliminate past civil rights abuses and current inequalities in education through such programs as Title I, busing, and affirmative action. These programs and policies were intended, at least in part, to use the power of the government to meet the obligations of society to treat all its citizens justly, something not always done between private individuals and by private business. The enactment of the Civil Rights Act of 1964 put the U.S. government in its role as a protector of civil rights at odds with the business community.[33]

Presenting vouchers—a program based on marketplace mechanisms—as the best means to advance civil rights redefines the right to a quality education away from a right of citizenship to something akin to a property right that must be exercised by a responsible consumer. In this language, the citizen-consumer's use of free enterprise—buying the service of education from the best school and leaving schools that do not provide good service—becomes the means to ensure one's civil rights. Thus, the citizen-consumer alone is responsible for "exercising" the right to a quality education. The government's responsibility extends only to protecting the free exchange of educational goods and services. In this framing, the government is an enabler of individual rights, but does not guarantee them. It has no direct responsibility for the individual, nor for creating a just society.

Jacoby's piece in the *Boston Globe* supports his call for vouchers by directly blaming the problems of urban education on the poor parental choices of minority parents and on bad government. Responsible consumers are the only solution. According to Jacoby, the quality of education would improve for poor, urban, minority students if education were treated more like "food or clothing or health care—where the market generates lots of options and parents are free to choose among them."[34] By this logic, a student's civil right to quality education is limited only by a parent's injudicious use of their voucher. Civil rights violations result only from bad individual choices, not unjust societal choices. The role of government, then, is to get out of the way. The business logic of property rights applied to civil rights is subtly supported by the presentation of urban educational problems as resulting from poor individual choices, as something akin to natural causes, or as simply existing of unknown cause. The concept that society as a whole might have a role in urban education problems, either directly or through related issues like unequal health care and employment opportunities, is denied or ignored. Government, therefore, has no direct responsibility to correct them.

The Wilgoren piece in the *New York Times* describes high dropout rates and illiteracy as "inner-city plagues."[35] Linking urban educational problems with the plague invites readers to view them not only as widespread and horrific, but also as unavoidable natural occurrences. Readers are not invited to see high dropout rates and illiteracy as societal creations. How differently might a reader perceive urban education problems if the *New York Times* were to present the illiterate student and the student who drops out of school as "cursed"—afflicted by something placed on one person by another?

Wilgoren also presents the problems in urban education as existing without cause. Inner-city students are described simply as "needy" and urban schools as "impoverished."[36] No cause is given. No actor or action caused the impoverishment or the neediness. They just seem to be that way. The reader is not invited to view society as being responsible.

The power of the language of any policy is that with repeated use over time, it can push out other policy options and limit what is considered in the public debate. Thus, as the language of voucher policies and their underlying business logic are repeated in the news, they become more commonplace, and eventually become the dominant language of reform. Vouchers, along with the business and marketplace logic that supports them, become the accepted commonsense start of the education reform debate. At this point even opponents of using vouchers to improve urban schools begin to contest them in business language.

Vouchers as a Trojan Horse

Critics of vouchers as the means to bettering urban schools predominantly use a version of the business language used by voucher proponents. Their contrary language is simply that vouchers do not work. Voucher critics do not question the business model of education, only whether vouchers will achieve the competitive equity that voucher proponents contend they will.

Consider a news article in the *New York Times* that described the Senate debate that ultimately defeated the Bush voucher proposal in his No Child Left Behind legislation.[37] In this article, titled, "Senate Rejects Tuition Aid, A Key to Bush Education Plan," opponents of vouchers for low-income city students present them as a Trojan horse sent to undermine public schools. The article does not explain why government-managed urban public schools are considered worth saving nor does it present an alternative vision of how the government might better advance civil rights than can the marketplace.

Republicans contend that publicly financed vouchers are an innovative way to give children in dead-end schools a better education and to force public schools to improve. Democrats who say the approach offers only false hope to children argue that vouchers are a threat to public schools, which will see some money steered to private schools.

"It sounds so good," said Senator Hillary Rodham Clinton, Democrat of New York, "but it has a number of serious flaws that doom it. Experiments have demonstrated absolutely no evidence that vouchers help improve student achievement.

"Secondly, we know that vouchers do not help the students who need the help the most. They do nothing to help improve public schools. Vouchers only further segregate and stratify our public schools."[38]

According to the Democrats referenced in this article, one should support government-managed public schools only because vouchers and the marketplace would perform even worse. There is no discussion of why public schools could be an important societal institution in and of themselves.

Similar language is used in a lengthy piece in the *New York Times* about New Zealand's experience with school vouchers.[39] In "A Cautionary Tale from New Zealand," professor of public policy Helen Ladd and her husband, Edward Fiske, an education consultant and former education editor of the *New York Times*, describe the failure of vouchers to improve "troubled urban schools" in New Zealand as a lesson for U.S. education policy.[40] They state that the New Zealand government's refusal to intervene to assist troubled urban schools, as called for under the theory of the educational marketplace, led to increased racial and economic segregation in schools. The result was that schools in middle- and upper-middle-income communities often improved, while schools with poor populations spiraled downward. To combat this, the New Zealand government eventually changed course and began to directly assist the troubled schools. It provided additional money for school health clinics and new equipment, and to buy out underperforming staff.

In this article, Fiske and Ladd criticize the logic of the education marketplace in property right language, but do not explicitly embrace the language of education as an entitlement right. Fiske and Ladd describe how the government had to take a direct role in providing quality education beyond the promoting and protecting marketplace. They conclude that vouchers and individual choice of school alone do not work for poor, urban students.

Still, Fiske and Ladd do not make clear the fundamental motivation behind the New Zealand government's decision to intervene. Did it intervene because it needed to temporarily correct this new program of marketplace management? Or did the New Zealand government intervene because it saw an active and mutual obligation between individuals and society that is best protected and advanced through government? In other words, was the New Zealand government fixing or replacing marketplace management? The news piece does not say.

In addition, Fiske and Ladd are unclear about the purpose of schooling. In their news article, Fiske and Ladd discuss "success in school" and indicate that schools can be "successful," but they do not define what these terms mean.[41] To help interpret these terms, as well as the government's intention in intervening on behalf of urban schools, it is best to consider them in light of the pervasive use of business practices and goals in education and other government activities.

THE LARGER CONTEXT

Two trends in U.S. society appear especially relevant to interpreting the language of urban education policy: the application of marketplace principles to an ever-growing share of society and the expansion of "equity" to mean all of U.S. education, rather than segments within it. The pervasiveness of these concepts makes their extension to education more likely.

Over the last twenty years, outsourcing government activities to private businesses has steadily increased.[42] The military is emblematic of the privatization of government activities. In Operation Iraqi Freedom, for example, private contractors prepare soldiers' meals, provide Internet services, and interrogate prisoners.[43]

The education marketplace has similarly expanded. Schools outsource their janitorial and food services. Vouchers, charter schools, tuition tax credits, and private educational management organizations like Edison Schools, Inc., have increased significantly in the last twenty years.[44] School districts sell public building space to soft drink manufacturers and other advertisers to raise funds for school programs.[45] International corporations like pharmaceutical giant GlaxoSmithKline provide free curricula and lesson plans to schools.[46]

Business leaders and business language increasingly set the education agenda. Since the Reagan Administration published "A Nation at Risk,"[47] the education debate has been inundated with notions of how schools can prepare students to be better workers and make the nation more economically competitive in the global marketplace. Referring to the need to maintain the "once unchallenged preeminence [of the United States] in commerce, industry, science, and technological innovation,"[48] "A Nation at Risk" considers other educational activities to be distracting and harmful:

Our society and its educational institutions seem to have lost sight of the basic purposes of schooling, and of the high expectations and disciplined effort needed to attain them. . . . That we have compromised this commitment is, upon reflection, hardly surprising, given the multitude of often conflicting demands we have placed on our Nation's schools and colleges. They are routinely called on to provide solutions to personal, social, and political problems that the home and other institutions either will not or cannot resolve. We must understand that these demands on our schools and colleges often exact an educational cost as well as a financial one.[49]

Business leaders, in turn, have taken an active role in shaping state and federal education policy. Describing and orienting education according to the needs and priorities of business and the marketplace are now common in the language and activities both outside and within the education community.[50]

"A Nation at Risk" also began to reshape the meaning of equity. Dating to the civil rights movement, education equity has concerned disparities within the U.S. educational system. Among these were the lack of funding and resources for urban schools. When "A Nation at Risk" condemned the entire U.S. educational system as failing to produce a competitive workforce, it specifically shifted the debate away from equalizing disparate funding, resources, and social conditions among school districts. Rather, it cast all school districts as burdened with problems affecting the nation's economic well-being:

All, regardless of race or class or economic status, are entitled to a fair chance and to the tools for developing their individual powers of mind and spirit to the utmost. This promise means that all children by virtue of their own efforts, competently guided, can hope to attain the mature and informed judgment needed to secure gainful employment, and to manage their own lives, thereby serving not only their own interests but also the progress of society itself.[51]

To support this statement, "A Nation at Risk" presented statistics on the failure of U.S. education as a whole. It did not separate out the high test scores of wealthy, white suburban students from the low test scores of poor, minority, urban students.[52] It presented equity as making U.S. students equal to students from competitor nations rather than setting as a goal the equalization of educational opportunities among poor urban students and their well-to-do suburban counterparts.

A Little of Both Leaves a Business Message

Some news pieces attempt to find a middle ground between proponents and opponents of vouchers for urban public schools. They draw bits from both camps—managerial innovation from the voucher proponents and more money and support for all schools from the voucher opponents. This mix of language, however, still presents a mostly pro-business model or property right view of education. It places the fulfillment of a right to quality education almost completely on the individual and only slightly on society. Further, it leaves unsaid the purpose of education, which in the current educational climate, makes it likely to be interpreted as economic competitiveness alone.

Take, for example, an opinion piece in the *Washington Post* by Professor Paul Hill of the University of Washington's Center on Reinventing Public Education.[53] In "Aha! School Choice Can Work in D.C.," Hill argues that a properly designed voucher system could go a long way toward providing quality education to impoverished children in poor-performing public schools, many of which are urban schools. One of the obvious requirements—which Hill lists in his "Well duh!" category—is that all schools should receive equal per-pupil spending. He writes:

In a public school setting, equal per-pupil spending—whether a child attends a traditional public school, charter school, magnet program or other option [like vouchers]—is critical to give families, particularly poor ones, not just alternatives but good alternatives to failing local schools.[54]

This type of equality—equal spending power—presents a property right, business model approach to education. All that is necessary for good education is parents acting as good consumers. Society is assumed to have achieved a level playing field and thus there is no obligation to go beyond the notion of "same as equal."

To the extent that poor, urban schools were to receive more from society in the language of a communal obligation to student learning, it comes in the form of bonuses to attract teachers to the most difficult schools. Hill puts it this way: "A few

creative incentives could work wonders: By using extra grant money to offer bonuses, school districts could lure excellent teachers to tough classrooms."[55]

Of further interest is the lack of specificity about what vouchers would improve in schools. Hill describes the improvement as "higher achievement" and "quality of academics"—but what do these terms mean? Do they mean making students better quality laborers as called for in "A Nation at Risk"? Or do they mean active citizens and reflective thinkers who also challenge and transform the status quo? Hill leaves these terms for the reader to interpret. Given the strong influence of the business community and the prevalence of business language in the current language of education generally and within discussions of vouchers specifically, it is more likely that readers will interpret ambiguous terms like "higher achievement" to mean the development of students as more globally competitive workers than as well-rounded, critical citizens.

CONCLUSION

Language matters in education policy. When newspapers and voucher supporters present vouchers as the best means to enhance urban students' civil right to equal educational opportunity, they extend the logic of the marketplace to the very core of the nation's social structure. Education is a property right. Civil rights are a property right. Government efforts to equalize social inequalities only make the situation worse. Equality through competition is no longer contradictory; it becomes common sense.

NOTES

1. van Dijk, T. (2000). Critical discourse analysis. In D. Schiffrin, D. Tannen, & H. Hamilton (Eds.), *The handbook of discourse analysis*. Oxford: Blackwell; Fairclough, N. (1995). *Critical discourse analysis: The critical study of language*. Harlow, UK: Longman; Herman, E. &

Chomsky, N. (1988). *Manufacturing consent: The political economy of the mass media.* New York: Pantheon; Kingdon, J. (1984). *Agendas, alternatives, and public policy.* Boston: Little, Brown.

2. Fairclough, N. (1995). *Media discourse.* London: Arnold; Lawrence, R. (2000). *The politics of force: Media and the construction of police brutality.* Berkeley, CA: University of California Press.

3. Ball, S. (1994). *Education reform: A critical and post-structural approach.* Buckingham, UK: Open University Press; Ball, S. (2002). *Class strategies and the education market: The middle classes and social advantage.* London: Routledge-Falmer; Fairclough, *Critical discourse analysis*; Smith, M. (2004). *Political spectacle and the fate of American schools.* New York: RoutledgeFalmer.

4. Lawrence (2000).

5. Fairclough. *Critical discourse analysis*; Foucault, M. (1980). *Power/knowledge: Selected interviews and other writings 1972–1977.* New York: Pantheon Books; Rosenblatt, L. (1994). The transactional theory of reading and writing. In R. Ruddell, M. Ruddell, & H. Singer (Eds.), *Theoretical models* and processes of reading (4th ed.). Newark, DE: International Reading.

6. See, e.g., Wilgoren, J. (2001, January 23). Education plan by Bush shows new consensus. *New York Times.* p. A1.

7. *Brown v. Board of Education,* 347 U.S. 483 (1954).

8. Fairclough. *Media discourse;* Fairclough. *Critical discourse analysis.*

9. Jacoby, J. (2004, May 30). Vouchers and equal education. *Boston Globe* p. D11.

10. Jacoby (2004).

11. Jacoby (2004).

12. Berliner, D., & Biddle, B. (1995). *The manufactured crisis: Myths, fraud, and the attack on America's public schools.* Reading, MA: Addison-Wesley; Meier, D. (1995). *The power of their ideas: Lessons for America from a small school in Harlem.* Boston: Beacon Press.

13. van Dijk (2000).

14. Jacoby (2004).

15. Jacoby (2004).

16. See, e.g., Ayers, W., & Ford, P. (1996). *City kids, city teachers: A* view from the front row. New York: New Press; Bracey, G. (2003). *What you should know about the war against America's public schools.* Boston: Allyn and Bacon.

17. Jacoby (2004).

18. Jacoby (2004).

19. Berliner & Biddle. *The manufactured crisis;* Rothstein, R. (2004). *Class and schools: Using social, economic, and educational reform to close the black-white achievement gap.* Washington, DC: Economic Policy Institute.

20. Steinberg, J. (2001, January 26). Adding a financial threat to familiar promises on education. *New York Times.* p. A17.

21. Steinberg (2001, January 26).

22. See, e.g., Zinn, H. (1980). *A people's history of the United States.* New York: Harper and Row.

23. See, e.g., Ball. *Class strategies;* Dale, R. (1989). *The state and education policy.* Oxford, UK: Oxford University Press.

24. Wilgoren (2001, January 23).

25. Wilgoren (2001, January 23).

26. Wilgoren (2001, January 23).

27. Wilgoren (2001, January 23).

28. Wilgoren (2001, January 23).

29. Wilgoren (2001, January 23).

30. See, e.g., Ayers, W., Hunt, J., & Quinn, T. (1998). *Teaching for social justice: A democracy and education reader.* New York: Teachers College Press.

31. The Elementary and Secondary Education Act, renamed the No Child Left Behind Act, 20 U.S.C. §§101–9601 (2002).

32. See, e.g., Campbell, C. (1997). *Civil rights chronicle: Letters from the South.* Jackson, MS: University of Mississippi Press.

33. Civil Rights Act of 1964, 42 U.S.C. §2000a et seq. (1964).

34. Jacoby (2004).

35. Wilgoren (2001, January 23).

36. Wilgoren (2001, January 23).

37. Alvarez, L. (2001, June 13). Senate rejects tuition aid, a key to Bush education plan. *New York Times.* p. A26.

38. Alvarez (2001, June 13).

39. Fiske, E., & Ladd, H. (2000, August 6). A cautionary tale from New Zealand. *New York Times: Education Life Supplement.* p. 34.

40. Fiske & Ladd (2000, August 6), p. 34.

41. Fiske & Ladd (2000, August 6), p. 34.

42. Savas, E. (2000). *Privatization and public-private partnerships.* New York: Chatham House.

43. Council on Foreign Relations. Iraq: military outsourcing. http://www.cfr.org/background/background_iraq_outsourcing.php; Singer, P. (2003). *Corporate warriors: The rise of the privatized military industry.* Ithaca, NY: Cornell University Press.

44. Bracey (2003).

45. Molnar, A. (1996). *Giving kids the business: The commercialization of America's schools.* New York: Westview Press; Saltman, K. (2000). *Col-*

lateral damage: Corporatizing public schools—A threat to democracy. Lanham, MD. Rowman and Littlefield.

46. GlaxoSmithKline. Dedicated to science education. http://www.gsk.com/education/11_19 years.htm.

47. National Commission on Excellence in Education. (1983). *A nation at risk.* Washington, DC: Government Printing Office. http://www.ed.gov/pubs/NatAtRisk/risk.html.

48. National Commission on Excellence in Education. *A nation at risk,* ¶1.

49. National Commission on Excellence in Education. *A nation at risk,* ¶¶3–4.

50. Anderson, G. (2001). Disciplining leaders: A critical discourse analysis of the ISLLC National Examination and Performance Standards in Educational Administration. *Int. J. Leadership in Education* 4 No. 3: pp. 199–216; Mulderrig, J. (2003). Consuming education: A critical discourse analysis of social actors in new Labour's education policy. *Journal for Critical Education Policy Studies* 1 No. 1. www.jceps.com/?pageID=article&articleID=2.

51. National Commission on Excellence in Education. *A nation at risk,* ¶11.

52. Berliner & Biddle (1995).

53. Hill, P. (2003, September 21). Aha! School choice can work in DC; Vouchers can't cure a crippled system, but they're a start. *Washington Post.* p. B1.

54. Hill (2003, September 21), p. B5.

55. Hill (2003, September 21), p. B5.

Research and Urban Education

UTILIZING *CARIÑO* IN THE DEVELOPMENT OF RESEARCH METHODOLOGIES

Jeffrey M. R. Duncan-Andrade

My mother ends her e-mails with the words *con cariño*. Cariño is often translated as *caring, affection*, or *love*, but much is lost in this translation. Cariño is more a concept than a word. It is the foundation of relationships among the poor and working classes—often the only thing left to give, in families raising children on substandard wages. Angela Valenzuela describes cariño in the context of schooling as *authentic caring*, a concept distinctly different from what she calls *aesthetic caring*. She explains that schools serving poor and working-class Latino/-a children often fail to develop reciprocal relationships whereby children are authentically cared for and, in turn, open themselves up to care about school. Drawing from the literature on caring in schools,[1] Valenzuela argues that "schools are structured around an *aesthetic caring* whose essence lies in 'an attention to things and ideas.'"[2] This leads to a culture of false caring, one where the most powerful members of the relationship define themselves as caring despite the fact that the recipients of their so-called caring do not perceive it as such. Ultimately, aesthetic caring results in pragmatic relationships between school officials and students, straining the teaching and learning process.

Not far removed from the practice of aesthetic caring is the technocratic jargon of educational discourse that encourages an "impersonal and objective language, including such terms as goals, strategies, and standardized curricula, that is used in decisions made by one group for another."[3] This discourse is largely shaped by education research agendas that view authentic caring as an afterthought. At their worst, these agendas promote scientific objectivity that frowns upon overt discussions of caring in an effort to mirror more traditional forms of research.

This chapter analyzes recent federal legislation that promotes traditional scientific research models in education. Emerging from this analysis is a call for educational researchers to blaze a new path in social science research—one that foregrounds the ethic of cariño while maintaining the rigor of established scientific research. Examples of education research agendas grounded in cariño are included to demonstrate the viability for future growth in this direction.

WHAT IS EDUCATIONAL RESEARCH?

The debate over what constitutes legitimate education research has been heavily influenced by the federal No Child Left Behind Act (NCLB). Shortly after NCLB was signed into law in January, 2002, the George W. Bush administration enacted the Education Sciences Reform Act of 2002. This act, in turn, established the Federal Institute of Education Sciences, which aims to transform education "into an evidence-based field in which decision makers routinely seek out the best available research and data before adopting programs or practices that will affect significant numbers of students"[4]

According to the Institute's guidebook on effective educational intervention, *Identifying and Implementing Educational Practices Supported by Rigorous Evidence: A User-Friendly Guide* (2003), practitioners can use research that is supported by "strong" or "possible" evidence of effectiveness to improve their schools.[5] A study can boast of strong evidence of effectiveness if its research is backed by quality (well-designed and implemented randomized controlled trials) and quantity (effectiveness in two or more similar school/classroom settings) evidence. If not supported by strong indicators of effectiveness, research backed by possible evidence of effectiveness may also be considered worthy of implementation. Possibly effective studies are defined as studies that show some promise using randomly controlled trials and/or using comparison-group studies with "very closely matched" focal groups. The Federal Institute of Education Sciences rubric asserts that educational researchers aiming to place their studies in either of these two categories should align their methodologies more closely with "the fields of medicine and welfare policy [which] show that practice guided by rigorous evidence can produce remarkable advances."[6] Inherent in this logic is the belief that research's "gold standard," based on random controlled trials, can elucidate what works in schools.[7]

At first glance, it is difficult to disagree with these ideas because educational research has long been considered pseudoscience and has produced little evidence to refute such critiques. Further, our tenuous position in the research community gives cause for looking long and hard at our methodologies and claims they produce. We should have consensus in the educational research community to use and expect rigorous evidence gathering and analysis as a precursor to our research based conclusions. We should also expect, as in medical and social welfare research communities, that our work produces meaningful and documented change in our spheres of influence.

On the surface, NCLB's direction for educational research seems logical and in the best interest of schools and the research community. Upon deeper examination, however, this direction for educational research steers us down a dangerous road, one that Emerson forewarns us to avoid:

There is a time in every man's education when he arrives at the conviction that envy is ignorance; that imitation is suicide; that he must take himself for better, for worse, as his portion; that though the wide universe is full of good, no kernel of nourishing corn can come to him but through his toil bestowed on that plot of ground which is given to him to till.[8]

The road that we, as educational researchers, must hoe is not the same as that of the other disciplines. The ground bestowed on us begs a different kind of nourishment than is required of other fields. Like the field of education itself, educational research should be grounded in authentically caring relationships, a culture of cariño.

A Brief Overview of Traditional Educational Research Paradigms

Burkhardt and Schoenfeld propose improving education research to make it more useful, more influential, and better-funded enterprise.[9] Their analysis of traditions in education research are worth exploring at length to paint a broad picture of the field. Burkhardt and Schoenfeld categorize education research paradigms under three main headings: humanities, science, and engineering.

Citing the Higher Education Research Funding Council for England and Wales, they describe the humanities process as:

[O]riginal investigation undertaken in order to gain knowledge and understanding; scholarship; the invention and generation of ideas . . . where these lead to new or substantially improved insights.[10]

Without empirical data to back these ideas and inventions, the humanities paradigm, despite being "the oldest tradition in education," rarely produces much more than "critical commentary."[11]

The science approach, although noted as having a hotly contested definition, is described as:

[F]ocused on the development of better insight; of improved knowledge and understanding of "how the world works" through the analysis of phenomena; and the building of models that explain them.[12]

Unlike the humanities design, the science approach uses empirical testing to investigate identifiable problems. This difference is cited as being imperative for the legitimization of the research findings. The shortcoming of this approach is that it does not produce practical solutions to the problems that it investigates.

For Burkhardt and Schoenfeld, the engineering approach is considered the best research method because it relies on empirical testing aimed at producing a practical impact. They again draw from the Higher Education Research Funding Council's definition:

[I]t [the engineering approach] can be described as "the use of existing knowledge in experimental development to produce new or substantially improved materials, devices, products, and processes, including design and construction."[13]

While reflecting the best practices of the humanities and science approaches (strong theoretical grounding and empirical testing), the engineering approach has the primary purpose of producing tools and processes that address the local problem. Although touted as the best of the three approaches, the engineering model does not produce solutions that can be easily implemented for large-scale change.[14]

TWO PROBLEMS WITH CONVENTIONAL EDUCATION RESEARCH

Burkhardt and Schoenfeld's summation of the main education research traditions is thorough and useful to the degree that it gives us a sense of where mainstream education research has been and where it is headed. They make important points: There is a need for more empirical studies that produce educational tools supported by documented and sustained change in schools; and educational research must produce more bang for the buck, and the way to do that is to produce research methodologies that link research and practice.[15]

Absent from this discussion and from many of the mainstream critiques on the state of educational research are two of the most significant problems facing educational research communities: (1) the continued effort to model educational research on other research-based fields, and (2) the absence of a prioritization of an ethic of authentic caring in educational research. Before discussing the first of these problems, it is important to revisit Emerson's sense that "imitation is suicide." Emerson explains that we cannot produce meaningful work except by hoeing the road we are given. For educational research this is not the road of medicine, social work, physics, or any of the other so-called respected research fields. The protocols of educational research laid out by the Bush administration's Department of Education (DOE) miss the mark with their suggestions that education should follow the lead of social welfare and medicine in their efforts to produce meaningful research. The consistent failure of educational research to produce meaningful local or national change, particularly in the urban communities of color that are most often studied and least served, is not for a lack of methodological rigor. The Department of Education's insistence on closer adherence to the protocols and products of science-based research (empirical testing, scaleable product development) is tantamount to professional suicide. This is not to say that educational research should altogether abandon the use of scientific methods. Instead, it is a critique of the field's identity crisis, one that cannot be solved by attempting to replicate the efforts of other research fields. We should continue to develop and demand rigorous research methodologies in our field, but not with an eye toward "lab-to-engineering-to-marketing linkages" typical of "the drug companies, Bell Labs, Xerox PARC and IBM."[16] Our field should not seek to legitimate itself through more efficient contribution to a market driven enterprise. Education research should not attempt to generate scaleable products for sale at market. We are a field that is charged with caring for and educating young people. We have never found a way to reconcile this purpose with our sense of research agendas and methodologies of inquiry. The resulting effect has been a professional identity crisis, one that has the field of education occupying the margins of academia and the research community, beholden to funding sources shallow enough to ensure that education research agendas remain complicit with a field that is defined for us rather than by us. The time has come for the educational research community to come of age; to heed Emerson's advice that for better, for worse, we can only be fulfilled when we foreground our portion on that which makes our field unique, an ethic of authentic caring.

In order to ground our work in an ethic of caring, we must ask ourselves two key questions: (1) What does authentic caring look like in educational research; and (2) What is the difference between authentic caring and aesthetic caring in a research agenda?

BREAKING THE MOLD: PUTTING CARIÑO FIRST IN EDUCATION RESEARCH AGENDAS

Authentic Caring in Educational Research

Education is a unique enterprise, one that is a far cry from controlled laboratories or county general hospitals. Educators interact with their students almost every day for nine months each year. The frequency of interactions between teachers and students significantly differentiates education interventions from the other enterprises that conventional thinking suggests are worth modeling ourselves after. The traditional educational discourse and research methodology, which focuses on things and ideas rather than people and material conditions, has largely resulted in an educational research paradigm that seeks to find the "one best system."[17] For poor and working-class children in particular, this effort to create cookie-cutter reform models has meant decades of educational stagnation and their resultant socioeconomic marginalization.

Some researchers are rethinking educational research by emphasizing reciprocal relationships with schools, leading to deeper commitments for researchers to the school's and community's welfare. These educational researchers understand that each school's unique set of stakeholders and material conditions requires a research methodology that recognizes these differences. Rather than aiming to develop a model that can be laid on top of any school, this educational research approach focuses on forming relationships that pay attention to the special needs of a particular school. This focus on relationships translates into a greater emphasis on producing real change in the schools where the research is taking place.

INTERVENTION FOR EMANCIPATORY CHANGE

An approach to educational research that emphasizes cariño has also been called action research and described as an intervention for "emancipatory change":[18]

In stark contrast to "policy studies," whose aim is to provide "useful," expert knowledge for institutional planning, the core of critical action research involves its participatory and communally discursive structure and the cycle of action and reflection it initiates. The knowledge enabled through such reflexive and shared study leads not to bureaucratic directives, but, more important, to the possibility for emancipatory change.[19]

The value of this type of critical research is its focus on empowering individuals as agents of meaningful, sustainable change. The direct aim of this type of research agenda is to positively impact the material conditions of those involved with the study; it is an approach to research that gives more than it receives. By focusing more directly on improving the immediate circumstances, it de-emphasizes the traditional method of searching for empirical truths that can be implemented on a large scale. Instead, it seeks to democratize the tools of research and knowledge creation.[20] This way, when researchers leave, they leave behind a sense of hope and promise, one that is directly tied to the individual actors' sense of themselves as capable change agents. Beyond a heightened awareness of the capacity to change, this kind of research also leaves behind a set of tools that can be used and reused to continually improve the conditions most in need of attention. This is unique, because traditional research methods leave these tools in the hands of the researchers; so when the researcher leaves, so do the tools to research and, to a large extent, so does the sense of agency.

Research agendas that are committed to collaboration with participants as colleagues rather than subjects can result in richer stud-ies. This approach reduces dependency based colonial models of knowledge production that have historically reproduced the status quo. By inserting multiple voices into the conversation, the process of identifying problems and researching solutions becomes more democratic. As well, this research program provides a grounded, structured form for individual and structural reflexivity that can serve as a mechanism for ongoing feedback and adaptation as new and different issues arise that need the attention of research. Perhaps most important, it recognizes the complexity of each individual set of conditions and encourages a sensibility of local agency and control for developing solutions for local problems. This is not to say that sites cannot learn from the research of others; this is not a subtractive model or a zero sum game. Instead, this is an additive model of educational research, which suggests that sweeping policy amendments will not be sufficient to bring about the local attention to change that is necessary in institutions like schools. What is necessary is a combination of progressive policy and more attention to localized research that allows for broad policies to be locally efficacious and relevant.

CARING RESEARCH METHODS IN PRACTICE

The Diversity Project

A growing group of researchers are employing the strategies of an action-oriented research methodology. One such example is the work in the San Francisco Bay Area of the Berkeley High School-based Diversity Project. Between 1996 and 2000, under the direction of former UC-Berkeley Professor Pedro Noguera, the project was a collaborative effort that included more than thirty teachers, students, parents, school board members, and university researchers.[21] As Noguera describes it:

We purposefully created a team including the various constituencies that make up the school because we wanted to ensure that our work would not contribute to further polarization. Our plan was to use findings generated from our research to guide and influence changes at the school.[22]

The project was initiated by a parent at Berkeley High School (BHS) with the aim of addressing persistent issues of racial inequality and disparate achievement for black and Latino/-a students. The logic behind using research to address this issue resided in the belief that the inquiry process itself could shed new light on ways to approach an issue that had become normalized at the school. For Noguera, this sort of collaborative research held the potential to do more than "document patterns of racial disparity," it stood to "bring about a change in student outcomes" by changing "the way in which people thought about racial patterns at the school."[23]

Four years later, the Diversity Project has not solved the issues of educational inequality at BHS, and no scaleable policy panacea has emerged from the data analysis. What has changed at BHS is the way that the least powerful groups participate in the direction of the school. Spurred on by the project's research, black and Latino/-a parents have become increasingly more organized around issues of educational opportunity. One organization, Parents of Children of African Descent (PCAD), used the project's research that showed high rates of failure in ninth-grade math to create a new course that supported these students. Their program proved largely successful and has worked to disrupt these previously accepted patterns of failure.[24]

The greatest strength of this approach to educational research is its tendency to create long-lasting collaborations because of its emphasis on developing caring relationships. This extended relationship shows a commitment to people rather than ideas and implies a stick-to-itiveness that is necessary for addressing the more complex problems of a school; this is particularly important when working to deconstruct problems that have been left unchallenged for decades. The other outcome of these types of extended collaborative research relationships is the democratization of the process. The sharing of the leadership responsibilities and the process has allowed BHS to continue the work long after the researchers are gone.[25]

THE LAAMP PROJECT

Another example of action-oriented research is the Los Angeles Annenberg Metropolitan Project (LAAMP). As a collaboration between UCLA's Institute for Democracy, Education, and Access (IDEA), and a local school district, LAAMP brought together a group of researchers to address a set of issues similar to those being addressed by Berkeley's Diversity Project. In an effort to address persistent rates of academic marginalization for black and Latino/-a students at Pacific Beach High School and districtwide, a group of university researchers, district-level officials, school officials, teachers, parents, and students collaborated on a multi-year research and equity project.

LAAMP situated its research methodology inside a framework that aimed to produce meaningful change while engaging in research that documented the process of school reform. Beginning in 1995, this work set up a series of inquiry groups as a way to start dialogue around issues of equity and access in the district, which was faced with the challenge of disrupting a bimodal school system. In effect, this meant addressing the fact that white and Asian students were finding high levels of success in the same school where high numbers of black and Latino/-a students were failing. Despite being inside the same school wall, this set of bimodel outcomes had become normalized across the district. Ultimately, the inquiry groups brought together parents, students, administrators, and school staff to discuss this pressing problem through a set of shared readings, and then used those discussions to conceive of ways to disrupt the issues of inequality. These inquiry groups were guided by "critical friends"—researchers and faculty from IDEA who helped give the participants a language for confronting these issues in productive ways.[26] As one elementary school teacher described it:

Inquiry has allowed me to reflect on my teaching practices with a group of teachers with whom I typically would not have the opportunity to sit and talk. . . . Topics of discussion centered around our school's two "essential questions": (1) "What can I do to ensure that the inequitable pattern of student achievement no longer exists?" and (2) "What can I do to ensure that there is student and parent voice in my classroom?"[27]

At the high school, the decision was made to also include students in the inquiry groups, further emphasizing the commitment to democratic participation in the school improvement efforts sparked by the project. To allow for more extended conversations, the project also researched the use of inquiry retreats; these were off-campus retreats where inquiry participants were able to dialogue and problem solve for lengthy periods of time.

Feeling like the project needed to have a more immediate impact on student learning, a classroom-based component was added in year three of the project. Beginning in 1997, a group of the university researchers from LAAMP partnered with a social studies teacher at Pacific Beach High School and began the Futures Project. From 1997–2001, the Futures Project gave year-round academic and social support to a cohort of 30 black, Latino/-a and Southeast Asian students from their 9th- through 12th-grade years.

By all predictive measures (i.e., standardized tests, socioeconomic status, race, and course enrollment), Futures students had mediocre prospects for completing high school, qualifying for entry into a four-year college, and suc-cessfully engaging in curricula leading to a baccalaureate degree.[28]

By providing students with additional support from the university research team, including access to summer research apprenticeship seminars at UCLA, this group of students was empowered to research and "challenge unjust policies and practices" that limit access for black, Latino/-a and other nonwhite student groups.[29] Over the course of the four years, the success of these students became a powerful counter-narrative, stimulating important conversations about the possibilities for groups that had traditionally failed at Pacific Beach High School. By the end of the four years, 29 of the 30 Futures participants graduated from high school, and 25 of them gained acceptance to four-year universities.[30]

By 2002, both LAAMP and Futures were finished. The research that came out of these projects continues to influence state and national academic and policy circles. Equally as important, this research continued to impact the Pacific School District, most particularly Pacific Beach High School, long after the researchers left. The work that resulted from the employment of this caring research methodology created school and community cultures more attentive to issues of equity.

Like the work at Berkeley, participants are quick to say that plenty of work remains to be done in the district. However, they also point out that the research helped to develop mechanisms for public reporting and a language of social justice that has continued on in the work of progressive-minded students, teachers, and community based organizations.

INDIVIDUAL RESEARCHER AGENCY

To this point, I have described university-based research projects that have brought to bear a variety of resources on school sites. However, I would suggest that individual researchers can also positively impact schools by employing a research methodology that privileges cariño. My own work in an Oakland, California, high school is an example of the impact that one researcher can have with a research agenda focused on addressing a school problem while they are researching it.

From 1997–2001, I directed and researched the efficacy of a sports-based academic and social support program called the Lady Wildcat Basketball Program (LWBP). As a way of investigating the role of youth culture in the academic and social development of urban youth, I designed and implemented a year-round basketball program that provided its thirty participants with continual academic and social support. The research model focused on working collaboratively with the high school participants, parents, teachers, university undergraduate tutors, community members, and community organizations to develop a college going culture to counter the rampant academic failure in Oakland schools.

Using traditional qualitative research tools, the research documented the progress of the program through attention to four focal students; three of the focal students started the program as ninth-graders in summer of 1997, and the other began as a ninth-grader in 1998. With the research as the backdrop, the LWBP became the most successful in the city, producing: back-to-back-to-back league championships, a top-ten state ranking and a 100 percent graduation and college admissions rate for its four-year participants.[31]

The overwhelming success of the program led to the creation of a set of expectations programwide. Parent and student participants came to expect that the young people would receive year-round social and academic support that would facilitate their matriculation to a college or university. A powerful counter-narrative to the school's grade point average of 1.6 for black students, college attendance became matter-of-fact for LWBP participants and its 75 percent black participants. For the students, the program became a site of intervention in their academic and personal lives that rivaled the most supportive of family structures:

Sandra: For me, it's been like my family. If I have problems or anything I know who to go to. I never really worry anymore about getting stuck . . . you know about not being able to get through things because I know people here can help me and that they want to help me.

Lizette: This isn't really like a team to me. It's more like a family. We do everything together . . . eat, study, travel, play . . . everything . . . even cry. We've come so far in the last four years that no one can really understand us. People say all the time to us that they wish they had friends like we have in this program. They ask me how we do it. I tell them we work hard at it (laughing).[32]

Many parents felt much the same as their children about the impact of the program on participants' academic and social lives:

Monica: I've seen my daughter's sense of herself and responsibility to others grow. In this program she has been provided with a second family . . . a group at school that I like her to spend time with. A real good group of friends that guide her right.

Linda: She (Mika) has a place she feels she belongs. Academically she has never done better. She has friendships and seems to feel comfortable with herself. She seems more accessible than many teens—less rebellious and angry. The attention to team building has developed this.[33]

The impact of the LWBP ultimately began to reverberate throughout the athletic department at the school. With the continuous combination of academic and athletic success, the athletic director and assistant principal began asking the other athletic programs to implement similar academic support programs for their participants. The boys' basketball program in particular invested heavily in the academic support model of the LWBP and found increasing academic stability and growth for its participants.

In addition to a shift in the institutional culture of athletic participation, the program acted as a conduit for several of the university undergraduate tutors to enter coaching and teaching in urban schools. Several student participants also began pursuing university degrees and activities that will allow them to return to urban communities as teachers and community organizers.

The LWBP did not produce schoolwide change, and for some its success was at the price of a unilateral focus on the program rather than on a more rounded high school experience. Other critics lamented that the program bred a closed-door community, inaccessible to those who lacked athletic potential or desire. There is much to be learned from these critiques; however, the successes of the program stand, nonetheless, as testament to the potential of action-based educational research to create caring projects that have immediate and lasting positive impacts on those involved in the research. Although it is helpful to have the resources of a project the size of the Diversity or Futures Projects, the LWBP shows that individual researchers can also implement effective educational action research.

Implications for Educational Research Agenda

Valenzuela's articulation of the concept of cariño, or caring,[34] as a central tenant of good teaching seems to have shot wide of many education researchers working in poor and nonwhite urban schools. Too often, these research agendas take no responsibility for improving the quality of services at research sites and have even less commitment to improving the lives of the subjects that reside there. The challenge to the educational research community is to rethink the merits of business as usual research agendas, now disguised under more progressive and convoluted titles such as No Child Left Behind. This calls for educational researchers to develop lines of questioning and data collection methods that foreground a sense of cariño rather than striving to simplify data acquisition.

NOTES

1. Gilligan, C. (1982). *In a different voice*. Cambridge, MA: Harvard University Press; Noddings, N. (1992). *The challenge to care in schools: An alternative approach to education*. New York: Teachers College Press; Prillaman, R., & Eaker, D. (1994). *The tapestry of caring: Education as nurturance*. Norwood, NJ: Ablex.

2. Valenzuela, A. (1999). *Subtractive schooling: U.S.-Mexican youth and the politics of caring* (p. 22). New York: SUNY Press.

3. Valenzuela (1999), p. 22.

4. U.S. Department of Education. (2005). About the *Institute of Education Sciences. Retrieved November 23, 2005, from Federal Department of Education Web site*: http://www.ed.gov/about/offices/list/ies/index.html.

5. Coalition for Evidence-Based Policy. (2002). *Identifying and implementing educational practices supported by rigorous evidence* (pp. 1–28). Washington, DC: U.S. Department of Education.

6. Coalition for Evidence-Based Policy (2002), p. iv.

7. Coalition for Evidence-Based Policy (2002), p. iii.

8. Emerson, R. (1841). *Self-Reliance*. Retrieved July 20, 2005 from http://www.emersoncentral.com/selfreliance.htm.

9. Burkhardt, H., & Schoenfeld, A. (2003). Improving education research: Toward a more useful, more influential, and better-funded enterprise. *Educational Researcher, 32* (9), 3–14.

10. Burkhardt & Schoenfeld (2003), p. 5.

11. Burkhardt & Schoenfeld (2003), p. 5.

12. Burkhardt & Schoenfeld (2003), p. 5.

13. Burkhardt & Schoenfeld (2003), p. 5.

14. Burkhardt & Schoenfeld (2003).

15. Burkhardt & Schoenfeld (2003).

16. Burkhardt & Schoenfeld (2003), p. 5.

17. Tyack, D. (1974). *The one best system: A history of American urban education*. Cambridge, MA: Harvard University Press.

18. Kincheloe, J., & McLaren, P. (1998). Rethinking critical qualitative research. In N. Denzin & Y. Lincoln (Eds.), *Handbook of research on qualitative research* (pp. 260–299). Thousand Oaks, CA: Sage.

19. McLaren, P., & Giarelli, J. (1995). Introduction: Critical theory and educational research. (1995). In

P. McLaren & J. Giarelli (Eds.), *Critical Theory and Educational Research*. New York: SUNY Press.

20. Nader, L.(1999). *Up the anthropologist— Perspectives gained from studying up*. In D. Hymes (Ed.), *Reinventing anthropology* Ann Arbor: University of Michigan Press.

21. Noguera, P. (2004). *City schools and the American dream*. New York: Teachers College Press.

22. Noguera (2004), p. 67.

23. Noguera (2004), p. 67.

24. Noguera (2004), p. 80.

25. Noguera (2004).

26. Oakes, J., & Lipton, M. (2003). *Teaching to change the world*. 2nd edition. Boston: McGraw Hill.

27. Oakes & Lipton (2003), p. 385.

28. Collatos, A., et al. (2004). Critical sociology in K–16 early intervention: Remaking Latino pathways to higher education. *Journal of Hispanic Higher Education, 3* (2), p. 165.

29. Collatos et al. (2004).

30. Collatos et al. (2004).

31. Duncan-Andrade, J. (under contract). *What urban schools can learn from a successful sports program: Ballin', best friends, and breakin' cycles*. New York: Peter Lang.

32. Duncan-Andrade (under contract).

33. Duncan-Andrade (under contract).

34. Valenzuela (1999).

TANGLING THE KNOT WHILE LOOSENING THE STRINGS: EXAMINING THE LIMITS AND POSSIBILITIES OF URBAN EDUCATION FOR AFRICAN-AMERICAN MALES

Anthony L. Brown and Keffrelyn D. Brown

Since the early twentieth century, educators have focused on the challenges associated with schooling in large, metropolitan settings. Whether this discussion targeted "city" or "urban" schools, such work sought to untangle the difficulties associated with providing effective schooling for all students. Both historically and in the contemporary context, one method used to accomplish this task is to identify and target specific students most likely to experience problems within the urban school environment. Although numerous categories have emerged over the last century to define and name these students (e.g., problem student, incorrigible, backward, culturally deprived, at-risk), this process relies upon a standard of normality in which certain children and adolescents (as well as families and communities) become positioned as normal, while others are seen as at worst, deviant or as at best, different from this imagined norm. Though these efforts are intended to correct or change the social conditions related to urban schooling, they often lead to the creation of normalizing discourses that both create and constrain the possibilities of thought and action by ascribing fixed, essentialized meanings about particular students.

The purpose of this chapter is to examine how normalizing discourses operate within and limit the possibilities of urban education research and practice, particularly in relation to African-American male students who since the 1980s have been positioned as both a problem and as at-risk. Drawing from the insights of Michel Foucault's analytics of power, the first part of this chapter outlines a conceptual framework for understanding the idea of normalizing discourse. The second part of the chapter examines how urban education research normalizes the African-American male student as both a problem and as at-risk. The chapter concludes by considering the implications of normalizing discourse on future urban education research and practice.

POWER AND DISCOURSES OF NORMALITY

In *The History of Sexuality: An Introduction*, Michel Foucault advances a conception of power that acknowledges its integral relationship with discourse, or the rules and ways of thinking and speaking. Here, discourse serves as a tool whereby societal knowledge, coupled with power relations, emerge and make possible the creation of subject positions (individual/group identity) as well as the concomitant ways of thinking and acting associated with those created subjects. Normalization, or the process in which people, things, behaviors, and ways of thinking and being become positioned as fixed and knowable is one manifestation of Foucault's analytics of power.[1]

The form of power discussed by Foucault is not located in a central or sovereign location, rather it manifests in multiple relations deployed in complex, often strategic societal networks that guide the possibilities of conduct and outcome.[2] Power has a productive quality in that it allows for "active, material practice in constructing the world."[3] One productive aspect of power is how it operates in the constitution of subjects, or the way in which people understand and become defined by others, as well as themselves. Foucault is concerned with how beings come to life—that is, how they become constituted as living, breathing entities with essentialized characteristics. This process is situated in a historical understanding of how a person becomes first categorized as an individual, marked by and attached to his or her own individuality, who then later embodies a self that is imposed by a law of truth that he or she is bound to recognize and acknowledge.[4]

That both the subject and others recognize and understand the subject through specific societal markers is a fundamental aspect of productive power relations that make normalizing discourses possible.

Within education research, discourses of normalization generally refer to how particular individuals or groups of students become positioned and understood by themselves and others, with a particular focus on marking those values and beliefs that differentiate between the normal and the abnormal.[5] While these works typically bound the research inquiry within the confines of schools and/or classrooms, the processes and knowledge that inform the construction of subjects circulates across sites outside of the conveniently bounded school or classroom space. Often in education research what constitutes normal becomes juxtaposed against what is considered abnormal or deviant. Within these educational settings it is assumed that understanding normalcy and deviance relies on relational thinking, as one cannot understand what is abnormal or deviant without first having a notion of what is normal.

In this chapter, the idea of normalizing discourse moves in a somewhat different direction from the way it is typically discussed in education research. Rather than focusing on the relational way in which some people and things get positioned as normal or abnormal, this chapter considers how normalizing discourses constitute particular subject positions (e.g., good teacher; bad parent; African-American males),[6] as well as how these positions become recognized as fixed, knowable, and fully understandable. These entities become fixed, or essentialized in relation to how they are discussed, recognized, and understood by others, often through: (1) populational reasoning that uses statistics to divide, classify, and understand the characteristics of groups,[7] and (2) the use of narratives, or what Homi Bhabha refers to as the "same old stories" told about these entities.[8] Normalizing discourses generally operate as unquestioned knowledge within a society and are presented in ways that assume common understanding over time and across wide groups of people.[9] In urban education research and practice, African-American males are often situated within normalizing discourses.

POWER, DISCOURSE, AND THE AFRICAN-AMERICAN MALE SUBJECT

Since the 1960s, urban education research has examined the challenges faced by African-American students. The 1980s ushered in a somewhat new concern: understanding and meeting the unique educational needs of African-American male students. For example, since this time there have been numerous books,[10] Congressional hearings,[11] and peer-reviewed articles focused on the African-American male student.[12] In addition, academic journals have devoted special volumes to the examination of black male students. In autumn, 1994, *The Journal of Negro Education* published a special volume, titled "Pedagogical and Contextual Issues Affecting African American Males in School and Society." In 2003, the *Urban Education* journal devoted two special volumes (July and September) on the challenges facing African-American male students.

How, then, does one go about examining the issues facing the black male in educational contexts? How is the African-American male subject constructed and understood across educational discourse? From what knowledge base does this work draw? Both sociological and educational research about African-American males has helped to construct a normalizing discourse about African-American male students. Throughout the early and mid-twentieth century, social science research explored three central themes that inform education discourses on the black male including their: (1) presumed lack of fathers and proper male role models,[13] (2)

(maladaptive) cultural adaptations in response to the larger social context,[14] and (3) material conditions in relation to other groups within the U.S. society (e.g., poverty, education).[15] Whereas this research suggested who the African-American male was and how he behaved,[16] it also made it possible to construct particular interventions fashioned specifically for this student, by explaining the condition or crisis he faced.

The following sections investigate how urban education research uses normalizing discourses by situating the black male student as an essentialized, fully knowable subject and then draws from this knowledge when developing unique interventions to meet his academic needs. This dual relationship does not have to occur in the context of any one piece of research to be considered a normalizing discourse and consequently is not presented in this paper in such a manner. In the discussion that follows, the authors present examples of the discourses deployed in urban education research that help to create the black male subject and later, how these same discourses get picked up by others when promoting specific educational interventions for these individuals. The first section explores how the African-American male subject is constituted through urban education research. The second section examines how these discourses get deployed in educational interventions for black male students.

CREATING THE AFRICAN-AMERICAN MALE SUBJECT

This process of creating the black male subject is often accomplished through the use of three types of rationales. On the basis of African-American males' presumed social status, identity construction, linguistic discourses, and styles of learning, these rationales are later used to justify the use of unique/alternative programs and curriculum and pedagogical strategies for these students. These rationales are: (1) statistical rationales, (2) behavioral rationales, and (3) cultural rationales.

When discussing the African-American male in research, authors typically use statistical evidence to illustrate the dire social conditions facing black males in the United States. This literature points to increased rates of homicide, homelessness, poor health (e.g., HIV/AIDS, drug addiction), incarceration and unemployment among African-American men.[17] In the specific case of urban education research, this strategy is employed to show the adverse circumstances faced by the African-American males in school, pointing to statistics that suggest black male students have high suspension, expulsion, and drop-out rates,[18] as well as disproportionately high placement in special education classes,[19] as well as high levels of illiteracy and academic underachievement.[20] This statistical strategy, although not unique to research on African-American males, is usually found in the opening sections of published work on this subject as a way to set up the relevance of the topic of study.[21]

Urban education research also draws on psychological rationales to explain the unique compensatory adaptations made by African-American males. Several scholars assert that African-American males have developed behavioral patterns to compensate for their psychological deficits, including, self-doubt, alienation, low self-esteem and distorted self-image.[22] Some researchers identify the following behaviors as characteristic of the urban African-American distorted male image: the "make one" image (i.e., fathering a child), "player of women" image (i.e., womanizing), and "take one" image (i.e., being tough or machismo).[23] James Patton argues that these behaviors are indicative of contemporary "nonfunctional" definitions of socialization and manhood.[24] Richard Majors and Jane Billson define these behaviors as *compulsive masculinity,* or typical black male masculine values that are reflected through "rigid prescrip-

tions for toughness, sexual promiscuity, manipulation, thrill-seeking, and a willingness to use violence to resolve interpersonal conflict."[25] Consequently, researchers claim that the African-American male establishes an African-American male behavioral and cultural norm that is antithetical and oppositional to mainstream models of behavior and interaction.[26] When this discourse is situated within a school context, researchers claim that African-American males form an *oppositional identity* or *cultural aversion* to learning that results in persistent levels of intellectual disengagement and academic underachievement. For example, Pedro Noguera highlights the need for policy interventions that address the problematic educational experiences of African-American males:

Institutionally, this may require programmatic interventions aimed at buffering and offsetting the various risks to which black males are particularly vulnerable. However, to be effective such initiatives must also involve efforts to counter and transform cultural patterns and what Ogbu (1987) has called the "oppositional identities" adopted by black males that undermine the importance they attach to education.[27]

Here, Noguera illustrates one common premise of education interventions for black males—the belief that such undertakings must specifically combat and reverse the problematic, self-imposed behaviors of these children and youth.

Cultural rationales focus on the cultural and linguistic differences of African-American males, suggesting that teachers implement pedagogical practices that build off these differences. What separates a cultural rationale from a psychological rationale is the specific attention given to speech, language, and discourse to explain the distinctiveness of African-American male students. Much of this work is premised on previous scholarship that suggests the African-American community has acquired unique and distinct discourse practices.

Several scholars have argued that schools need to understand the acculturated experiences of African-American children and implement strategies conducive to their unique linguistic discourse.[28] For example Peter Murrell points out that:

Discourse practices and the communicative features within the African American community, particularly the powerful oral traditions, can serve an important role in the educative process.[29]

This perspective suggests that through the use of African-American discourse practices teachers can promote conceptual learning in literacy. Since the 1960s, researchers have examined the verbal games and exchanges that occur between African-American males such as "jonin'" and "playing the dozens."[30] "Jonin'" and "playing the dozens" are rapid-fire, playful verbal contests between African-American males in which the goal is to develop clever metaphors that signify elements of truth, myth, and hyperbole. While stating that he does not condone the negative aspects these communication styles often employ, Jawanza Kunjufu adds, "[I]f we want to save black boys, we must transfer their cultural strengths into the classroom experience."[31] Accomplishing this, however, is not an easy task.

It is not uncommon for urban education research to show how culturally specific forms of communication between African-American male students is both unrecognized and underutilized in the traditional school setting. For example, when discussing African-American students generally and black males in particular, Peter Murrell points out that "teacher preparation programs lack access to pedagogical expertise drawn from the culture, language, and history of African Americans."[32] Murrell suggests that this lack of specific cultural knowledge about the black male places this student at a severe learning disadvantage. In addition, when drawing from his research with preadolescent African-American males, Jabari Mahiri suggests the

need for "approaches that schools can take to better reflect and accommodate the unique ways that literate behaviors and literacy skills are developed and practiced in a communicative style that is culturally based," because "the language uses . . . observed among the boys [African-American males in the study] are strikingly different from the passive transmission model of learning that is commonly employed in mainstream school literacy efforts."[33] The research from Murrell and Mahari imply that in order to close any potential cultural gap or incongruence between African-American male students and school knowledge, teachers need to scaffold instruction in relation to the *specific* ways that black American males communicate.[34]

In relation to the above statistical, psychological, and cultural rationales, who then is the African-American male? How do these discourses constitute his subjectivity? While statistical rationales drawn from census data render the black male as at-risk and endangered, these discourses also situate him as a problem that requires urgent and immediate intervention. Psychological rationales suggest that because of his social reality, the black male possesses a distorted and abnormal sense of self. Finally, cultural rationales position the African-American male as verbally gifted, poetic, and metaphorically clever. These gifts emerge in relation to the everyday realities and experiences faced by black males, as well as the cultural legacy of the larger African-American community.

EDUCATION INTERVENTIONS FOR THE AFRICAN-AMERICAN MALE

Recognizing the material challenges facing African-American males as a result of centuries of discrimination, political violence, and oppression, as well as the perennial struggle for equitable education opportunities in the United States, researchers during the 1980s began to develop education interventions specifically for these students. That these interventions relied upon existing perspectives on what constituted the African-American male is evident in the solutions they offered. As a result of the statistical, psychological, and cultural rationales advanced in urban education research on black males, the education community is given a normalizing frame to see, talk about, and—ultimately—act on this subject. The next section examines some of the popular interventions proposed for African-American male students.

Education interventions proposed for African-American males have been situated both within and outside of the school context, and many of the statistical, psychological, and cultural rationales outlined previously justify the kinds of interventions offered. When discussing general education interventions proposed for African-American males, Noguera points out:

[T]he common theme underlying each of these initiatives is an assumption that the needs of black males can best be served through efforts specifically targeted at them, even if those efforts require isolating black males in order to apply the intervention.[35]

One intervention for African-American males that has received considerable attention is the creation of rites of passage and mentor programs.

The goal of rites of passage and mentor programs is to provide guidance for black males as they transition into manhood. Rites of passage programs utilize similar Afro-centric principles and pedagogies to develop the appropriate behaviors of African-American males. These programs are designed to combat the unhealthy behaviors of African-American males— such as drug abuse, violence, and gang activity.[36] These programs also assume that when students are provided pedagogies that speak to their concerns, their self-confidence and pride increases, thus leading to heightened levels of academic success.[37] Mentoring programs, on the

other hand, often vary across settings. For example, the 100 Black Men mentor program expands the traditional one-on-one mentoring by utilizing groups to facilitate their mentees' goals.[38] Other mentor programs, such as Project 2000, arose out of the belief that black boys needed more extensive opportunities to work directly with black male adults in school settings. About these programs, Spencer Holland states, "[T]he primary objective of the program is to provide positive adult male role models, particularly African-American men, in the daily life of African-American boys."[39]

In terms of classroom strategies, one of the earliest attempts in the mid-1980s to address the expressive discourse or learning style of African-American males came from the observations of Jawanza Kunjufu. From these observations, Kunjufu found that African-American males possess a unique style of expression when playing the dozens that could be transferred to the classroom. He asserts that through these activities, black males possess the following linguistic strengths: (1) quick thinking skills, (2) rhythmic understanding, (3) expansive vocabulary, and (4) public speaking potential. Kunjufu also emphasizes the need for teachers to understand the various expressive patterns of African-American boys, but further suggests that educators need to channel these strengths into more positive academic activities, such as spelling bees, spelling through rhyming and debates.[40] Likewise, Janice Hale-Benson argues that black males possess unique learning styles that should be accounted for when trying to improve academic achievement. She argues that teachers and schools must acknowledge that black males and black children have unique cultural orientations that are generally people-oriented, feeling-oriented, and non-verbal.[41]

Murrell also focuses on the unique discourses of African-American males. He argues that teachers who acquire more knowledge of African-American male cultural expression can more effectively address these students' educational concerns. Murrell asserts that *responsive teaching* identifies the specific speech activities that promote the development of African-American males, as well as assist in their academic achievement. According to Murrell, these speech activities "frame the discourse" within which African-American males routinely operate. These include: (1) a question-posing, teacher-challenging approach; (2) a preference for request-for-information teacher inquiries; (3) an eagerness to show off the information they possess; (4) a penchant for extended application; and (5) a preference for "getting over" rather than admitting ignorance.[42]

Relating discourse with athletics, Mahiri found that the linguistic discourse of African-American males could also be identified in sports activities such as basketball. Mahiri argues that when African-American males play basketball, they convey a set of complex literacy discourses that requires them to manipulate discrete elements of text. He calls these ways of communicating as the *discourse of basketball*, which refers to specific language terms, cognitive images, and interactional modes of speech associated with the game of basketball. For Mahiri the discourse of basketball takes place on and off the basketball court and involves topics, discussions, literacy, and analysis of several elements of the game, such as actual play, college and professional statistics, and the detailed and analytical literacy used to understand basketball video games. Mahiri goes on to suggest that because basketball has high motivational value for black boys, incorporating the discourse of basketball into classroom pedagogy will motivate these students to engage in literacy learning and improve their overall academic achievement.[43]

Another common intervention for black males is the development of African-American male immersion schools.[44] The development of all-male academies is premised on three core beliefs about the black male: (1) they have no adequate role models, (2) they live in absent-father homes, and (3) they suffer from feelings of inadequacy and low self-esteem and consequently engage in compensatory masculine behaviors. To address these concerns, all-male academies ideally would hire black male teachers who would act as role models. In addition, these schools would provide alternative curricular programs that combat and challenge the maladaptive student behavior. Although in recent discussions, immersion schools have received less attention because of legal constraints, education researchers and practitioners have continued to discuss the need for gender-specific education for African-American males.[45]

As the previous section illustrates, intervention arguments for African-American males are generally guided by a fixed conceptual reasoning about the cultural and psychological contexts of these individuals' lives. While it is for certain that many African-American males share these contexts, across educational literature it is common to find interventions that position African-American males as a homogeneous group. To this extent, we suggest that rationales used to explain the social and educational lives of black boys, coupled with arguments made for intervening on them, unintentionally help to reproduce a normalizing discourse that fastens in place how one can conceptualize and act on behalf of African-American male students.

CONCLUSION

The previous discussion illustrates how normalizing discourses operate in urban education research focused on African-American male students. Normalizing discourses help construct a particular subject—in this case the African-American male—in a way that frames the possible ways of looking at, understanding, and ultimately intervening on his behalf. Returning to Foucault's analytics of power, normalizing discourse is a power relationship that relies on the circulation of multiple discourses and relationships (e.g., social science research, urban education research, social and material realities, and cultural-historical practices) that converge and make possible the creation of people, things, and ways of thinking and being. Concerning power, Foucault states:

[It] must be understood in the first instance as the multiplicity of force relations immanent in the sphere in which they operate and which constitute their own organization; as the process which, through ceaseless struggles and confrontations, transforms, strengthens, or reverses them; as the support which these force relations find in one another; and lastly, as the strategies in which they take effect, whose general design or institutional crystallization is embodied in the state apparatus, in the formulation of the law, in the various social hegemonies.[46]

Here, "[p]ower is everywhere; not because it embraces everything, but because it comes from everywhere."[47] This suggests that power relations are necessary and inevitable, as Foucault argues, "[a] society without power relations can only be an abstraction."[48]

Power relations become evident in the research and intervention process undertaken by social scientists and educators who, both in the past and present, attempt to address the adverse material conditions facing the African-American male. While it is clear that, given the sociopolitical circumstances facing this subject, such work seemed (and perhaps, continues to seem) necessary, this work relies on past historical and empirical discourses that tend to position the African-American male as essentially endangered and in crisis. And while for the most part, there has been a shift away from positioning the black male as innately deviant, culturally deprived, and responsible for his own condition, discourses about his subjectivity fashion him as fundamentally at-risk and culturally homogenous even when theorizing about him from a cultural difference perspective

(e.g., culturally distinct patterns of behavior) or through a structural analysis (e.g., addressing material realities created by institutional practices).

The concerns raised in this chapter are not novel. During the early twentieth century, black scholar Alain Locke challenged intellectual perspectives that essentialized what constituted African Americans, as well as how to best meet their educational needs. This prominent African-American thinker took a lead in questioning the then popular belief that race and culture were innately determined. Locke's insistence that "race operates as tradition, as preferred traits and values" indicates some agreement with the belief that social reality helps to shape African-American culture and behavior. However, Locke's concern that cultural explanations for behavior might lead to essentializing discourses that overly determine the constituted black subject is implied in his comments about these intellectual explanations.[49] Locke cautions in this regard, "[b]ut a school of thought or art or social theory that lays claim to totalitarian rectitude must, I think, be challenged."[50]

Challenging potential normalizing discourses is a necessary activity in any society concerned with the effects of power relations. Since power relations are inevitable in society but do not possess any predetermined, specific configuration, the impetus for interrogating existing relations of power through "analysis, elaboration, and bringing into question"[51] how these relationships operate becomes the task of its citizens. In the case of urban education research, this chapter has tried to question the role normalizing discourses play in creating a seemingly static, knowable African-American male subject who requires a particular kind of education intervention. What this work points to are the unintended consequences that emerge when trying to change and address the material, everyday realities facing black men and boys. Since the

1990s, urban education theorists have illuminated the potential unintended effects of normalizing discourse on African-American males in urban education research.[52] These authors suggest the need to move beyond perspectives that essentialize or offer generalized prescriptions for how to work with these individuals. Additionally, normalizing discourses also make it difficult to address the challenges facing black males who do not fall within the typical, or "same old stories"[53] told and understood about them as a collective group. James Earl Davis states:

Not all Black boys are the same. This simple point is not an obvious one given most of the discussions about the so-called Black boy problem in American schools. But where are the high-achieving African-American boys? It is apparent from the national conversation on troubled boyhood that the inclusion of high-achieving Black boys' experiences muddles the discussion . . . Racism, stereotypes, lower expectations, and pervasive peer and popular culture define the "other" boyhood crisis that many Black boys face daily.[54]

Additionally, Garrett Duncan suggests the need to listen more closely to the voices of African-American males to note the differences in their experiences and behaviors, even when these students appear to come from similar backgrounds.[55] Such an approach would help researchers, policy makers, and school personnel move away from simple, unquestioned perceptions of what it means to be black and male in U.S. schools and society.

Indeed, the proverbial tangled knot that researchers, policy makers, and educators attempt to untangle when addressing the material conditions and educational challenges faced by African-American males becomes more twisted and harder to unravel when normalizing discourses are taken into account. While this dilemma does not and should not debilitate the work of those concerned with the plight of African-American males, it does promise to make educational research and practice a more difficult, and clearly a less certain, task.

NOTES

1. Foucault, M. (1990). *The history of sexuality: An introduction.* New York: Vintage.

2. Foucault, M. (1983). Afterword: The subject of power. In H. Dreyfus & P. Rabinow (Eds.), *Michel Foucault: Beyond structuralism and hermeneutics* (2nd ed., pp. 208–226). Chicago: University of Chicago Press.

3. Popkewitz, T. (2000). Globalization/regionalization, knowledge, and the educational practices: Some notes on comparative strategies for educational research. In T. Popkewitz (Ed.), *Educational knowledge: Changing relationships between the state, civil society, and the educational community* (p. 16). New York: State University of New York Press.

4. Foucault (1983).

5. Ferguson, A. (2001). *Bad boys: Public schools in the making of masculinity.* Ann Arbor: University of Michigan Press; Goldstein, R. (2004). Who are our urban students and what makes them so "different"? In S. Steinberg & J. Kincheloe (Eds.), *19 urban questions: Teaching in the city* (pp. 41–51). New York: Peter Lang; Marsh, M. (2003). *The social fashioning of teacher identities.* New York: Peter Lang; Perry, P. (2002). *Shades of white: White kids and racial identities in high school.* Durham, NC: Duke University Press; Popkewitz, T. (1998). *Struggling for the soul: The politics of schooling and the construction of the teacher.* New York: Teachers College Press.

6. Hacking, I. (2002). *Historical ontology.* Cambridge, MA: Harvard University Press; Marsh (2003); Popkewitz (1998).

7. Popkewitz (1998).

8. Bhabha, H. (1994). *The location of culture.* London: Routledge.

9. Perry (2002).

10. Brown, M., & Davis, J. (2000). *Black sons to mothers: Compliments, critiques, and challenges for cultural workers in education.* New York: Peter Lang; Gibbs, J. (1988). *Young, black and male in America: An endangered species.* New York: Auburn House; Polite, V., & Davis, J. (1999). *African-American males in school and society: Practices & policies for effective education.* New York: Teachers College Press.

11. United States Commission on Civil Rights. (1991, March 19). *The crisis of the young African*

American male in the inner cities: Congressional Report 1.2: AF 8/v. 1.v. 2. Washington, DC: Government Printing Office.

12. Garibaldi, A. (1992). Educating and motivating the African-American male to succeed. *Journal of Negro Education, 61* (1), 4–11; Leake, D., & Leake, B. (1992). Islands of hope: Milwaukee's African American immersion schools. *Journal of Negro Education, 61* (1), 24–29.

13. Frazier, E. (1940). The Negro family and Negro youth, *Journal of Negro Education, 9* (3), 290–299.

14. Clark, K. (1965). *Dark ghetto: Dilemmas of social power*. New York: Harper & Row.

15. Moynihan, P. (1967). The Negro family: The case for national action. In R. Rainwater & W. Yancey (Eds.), *The Moynihan report and the politics of controversy* (pp. 47–132). Cambridge, MA: M.I.T.

16. Kelley, R. (1994). *Yo' mama's dysfunctional! Fighting the culture wars in America*. Boston: Beacon.

17. Gibbs (1988); Lee, C. *Empowering black males*. Available from http://www.ericfacility.net.

18. Lee (1991); Majors, R. (2001). *Educating our black children: New approaches*. New York: Routledge; Murrell, P. (1994). In search of responsive teaching for African American males: An investigation of students' experiences of middle school mathematics curriculum. *Journal of Negro Education, 63* (4), 556–569.

19. Murrell, P. (1993). Afrocentric immersion: Academic and personal development of African American males in public schools. In T. Perry & J. Fraser (Eds.), *Freedom's plow: Teaching in the multicultural classroom* (pp. 231–259). New York: Routledge; Murrell, 1994.

20. Slaughter-Defoe, D., & Richards, H. (1995). Literacy for empowerment: The case of black males. In V. Gadsen & D. Wagner (Eds.), *Literacy among African American youth: Issues in learning, teaching, and schooling* (pp. 125–147). Cresskill, NJ: Hampton; Holland, S. (1996). Project 2000: An educational mentoring and academic support model for inner-city African American boys. *Journal of Negro Education, 65* (3), 315–321; Lee, (1991); Reed, R. (1988). Education and achievement of young black males. In J. Gibbs (Ed.), *Young black, and male in America: An endangered species* (pp. 37–93). Westport, CT: Greenwood.

21. Holland (1996); Mahiri, J. (1994a). African American males and learning: What discourses in sports offer schooling. *Anthropology & Education Quarterly, 25* (3), 364–375; Murrell (1993).

22. Majors, R., & Billson, J. (1992). *Cool pose: The dilemmas of black manhood in America*. New York: Touchtone; Patton, J. (1995). The education of African American males: Frameworks for developing authenticity. *Journal of African American Men, 1* (1), 5–26; White, J., & Cone, J. (1999). *Black man emerging: Facing the past and seizing the future in America*. New York: Routledge.

23. Patton (1995); Oliver, W. (1989). Black males and social problems: Prevention through Afrocentric socialization. *Journal of Black Studies, 20* (1), 15–39.

24. Patton (1995).

25. Majors & Billson (1992), p. 34.

26. Majors & Billson (1992); Noguera, P. (2003). The trouble with black boys: The role and influence of environmental and cultural factors on the academic performance of African American males. *Urban Education, 38* (4), 431–459; Patton (1995).

27. Noguera (2003), p. 437.

28. Kunjufu, J. (1986). *Countering the conspiracy to destroy black boys* (Vol. 2). Chicago: African American Images; Mahiri, J. (1994b). Discourses in sports: Language and literacy features of preadolescent African American males in a youth basketball program. *Journal of Negro Education, 60* (3), 364–375.

29. Murrell (1993), p. 247.

30. Kochman, T. (1967). Rapping in the ghetto. In L. Rainwater (Ed.), *Soul* (pp. 51–76). New York: Aldine; Liebow, E. (1967). *Tally's corner: A study of Negro streetcorner men*. Boston: Little, Brown and Company.

31. Kunjufu (1986), p. 16.

32. Murrell (1994), p. 556.

33. Mahiri (1994a), p. 306.

34. Murrell (1994); Mahiri (1994a).

35. Noguera, P. (1996). Responding to the crisis confronting California's black male youth: Providing support without furthering marginalization. *Journal of Negro Education, 65* (2), 221.

36. Alford, K., McKenry, P., & Gavazzi, S. (2001). Enhancing achievement in adolescent black males: The rites of passage link. In R. Majors (Ed.), *Educating our black children: New directions and radical approaches* (pp. 141–156). New York: Falmer Routledge.

37. Fashola, O. (2003). Developing the talents of African American male students during non-

school hours. *Urban Education, 38* (4), 390–430; Watts, R., & Jagers, R. (Eds.). (1997). *Manhood development in urban American communities.* New York: Hayworth; Warfield-Coppock, N. (1992). The rites of passage movement: A resurgence of African-centered practices for socializing African American youth. *Journal of Negro Education, 61* (4), 471–482.

38. Dortch, T. (2000). *The miracles of mentoring: How to encourage and lead future generations.* New York: Doubleday/Broadway Books.

39. Holland (2000), p. 317.

40. Kunjufu (1986).

41. Hale-Benson, J. (1986). *Black children: Their roots, culture, and learning styles* (2nd ed.). Baltimore, MD: John Hopkins.

42. Murrell (1994).

43. Mahiri (1994b).

44. Leake & Leake (1992).

45. Cooper, R., & Jordan, W. (2003). Cultural issues in comprehensive school reform. *Urban Education, 38* (4), 380–397.

46. Foucault (1990), pp. 92–93.

47. Foucault (1990), p. 93.

48. Foucault (1983), pp. 222–223.

49. Locke, A. (1968). *The new negro.* New York: Athneum.

50. Locke, A. (1989). Who and what is "Negro"? In L. Harris (Ed.), *The philosophy of Alain Locke: Harlem Renaissance and beyond* (p. 211). Philadelphia: Temple University.

51. Foucault (1983).

52. Davis, J. (2003). Early schooling and academic achievement of African American males. *Urban Education, 38* (5), 515–537; Duncan, G. (2002). Beyond love: A critical race ethnography of the schooling of adolescent males. *Equity & Excellence, 35* (2), 131–143; Gordon, E.T., Gordon, E.W., & Nembhard, J. Social science literature concerning African American men. *Journal of Negro Education, 63* (4), 508–531; Noguera (1996).

53. Bhabha (1994).

54. Davis (2003).

55. Duncan (2002).

MULTISITED ETHNOGRAPHIC APPROACHES IN URBAN EDUCATION TODAY

Greg Dimitriadis and Lois Weis

CULTURE AND EDUCATION

Studying out-of-school culture is nothing new. A long and venerable history of work in the "anthropology of education" contextualizes the practice of education in specific cultural sites and settings.[1] Formal schooling is seen as one tool of socialization, one way culture is transmitted from generation to generation. But, as Spindler and others point out, it is not the only such tool. Older and younger people engage in multiple practices of enculturation—for example, through storytelling or dinner table talk—that have critical educative implications. This work has been largely comparative. George and Louise Spindler, for example, studied several different Native American groups in the United States, highlighting the "cultural variations that mark education in every society in relationship to every other."[2] Much of this work has been concerned with uncovering cultural mismatches between home and school settings. The goal, here, is to help educators in "overcoming defenses by bringing unconscious motivations, assumptions, orientations to conscious awareness,"[3] ultimately helping to eliminate racial bias in education through radical contextualization and cultural sensitivity.

Such work relies, of course, on specific ideas or theories about culture itself—namely, that culture is a bounded object of study and can be understood as such; in other words, that it is discrete and can be contained. Yet, notions of cultural containment belie the contemporary reality of migration, mediation, and complex cultural transactions so much a part of the quotidian for many youth in the United States and beyond. Culture—as so much work in globalization has made clear—is interconnected, in transit, the result of various often unequally situated and disjunctive flows and trajectories.[4] As Eisenhart argues, these new tensions around culture have helped to muddle debates around ethnographic methodology.[5] If culture can no longer be contained in discrete sites and settings, the traditional tools of qualitative inquiry need re-thinking.

Multisited ethnography offers a key response to this muddling that Eisenhart highlights.[6] Doing multisited ethnography, according to George Marcus, means "tracing and describing the connections and relationships among sites previously thought incommensurate."[7] The multisited ethnographer must, in any project, "keep in view and mind two or more ethnographically conceived sites juxtaposed."[8] By way of direction, Marcus offers the diction: "follow the people," "follow the thing," "follow the metaphor," "follow the plot, story, or allegory," "follow the life or biography," and "follow the conflict."[9] All imply different starting points for tracing connections across and between different sites—individual biographies, objects, and/or stories. As he notes,

Multisited research is designed around chains, paths, threads, conjunctions, or juxtapositions of locations in which the ethnographer establishes some form of literal physical presence, with an explicit, posited logic of association or connection among sites that in fact defines the argument of the ethnography.[10]

In other words, the researcher defines a question and then draws links intuitively across different, tangible sites. This has resulted in ethnographic work in anthropology that has followed the same population across locations, as in, say, nurses traveling between India and the United States, or software developers from Ire-

land engaging in work for companies in the United States.[11] In education, it has meant studies like Eisenhart and Finkel's *Women's Science*,[12] which looked at the multiple sites (e.g., alternative high schools, classes, and local activist groups) where women learn to become scientists.

Yet, multisited ethnography is not simply "a set of *methods* that are very specifically prescriptive for the conduct of fieldwork."[13] It has also challenged us to re-think our *research imaginary* more broadly, implying a kind of self-reflexivity about how particular ethnographic sites are imagined, how objects are delimited. Marcus argues, in fact, that multisited ethnographies can be constructed around a single, strategically selected locale. Such ethnographies treat "the system as background," although they try not to lose sight of the fact that "it is integrally constitutive of cultural life within the bounded subject matter."[14] As a key example of this kind of reconfigured multisited ethnography, Marcus offers the well-known school ethnography, *Learning to Labor*. Although the primary site for this research is a single school, Willis juxtaposes and explores (largely through self-report data) a small group of working-class lads, as well as working-class conformist youth across sites including school, the shop floor, home, the dance hall and local bars. All sites are put into dialogue with one another in order to explain how class structures are reproduced and validated through and in everyday cultural practices. Willis makes every effort to explain larger issues of class through his rich ethnographic description of young people—though, as Marcus points out, without similar immersion in multiple sites, Willis risks reproducing "canned visions of capitalism," a point we will return to toward the end of this chapter.[15]

In sum, multisited ethnographic work—even work focused on a single, strategically selected locale—has challenged us to re-think fundamentally our research imaginary in school research in ways that push the borders of the home-school nexus. Here, we interrogate two sites that resonate deeply in contemporary ethnographic research in education—community-based learning sites and popular cultural texts. We call attention to the new critical energies at work in the sites and the particular challenges they offer contemporary education researchers. Both are sites where young people's lives are being explored in ways that look beyond simple home–school binaries. Both also reflect our own particular research agendas.[16] As such, we explore them both for their own unique potential as well as the ways in which they are illustrative of a larger set of issues, hoping to wedge open discussion and broader theoretical concerns. We begin with a look at community-based organizations and safe spaces.

COMMUNITY-BASED LEARNING SETTINGS AND SAFE SPACES

Shirley Brice Heath's *Ways with Words* is, of course, a germinal text in the area of home/school connections.[17] Here, Heath looks at home language practices across three differently situated communities, noting which kinds of practices prepare students in what kinds of ways for success or failure in school. Different students possess different kinds of literacy skills, rooted in home practices that are differentially valued or validated in school. Focused on the variable nature of literacy, this work opens up a range of questions and concerns related to language, learning practices, and specific institutions, including cross-case comparisons between and across dominant and non-dominant learning settings.

Heath and her colleagues have extended this work over the past several years to focus on what they call community-based organizations (CBOs), highlighting the ways in which community is the "third area beyond school and family" for school

researchers.[18] Focusing on the organizations young people identified as most successful, and deploying what they call "guerilla ethnographers," Heath and McLaughlin spent five years looking at sixty different organizations, gathering data from 24,000 youth in predominantly low-income and marginalized community settings across the country.[19] This research serves to establish the critical importance of these sites as well as identify key characteristics of the most successful such organizations,[20] stressing the key notion that CBOs are not bureaucratic institutions, as (typically) are schools, but emergent and unpredictable ones. Such institutions draw on the strengths of particular young people, working with particular adults, on specific tasks, with real risks and real consequences in specific settings. CBOs typically offer young people the opportunity to work through real-world activities that demand their full participation. As Heath notes:

Community organizations that create positive learning environments exhibit these same features. Work takes place within a "temporal arc," with phases that move from planning and preparation for the task ahead; to practice and deliberation along with ample trial-and-error learning, to final intensive readiness for production or performance; and, ultimately, to a culminating presentation of the work that has gone before.[21]

Community-based organizations may include arts-based activities, such as theater, dance, and music,[22] as well as sports-based activities, such as gymnastics, baseball, and basketball.[23] For example, while putting on a drama to raise money for a trip, young people have to decide (among other things) who will design the costumes; who will design the sets; who will act, write, advertise, and manage the finances; and so forth. These activities unfold under the guiding hand of older, better skilled community workers, or "wizards,"[24] individuals who see young people as resources to be employed, not problems to be managed.[25]

By way of example, Heath looked at the everyday talk of a coach (Victor Cage) and his community center based basketball team (the Dynamos) as they worked through their season. Here the coach modeled conditional "what if" phrases as they worked to co-create a set of flexible rules and strategies to accomplish specific tasks. This kind of work depends on "carrying distributed knowledge, shared skills, and discourse patterns through a project over a period of time."[26] As Heath notes, the team internalized a set of rules that they were able to adapt flexibly when the coach transgressed them. Ultimately, the team created a "sense of place with a keen notion of the role of rules and ways of planning and talking about relations between rule setting and rule breaking."[27]

This work has been marked by a split between school and nonschool settings. According to Heath, schools often prefigure relevant curricula based on simple notions of identity, assuming, for example, that young people desire activities defined by adults as ethnically or culturally relevant. According to Heath and McLaughlin, CBOs thrive on the complex, already existing social networks of young people—on their ability to mobilize specific sets of personal resources to deal with concrete concerns and challenges. Lived identities in these organizations, as Heath and McLaughlin argue, are "complex, and embedded in achievement, responsibility, and . . . immediate support network[s][28] in ways that exceed the easy delineation of (multi)cultural borders and boundaries." There is nothing predicable or stable about the ways ethnicity and identity play out in these organizations, nor do these organizations make a priori assumptions about young people and culture.[29]

Community organizations, particularly those in which the arts are intensely integrated, generate unexpected contexts and collaborations that often add up to some outcomes that are tough to achieve elsewhere, blurring lines of racial and ethnic division and crossing linguistic barriers.[30]

For the most part, then, Heath and her colleagues have not situated their research in schools. One gets the sense—with only occasional exceptions[31]—that schools are a vestige of another era and that for disenfranchised youth, in particular, the most interesting and important kind of education is happening outside of school. They sum up with the observation, "Schools are experienced as hostile and demeaning environments where neither inner-city youth nor their interests are taken seriously."[32] Furthermore, schools are no longer training youth for the kinds of flexible problem-solving activities that are so necessary for job readiness in the information age. Such work, again, is happening in community-based organizations.

Although less focused on skills, similar ideas have been developed by Michelle Fine, Lois Weis, and colleagues on safe spaces.[33] Not marked by the same split between in-school and out-of-school settings, Fine and Weis' work has focused on the imaginative resources young people use to carve out spaces for themselves in different settings, both inside and outside of school. Young people, they argue, carve these safe spaces in a variety of sites—in school and out of school—creating "counterpublics," to use Nancy Fraser's term, ironically out of the very exclusionary practices of the public sphere.

These spaces are not just a set of geographical/spatial arrangements but, rather, theoretical, analytical, and spatial displacements—a crack, a fissure, a fleeting or sustained set of commitments. Individual dreams, collective work, and critical thoughts are smuggled in and reimagined.[34]

Refusing the school–non-school binary, these authors explore how young people take up public spaces[35] and how within the context of great poverty and the dismantling of the public safety net, they carve out private ones.

By way of example, the authors juxtapose two sites: Molly Olga, a neighborhood arts center in Buffalo, and an Orisha spiritual community in New York City.[36] In the first site, a diverse group of participants meet in an urban community to work under the tutelage of its director, Molly Bethel. Molly Olga's poly-vocal feel encourages people who do not normally interact with each other—from poor black youth to white upper-middle-class housewives—to discuss common concerns. It is a thriving "community of difference" constituted through aesthetic practice. In the second example, the authors highlight the micro-moves of a "self-consciously heterogeneous spiritual community" in New York City as participants invent and reinvent religious practices of the African and Cuban Diaspora, making them relevant for broad groups of urban dwellers. In both cases, the authors highlight "spaces in which 'difference' signals interest, engagement, commitment, and opportunity" that look beyond the "walls of school."[37]

Additional work focuses more specifically on school culture. Weis and Fine, for example, juxtapose the powerful day-to-day work within two in-school sites—an abstinence-based sex education program and a de-tracked and racially integrated World Literature class—both located in Northeastern urban schools.[38] In the first example, the authors demonstrate how the program participants stretch beyond the official intent of the program (abstinence only) to "traverse a variety of subjects regarding race, gender, sexuality, and men." Under the guidance of the program's leader, Doris Carbonell-Medina, this weekly meeting becomes a safe space for these young women as they discuss salient issues in honest and personally meaningful ways. In the second example, the authors show how a World Literature class can be a powerful space in which to engage questions of identity and difference. They write:

Students have learned to engage in this space, for 45 minutes a day, with power, "difference," and a capacity to re-vision. Some with delight and some still disturbed, they know that everyone will get the chance to speak and be heard."[39]

The authors go to great lengths to trace the discourse as it evolves over a year-long period as students discuss books like *Of Mice and Men, Two Old Women,* and *La Llorana:*

Rather than assuming a priori parameters, work on community-based organizations and "safe spaces" raises important questions as to where "education" is happening today. Juxtaposing in-school and out-of-school sites, this work powerfully reframes contemporary educational questions and agendas. For Heath, McLaughlin, and colleagues, this has meant an elaborated discussion of what kinds of "skills" are fostered in these sites, and how these skills translate across the kinds of tasks most associated with our contemporary information age. For Weis, Fine, and colleagues, this has meant looking at how a variety of young people "homestead," or claim authentic and meaningful spaces and identities within a variety of sites, both in school and out of school. This work intentionally de-centers the home–school binary in educational research, evoking the myriad of ways in which "community" is a "third area" of study.[40]

POPULAR CULTURE

Further pushing the question of contemporary out-of-school curricula, recent research has stretched well beyond the home–school binary in its growing focus on popular cultures and technologies. Paralleling research on alternative learning sites, this work has challenged our assumptions about what counts as educational curricula or texts for young people. Indeed, as a range of scholars have argued, popular culture increasingly offers a terrain upon which young people are navigating their lives and meeting their everyday needs and concerns.[41] These cultural texts are proliferating in complex ways in and through video, film, television, and music technologies, as well as computers and the internet—all of which have increasingly complex relationships to and with each other.

Recent work on popular culture and education has looked at how young people have used these texts in practice or performance.[42] David Buckingham and Julian Sefton-Green, for example, have treated media literacy as a kind of symbolic social action. Their work has explored how young people mobilize popular texts as discursive resources in particular and meaningful ways, using them to negotiate senses of self and community. In *Cultural Studies Goes to School*,[43] the authors offer several case studies of young people using the media to create personally relevant texts—from magazines to photographs to popular music—as they "author" their lives, so to speak. They write,

In adopting 'critical' positions in discourse, in staking out their tastes and identities, and in intervening directly in popular cultural forms, these [youth] are actively defining themselves in relation to wider social, cultural, and ideological forces.[44]

This is a less defensive approach than are many current media literacy approaches.[45] In fact, Buckingham has noted that this kind of work often invites problematic kinds of pleasures from students.[46] Even these—perhaps especially these—must be understood if we are to engage with the lives of young people in authentic ways.

Sefton-Green extends this work, focusing on the relationship between popular media culture, the arts, and the internet.[47] In *Young People, Creativity and New Technologies*, Sefton-Green gathers recent theoretical and empirical work "to describe the opportunities digital technologies offer for communicating, disseminating and making culture as well as acting as a vehicle for personal and collective self-expression."[48] Among other topics, contributors discuss multimedia memoirs, self-produced CD-ROMs, on-line school scrapbooks, and personal Web pages. These new and creative uses of information technology are part of a broader redefinition of youth culture that has implications for all manner of educational practice—from the classroom to the dance floor and beyond.[49]

More recently, scholars in education have moved toward less prefigured, ethnographic approaches that look at the ways young people construct identities through popular culture and their implications for school life.[50] For example, Dimitriadis's recent work looks at how young people construct notions of self, history, and place through their uses of hip-hop texts, focusing on how these young people use these texts in concert with—and in counter-distinction to—school texts. For example, Dimitriadis looked at the ways in which two teenagers constructed notions of a Southern tradition through their use of Southern rap texts; how young people constructed notions of history through viewing the film *Panther*, a film they connected to hip-hop culture more broadly; and how young people constructed powerful senses of self through talk about the life and death of icon Tupac Shakur. All are examples of popular culture's reach and power. He writes, "We see popular culture more and more, providing the narratives that young people are drawing on to deal with the issues and the concerns most pressing in their lives." He shows, "These investments played out in often unpredictable ways."[51]

Dolby and Yon have developed similar ethnographic projects in the field of education, though both have looked to settings outside the United States. Dolby,[52] in a particularly fascinating study, looks at how young people at a high school in South Africa (Fernwood High) negotiate ideas about race in the aftermath of apartheid. Here, music and fashion became ways to carve out ideas about being white, black, and colored, at a moment when a priori racial categories are called into question. These popular symbols circulated and were ascribed different meanings at different times. Rave music, for example, "is understood specifically as 'white' music. A colored student who listens to rave would be ostracized by her or his classmates, and seen as a threat to 'colored' identity."[53] In sum, she argues:

"Race" at Fernwood reinvents itself (as it does constantly) as a site of identification that takes its meaning, in large part, from affect and affective investments. Students are invested in the emotions of desire that surround consumptive practices, particularly the practices of global youth culture.[54]

Yon, in turn, looked at a multiethnic high school in Toronto (Maple Heights), focusing on the ways in which young people negotiate their day-to-day identities. Yon offers portraits of different young people and the creation of complicated identities through their investments in popular culture. He writes:

Many of the signs and symbols of the popular cultures of these youth, like dress codes and musical tastes, are racialized. This means that the signifiers of race can also change with the changing signs of culture and identity, and what it means to be a certain race is different from one context to the next.[55]

He offers several examples of young people constructing notions of self through popular culture. These include a Canadian-born black, a white youth who identifies with black culture, as well as a black immigrant from the Caribbean—all of whom use popular culture to negotiate and stake out particular senses of self.

In sum, Dimitriadis, Dolby, and Yon make it clear that we cannot understand young people's identities in predictable ways. More and more, as this work makes clear, we must ask ourselves what kinds of curricula—broadly defined—young people draw on to understand, explain, and live through the world around them. This is messy terrain, one that extends beyond a priori notions about identity often privileged by educators. As these authors make clear, the multiple uses to which popular culture is put challenge and belie easy notions of cultural identification. Young people in the United States and around the world are elaborating complex kinds of social and cultural identifications through music like hip-hop and techno in ways that challenge predictive notions about texts, practices, and identities. "The global context of popular culture," Dolby writes, is critical for "the marking of racialized borders, and for their subsequent displacement and rearrangement."[56]

NEW DIRECTIONS

As this research demonstrates, and as anthropologists have long noted, education takes place both within and beyond the boundaries of school. Today though, education is an increasingly emergent phenomenon, unfolding across numerous sites and settings with and in between multiple texts. It is the "in-between"—the moving back and forth between sites and texts—that increasingly defines our children's lives and cultural landscapes and must, therefore, define our research agenda.

Yet, multisited work in education has not, for the most part, explored these sites, literal or otherwise, as existing in dynamic interrelation to other sites in specific and particular ways. While we have many studies of single sites, we do not have a sense of how these sites are enmeshed in particular ways in complex webs of relationships for their participants. We have one kind of mapping here; one where sites take on meaning in the context of other isolated sites as well as self-report data on the backstage knowledge of participants. Missing, it seems, are more relational kinds of studies—studies that, for example to return to Marcus, "follow the people," "follow the biographies," or "follow the story" in complex and inevitably unpredictable ways.

Indeed, while Heath and McLaughlin have suggested looking away from traditional schools and focusing only on CBOs, there seems a danger of reifying these sites as objects of study. Just as *Learning to Labor* often reproduced canned ideas about capitalism, we are perhaps in danger here of reproducing clichés about what happens in schools if we rely only on participants' self-report data about these sites. Instead of turning away from the study of schools, we suggest figuring out, in particular and situated ways, the relationship *between* multiple sites—schools, community centers, job sites, and so forth—and the skills they encourage and enable for young people. This means actually doing the research cross-site in a way that we have not done before. Additionally, while Weis and Fine have included in-school and out-of-school sites in their work, there is a parallel danger of focusing on single-sited studies in isolation from one another, as Weis and Fine tend to do. While these authors have taken great pains to show internal dynamism around identity within these sites, we have little sense of how participants live their lives *across* and *between* sites. If identity is always an emergent construction, we need to understand more clearly how these identities play out in relation to and with each other in the space of the "in between."

Like work on CBOs and safe spaces, work on popular culture and education has overwhelmingly been single-sited. For example, studies by Dimitriadis, Dolby, and Yon focus on single settings—a community center and two high schools, respectively.[57] In each case we gain a clear picture of a particular educational site and a specific group of young people. In each of these cases, we are asked to expand our notion of education—where it happens and with what texts. Yet, we get little sense of how different sites—understood on their own terms—invite the working across that we discuss here. For example, while Dimitriadis talks about his participants' experiences in traditional schools, he relies largely on self-reported data rather than entering the school site first hand. In turn,

neither Dolby nor Yon look at young people's uses of these texts in ways that extend beyond school settings. Missing, it seems, is research that follows individuals and groups as they traverse a wide range of texts in different settings, and perhaps at different times of their life.

Re-engaging with the power and limitations of the work discussed throughout, we offer here a beginning set of imagined possibilities for engaging in the kind of ethnographic work discussed above. Ethnographies that recognize and take seriously into account the many sites of education can help to work against naturalized frames, categories and theories in education—offering an important advance in our thinking about youth and schooling. Indeed, we must be responsible for the questions we ask and stretch beyond the taken-for-granted categories and assumptions. There is no neutral terrain here. How we frame problems and objects of study can very well reproduce unfair power relationships in our work. With multisited ethnography, we can both de-naturalize our object of study and conduct powerful work in the field—a twin imperative for our continued relevancy. We ask you, the reader, to imagine with us what such work might look like and invite continued discussion. Our list below, then, for imagined possibilities, is meant only as a beginning.

1. We begin by calling for more studies of different groups in ostensibly the same space. In other words, it is critically important that we understand how teen men and women appropriate an array of popular cultural texts and/or programs, for example. This project must be stretched to involve teen men and women of different races, ethnicities, sexualities and/or social class—all the time, following Heath, Dimitriadis, McCarthy, and others, questioning our a priori assumptions here. Understanding how different groups across and within race, for example, make meaning of texts or programs is an important project. We know from our own work that there is

no one African-American, for example, appropriation of a text. Rather, different groups *within* any given category, work, texts vary differently. This needs to be built within a new research imaginary.

2. As noted throughout, we would also encourage more studies of youth across spaces such as community centers and popular culture, as well as school, family, and so forth. Often we go into one such site, while ignoring all others, or rely upon self-reported data as to individual/group behavior in sites other than the one in which we are physically immersed. We have engaged in such single-site studies ourselves (Dimitriadis in community centers and with popular culture; Weis in community centers and schools) and understand full well the difficulties of following youth through varying zones of action. Nevertheless we would suggest that we must begin to do this work. This might involve a team of researchers, perhaps one person in the school, one in the families, and so forth. Again we understand full well the difficulties of establishing rapport and trust, even for one person, much less a team of people. But we would argue that we must begin to think along these lines in order to explore the range of action in youth's lives and urge others to join with us as we pursue these ideas.

These two suggestions are grounded largely in the above discussion. It is important to note, however, that multisited work has an important temporal and regional component, as well. As George Marcus notes, it gives us important ways to understand the often disjunctive and uneven distribution of social, cultural, and material imperatives.[58] Suggestions (3) through (5) offer ways to push further the important implications of multisited ethnography, in ways we have not yet discussed.

3. As we indicated throughout, we see great possibilities in "following the people" or "following the individual" across sites and texts. Most ethnographic studies, however, are inevitably done at a single point in time at a single site. While we learn a great deal from such studies, what we do not know is what happens to them after they leave these specific locations. Culturalist theoretical challenges, although important, do not enable us to probe the linkages between actual school experiences as explored by ethnographers, and life chances and choices in other sites. Thus, multisited work in education could powerfully be conducted over time as well as space. We have some examples of follow-up studies, such as Jay MacLeod's *Ain't No Makin' It*, Claire Wallace's *For Richer, For Poorer*, and Paul Willis' *Learning to Labor*. These studies, however, tend to be short-term follow-ups. Willis, for example, followed his subjects only briefly into the work force. Although we certainly understand why investigators do not engage in long-term follow-up studies, such studies would go a long way toward unpacking the ways in which individuals and/or groups move through different spaces. It is only through such long-term follow-ups that we can begin to understand the interlocking connections between and among race, social class, gender, schooling and the new economy, engaging theoretical debates in this area and going far beyond what we know to date. Lois Weis begins such long-term work in *Class Reunion: The Remaking of the American White Working Class* (2004), her 15-year follow-up of white working-class students who originally appear in *Working Class Without Work: High School Students in a De-industrializing Economy* (1990). We all for many more such studies across social class and race/ethnicity.[59]

4. Stretching further we would like to see increased studies of groups similar in race, class, and gender across geographic sites within the United States. Michelle Fine and Lois Weis, for example, map experiences and practices since leaving high school among African-American, Latino/Latina, and white men and women in the urban Northeast.[60] Based on their data, Fine and Weis come to conclusions regarding the economy, body politic, and the state. Yet, as Peter McLaren reminds us, Los Angeles is a wholly different space, no doubt producing different scenarios.[61] And Atlanta has

a far more thriving economy than the Northeast, where Lois and Michelle worked, as well as a different kind of racial history. Asking the same kinds of questions in varying geographic contexts within the United States will go a long way toward understanding the relationships between the state and economy and the ways in which individuals and/or groups forge their lives.

5. Along the lines outlined above, we must also begin to situate our studies globally. Groups can be studied between and among countries such as the United States, Australia, and England, for example, and more time needs to be taken contextualizing what we find within the global economy and meaning systems. In addition, we can usefully explore concepts like race, for example, by focusing carefully on groups within different national contexts. Nadine Dolby, for one, has begun this work in South Africa, and we would encourage others to pursue her agenda.[62]

FINAL (FOR NOW) THOUGHTS

The above demand a different set of understandings as to what constitutes what we call "the research imaginary" in education, how we contextualize and understand what we envision as education, and how we think students get it. Indeed, if we accept a notion of education that implies only traditional school sites and curricula, our work potentially ignores a variety of important complexities in young people's lives—how education happens outside of school; what students bring to the school; and how this intersects with what school offers. At worst, if we uncritically accept a priori parameters for what education is, we are in danger of simply reproducing the same set of questions, problems, and issues we have inherited. As Jan Nespor writes in *Tangled up in School*,

When groups and processes are analytically detached from each other . . . it becomes easy to slide into the bleak loops of contemporary educational debate. . . . The debate becomes less

simple, but more constructive, when we focus on dense interconnections among various actors and processes.[63]

We have, we argue, an imperative to reimagine our object of study—one that forces us to re-engage with the lives of youth on fresh terrain, simultaneously challenging predictable notions of culture and identity. This demands cross-site and cross-space collaborative work in forms that we have not previously engaged—2004 is a very different space for all of us than thirty years ago. We invite this conversation to continue as we all imagine what research around these issues might look like in the next decade.

NOTES

1. Spindler, G. (Ed.). (2000). *Fifty years of anthropology and education: 1950–2000*. Mahwah, NJ: Erlbaum.

2. Spindler (2000), p. 30–31.

3. Spindler (2000), p. 30.

4. Appadurai, A. (1996). *Modernity at large: Cultural dimensions of globalizations*. Minneapolis, MN: University of Minneapolis Press; Massey, D. (1994). *Space, place, and gender*. Minneapolis: University of Minneapolis Press.

5. Eisenhart, M. (2001). Educational ethnography past, present, and future: Ideas to think with. *Educational Researcher, 30* (8), 16–27.

6. Burawoy, M., et al. (2000). *Global ethnography*. Berkeley: University of California Press; Marcus, G. (1986). Contemporary problems of ethnography in the modern world system. In J. Clifford & G. Marcus (Eds.), *Writing culture: The poetics and politics of ethnography* (pp. 165–193). Berkeley: University of California Press; Marcus, G. (1998). *Ethnography through thick and thin*. Princeton, NJ: Princeton University Press.

7. Marcus (1998), p. 14.

8. Marcus (1998), p. 14.

9. Marcus (1998), pp. 90–95.

10. Marcus (1998), p. 90.

11. Burawoy et al. (2000).

12. Eisenhart, M., & Finkel, E. (1998). *Women's science: Learning and succeeding from the margins*. Chicago: University of Chicago Press.

13. Eisenhart & Finkel (1998), p. 6.

14. Marcus (1998), p. 172.

15. Marcus (1998), p. 45.

16. Dimitriadis, G. (2001). *Performing identity/ performing culture: Hip hop as text, pedagogy, and lived practice.* New York: Peter Lang; Dimitriadis, G., & McCarthy, C. (2001). *Reading and teaching the postcolonial: From Baldwin to Basquiat and Beyond.* New York: Teachers College Press; Dimitriadis, G., & Weis, L. (2001). Imagining possibilities with and for contemporary youth: (Re)writing and (Re)visioning education today. *Qualitative Research, 1* (2), 223–240; Fine, M., & Weis, L. (1998). *The unknown city: Lives of poor and working-class young adults.* Boston: Beacon Press; Weis, L., & Fine, M. (2001). Extraordinary conversations in public schools. *International Journal of Qualitative Studies in Education, 14* (4), 497–524.

17. Heath, S. (1983). *Ways with words: Language, life, and work in communities and classrooms.* Cambridge: Cambridge University Press.

18. Heath, S. (2001). Three's not a crowd: Plans, roles, and focus in the arts. *Educational Researcher, 30* (7), 10–17.

19. Heath, S., & McLaughlin, M. (Eds.). (1993). *Identity and inner-city youth: Beyond ethnicity and gender.* New York: Teachers College Press.

20. McLaughlin, M., Irby, M., & Langman, J. (1994). *Urban sanctuaries: Neighborhood organizations in the lives and futures of inner-city youth.* San Francisco: Jossey-Bass.

21. Heath (2001), p. 12.

22. Ball, A., & Heath, S. (1993). Dances of identity: Finding an ethnic self in the arts. In S. Heath & M. McLaughlin (Eds.), *Identity and inner-city youth: Beyond ethnicity and gender* (pp. 69–93). New York: Teachers College Press.

23. Heath, S. (1991). Inner-city life to literature: Drama in language learning. *TESOL Quarterly, 27* (2), 177–192; Mahiri, J. (1998). *Shooting for excellence: African American and youth culture in new century schools.* Urbana, IL: National Counsel of Teachers of Education.

24. McLaughlin, Irby, & Langman (1994).

25. Dimitriadis & Weis (2001).

26. Heath, S. (1996). Ruling places: Adaptation in development by inner-city youth. In R. Jessor, A. Colby, & R. Schweder (Eds.), *Ethnography and human development: Context and meaning in social inquiry* (pp. 225–251). Chicago: University of Chicago Press.

27. Heath (1996), p. 246.

28. Heath & McLaughlin (Eds.) (1993), p. 32.

29. Heath & McLaughlin (Eds.) (1993), p. 20.

30. Heath (2001), p. 16.

31. Heath & McLaughlin (Eds.) (1993).

32. McLaughlin, M., & Irby, M. (1994). Urban sanctuaries: Neighborhood organizations that keep hope alive. *Phi Delta Kappan, 76* (4), 305.

33. Dimitriadis & Weis, 2001; Fine & Weis, 1998; Hall, J. (2001). *Canal town youth: Community organization and the development of adolescent identity.* Albany: SUNY Press; Weiler, J. (2000). *Codes and contradictions: Race, gender identity, and schooling.* Albany: SUNY Press; Weis & Fine, 2001.

34. Fine, M., Weis, L., Centrie, C., & Roberts, R. (2000). Educating beyond the borders of schooling. *Anthropology & Education Quarterly, 31* (2), 132.

35. Kelly, G. (1997). *From Vietnam to America: A chronicle of the Vietnamese immigration to the United States.* Boulder, CO: Westview Press.

36. Fine, Weis, Centrie, & Roberts (2000).

37. Fine, Weis, Centrie, & Roberts (2000), p. 149.

38. Weis & Fine (2001).

39. Weis & Fine (2001).

40. Heath (2001), p. 15.

41. Dimitriadis (2001).

42. Buckingham, D. (1993). *Children talking television: The making of television literacy.* London: The Falmer Press; Buckingham, D. (1996). *Moving images: Understanding children's emotional responses to television.* Manchester, England: Manchester University Press; Buckingham, D. (Ed.). (1998). *Teaching popular culture: Beyond radical pedagogy.* London: UCL Press; Buckingham, D., & Sefton-Green, J. (1995). *Cultural studies goes to school: Reading and teaching popular media.* London: Taylor & Francis; Tobin, J. (2000). *Good guys don't wear hats: Children's talk about the media.* New York: Teachers College Press.

43. Buckingham & Sefton-Green (1995).

44. Buckingham & Sefton-Green (1995), p. 82.

45. Brunner, C., & Tally, W. (1999). *The new media literacy handbook: An educator's guide to bringing new media into the classroom.* New York: Doubleday.

46. D. Buckingham (Ed.) (1998).

47. Sefton-Green, J. (Ed.). (1998). *Digital diversions: Youth culture in the age of multimedia.* New York: Routledge; Sefton-Green, J. (Ed.). (1999). *Young people, creativity and new technologies.* New York: Routledge.

48. Sefton-Green (Ed.) (1999), p. 1.

49. Sefton-Green (Ed.) (1998).

50. Dimitriadis, 2001; Dolby, N. (2001). *Constructing race: Youth, identity, and popular culture*

in South Africa. Albany: SUNY Press.; Yon, D. (2000). *Elusive culture: Schooling, race, and identity in global times.* Albany: SUNY Press.

51. Dimitriadis (2001), p. 120.

52. Dolby, N. (2000). Changing selves: Multicultural education and the challenge of new identities. *Teachers College Record, 102* (5), 898–912; Dolby (2001).

53. Dolby (2000), p. 206.

54. Dolby (2000), p. 203.

55. Dolby (2000), p. 71.

56. Dolby (2001), p. 9.

57. Dimitriadis (2001); Dolby (2001); Yon (2000).

58. Marcus (1998).

59. Weis, L. (1990). *Working class without work: High school students in a de-industrializing economy.* New York: Routledge; Weis (2004). *Class reunion: The remaking of the American white working class.* New York: Routledge.

60. Fine & Weis (1998).

61. McLaren, P. (1997). *Revolutionary multiculturalism: Pedagogies of dissent for the new millennium.* Boulder, CO: Westview Press.

62. Dolby (2001).

63. Nespor, J. (1997). *Tangled up in school.* Mahwah, NJ: Erlbaum.

OBJECTIVITY IN EDUCATIONAL RESEARCH: THE QUEST FOR CERTAINTY BETWEEN THE 1950S AND 1970S

Greg Wiggan

BACKGROUND: MAPPING THE SOCIAL LANDSCAPE

After World War II, there was a growing belief in the desirability of social equality. This belief was advocated by African Americans who fought in the war, hoping that white Americans would reward them for their patriotism by granting them civil rights and equality. During the war, school segregation continued to belie the basic premise of equality in public education.[1] As late as 1951, most states had laws that permitted separate education for black and white children. However, the 1954 *Brown v. Board of Education* case transformed American history. In the case, the National Association for the Advancement of Colored People (NAACP) represented Linda Brown, a black student who was forced to attend school several miles from her home because coeducation of black and white children was prohibited. The Supreme Court ruled that separate education was inherently unequal; therefore, public schools had to be desegregated.[2] The NAACP's victory in *Brown v. Board of Education* was the turning point in the struggle for civil rights. The victory reassured advocates of equality and civil rights that their activism could effect social change.[3]

Although it was met with great resistance, the ruling in *Brown v. Board of Education* brought hopes of transforming public schools as well as the social and economic landscape. However, fifty years after *Brown v. Board of Education*, today's public schools are still segregated; and more importantly, the issue of inequality continues to be a concern not only in schools, but also in the social and economic system. For some, the idea of improving school equity means that students are simply bused to schools in other neighborhoods. While that might be a noble goal, yet it does little to improve the racialized structure of public education and the cycle of school failure. Rather than providing a quality education to all children regardless of their race or social class (like the victory in *Brown v. Board of Education* was supposed to accomplish), the current system forces the poor as well as black and brown parents to chase after the carrot (quality schools) on a stick (neighborhoods) that is always in sight, but they are never able to catch up to it.

OBJECTIVITY ENTHRONED

After the *Brown* case, there was an enormous growth in public school expenditure and programs aimed at addressing social inequality. There was an eagerness on the part of policy makers to base institutional reform on objective (empirical) research. This led to an influx of social science researchers attempting to investigate social and educational inequality for the purpose of creating social change. The involvement of members of the academy in research aimed at policy making perpetuated a noble dream of objectivity in school research.[4] By objectivity, I am referring to the presumption that social phenomenon can be perceived independent of experience. In other words, it is the belief that the truth about a phenomenon can be known if subjectivity is avoided. Objectivity emphasizes empirical methods of investigation, focusing less on personal accounts and more on quantifiable measures. Research was not only being produced as scholarship, but also for policy recommendations. As a result, questions of objectivity and legitimate scholarship became more central in educational discourse.

As the policy implications of school research grew, the government became one of the major sources of funding for educational research, and it favored policy-oriented studies that were quantitatively based.[5] The government reified quantitative research as the standard for school and policy evaluation.[6] Because the primary goal of government supported research was policy making, it had to be uniform and objective so that decisions could be made based on empirical data.[7] During this time, the prevailing notion was that government resources were better used to fund quantitative rather than qualitative research,

because the former involved less researcher bias and subjectivity, which were believed to be inherent in qualitative studies. Qualitative research was viewed as being open-ended and flexible; therefore, it was unable to reveal the facts about student achievement and school inequality issues. In addition, qualitative research was not as generalizable, which limited its utility in public policy areas. Hence, quantitative studies were not only viewed as being most reliable, but were ultimately enthroned as the standard for school research.

The emphasis on quantitative research presumed a form of direct realism, supposing that researchers could perceive social phenomenon free of intermediary subjectivity.[8] Due to the demand for objectivity, what qualitative research could reveal about personal experience and enlightenment was regarded as inferior to the knowledge provided by systematic and quantifiable measurements, which was being called objective.[9] This approach to objectivity was somewhat of a naïve way of viewing social phenomenon, which undermined personal accounts and led to extremism in educational research.

REPOSITIONING FOR OBJECTIVITY

In 1963, the founding of the American journal *Sociology of Education* marked the formal recognition of the growing prestige of the discipline.[10] Although there was a previous attempt to unite sociology and education, namely in 1927 with the *American Journal of Educational Sociology*, the journal reflected less sociological principles and more general concerns about education. During this time, most educational sociologists were in schools of education rather than sociology departments. Due to the low esteem that was generally associated with educational researchers, there were barriers concerning the respectability of the discipline.[11] Schools of education were generally viewed as sites where practitioners were trained, rather than places of rigorous academic studies for serious intellectuals.[12] The consensus was that schools of education lacked an academic discipline and offered low-level university curriculum.[13]

As a result of the lack of esteem assigned to schools of education, educational sociologists attempted to enhance the image of their field. More educational sociologists worked out of sociology departments, as opposed to schools of education. Furthermore, rather than referring to themselves as educational sociologists, they called themselves sociologists of education and attempted to prove that their work warranted scholarly merit.

In 1964 the U.S. Congress passed the Civil Rights Act, and it directed the Commissioner of Education to study inequality of educational opportunity among racial groups. This was intended to be a two-year study sponsored by the government. Furthermore, the findings of this study, documenting what the problems were in public schools, were to be presented to the President and Congress. James Coleman, a professor of sociology at Johns Hopkins University, headed the committee on education. The study began promptly, and in 1966 the report, titled *Equality of Educational Opportunity*, was published by the Government Printing Office.[14] The report examined material differences between school districts, comparing such things as school and class size, student background, teacher training, learning facilities, and student expenditure. In the report, Coleman found that the characteristics of school districts were not significantly related to school achievement as much as were the problems in students' families and communities.[15] Coleman's study marked the beginning of large quantitative research aimed at providing overreaching generalizations about public education.

After the Coleman report, Blau and Duncan's study, *The American Occupational Structure*, became one of the most influential works in education. The authors' work reinforced the belief that objectivity could be attained in research. This study was intended to examine education and occupation mobility. The authors proposed that the occupational structure is the basis of the stratification system in contemporary industrial societies.[16] Sampling 20,700 males between ages 20 and 64 and applying multivariate analysis, they found that the impact of educational factors was the single largest contributor to one's life chances. Blau and Duncan developed a statistical model to predict how much education contributed to individual occupational attainment. This research had a profound influence on the future of educational research.[17] Like the Coleman report, this study was used to make broad generalizations about schools. Although Blau and Duncan excluded minorities from their sample, their study was heralded as objective scholarship with wide implications for educational policy.

Similarly, in 1969 a study published by Arthur Jensen drew much attention. Jensen argued that educational and social policies should be based on the premise that the intellect of minorities, particularly African Americans, was genetically inferior to Caucasians.[18] Jensen posited that educational attainment was linked to genetic determinants, which were quantifiable, but could not be mediated through social programs. Although Jensen's study was quantitative, his research was racially charged, and may have cast doubt on the belief that quantitative research was more objective than qualitative inquiry. However, his work drew an enormous amount of attention. And similarly, more recent scholars arguing for racial and or genetic deficiency continue to receive applause (see Herrnstein and Murray's *Bell Curve* and Lynn and Vanhanen's *IQ and the Wealth of Nations*).

By the 1970s, other studies contributed to the practice of objectivity in educational research. In 1972, Christopher

Jencks et al. published *Inequality: A Reassessment of the Effect of Family and Schooling in America*. Like the other studies before it, these researchers exemplified the new way of doing objectivity in educational research. The new way of doing research not only entailed quantitative data, but also the use of large samples aimed at making generalizations for public policy.[19] Support for this study came from a number of sources including the United States Office of Education and the Massachusetts State Department of Education.[20] This study was aimed at informing neighborhood and school decision-making processes.[21]

Jencks et al. argued that the growing belief that social equality could be achieved through educational equality was problematic. During the 1960s, a popular way of viewing school failure was to examine the inequality in financial resources available to minority students, as well as the differential treatment they received in schools.[22] Jencks et al. postulated that reform strategies focusing on education were not only inadequate, but also misguided. Education reformers were devoting their efforts to addressing the War on Poverty by providing resources to create equity in schools. However, the authors questioned the effectiveness of this approach.

According to Jencks et al., equalizing the resources and the time spent in school would not be sufficient to reduce economic difference in students' homes. They argued that there was no evidence that school reform could substantially reduce social inequality or differential school performance. Rather, they proposed that these differences could be understood in terms of students' family characteristics.[23] In addition, they argued that a realistic solution to inequality would be to redistribute wealth and create more equity in parents' income.[24]

In 1974 Raymond Boudon produced a study titled *Education, Opportunity, and Social Inequality*. In the same tradition as its precursors, this study was a quantitative investigation, which was funded in part by the U.S. Office of Education. The main question in this study was whether rates of occupational or social mobility across generations were altered by improvements in education. Using a quantitative model, Boudon concluded that stratification was the principal factor responsible for inequality of educational and social opportunities. In addition, he argued that reduction in economic disparities would have the greatest impact on educational and social inequalities.[25]

Like the other studies, Boudon's work reflected the belief that quantitative work provided more precise descriptions of social phenomenon. Sponsors of educational research were interested in scholarship that could inform public policy or legitimatize their decision making process. Only the most rigorous work could receive consideration for funding, because the scholarship would be used as the scapegoat for policymakers engaging in public debates and political processes.

By the mid-1970s, the sociology of education literature was filled with quantitative works of objectivity. However, in the late 1970s scholars began to recognize that the literature was lacking personal accounts and interpretations from participants' viewpoints. With the growing influence of symbolic interactionism, ethnomethodology, phenomenology, and other interpretive perspectives that challenged objectivity and positivistic claims, education research would soon reflect more interpretive perspectives. There was a resurgence of qualitative inquiry in the school achievement debate when researchers like John Ogbu, Ray Rist, and August Hollingshead published major interpretive works in the field. Finally, the sociology of education literature regained some balance between quantitative and qualitative studies, as some of the clout surrounding the earlier perspective was challenged and influenced by interpretive frameworks.

CONCLUSION

Between the 1950s and 1970s, the problem of objectivity was one of the most fundamental challenges that faced the social sciences.[26] Researchers struggled to understand how biases could be avoided in social research. During this time, there was a demand for educational researchers to produce policy-oriented studies. These studies where supposed to be objective, where objectivity was being equated with quantitative, empirical investigation. As a result, a series of studies were conducted with the aim of objectivity. These studies, however, scarcely relied on the personal accounts of individuals, while privileging statistical modeling used to predict future outcomes. The perception was that quantitative studies were less biased and therefore more objective. Furthermore, these studies seemingly allowed for broad generalizations and public policy perspectives.

Although quantitative and qualitative research are different in terms of the way they inform our understanding of social phenomenon, they are both important methods of investigation.[27] However, while researchers were pursuing objectivity, they failed to embrace the value of interpretive research. The noble dream of objectivity was reinforced by the governments' sponsorship of quantitative studies. As research was conducted, policy was created and implemented, and in some cases it failed to produce desired outcomes. Soon it was evident that objectivity in educational research was like nailing jelly to the wall.[28] Therefore, the only meaning that objectivity could have was doing rigorous research by documenting and supporting one's arguments and making explicit the values premises underlying one's research.

For today's educational researcher, the issues of low student achievement and school failure reemerge as social problems in the field of education. While researchers generally use social and genetic perspectives (student opposi-

tional identity, social class and/or culture of poverty, and biological models) to explain school achievement and school failure issues, there are important areas that still need to be addressed. These specific issues have to do with the examination of students' beliefs about the quality of their education, as well as investigating the educational progress students believe is necessary to improve school achievement.

While much attention has been given to survey research, students' perspectives need to be understood more precisely so that intervention programs can be developed more effectively. Rather than simply producing scholarship to serve the interest of political parties or agencies, researchers must maintain the integrity of their work. Furthermore, individual experiences must be taken more seriously if we are to improve our understanding of social phenomenon.

NOTES

1. Tyack, D. (1967). *Turning points in American educational history* (p. 274). Waltham, MA: Blaisdell Publishing.

2. Tyack (1967), pp. 274, 304–308.

3. Karenga, M. (1993). *Introduction to black studies* (2nd ed., p. 168). Los Angeles: University of Sankore Press.

4. Karenga (1993); Karabel, J., & Halsey, A. (1977). *Power and ideology in education* (p. 5). New York: Oxford University Press; Novick, P. (1988). *That noble dream: The "objectivity question" and the American historical profession* (pp. 1–17). Cambridge: Cambridge University Press.

5. Karabel & Halsey (1977), pp. 5–6; McCartney, P. (1971). *Effect of financial support on growth of sociological specialties* (pp. 395–406). In E. Tiryakian (Ed.), *The phenomenon of sociology*. New York: Appleton Century-Crofts.

6. Dresch, S. (1975). A critique of planning models for postsecondary education: Current feasibility, potential relevance, and a prospectus for further research. *Journal of Higher Education, 46* (3), 245–286; Sussmann, L. (1967). Educational research programs of the Office of Educa-

tion: An interview with Dr. R. Louis Bright, associate commissioner for research, *Sociology of Education, 40* (2), 158–169; Brown, F. (1975). Assessment and evaluation of urban schools. *Journal of Negro Education, 44* (3), 377–384.

7. Eisner, E. (1994). *The educational imagination of the design and evaluation of school* (3rd ed., p. 215). New York: Macmillan.

8. Pojman, L. (2001). What can we know? An introduction to the theory of knowledge (2nd ed., pp. 64–79, 343). Belmont, CA: Wadsworth.

9. Saha, L., & Zubrzycki, J. (1997). Classical sociological theories of education. In L. Saha (Ed.), *International encyclopedia of the sociology of education* (pp. 241–246). Canberra, Australia: Pergamon.

10. Karabel & Halsey (1977), p. 3.

11. Karabel & Halsey (1977), pp. 3–4.

12. Bartky, J. (1955). The school of education and the university, *Journal of Higher Education, 26* (5), 254–260.

13. Bartky (1955), p. 255.

14. Kent, J. (1968). The Coleman report: Opening Pandora's box. *Phi Delta Kappan, 49,* 242–245.

15. Coleman, J. (1966). *Equality of educational opportunity* (pp. 316–317). Washington, DC: U.S. Government Printing Office.

16. Blau, P., & Duncan, O. (1967). *The American occupational structure* (p. vii). New York: John Wiley & Sons.

17. Bennett deMarrais, K., & LeCompte, M. (1995). *The way schools work: A sociological analysis of education* (p. 183). White Plains, NY: Longman Publishers.

18. Jensen, A. (1969). How much can we boost IQ and scholastic achievement? *Harvard Educational Review, 39* (1), 1–23.

19. Coleman, J. (1973). Review of the book *Inequality: A reassessment of the effect of family and schooling in America* by C. Jencks, M. Smith, H. Acland, M. Bane, D. Cohen, H. Gintis, B. Heyns, and S. Michelson, *American Journal of Sociology, 78* (6), 1523–1544.

20. Jencks et al. (p. vi).

21. Cain, G. (1974). Socioeconomic background and achievement. *American Journal of Sociology, 79* (6), 1497–1509.

22. Bennett deMarrais & LeCompte (1995), p. 237.

23. Jencks et al. (1972), p. 8.

24. Jencks et al. (1972), pp. 253–265.

25. Boudon, R. (1974). *Education, opportunity and social inequality: Changing prospects in Western society* (pp. 193–201). New York: John Wiley & Sons.

26. Myrdal, G. (1969). *Objectivity in social research: The 1967 Wimmer lecture* (pp. 3–5). New York: Random House.

27. Eisner (1994), pp. 235.

28. Novick (1988), pp. 1–17.

Aesthetics and Urban Education

IN THE MIDDLE: AN ARTIST/RESEARCHER EXPERIENCES URBAN REFORM

Joanne Kilgour Dowdy

INTRODUCTION

The black female community activists who founded schools in the late nineteenth century and twentieth century saw their commitment to the education of women as the means to improve the condition of all blacks. Their shared philosophy was based on three tenets: (1) the moral superiority of women; (2) the view that the black woman was entirely responsible for the development of all blacks; and (3) the expectation that black women would attend to the needs of their (black) sisters.[1] Publications such as Anna Julia Cooper's book, *A Voice from the South*,[2] in which she wrote on womanhood, and her 1899 presentations at the Hampton Negro Conference, are testimonials to the concern that educated black women expressed at the time regarding moral development in girls and women in their urban American communities.

These "club women," as the progressive black women have been referred to, were important to the transformation of the image of black women after abolition in 1865. They were determined to erase the stereotype of black women as licentious because of their historic subjugation to white slave masters.[3] Giddings also describes the development of the "cult of true womanhood" as it was translated from the white community by black club women who worked to change the material and moral conditions of the post-slavery black community.[4] Mary McLeod Bethune, an educator and activist, claimed that black women "recognized the importance of uplifting [their] people through social, civic, and religious activities."[5] Mary Church Terrell, educator and writer, declared war on immorality and low socioeconomic status among blacks by insisting that the more intelligent and influential blacks had a responsibility to "uplift those beneath them."[6] Nannie Burroughs, school principal and activist, spoke and wrote about the "respectability" of the working-class woman, encouraging club women who were involved in social uplift programs to find the "ordinary, common-sense, spirit-filled, everyday woman" and involve her in the movement for racial uplift.[7]

The abolition of slavery led to a demand for improved educational resources. It was in this national environment of re-envisioning the future of black people that the women leaders began organizing schools that gave children the experiences that enabled them to carry out work beyond menial tasks. Reading, writing, and arithmetic were foundation courses for all blacks enrolled as beginning students, regardless of age and former experience. Through their activism, these female community leaders managed to mobilize forces that transformed the post-slavery population. Community activity in the minds of these "club sisters" represented a hands-on approach to changing the conditions created by the forces of racism, sexism, and classism.

THE UNIVERSITY FELLOW

The work of the University Fellow, or "inspector"—the person responsible for the least well-served African-American students in Middle School—was to ensure that students who were failing classes would receive the academic support needed to improve their performance. I had the privilege of serving as a present-day University Fellow, and the five-week drama/writing/workshop I implemented allowed me to work with teachers committed to enhancing their teaching philosophy so that all their students would have a better chance of succeeding.

In my job as a University Fellow, between 1997 and 1999, I investigated problems and then actuated solutions that would lead to more successes. I provided an opportunity for all the children to focus on improving their writing skills through experiences with the dramatic arts. This was a space in which I could make practical inroads into the teachers' pedagogy and advance the agenda of the urban reform initiative. Like my black sisters of the nineteenth-century club movement, I made sure that a group of urban black children experienced success in mainstream literacy. School improvement that was aimed at one group of students, the

least well-served, allowed other participants in the class to benefit from this new, drama-based pedagogy.

The teachers' belief in the potential of students was most evident in the attitude of a white, male colleague who implemented the drama/writing workshop in his eighth-grade classroom. Mr. Grady worked as a co-learner with the students and was willing to admit that he was growing in expertise as the class proceeded. His resistance to fear and lack of confidence among the students encouraged an atmosphere of cooperation and adventure in the children. He demonstrated his commitment to students' learning by doing rather than by listening to him lecture or by completing written exercises in their notebooks.

THE URBAN ATLANTA COALITION COMPACT

In the tradition of the club women of the post-slavery era, the Urban Atlanta Coalition Compact (UACC) was created to serve the least successful African-American students in seven public schools of metropolitan Atlanta from 1997 to 2001. At each of these schools a University Fellow (UF) was the liaison between Sherman State University and the school. The UF's duties included: (1) creating a school profile based on interviews with a broad representation of students, faculty, support staff, and parents; (2) facilitating communication between the director of the UACC and the leaders of the Action Team, a school-based teacher group; and (3) working in individual classrooms as the need for her expertise arose. For example, as a language arts specialist, I was expected to provide classroom support for the faculty in that unit. An important responsibility of the UF was to relay information efficiently between the individual school and the university as planning for school activities and other UACC business was conducted. The UF worked with the

Action Team to promote the implementation of the reform initiatives that had been created to improve the education of the least well-served African-American students in the urban school.[8]

In my role as University Fellow at Middle School, the only middle school in the Urban Atlanta Coalition Compact, I implemented several key elements for successful involvement in urban education by the faculty and students. These benchmarks are described in Delpit's "Ten Factors Essential to Success in Urban Classrooms." (See Table 5.)

In one eighth-grade classroom I, as the UF, along with a group of teachers from the language arts faculty, implemented a drama initiative. This project developed into a five-week unit of drama exercises and writing activities that supported the development of the writing skills of low-achieving students in two classes. In two other classes we introduced a unit where students worked to collect and translate the slang terms and idioms from their home language into standard English versions. The point of the exercise was, first, to create a space in the classroom where students felt free to bring in their home language and celebrate it. Secondly, we wanted to build a bridge to standard English so that students could feel comfortable going back and forth from one form of the language to another, enriched by the knowledge that they had more than one mode of communication available to them. We also implemented a nine-week poetry and performance workshop.[9] The Action Team also supported a plan for training teachers in anti-racism techniques, and in an individualized academic program for students who had been retained at Middle School in the year that the UACC reform initiative arrived at the urban school.

Middle School represented a microcosm of the city in which it was situated. Even though 80 percent of the teachers and staff at Middle School voted to become involved with the UACC, I still feel that my presence in the school generated a cautious attitude among the faculty. This perceived reservation made me feel like a club woman of the nineteenth century, an "inspector" of the least well-served urban students. The high percentage of children from lower economic neighborhoods, and the way in which the faculty were developing measures to ensure the success of the failing African Americans in their charge, were only two of the hot issues that I had to negotiate over the first year.

Table 5.
Dr. Lisa Delpit: Ten Factors Essential to Success in Urban Classrooms

1. Do not teach less content to poor, urban children, but understand their brilliance and teach more!
2. Whatever methodology or instructional program is used, demand critical thinking.
3. Assure that all children gain access to "basic skills," the conventions and strategies that are essential to success in American education.
4. Provide the emotional ego strength to challenge racist societal views of the competence and worthiness of the children and their families.
5. Recognize and build on strengths.
6. Use familiar metaphors and experiences from the children's world to connect what they already know to school knowledge.
7. Create a sense of family and caring.
8. Monitor and assess needs and then address them with a wealth of diverse strategies.
9. Honor and respect the children's home culture(s).
10. Foster a sense of children's connection to community to something greater than themselves.

My job as the UF led me to ask questions about students who were not performing at grade level in reading and writing, involving me in situations that pitted my sense of moral responsibility against the "conventions" of the white-dominated parent association. In the presence of this powerful group of professionals, it was difficult to feel comfortable in the school. My feeling of being an interrupter of the school culture, or inspector of the premises where black children were being educated according to white middle-class values,[10] can best be explained through some of the comments that I documented during the initial self-study that the school did in 1998. The quotes from teachers, parents, and staff members that stand out to me after seven years include: "Even though this [black] kid may have a 'B' average and the white kid has a 'B' average, more time is spent with the white one" (staff); and "There are [teachers] who are victims of their training and think that the issue with the African-American child is impenetrable" (parent). From the staff I heard: "Looks like almost two schools, white school here, black school there"; and "There is a lack of understanding of the different cultures that we have here, primarily lack of understanding between the black and white cultures." The strongest comment came from a mother who protested that "The school should not "discount me as a black parent 'cause I'm just as concerned about my child. I will not allow [them] to bring down . . . his self-esteem."

THE MIDDLE SCHOOL DRAMA WORKSHOP

Middle School is part of a small municipal school cluster. There are seven elementary schools, one middle school, and one high school in this urban environment. The elementary schools have traditionally housed populations of children of the same racial background. When the students arrive at Middle School it is usually the first time that they encounter children of a different racial background in their classrooms. There is also a wide range in the economic levels of the children from the black and white majority neighborhoods. These differences in racial and economic status create an undercurrent of tension in the school. Interviews with black and white students conducted by a research team did reveal several instances where teachers of both races gave unstintingly to the black children who graduated to Middle School from a predominantly black elementary school.[11]

Middle School has 622 students, of whom 55 percent are black, 41 percent are white, 1 percent are Latino, and 3 percent are multiracial and international. Of the total, 39 percent are eligible for free or reduced-fee lunches.[12] The divide between the social backgrounds of the black and white children may be partly explained by the fact that many of the black children live in public housing, while the white children live in middle-class homes. Both of these groups live within easy reach of the school and can be seen walking, cycling, traveling in school buses, or being driven by their parents and guardians.

In my role as University Fellow I had worked on UACC, the urban school reform project, at Middle School for a few weeks before the drama/writing workshop was launched in October, 1997. The teachers who were interested in doing drama in the reform project were in the language arts classrooms. We formed a small study group and began meeting at off-hours in order to try out exercises that teachers would later do in their classrooms. This kinesthetic approach to teaching became an opportunity to see teachers from another perspective.[13] They were not only interested in student success in the traditional curriculum, but also wanted to see their charges come into their own and take pride in their heritage as black people with a history of achievement in the sciences and arts. The dramatists were club women and men in their own right. They created the acting workshop to improve the chances of reaching those students not being served by traditional classroom pedagogy.

The Philosophy behind the Drama/ Writing Workshop

It was important for me to get into a classroom during my first month's work at Middle School, to collaborate with a teacher, and to make a difference in the individual lives of the urban students. Teachers, especially those engaged in the drama group, had to demonstrate their commitment to the philosophy of high expectations for the least well-served African-American students in order to realize the practical phase of the reform agenda. As an acknowledged black club woman working at the end of the twentieth century, I was impatient to see children who had been suffering under the restraints of the desk/pencil/paper traditional mode of teaching move over to an experiential way of learning. I knew that the children who learned best by being active during the lesson, as well as the teachers in the drama group, were ready for engagement through UACC-inspired teaching.

One teacher in the language arts faculty had a need to learn new methods of literacy instruction. Mr. Grady, a white, male teacher, wanted to engage the failing students in his class so that they could succeed at the level he believed was necessary for passing the state-mandated test at the end of the school year. He first described these children to me as the ones who had "free lunch" and those who came from "bad neighborhoods." At a later point in our discussion, he admitted that he did not know what kind of music the children enjoyed, if they did any leisure reading, or whether they attended church with their parents or extended family. Our

first discussion gave me a good idea about the kind of work that was necessary to build a solid community feeling in Mr. Grady's classroom.

During my second discussion with Mr. Grady, in his planning period, I decided to introduce him to some principles of drama for the language arts classroom. When Mr. Grady invited me to mentor him in his language arts classes, I was able to demonstrate some of the drama activities that could be included in a writing workshop. In collaboration with Mr. Grady and the urban students in his eighth-grade class, I developed a series of lessons that helped students explore writing from an actor's perspective. The progressive steps facilitated the students' ability to identify the characters in a piece of writing, turn the story into a script, and then to demonstrate their understanding of the characters through the performance of an improvised dramatic work. Mr. Grady was encouraged to videotape the student improvisations and use the recordings as texts that the students could review, discuss, write about, and reflect on as they developed their writing skills.

Because I believe, along with others, that we all participate in "play-acting" from early childhood to well into our mature years,[14] I worked with Mr. Grady to create a classroom that was highly responsive to dramatic experiments. Encouraging students to improvise lines based on the text that they were reading, to come up with dialogue based on character descriptions that the writer had offered in the novel, or to feed off of each other in small scenes that were based on some pivotal event in a story, all led them to experience excitement and to invest in the drama and writing exercises. This new enthusiasm for the drama/ writing class also led Mr. Grady to change the look of his classroom by bringing in a couch from his home and setting up reading corners where students could relax with a book, or write when they felt inspired after a dramatic exercise.

Coaxing people to act "as if" allows them the opportunity to reveal their feelings, to commit to the project at hand, and to experience the support of a group as they develop their creative responses to a poem or other text.[15] With these ideas in mind, I provided exercises that I had garnered from my acting training at the Julliard School. Students were asked to write letters in character, to talk as characters in particular attitudes (anger, sadness, distress), or to mime scenes that would show their characters' attitudes.

The levels of actor training explored gave students a chance to find their own space for engagement—i.e., the kinds of experiences that they were willing to "act out" in public. The topics covered in the drama improvisation workshops included, among others: friendship, loneliness, racism, domestic abuse, women's rights, parent/children relationships, and love. The wide range of emotions evoked through this kind of dramatic exploration enabled the students to find words and actions to show the attitudes that they wanted to demonstrate. The students got to decide which emotions to deal with under the given circumstances of their mood, experience, and interest at the time of the training.

The drama/writing workshop also gave me an opportunity to "operationalize" Delpit's Ten Factors Essential to Success in Urban Classrooms. During the time we worked in the UACC, Dr. Delpit had repeatedly referred to our "marching orders," which included such imperatives as: develop content-rich classes; encourage critical thinking; use "basic skills" as a fact of formal education; allow students to develop the "ego strength to challenge racist societal views" of their potential; build on strengths; use children's home language to build a bridge to formal school English; create a family atmosphere in the school; address diverse needs and attend to them with various strategies; honor the children's home culture; and develop a sense of connectedness to the community so that children can perceive themselves as more than individuals.

Details of the Drama/Writing Workshop

Mr. Grady and I agreed on a list of guidelines at the start of the collaboration. I also met with the language arts teacher before he began each step in his drama/writing workshop. We decided to follow the lead of the students once we introduced them to the principles of character analysis and improvisation of dramatic scenes based on scene study. Mr. Grady also used dramatic principles based on his own experience with the drama group, which he met with in the early-morning sessions that I organized for teachers in the building. His first objective with the eighth-grade class was to get the students interested in performing scenes based on the literature they read from the syllabus. From that step we shaped the drama/writing unit for student success by asking the students to rewrite scenes they had read after thinking about the beginning, middle and end of each scene. Mr. Grady did not tell the students how to fill the scenes with content since he trusted that their imaginations would suffice. Also, when some students showed a greater inclination to direct scenes that were written in class, or run the video camera when scenes were being recorded, Mr. Grady assigned student director roles that would use these talents.

One of the exercises that evolved from working with student responses to the written text and their development of scripted scenes from these stories was the mask exercise. Mr. Grady had students read a portion of a novel and choose characters that were interesting to them. Each student would look for all the characteristics of the personality he or she chose as the writer described them, and then create a written composite of that person. After the details of the characters' lives and abilities were established, the students were encouraged to create masks with papier-mâché. The art teacher was enlisted to provide materials and support while the students constructed their masks and later decorated them to show the outstanding personality traits that the novel described for their characters' lives. This activity led to scenes between characters in mask, an extensive writing response to the work of creating the masks, and then writing as if the students were the characters themselves. All of the performance products were videotaped by the students.

Lessons Learned
Multiple Ways of Knowing

There are many ways of "knowing" and expressing our experience. Harste reminds us that different symbol systems used for communication among human beings represent ways we "make and share meaning."[16] It is this incentive to find various expressions and connect with the journey of human experience that guided Middle School students' efforts to "hear" the voice of characters. To challenge Mr. Grady's class, we needed to expand "ways of knowing" for both Mr. Grady and his students. Through drama, art, video production, and language communication, we encouraged the students to analyze written texts for more successful learning inside and outside the classroom.[17]

Mr. Grady began using different aspects of his training that formerly he had found neither time, interest, support, nor enthusiasm to use in the language arts classroom. For example, he was able to share a large jazz music collection with the students when they began to read literature that mentioned certain musicians. This music contributed to the atmosphere that Mr. Grady used to create an inviting classroom where the urban students felt welcomed and appreciated. He also demonstrated his fondness for acting

when he dramatized characters and explained the ways in which he identified with certain stories that he read in class. Mr. Grady began writing every morning before the class began, and was able to tell students about his struggle with certain aspects of his creativity as the semester progressed. He found himself being challenged to commit his imagination and emotion to the creation of characters. Mr. Grady also displayed his artistic taste when he decided to bring in a sofa and carpet to recreate the classroom. I imagine that the students felt their teacher had suddenly become more "human," less an authority figure and more a "club" member who supported children's learning in the way that a club woman would do. By bringing his sincere interest in writing, acting, video production and reading to the task of teaching urban students, Mr. Grady enhanced his potential for success as a teacher.

Realizing the Urban Reform Agenda

Clearly, the expectations in relation to the students and teachers in Middle School's classrooms that the UACC urban reform agenda had primed me to have were realized in this drama/writing workshop. It was no accident that some male students, mostly black, began to participate in the project. Before the UACC they may have felt invisible in the classroom with their white teacher, Mr. Grady. They may have had a similar experience to the graduate students who described themselves as "noises in the attic" within the white academic environment of higher education.[18] Or, the urban students might have identified with Carter Woodson's description of the "mis-education of the Negro" and what it was like to feel ill-fitted as a black person in a Eurocentric culture.[19]

The drama/writing project ensured that all the students were invited to bring their experiences and creativity to the language arts classroom. In Mr. Grady's class, they participated as artists of equal status. This urban classroom valued the students' culture and used their experiences as a bridge to new knowledge through the use of their home community's languages and experiences.[20] The use of each student's home language in describing and performing the characters in the readings created space for the different cultures to co-exist in Middle School.

Critical thinking was also a necessary part of the journey to performing the characters. The students had to ask questions of the writer, the story, themselves, and their classmates in order to construct realistic personae for their dramatic improvisations and literary products. Individual learners showed their life experiences and needs as students, which allowed Mr. Grady, and myself, to learn more about students and to respond on a more personal basis to them as artists. A family atmosphere developed in the classroom as a result of the kind of listening students did for performances created around literary characters. Quiet students found ways to show their emotional life, and outgoing students developed ways to use words to help them paint their intimate realities. Previously retiring students found voices to communicate through their contributions as designers of sets, rehearsal directors, or video-camera operators. A climate based on mutual respect for each other's work became the norm in the writing workshop.

More important for the student participants and for Mr. Grady, high expectations of performances in the drama/writing workshop became the natural order of business. These changes were captured in our videotapes of the classes when students performed their written creations. The video presentations allowed the students, Mr. Grady, and myself to appreciate the growth of students in the many dimensions that the drama/writing workshop facilitated. The students had evolved in their willingness and ability to be physically involved in character representations and more comfortable with the idea of sharing their life experiences through the writing and performance of their creations.

The drama/writing workshop made it possible for this University Fellow to find a practical way to put the UACC urban reform agenda to work. As a modern-day club woman and artist/researcher, I fortunately found it impossible to avoid the call for social uplift at Middle School. I was compelled to be a community organizer on behalf of the least well-served children, and to enlist Mr. Grady in the effort to make success possible for all his charges. More importantly, we were both motivated to take action in the language arts classroom, and to implement teaching methods that would improve chances of success among the least well-served African-American students. In the service of the legacy of the club women, we achieved many of the marching orders Dr. Delpit gave us to assure the improvement of the education of the children. By introducing a kinesthetic approach to teaching the urban middle-school students,[21] I encouraged Mr. Grady to find ways to ensure that his students could creatively demonstrate their understanding of life.

CONCLUSION

Teachers who embrace multiple ways of knowing and encourage students to participate in activities leading to new ways of communicating develop a philosophy of teaching that informs all their experiences. Consequently, the ten factors that Delpit advances to promote successful classrooms for urban children become a challenge that teachers can meet effectively. By encouraging this kind of pedagogy, the artist/researcher creates a space where positive attitudes facilitate creative learning.

This article represents the concerted effort to review the plans, methods and successes that resulted when Mr. Grady and I developed a common "language" to facilitate the arts-based pedagogy in the middle-school urban classroom. Students video-taped doing their dramatic scenes demonstrated their understanding of the steps that led them to identify with and perform their characters using the text from novels or their original scripts. The individual performances videotaped so that the students and Mr. Grady could review and appreciate the work. Mr. Grady was pleased enough with the student work to show an excerpt of the videotape with students in masks to his graduate colleagues at the university where he was studying literacy methods for middle school. Mr. Grady also wrote a term paper, and later presented a workshop for teachers, based on his research on kinesthetic learning principles and the need for students to be physically engaged in what they study in classrooms.

Throughout this country's history, most blacks have lived near or below the poverty line,[22] and this disadvantage is exacerbated by other factors in the educational environment of black children. We must, therefore, salute the success of any classroom initiative that increases the learning potential of the least well-served students in our urban schools. Since most black children live with a single parent, usually a mother, it is imperative to provide schooling that will enhance the children's chances of overcoming the effects of straitened economic and social circumstances. Also, the students must have positive role models who are black, female, and literate. As the artist/researcher working with Mr. Grady, I was able to provide this example.

As a researcher/teacher/artist, I claim my heritage from the order of black women community workers who include Mary McLeod Bethune, Frances Ellen Watkins Harper, Fannie Barrier Williams, Anna Julia Cooper, Fannie Jackson Coppin, Sarah J. Early, and Hallie Q. Brown.[23] The acknowledgement of my ancestors as I worked with Mr. Grady and his students as a University Fellow in the Urban Coalition

Compact ensured my alertness to opportunities to create successful experiences in that eighth-grade urban classroom. I became aware of the importance of my role as "inspector," and determined to play that role well. I am glad that I adopted this title for myself after realizing that my arrival at Middle School was a signal to the staff and teachers of the school that those children least well-served were my wards. It is equally important to me that, as a club woman, that I grew in knowledge about how I could facilitate reform in an urban middle school. It was a revolutionary experience for me, for Mr. Grady, and for his students when we held hands as collaborators. This experience is a testimony to the improvements that a few committed people can make in the service of African-American students.

NOTES

1. Perkins, L. (1980). Black women and the philosophy of "race uplift" prior to emancipation. Working paper, National Institute of Education (ED). Washington: ERIC Document Reproduction Service No. ED 221 444.

2. Cooper, A. (1892). *A voice from the South.* Xenia, Ohio: Aldine Printing House.

3. Batker, C. (1998). Love me like I like to be: The sexual politics of Hurston's *Their eyes were watching God;* the classic blues, and the black women's club movement. *African American Review, 32* (2), pp. 199–213.

4. Giddings, P. (1984). *When and where I enter: The impact of black women on race and sex in America.* New York: Bantam Books.

5. Lerner, G. (Ed.). (1973). *Black women in white America: A documentary history.* New York: Random House.

6. Higginbotham, E. (1993). *Righteous discontent: The women's movement in the black Baptist church: 1880–1920,* p. 206. Cambridge, MA: Harvard University Press.

7. Higginbotham (1993), p. 208.

8. Obidah, J. (1999). First-year documentation and evaluation report of the Urban Atlanta Coalition Compact. Atlanta: Georgia State University, Alonzo A. Crim Center for Educational Excellence.

9. Dowdy, J. (2002). Ovuh Dyuh. In L. Delpit & J. Dowdy (Eds.), *The skin that we speak: Thoughts on language and culture in the classroom*, pp. 3–14. New York: The New Press.

10. Delpit, L. (1995). *Other people's children: Cultural conflict in the classroom.* New York: New Press.

11. Meyers, B., Dowdy, J. & Paterson, P. (2000). Finding the missing voices: Perspectives of the least visible families and their willingness and capacity for school involvement. *Current Issues in Middle Level Education, 7* (2), pp. 59–79.

12. (1999–2000). Georgia Public Education Report Card.

13. Dowdy, J. (1999). Becoming the poem: How poetry can facilitate working across differences in a classroom. *The Change Agent. Adult Education for Social Justice: News, Issues, and Ideas.* New England, MA: Literacy Resource Center.

14. Lederer, H. (1981). The play's the thing: The use of theater in language teaching. *Studies in Language Learning, 3*, pp. 35–41.

15. King, N. (1981). From literature to drama to life. In N. McCaslin (Ed.), *Children and Drama*, pp. 164–177. New York: Longman Inc.

16. Harste, J. (1994). Visions of literacy. *Indiana Media Journal, 17* (1), pp. 27–32.

17. Short, K., Harste, J. & Burke, C. (1996). *Creating classrooms for authors and inquirers.* Portsmouth, NH: Heineman.

18. Dowdy, J., Givens, G., Murillo Jr., E., Shenoy, D. & Villenas, S. (2000). Noises in the attic: The legacy of expectations in the academy. *International Journal of Qualitative Studies in Education 13* (5), pp. 429–446.

19. Woodson, C. (1994). *The mis-education of the negro.* Newport News, Virginia: United Brothers and Sisters Graphics and Printing.

20. Delpit, L. (2002). No kinda sense. In L. Delpit & J. Dowdy (Eds.), *The skin that we speak: Thoughts on language and culture in the classroom*, pp. 31–48. New York: The New Press; Baker, J. (2002). Trilingualism. In L. Delpit & J. Dowdy (Eds.), *The skin that we speak: Thoughts on language and culture in the classroom*, pp. 49–62. New York: The New Press.

21. Gardner, H. (1983). *Frames of Mind.* New York: Basic Books; Barbe, W. & Milone, M. (1980, January). Modality. *Instructor*, pp. 44–49; Reiff, J. (1992). *Learning styles: What research says to the teacher.* Washington: National Education Association.

22. Farley, R. (1997). Racial trends and differences in the United States 30 years after the civil rights decade. *Social Science Research 26*, pp. 235–262.

23. Robinson, L. France Ellen Watkins Harper. Retrieved from http://www.africana.com/Articles/tt_289.htm.

AESTHETICS AND URBAN EDUCATION: URBAN LEARNERS' AFFIRMATION AND TRANSFORMATION THROUGH ARTS AND HUMAN DEVELOPMENT EDUCATION

Kent Seidel with Imelda Castañeda-Emenaker

The purpose of art is to lay bare the questions that have been concealed by the answers.

—*James Baldwin, author*

The term "aesthetic" is most commonly associated with the discussion of beauty, often related to the meaning and value of an artistic effort. The word comes from the ancient Greek meaning "sense perception" and "to perceive." We will use the term "aesthetics" instead of arts, humanities, or liberal arts because our discussion will address several dimensions of aesthetic perception in education and urban communities. We will (1) address the current status of the arts in education and the community; (2) look at some of the theories underlying the transformative potential of the arts and aesthetic experience; and (3) discuss ways in which the arts and humanities can transform both education and community so that both are more successful.

In the deepest sense, we suggest that the arts and humanities can work together with education to alter how urban communities are perceived by their residents, neighbors, and visitors. Urban centers are too often viewed through a lens of deficits, focusing on high poverty, decay, and the migration of the wealthier, predominately white population to the suburban fringes. Yet urban areas remain our centers of civilization, with great resources to counter the deficits. An aesthetic focus has the potential to change perceptions of our urban core, in ways more profound than merely improving appearance with well-placed art, although that is a part of it.

Echoing the sentiments about urban settings, the arts have most frequently been brought to education to address deficits–to reach students that are outside the mainstream; to validate "other," minority cultures and help "at-risk" students find a place in school; to provide alternatives for learning "core subjects" to students who do not learn well via "traditional" approaches. Research provides evidence that the arts *are* effective in doing these things, even where deficit thinking was the motivator. Why, then, are we not educating all students with the arts, especially in our "at-risk, high-need" urban communities? We suggest that the arts are most effective when they truly transform the teaching and learning process, giving both voice and perceptive insight to all members of the learning community. This is a difficult transformation, however, and one that tends to unsettle the status quo.

Some scholars (e.g., Goodwin, Hilliard, Ladson-Billings) suggest that things will not change educationally for at-risk youth until we look at our own beliefs about and choices of interaction with these children. The same may be true for our urban communities, and we offer a theoretical line of reasoning for thinking transformationally about urban communities and education–using the arts and humanities not to fix what is wrong, but to embrace what can be right. It is a subtle, but incredibly important, difference in perception.

THE ARTS IN EDUCATION AND THE COMMUNITY

There is nothing worse than a sharp image of a fuzzy concept.

—*Ansel Adams, photographer*

In recent decades, arts advocates have been vocal regarding the importance of the arts as an integral, substantive part of the education of every individual. Although the research has many challenges ahead, there is strong evidence of the value of education that incorporates a strong arts element. Such education may occur in a traditional public school, or it may take place less formally within a healthy learning community. We also encourage the reader to consider a broad spectrum of artistic endeavors—not only classical traditions in dance, literature, music, theatre, and visual arts, but also arts rooted in folk, family, street and community which have not yet found their way into the established academy; not just museums, symphonies, and theatres, but any community collective committed to creative effort.

Each of the arts education examples highlighted in this chapter emphasizes a strong community connection as central to its success. This brings to the fore a concern, however: if the arts are to have a positive impact on our schools and communities, they must be present in our schools and communities. In reviewing the research, one finds many assertions that the arts are disproportionately leaving urban areas. Fortunately, a close look at the evidence suggests hope.

AESTHETIC OPPORTUNITIES: WEAK, POLARIZED, BUT POSSIBLE

Most schools still offer some music and visual arts instruction, and urban centers still boast a plethora of diverse arts opportunities, even if these are often burdened by resource limitations. The 1999 National Center for Education Statistics survey of U.S. public schools found that nearly all elementary schools (94 percent nationally, 96 percent in city locales, defined as "a large or mid-sized central city of a Metropolitan Statistical Area")[1] offer music instruction, and 87 percent offer visual arts (85 percent in cities). Fewer offered dance (20 percent, 23 percent in cities) or theatre (19 percent, 22 percent in cities).[2] At the secondary level, 90 percent of schools offered music (same for cities) and 93 percent (96 percent cities) offered visual arts instruction. Again, dance and theatre lag behind, with dance in 14 percent of schools nationally (but in 22 percent of city schools) and theatre offered in 48 percent of schools (50 percent of city schools).[3] There is a discrepancy for schools with a high percentage of students in poverty (75 percent or more qualified for free or reduced-price lunches), but it is fairly negligible with the exception of elementary music (88 percent offering instruction, vs. 94 percent nationally); elementary visual arts (79 percent vs. 87 percent); and secondary level visual arts (85 percent vs. 93 percent) and theatre (36 percent vs. 48 percent).

The true difference in arts instruction for many urban schools, which tend to have a higher percentage of poor and minority student populations, is in the *quality* of instruction and in the students' individual likelihood of participation in the arts that are offered. The report finds that elementary schools with the lowest minority enrollments and schools with the lowest poverty concentration were more likely to have dedicated rooms, special equipment, district curriculum guides for music and visual arts, and input from arts specialists on staff hiring, curriculum, and allocation of arts funds.[4] At the secondary level, schools with the lowest minority enrollments and schools with the lowest poverty concentration were much more likely to receive outside funding for music programs, to have two or more full-time visual arts teachers, and to have a dedicated space with special equipment for visual arts.[5] Combine these differences with the likelihood that students must have time, support, and resources for after- or before-school arts participation, and that they must stay in school to participate, and it is not surprising that arts education is becoming more polarized.

This polarization is not trivial if one considers creative expression, education, and the participation in community that attends these endeavors to be important human rights. The 1997 National Assessment of Educational Progress found evidence of polarization among groups of students as well, with "white and Asian students" attaining higher average scores than "black or Hispanic students."[6]

The NAEP study also found that higher levels of parental education were associated with higher levels of student performance for music, visual arts, and theatre. Education levels are also directly associated with adult participation in the arts. According to the National Endowment for the Arts,[7] there is a significant difference and direct correlation between level of education and arts participation and attendance. The differences are not as extreme overall for income level differences, however, except for the lowest income bracket and for certain art forms.

The polarization that we see among populations that are privileged and educated and those who are less so creates a difficult dichotomy for our urban centers in particular. The majority of large arts and humanities institutions are in urban sites. Museums are natural partners for education, with 88 percent providing K-12 educational programming, usually based on local and state curriculum standards.[8] There are only 75 dance companies with annual budgets of $1 million or more, but all are in major urban centers. Cities also have numerous community and "fringe" venues. Chicago, for example, has "at least 258 dance-making entities," and Washington, DC has 186 dance-making entities, predominately "culturally-specific" (41 percent) or modern dance (30 percent) in nature.[9]

Unfortunately there is often a disconnection, or at best a lack of mutual awareness, among these resources. As we discuss later, these entities participate in different aesthetic communities, so a disconnect is not surprising. However, if urban communities hope to tap the power of aesthetics in education and renewal, the trend data indicate that their many arts, community, and school entities must connect. This connection is perhaps the only commonality among every arts education success story that we have found in urban settings.

HUMANIZING OUR CENTERS OF CIVILIZATION

All our knowledge has its origins in our perceptions.

—*Leonardo da Vinci*

In this section we discuss cognitive aspects of creativity and the role of education in our society, considering each with regard to the relationship of the individual with the community. The interaction of creativity and education, and the power of expression that they can give to members of the learning community (both in-school and at-large), are an important concept underlying why the arts can be so effective in transforming lives and schools. The connection of creativity, education, and community is particularly crucial for our urban areas, as these places have the diversity, human concentration, and variety of resources to succeed as strong centers of healthy civilization.

CREATIVITY AND THE ACADEMY

Mihalyi Csikszentmihalyi, arguably the leading scholar on creativity, notes that very little separates humans from other animals. One finds in the animal kingdom communication, communities and social structures, divisions of labor, nurturing families, ability to learn, and tool use. What one does not find, at least so far, is the ability to create a long-term record of these things, and to build upon them over time. It is this ability to pass knowledge and skills from one to another and from generation to generation which produces what Csikszentmihalyi calls "big-C creativity," as well as education, the arts, and historical record. "Big-C creativity" refers to artistic and scientific efforts that build upon prior knowledge to advance the field, as opposed to the personal, "small-C creative" activities that we may pursue to enrich our lives–painting a picture, decorating a house, and the like.

Creativity (and, we will argue, artistic expressions of creativity in particular) and education are inextricable, and both rely on their interaction with a community of peers to flourish. For clarity, we will call this aesthetic community of peers the "academy."

Creativity . . . is a process by which a symbolic domain in the culture is changed. New songs, new ideas, new machines are what creativity is about. But because these changes do not happen automatically as in biological evolution, it is necessary to consider the price we must pay for creativity to occur. It takes effort to change traditions. For example, a musician must learn the musical tradition, the notation system, the way instruments are played before she can think of writing a new song; before an inventor can improve on airplane design he has to learn physics, aerodynamics, and why birds don't fall out of the sky.[10]

The individual learns from the traditions of the past and from those around her; her work is reviewed by her colleagues in the academy; that which is deemed worthy of attention will move beyond the academy to gain societal value and acceptance and, in so doing, will become part of the record for future creators. This reiterative process engages individuals with many communities, present, past, and future. It can be argued that no creative or aesthetic progress can ever be made without these communities, and the interaction requires education, whether formal or informal. Even the most radical and rebellious work gains some part of its identity from the community and preceding bodies of work. Note, too, that the process of working with an academy of creative peers is similar regardless of the aesthetic endeavor. What varies is the relationship of the various academies with society at large and with each other. An example from music: there is a formal classical tradition that may come to mind immediately as "The Academy"—an entire system resulting in orchestras, operas and symphonies, and traditional music education. But one also finds an academy of aesthetic peers among street rappers, church choirs, and coffee-shop musicians. Hip-hop and rap are an example of an academy that has radically changed in its recognition by society.

In recent decades, the field of education has attempted to define the disciplinary traditions that will provide the best educational background for our youth. Standards for "what every child should know and be able to do" have been created for nearly every subject taught in the schools, including the arts. Discussion of these standards is beyond the purview of this chapter; but the notion of a discipline of learning shaped by an academy, and traditions that will ground students in cognitive representations of the world, is important. Howard Gardner identifies a shift in thinking about thinking that is certainly key to educators:

The key notion of the cognitive revolution is "mental representation." Cognitive psychologists believe that individuals have ideas, images, and various "languages" in their mind-brain; these representations are real and important, and are susceptible to study by scientists and to change by educators. . . .

The simple shift to representations brought about a revolution in thinking about the two earlier strands of psychology. No longer did one focus simply on behaviors. Indeed, one might almost think of behaviors as being epiphenomena (that is, as being the shadows of our determining mental representations).[11]

Echoing the broadest sense of the aesthetic, Gardner equates these mental representations of the world to disciplines of study, lenses that shape how one interprets the world and how one creates new knowledge. He suggests the importance of teaching students to think like a scientist, an artist, an historian—in other words, to master the skills, knowledge, and traditions of thought that will provide learners with access to the academy, which will in turn provide them with the ability to create.

The discipline traditions focus attention in particular ways, and attention is the key to both creativity and education, according to Csikszentmihalyi. "If we want to learn anything we must pay attention to the information to be learned. And attention is a limited resource."[12] Attention provides both impetus and possibility for the creative effort to succeed. We can process only so much information at any given time, and our cognitive processes have evolved to provide us with remarkable capacity for "chunking" and organizing information in contextual ways.[13] The disciplines help with this. One might argue that the ability to focus attention is the essential core skill of education.

If creativity and education make us unique as humans, then creative expression and education—the connection to the communities of the past, present, and future—are not a privilege or a frill, but a most basic human right. The arts and humanities in particular are records of cultures and of individuals within those cultures. Just as "history belongs to the winners," so cultures and individuals become important or marginalized as their aesthetic voice is included or excluded from society's "attentional record." Selection of the curriculum and the inclusion or exclusion of the voices attended to (or not) by the school will in turn affect the attention of the community and the status of the many creative academies within society at large. The arts can transform education not because they "reach" a student and assimilate him or her into the majority culture, but because they *connect* students (and adults) to the knowledge and traditions of the larger community in a way that also encourages participation and expression of individual voices.

SEEING WITH INTELLIGENT EYES, HEARING ABSENT VOICES

Education is the ability to listen to almost anything without losing your temper or your self-confidence.

—Robert Frost

Urban communities are diverse communities, and to be healthy they must find ways to embrace that diversity as a strength. The arts have great potential to foster the interaction of the individual and the group. They educate by giving voice to the individual while respecting and embracing diversity of expression and ideas. By learning to bring both experience and reflection to our seeing, we can honor community as well as the creations of other cultures.

The Intelligent Eye: Understanding "Other"

The arts and humanities are a way for educators to reach students different from themselves, and can bring communities together by fostering understanding of multiple cultures. One cannot become the "other," but one can gain a reasonably good—and respectful—understanding of

the other by learning to see reflectively through the arts. David Perkins puts it this way:

Experiential intelligence . . . specializes in the quick take. It thrives on the expected. It honors the predictable over the adventurous, and the simple over the subtle. . . . Reflective intelligence refers to the knowledge, skills, and attitudes that contribute to mental self-management. . . . At the broadest level, this controlling role of reflective intelligence can be viewed as a matter of dispositions—to give looking time, to look broadly and adventurously, to look clearly and deeply, and to look in an organized fashion.[14]

To foster community, we must move from defining others using experiential intelligence, to understanding others—and ourselves—using reflective intelligence. Aesthetic artifacts are an effective subject for reflective intelligence. The artistic record of an individual and, collectively, of a culture, lend incredible insight into history, beliefs, values, and present and future potential. Reflective seeing also encourages us to define ourselves as individuals, instead of defining ourselves through rejection of others who do not, experientially, seem like us. Stereotypes come from the "quick take" of experiential intelligence, using a pattern of assumptions about culture and group to simplistically classify individuals. Aesthetic activities can teach us to think beyond the quick take of cultural background, as Maxine Greene describes:

Cultural background surely plays a part in shaping identity; but it does not determine identity. It may well create differences that must be honored; it may occasion styles and orientations that must be understood; it may give rise to tastes, values, even prejudices that must be taken into account.[15]

Finding Voice

For both education and community transformation, the aesthetic affirmation of the individual voice may be the most effective way to ensure participation in the learning community. For many students, participation in the group is more or less assured. They are not absent from the status quo or the expectations of student achievement. Even if they do not value education or school, they understand that by participating they will be better suited to take their place in a community that they already "own." Marginalized students are a different story. They must see the real possibility of reward from education by seeing how their voices contribute to society. This is the territory, unsettling to some, to which the transformational aesthetic takes us. By noticing the previously silent, we affirm the potential of the individual to be a force in the creative academy, and to change the academy's relationship with society's attentional record. This is a way to have a voice that might actually be heard. Maxine Greene again:

To help the diverse students we know articulate their stories is not only to help them pursue the meanings of their lives—to find out *how* things are happening and to keep posing questions about the why. It is to move them to learn the new things, to reach out for the proficiencies and capacities, the craft required to be fully participant in this society, and to do so without losing the consciousness of who they are.[16]

This is not merely an issue of motivating students by somehow connecting the curriculum with their life experiences; this is about offering them the real possibility of reward from education by helping them to see how their voices exist within, and contribute to, society. Our students' voices can either be implied by their absence, or included as valuable contributors to our definitions of student achievement.

The reiterative process of artistic creation, "big-C Creativity" and its interplay with academies and society, when considered with the concept of reflective intelligence, presents something of a paradox. Artistic efforts *must* be about the individual or individuals who create; they can be inspired by the "other," but cannot be "other." However, it is learning to see and understand the creative efforts of others that enables us each to

know something of substance about community members who are unlike us. In so doing, we all join the community.

To illustrate the individual's role in the aesthetic process, consider "protest theatre" such as that of Brecht, Boal, and recent South African artists. These artists focus on drawing attention to the creative work in order to cause those outside of it—the spectators, or "spect-actors," as Boal calls them—to question the status quo. They do not seek to arouse empathy, a sense of "belonging with" the actors, but rather a distancing that will foster introspection and analysis. These artists understand that their voice must always be interpreted by others through their own experiences. Here is Brecht instructing actors:

The actor must play the incidents as historical ones. Historical incidents are unique transitory incidents associated with particular periods. The conduct of the persons involved in them is not fixed and "universally human"; it includes elements that have been or may be overtaken by the course of history, and is subject to criticism from the immediately following period's point of view. The conduct of those born before us is alienated from us by an incessant evolution.[17]

Consciously bringing aesthetic voice to all members of the urban community has potential to help each member find and express his or her voice. As records of our sense perceptions, the arts and humanities allow ideas to take concrete form, providing an important artifact of the community's transformation and reminding individuals of their parts in it.

TRANSFORMING OUR PERCEPTIONS: THE AESTHETIC URBAN LEARNING COMMUNITY

Too much sanity may be madness. And maddest of all, to see life as it is and not as it should be!

—*Miguel de Cervantes*

In this section we look at the research record of the effects of arts education, and discuss how the aesthetic can, indeed must, move beyond the school walls to embrace and transform the community. In doing so, we define urban education broadly to mean the education of all members of the urban community. As school entities, we are almost uniquely suited to the task of mitigating the "mass-market" forces of policy—those that are concerned about preparing workers, maintaining current rules, reinforcing historical power structures. We are in a unique position to help our students and community members engage in learning and creating. Of all pursuits, the arts and humanities may lend themselves best to lifelong learning. They are able to include adults and youth on equal footing, learning and doing side-by-side.

Urban communities are often faced with challenging educational tasks, possessing disproportionate numbers of disadvantaged students, greater extremes of poverty, and greater strains on available resources than their suburban counterparts. We noted above that the arts have most frequently been incorporated to address such problems. Consider that of 62 studies summarized in the *Critical Links* report,[18] nearly all that address inner-city study sites and/or urban issues do so from the perspective of using the arts to address learning or social problems in these settings. That the arts are effective in addressing problems within the schools is to be celebrated, but we urge mindfulness so that we do not limit our understanding of the aesthetic dimension of education to that of a prescription for student and school deficits.

Transforming Academic and Social Development

There is already much evidence of a definitive correlation, if not a proven causal connection, between arts participation and factors key to academic and social development. We do not feel it necessary to make a strong distinction between the two here. Should the arts be a causal factor in success

for young people, the implications are fairly obvious regarding the inclusion of arts for all students. But correlations as strong as those identified in numerous studies indicate that there is at least a relationship of privilege between the aesthetic dimension and success in life. It is this relationship that is relevant to our discussion, and it is a relationship surely worth further study.

Time and again, research shows a strong correlation between academic success and arts participation, especially in the areas of mathematics and language. For example, math, verbal, and composite SAT scores are strongly correlated with increased participation in arts classes.[19] A comparative study of thousands of students in the National Educational Longitudinal Survey (NELS) showed that students (in general and those in low socio-economic status subgroups) with consistent high levels of involvement in music in middle- and high-school years had significantly higher levels of mathematics proficiency by grade 12. In addition, sustained involvement in theatre was associated with gains in reading proficiency, self concept and motivation, and higher levels of empathy and tolerance for others.[20] Although it may be hypothesized that students with strong verbal and math skills tend to self-select into arts classes, there are independent studies that support causal links between theatre and music in particular and learning verbal and mathematics skills, respectively.[21] Certain social and developmental benefits are found consistently in the research as well. For example, a case study project involving 2,269 11th-year students found that arts classes resulted in enjoyment, learning about social and cultural issues, development of creativity and thinking skills, enriched expressive skills, self confidence, and social development.[22] These types of benefits appear throughout the literature.

Many artists and educators cite the open-ended, risk-taking nature of the arts as key to developing students' personal and academic abilities. Veteran arts educator Jessica Hoffman Davis discusses the value of failure:

Arts encounters with mistake making, with facing and building on what's wrong, have tremendous implications for learning in other disciplines. But they are uniquely accessed in the safety of arts classrooms where, perhaps ironically, risk taking and failure may fruitfully abound. Safe from the hard edges of right and wrong answers, safe from agendas that exclude multiple perspectives, safe from assessments that are sure of themselves, arts classrooms provide opportunities for students to explore the messy uncertain realities that preoccupy their lived lives within and beyond the world of school.[23]

Such perspectives on engaging the world and learning are consistent with research on creativity and cognitive science.

Transforming Teaching and Learning

Inclusion of the arts and humanities in substantive ways puts students and teachers into interactive roles different from what one might expect to find in the traditional American classroom. These interactions lead to the transformation of the teaching and learning process, which seems to be essential for the benefits to students to reliably occur. Some examples of these noted changes in practice include:

- Being more student-focused, with teachers acting as coaches and facilitators of learning[24]
- Expanded teaching strategies, emphasizing risk taking, revision, and improvement; and inquiry-based and hands-on approaches that let students engage problems and test their own solutions[25]
- Finding options for assessing students progress and gaining new insights into student learning that teachers may otherwise have overlooked[26]
- More collaboration among teachers, and by teachers with the community and community arts resources[27]
- Valuing young people and placing them in positions of high expectation and responsibility in collaboration with adults[28]

The transformation of the relationship between learner and teacher cannot be emphasized strongly enough. Not only does it change the way a student works at learning, it provides life role models. In a study of 811 high school students, the proportion of minority students identifying a music teacher as a role model was significantly larger than for any other discipline—36 percent as opposed to 28 percent of English teachers, 11 percent of elementary teachers, 7 percent of physical education/sports teachers, and 1 percent of principals.[29]

Transforming the Connection of School to the World

There is also consistent evidence that the arts connect the educational effort to the "real world" and to the community in powerful ways. The Champions of Change report notes that "The arts experiences described in the research show remarkable consistency with the evolving workplace. Ideas are what matter, and the ability to generate ideas, to bring ideas to life and to communicate them is what matters to workplace success."[30] Evaluators of the "Transforming Education Through the Arts Challenge" found that teachers were exposed to, and learned to work with, a wide variety of community and arts resources.[31]

Transforming the Urban Site into an Aesthetic Learning Community

Artists and scholars suggest that a transformation can occur by giving the arts and humanities an active role in the education of all members of the urban community. According to Seana Lowe, several elements are needed for art to serve as an effective tool for community development, such as: (1) a "safe and fun" mood, coming together for the purpose of "artistic and community-building processes," and (2) "shared goals of community building and art."[32] The artist is a key catalyst, and Lowe compares the process to ritual:

Community art can affect personal and social transformation if utilized as a model for ritual interaction because of the combined influence of ritual and art. Ritual is a unique type of social interaction that serves as a context for possible change, and art uniquely inspires openings in imagination and need fulfillment.

Supported by the transformative influence of the artist's role, ritual has the capacity to recreate social frameworks by engaging human sentiment, and the symbols it produces can create social facts.[33]

In their introduction to the special issue of *Education and Urban Society* focusing on art education, Debra Holloway and Beth Krensky note that:

Transformative art education that provides students with opportunities to develop voice and make positive changes in their lives is rare, yet it does exist in schools and community centers in urban settings throughout the United States. . . . There are particular art education pedagogies that promote social responsibility, including community-based, feminist, moral/ethical, critical, and multicultural art education.[34]

It is interesting to note that the particular approaches cited by Holloway and Krensky have in common a conscious effort to make the voice of a marginalized academy heard within the larger society. The interplay of our creative academies is something of an intellectual evolution, but it does not need to be a competitive survival of the fittest. Unlike biological evolution, which may threaten the individual in service of the greater good of the species, creative evolution values and validates the individual voice. If we hope to make schools work for all children in our communities, we must move beyond the quick take to use our reflective intelligence to see each individual and his or her potential to contribute to the intellectual and creative evolution. This is an enormous challenge to each person in the community, but our urban centers in particular must rise to meet it. By including a true aesthetic dimension throughout our urban schools and communities, we will be better able to educate all our children effectively and strengthen our centers of civilization.

EXAMPLES OF PROJECTS THAT USE THE ARTS TO IMPROVE URBAN COMMUNITIES AND EDUCATION

Project ACE: Arts in Community Education— Milwaukee, Wisconsin

Arts in Community Education (ACE) brings learning through music into the classroom every day for Milwaukee children. The program integrates the arts with all subject areas in grades K–5, and supports school curricula in music and arts in grades 6–8. It serves more than 7,500 students and their parents. More than 400 teachers and professional musicians have been involved with the program. ACE was recognized by the Wisconsin Department of Public Instruction as a powerful enhancement of young people's education.[35]

CAPE: Chicago Arts Partnerships in Education—Illinois

The Chicago Arts Partnerships in Education brings together 37 schools, 53 professional arts organizations, and 27 community organizations. Evaluation indicated the value of the partnerships, demonstrated by the success of the collaboration of artists, schools, and the larger community. Six years into the project, teachers were fully integrating the arts into their subjects. Classroom and school climate improved, and students made significant gains in achievement as measured by Illinois standardized tests, the Iowa Test of Basic Skills, and subject and grade-level assessments. CAPE has been replicated across nine cities in the United States, Canada, and England.[36]

Art in the Market Project—Cincinnati, Ohio

Art in the Market is a partnership of the Community Design Center at the University of Cincinnati with two other organizations—the Citizen's Committee on Youth and Impact Over-the-Rhine—designed to serve at-risk youth aged 14–18 in Cincinnati's inner-city "Over-the-Rhine" community. Findlay Market, located in Over-the-Rhine, has been the site of Art in the Market projects since 1996. More than 200 youths have participated. The art products from the project are considered a welcome addition in the Over-the-Rhine community, and participants reported a greater willingness to work in their community. Representatives of the community, market vendors, the advisory council, parents, and the Art in the Market staff were all pleased with the results of the project.[37]

Pudding and Puppets: Using Accessible Art to Promote Family Literacy—Louisville, Kentucky

Using materials as varied as cookies with instant-pudding icing and paper bags transformed into puppets, arts educators from the Speed Museum work with recently arrived refugee children and their parents to promote family literacy. The emphasis is on having fun and finding simple, affordable ways to build literacy into everyday activities. The family literacy program of Catholic Charities Migration and Refugee Services serves multiple refugee communities, but most recently has welcomed a large number of Somali Bantu families. With little or no formal education experience and no English language skills, these parents face incredible challenges as they endeavor to support their children's schooling. Arts-based family literacy programs such as this partnership offer examples of the ways in which parents can encourage learning and the exploration of ideas. Other recent projects at the resettlement center have used photography and indigenous fiber arts to encourage self-expression and community involvement among recently arrived refugee families.

Rainier Vista Arts Program—Seattle, Washington

This year-round Arts Program for the young residents of the Rainier Vista public housing community is a partnership of the Seattle Housing Authority and the Children's Museum of Seattle. The program focuses on the arts of specific cultures and brings in guest artists, actors, musicians, and dancers to instruct the children and develop exhibits and performances. The afterschool program offers hands-on experience in the visual, performing, and literary arts supplemented with field trips to museums, libraries, cultural institutions, galleries, and artists' studios. In the summer program, students are provided with breakfast and lunch and participate in discipline-specific classes. The program has been cited by the U.S. Department of Housing and Urban Development as a model for public housing communities.[38]

The 52nd Street Project—New York City

"The purpose of the 52nd Street Project is to give every child the experience of success through writing and performing his or her own plays. Economically disadvantaged children from the Hell's Kitchen neighborhood of New York City are paired with professional theater artists to create, mount, and perform original theater pieces. Workshops take place in local community centers and theaters, as well as out-of-town retreats. The 52nd Street Project has written a practical guide to teaching theater arts to children."[39]

The Partnership for Arts, Culture, and Education—Dallas, Texas

The Partnership for Arts, Culture, and Education (PACE) brings more than fifty arts and cultural organizations together to facilitate arts and cultural programming for students. In a four-year assessment project, PACE found that integrating community-based arts and cultural enrichment into the core curriculum improved student achievement. Their study found significant differences in academic achievement in language arts as measured by standardized state-mandated tests. Teachers collaborated to align core subjects through thematic units that served as the basis for selecting community arts experiences for the students.[40]

NOTES

1. U.S. Department of Education, National Center for Education Statistics (NCES). *Elementary School Arts Education Survey: Fall 1999*, p. A-14. Washington, DC: U.S. Government Printing Office.

2. U.S. Department of Education, NCES (1999).

3. U.S. Department of Education, NCES (1999).

4. U.S. Department of Education, NCES (1999), p. 89.

5. U.S. Department of Education, NCES (1999), p. 89.

6. U.S. Department of Education, Office of Educational Research and Improvement. (1999). The *NAEP 1997 arts report card*, p. 142. Washington, DC: U.S. Government Printing Office.

7. Nichols, B. (2003). *Demographic characteristics of arts attendance, 2002*. Research Division Note #82. Washington, DC: National Endowment for the Arts.

8. American Association of Museums. (2003). *Museums working in the public interest*. Retrieved December 10, 2004, from http://www.aam-us.org/resources/general/publicinterest.cfm.

9. DanceUSA. (2004). *Facts and Figures*. Retrieved November 12, 2004, from http://www.danceusa.org.

10. Csikszentmihalyi, M. (1996). Creativity: Flow and the psychology of discovery and invention, p. 8. New York: HarperCollins.

11. Gardner, H. (1999). *The disciplined mind: What all students should understand*, p. 67. New York: Simon & Schuster.

12. Csikszentmihalyi, Creativity: flow and the psychology of discovery and invention, p. 8.

13. Bransford, J., Brown, A., & Cocking, R. (Eds.), (2000). *How people learn: Brain, mind, experience, and school (Expanded Edition)*. Washington, DC: National Academy Press.

14. Perkins, D. (1994). *The intelligent eye: Learning to think by looking at art*, p. 82. Santa Monica, CA: The J. Paul Getty Trust.

15. Greene, M. (1995). *Releasing the imagination: Essays on education, the arts, and social change*, p. 163. San Francisco: Jossey-Bass.

16. Greene (1995), p. 5.

17. Brecht, B. (1967). A short description of a new technique of acting which produces an alienation effect. In S. Clayes (Ed.), *Drama and Discussion*, p. 322. New York: Meredith Publishing Co.

18. Deasy, R. (Ed.). (2002). *Critical links: Learning in the arts and student academic and social development*. Washington, DC: Arts Education Partnership.

19. Deasy (2002), p. 96.

20. Catterall, J., Chapleau, R., & Iwanaga, J. (1999). Involvement in the arts and human development: General involvement and intensive involvement in music and theater arts, p. 2. In E. Fiske (Ed.), (1999). *Champions of change: The impact of arts on learning*. Washington, DC: Arts Education Partnership and the President's Committee on the Arts and Humanities.

21. Kase-Polisini, J. (Ed.). (1985). *Creative drama in a developmental context*. New York: University Press of America; Deasy (2002); Fiske (1999); Podlozny (2000). Strengthening verbal skills through the use of classroom drama: A clear link, pp. 239–276. *The Journal of Aesthetic Education*, 34 (3–4); Welch, N. (Ed.). (1995). *Schools, communities, and the arts: A research compendium*. Washington: National Endowment for the Arts.

22. Deasy (2002), p. 76.

23. Davis, J. (2003, October 8). In defense of failure. *Education Week*.

24. Horowitz, R. (2004). *Summary of large-scale arts partnership evaluations*, p. 22. Washington: Arts Education Partnership.

25. Horowitz (2004), pp. 22–24; Seidel, K. (1995). *Leaders' theatre: A case study of how high school students develop leadership skills through participation in theatre*. Unpublished doctoral dissertation, University of Cincinnati, OH; Fiske (1999), pp. ix–x.

26. Horowitz (2004); Weitz, J. (1996). *Coming up taller: Arts and humanities programs for children and youth at risk*. Washington: President's Committee on the Arts and Humanities.

27. Horowitz (2004), pp. 23–24; Seidel (1995); Fiske (1999); Castañeda, I., & Zorn, D. (2001). *AAAE Arts Connections longitudinal study: A technical report*. Cincinnati, OH: University of Cincinnati Evaluation Services Center.

28. Seidel (1995); Fiske (1999); Weitz (1996); McLaughlin, M. (2001). Community counts. *Educational Leadership, 58* (7), pp. 14–18.

29. Hamann, D., & Walker, L. (1993). Music teachers as role models for African American students. *Journal of Research in Music Education, 41*.

30. Fiske (1999), p. x.

31. Killeen, D., Frechtling, J., & Perone, D. (2002). *Transforming education through the arts challenge, final evaluation report.* Columbus, OH: The National Arts Education Consortium, Ohio State University. Available online at http://www.aep-arts.org.

32. Lowe, S. (2001). The art of community transformation. *Education and Urban Society, 33* (4), p. 468.

33. Lewis, A. (1980). The ritual process and community development. *Community Development Journal, 15* (3).

34. Holloway, D., & Krensky, B. (Eds.), (2001). The arts, urban education, and social change, p. 359. *Education and Urban Society, 33* (4).

35. Milwaukee Symphony, Education programs. (2004). Retrieved from http://www.milwaukeesymphony.org.

36. Catterall, J., & Waldorf, L. Chicago arts partnership in education: Summary evaluation. In Fiske (1999), pp. 38–62

37. *Evaluation reports on the Art in the Market Project prepared for the community design center.* (2000, 2001, 2002, 2003). Cincinnati, OH: University of Cincinnati Evaluation Services Center.

38. Weitz (1996), p. 69.

39. Weitz (1996), p. 86.

40. Tunks, J. (1997). Evaluation Report: *The partnership assessment project: Changing the face of American education.* Dallas, TX: Partnership for Arts, Culture, and Education.

AESTHETIC CONSCIOUSNESS AND DANCE CURRICULUM: LIBERATION POSSIBILITIES FOR INNER-CITY SCHOOLS

Donald Blumenfeld-Jones

In this chapter I explore how teaching modern expressionist dance to inner-city school children might be part of a liberation educational practice. In the context of teaching the arts, "liberation" means: people developing an "aesthetic consciousness" which provides the ability to come to grips with the emotional and physical constituents of their realities in ways that allow them to more consciously experience those realities (which are often, in the midst of living them, opaque to understanding). Through such encounters they may be able to think of new ways to be in those realities that lead to a greater range of possible lives they might lead, lives that would not be merely a pursuit of individual happiness but understood as ensconced within a communal context of responsibility for each other. In the specific case of teaching dance, liberation could take place through students creating their own dances out of the material of their own lives as the vehicle for developing aesthetic consciousness.

I will explore this liberation possibility in a number of steps. First, I will develop the concept of "aesthetic consciousness" in real-world social contexts related to what it means to be a cultured person and a person with taste, developing an awareness of the relation between aesthetics, class, and race. Second, I will connect these ideas to identity politics, laying out the terrain of modern dance possibilities as species of identity politics. I will do this for one particular population, African-American children. Last, I will describe a project I enacted in an African-American public inner-city middle school in Durham, North Carolina. Through these steps I will try to show how a certain form of identity politics provides the possibility for what I term an "authenticating" aesthetic practice, in which lies the aforementioned experiential possibilities. While the specific focus is on an African-American inner-city project, I hope the reader will be able to read "outward" to other contexts by considering how the discussion resonates with her/his experience and/or thinking.

AESTHETICS, LIVING AESTHETICALLY, AND SOCIAL CLASS/RACE

I will begin by clarifying what I mean by "aesthetics." The word derives from the Greek and means "sense perception or sensation" and is, in philosophy, "the study of what is immediately pleasing to our visual or auditory perception or to our imagination" as well as "the study of the nature of beauty." More conventionally, it is usually associated with the arts and is the study of "taste and criticism in the creative and performing arts."[1] The basic aesthetics questions are "What is beauty?" and "What is imagination and how does it function?" and, for the arts, the subquestions are, for instance, "How do the arts deal with beauty?", "What is art?", and "What are the criteria for assessing the quality of a specific work of art?" The art questions, and their answers, are designed to help viewers of art understand art and for artists to ground their practices in an intelligible understanding of what they are trying to accomplish. The answers to these questions have, of course, varied over the centuries according to differing social and political contexts.[2]

The questions of beauty and sensation, however, are not restricted to the arts. For instance, the degree to which people attend to their likes and dislikes in personal style in the areas of clothing, housing, furnishings, food, and so on, and attend to ways of being with others,[3] to that extent they are concerned with beauty, sensation, and sensual awareness, and can be said to be "living aesthetically." Conventionally, people today make their aesthetic choices with a consumerist consciousness, connecting beauty and sensation with buying the right food, clothing, makeup, movies, music, books, and so forth, in order to feel as if they are living the beautiful life, leading to improving their chances at success in life. Such consumerism is not confined to any one social class. For each social class people are known by what they wear, where they live, what vehicle they drive, what kind of food they eat, what kind of entertainment they consume, and they establish public identities in terms of how particular goods bestow particular social status, connecting them to a particular community. In all of this, aesthetics is at work.

"Beauty," the fundamental aesthetic concern, informs the above-mentioned choices. When people choose to dress in a certain way, that choice is meant to convey beauty to others (and to make themselves feel beautiful as well), not in any conventional sense of "beauty" but in the sense that their particular community would see as "beautiful." However, people do not, generally, construe their choices for becoming beautiful with aesthetics. Rather, as I have already noted, they construe aesthetics and art to be synonymous. In this synonymity, art is not merely "art" but, is, rather, high art,[4] which represents real beauty and is part of what Raymond Williams termed the "selective tradition."[5] This "real art" is consumed by those who occupy the power centers of society, as they attend symphonies, the theater, museums, and so forth, filling their lives with socially sanctioned beauty. It is not necessarily the case that they always like "high art," but it is with "high art" that they are most associated. It is the wealthy who pay millions for a Van Gogh painting; who attend charity functions for the opera and symphony; who pay large sums to attend symphony, opera, and theatrical productions; and who attend museum and gallery openings. These individuals subscribe to the aesthetic of the selective tradition and have access to and, supposedly, appreciation for it. Such subscription sanctions them as cultured and, in turn, as natural wielders of social power. On the other side of culture is Gans's "popular culture" designation. This tacitly references people who value country-western music, television game shows, soap operas, MTV, hip-hop culture, rock and roll, and the like, and who purchase paintings of dogs playing cards, of bucolic fields, of clowns, and of doe-eyed children, and enjoy painted velvet paintings. Such people tend to be members of the middle and working classes. People who claim enjoyment of country-western music, television game shows, and so forth, do not identify their interests in these objects as an interest in "the arts," and they do not subscribe to the value of aesthetics in their lives, for while they may enjoy their own form of beauty, it is not beauty in the aesthetics sense. This tinges their interests with a distinctly déclassé flavor, even to them. The distinction between what is really art (really beautiful) and what is neither art nor beautiful is based on a class definition of art and beauty. Pierre Bourdieu's *Distinction*[6] explicitly laid out this terrain as he explored the different social classes' view of what it means to have "good taste" and ably showed the social structures that resulted in the working-class membership viewing itself as having no aesthetic taste but enjoying its lack since the "having of social taste" was onerous. Nevertheless, it should be understood, in my thinking, that the working class in that study and the working class, the working poor, and the lower middle class do not lack aesthetics but possess, rather, a certain view of the value and meaning of aesthetics cultivated throughout society such that their hegemonized consciousness labels their taste as invalid or illegitimate as they subscribe to the inferiority of their own taste. The selective tradition that performs this labeling is found in school rules and curricula, which maintain and nurture the high/low culture distinction and are used to distribute valued school goods (students who appreciate high art are more likely to receive better teaching and better curricula), which, in turn, are used to distribute social goods. The elite class, who most benefits from such thinking, and whose representatives (school administrators and faculty) administer this thinking, view popular culture as dangerous and in need of being eliminated from school experience. In this way, the selective tradition is not only the most valued tradition but, also, the only tradition of real value.

Getting more specific about the relation between aesthetic living, popular culture, and danger, African-American children who live in or around the official poverty line in urban settings clearly have very specific aesthetics in terms of clothing and music, which are obviously important to them (given the percentage of their income they spend on such things). This communal popular culture aesthetic has been seen by society outside their communities as representing social danger (although this "ghetto" culture has become increasingly popular with middle-class white youth, to the dismay and fear of their parents). The hip-hop aesthetic is exemplary of this and the ways in which schools deal with this culture informs us of the meanings ascribed to the aesthetic by those outside of it. Succinctly, the hip-hop aesthetic is associated, by the larger society, with criminality and with encouraging anti-authority attitudes and is seen to lack social propriety and the ability to help young people succeed in life. This translates, in schools, into the banning of baseball caps worn turned to the side and the banning of certain other clothing.

An excellent example of this occurred recently in a Scottsdale, Arizona, school where an outstanding African-American student, Marlon Morgan (nominated for Youth of the Year by his local Boys and Girls Club, longtime Boys and Girls Club volunteer, editor of the school newspaper sports section, and fine student), was arrested on campus for wearing his hat sideways after refusing an order by campus security guards to turn it forward and then refusing to go to the assistant principal's office. Marlon pointed out that other youths (white) were wearing their hats sideways and weren't being asked to change. He was subsequently jailed for disorderly conduct, insubordination to police, and trespassing (he was eating lunch in his school cafeteria), and was suspended from school for three days. When he protested his differential treatment, the school and district officials replied that wearing his hat in that way was a sign of disrespect for authority (he broke the school dress code) and of being a gangbanger. (This despite much evidence to the contrary.) The National Association for the Advancement of Colored People (NAACP) became involved and his mother protested, eventually getting his suspension shortened to one day. Then, at the end of the school year a picture appeared in the student newspaper with Marlon and another African-American student who was wearing his hat sideways. The school administration seized all the newspapers and ordered the newspaper staff (including Marlon, the incoming sports editor for 2004–05) to tear the picture out of all the copies. They would have done the same for the yearbook (from which the picture was taken) if it hadn't been too costly to produce new yearbooks.[7]

We may ask why the administration of the school was so adamant in its policy and why the policy existed in the first place. Clearly they had labeled an aesthetic choice "subversive and dangerous," and even though an upstanding citizen of their school was wearing the clothing, he was accused of potentially provoking violence and danger. Obviously the school administration and school district (which are beholden, through the governing board membership and the most powerful voices speaking out at board meetings, to the power elites in the community) believe in the power of an aesthetic to be resonant with a deep consciousness that pervades all actions. Marlon was seen to be potentially violent and dangerous even though he had never shown signs of such behavior. Thus, his community's aesthetic was banned from the school (even though others, wearing hats in the same fashion, were not harassed). Beyond this specific set of incidents, while school people continue to condemn the hip-hop aesthetic (the school has maintained its dress code policies), they also fail to make "proper" aesthetics a central part of the curriculum. In the present environment of high-stakes testing, the arts are usually the first programs to be eliminated from schools. Aesthetics is clearly seen as a frill for inner-city children living in or near poverty, too rarified to be useful to people living in difficult economic, service-poor settings with lack of access to social resources. These children need to pass the basic academic testing program before money can be devoted to the arts in the schools. In short, the community's aesthetics are kept out of the school, but aesthetics of any kind is also not present in the curriculum.

In the face of these kinds of issues and arguments around aesthetics for inner-city children, how can we address developing an "aesthetic consciousness" in an urban setting? One obvious answer is to break down the barriers between the students' everyday lives and school life. In this case, allow hip-hop culture to be in the schools, acknowledging it as a legitimate form of aesthetic life. Use it as one base for developing art and art "appreciation." Open up the canon to critique. In these ways, the community's culture becomes the basis for curriculum rather than being adjunct or ignored. Another approach focuses not on popular culture but on using the making of art to explore the sensual aspects of life as markers of meaning in terms of how we are living our present lives. Rather than inculcate people with the knowledge of what is valued and what is not (a focus on high art), people make art in order to discover the life and beauty in their lives. Through such a mode of education, art might become critically useful and not just "a document of barbarity,"[8] institutionalizing the privilege of some on the backs of the massive others. Larger issues of life can be explored, which can, even, critique how art is bought and sold by those with the wealth and power. My task is, now, to develop this reasoning for liberation education through a more concrete and detailed discussion of, first, the relation between identity politics and possible dance resources and, then, through describing and discussing my particular project within the middle school.

DANCE AND THE AFRICAN-AMERICAN COMMUNITY: THE VARIETY WITHIN IDENTITY POLITICS

What are the possible dance resources that would be available for use in the school in which I taught? While some of the resources I will discuss were, in fact, not available to the students, because they exist in the world, they might have been available and are, therefore, pertinent to the discussion. One point should be made about "identity politics" as a guide to curriculum thinking. Such politics already exist through the above-mentioned "selective tradition" that informs the school curriculum, a tradition redolent with white privilege. "African-American" is the racially marked condition of unmarked "whiteness" (to borrow the discourse analysis in which being unmarked is the power position), and curriculum decisions are already made with whiteness tacitly in mind. To focus on African-American dance artists, as such, is to honor a tradition in the dance art absent from school life (except for the first species of identity politics dance art which I shall discuss) but which has a great deal to offer. Ironically, in thinking of identity politics and dance, African-American dance artists are no more monolithic than white dance artists, and the variety tells us that identity politics is not a neat and easily bounded term. Thus, even though some African-American artists do not choose to make art in reference to their racial/ethnic identity, they are yet marked by their status by others (reviewers, audiences, funding agencies). There is no escaping race in the United States.

One of the resources directly available to the children in this Southern city was a local dance company, headed by Chuck Davis, a dancer who had lived in New York City prior to moving to Durham, North Carolina, originally through the auspices of the American Dance Festival before he decided to take up permanent residence there and create a dance company. Mr. Davis had, for many years, taught for the National Endowment for the Arts through their "Dancers in Schools" program and was very experienced working with young people in schools. The company he established in Durham focused on performing dances of Africa and on teaching these dances in workshops and through outreach work into schools. He represented that segment of the African-American community who want to vivify the ancestry of today's African Americans, strengthening the individual's sense of valuable self, by focusing on who they were, as various peoples, prior to their imprisonment in Africa and subsequent enslavement within the United States. Various projects of Henry Louis Gates, Jr., (his TV series touring Africa and his *Encyclopedia Africana*) are other examples of this movement. Mr. Davis's company represented the only specifically African-American dance resource available to the community. I would argue that such dance fits easily, as an adjunct, occasional experience, within school settings because it is sufficiently exotic and distant from everyday life, that it poses no danger of altering that everyday life.

A second dance approach to African-American experience is exemplified in the work of Katherine Dunham. This approach to aesthetics and the African-American community has a strong anthropological cast (Dunham holds a PhD in anthropology), as the works that are produced are highly influenced by anthropological study of various black cultures, with a special focus on Haitian culture. Her study of the movement of these cultures was mixed with ballet and modern dance to produce a distinctive approach to movement that became known as the Katherine Dunham technique. This technique was rendered choreographically into spectacular theater, which Ms. Dunham characterized as "revues." She did not intend to reproduce "authenticity" in Davis's way, so much as communicate about culture through her art. She also differs from Davis in that at the time she was choreographing for and touring with her company (in the 1940s, '50s, and '60s), her dance was celebrated for its sensuality and aliveness but also, sometimes, branded as lascivious and teetering on the brink of obscenity. Although she became world-renowned and celebrated, her sensual work was seen as dangerous in its frank portrayal of such sensuality. As with Davis's heritage approach, Dunham invigorated a positive identity through making aesthetically legitimate the sensual life.[9]

Moving away from a heritage perspective, the focus shifts to celebrating the strength and vitality of African-American culture here in the United States. This is exemplified by the work of Alvin Ailey, who thematically explored "cultural" aspects of African-American life through such signature works as *Cry* (dealing with a black woman's grief), *Revelations* (dealing with the Southern experience, postemancipation), and solo studies of various great African-American musicians; and in the work of Donald McKayle, who choreographed numerous works based on street life in the African-American community. Ailey derived his movement vocabulary and dance technique from Lester Horton, a white maverick choreographer working in Los Angeles rather than New York City, who was the first choreographer to thoroughly integrate a dance company. With Horton's presence, identity politics presents a useful (something positive is achieved through it) but complex concept.

A fourth possible position takes a more or less race/ethnicity neutral stance toward dance and is exemplified by such artists as Bebe Miller and Bill T. Jones, both of whom may or may not explore what it means to be African American. Their focus is on their life experience in many guises, and they do not draw upon anthropological understandings as a base or upon culturally explicit forms. Rather, they function from a more or less "pure" modern dance base, as they are more interested in movement, music, and humanness than in speaking directly to people through conventionally legible forms (such as gospel music or dances about prostitutes in the community or the character of a jazz musician, and so forth). For instance, according to a 1999 *Dance Magazine* review of Bebe Miller:

[Miller] may be creating a new genre of dance: black urban flamenco. . . . From the get-go, Miller directs provocative questions toward the audience. She slyly asks if anyone is looking for the gay dancers on the stage, and she wonders aloud how many times the conversation shifts toward the fact that the company director is an African-American woman. Her troupe, composed of people of many colors, could be a microcosm of New York City—and she addresses her choreography toward the crazy quilt of city living.[10]

This reviewer reflects Miller's simultaneous awareness of her racial status, her questioning of any racial categories through her pastiche of references (black, urban, flamenco), and her direct acknowledgment of the salience of race in this society. She does not, as with Chuck Davis, Katherine Dunham, and Alvin Ailey, actively embrace her African heritage or African-American heritage, but she is more critical than they. In a similar example of postmodern pastiche, Bill T. Jones acknowledges publicly the influence of his Buddhist beliefs on his work. Jones has adopted the "postmodern" dance practice, drawing from ballet, a variety of modern dance vocabularies, and everyday movements, put together in idiosyncratic ways that reflect his individuality rather than his consciousness as an African-American choreographer. And yet, Jones has explored the issue of being African American in his choreography, particularly in his evening-length dance, "Last Supper at Uncle Tom's Cabin/The Promised Land." He has also been deeply involved, artistically, with the AIDS epidemic and homosexuality as issues. He creates work that is explicitly "political" in these regards, but that is rarely explicitly African American in theme. Nevertheless, Jones, as with Miller, is usually viewed as an African-American choreographer, rather than just a choreographer.

I will now turn to describing the project I enacted in the context of the above possibilities.

A MODERN DANCE PROJECT FOR THE MIDDLE SCHOOL

The program that I designed and produced was sponsored by the National Endowment for the Arts during the fall of 1981. It lasted six weeks and took place in a middle school in the eastern part of town, which was populated almost exclusively by African Americans. The school was nearly entirely African American although the faculty was predominantly white. Under the terms of this grant, my responsibility was to teach dance to the entire school. I had all morning every day of school, and I had each class (sixth, seventh, and eighth grades) for approximately forty minutes twice a week. I also arranged to have a special group on Fridays who would volunteer to have an extra class. In this extra class the students would create choreography that would be presented at a school assembly at the end of the six weeks. This arrangement was not part of the original grant (which had been secured by someone else), but was central to my version of the project. I

wanted young people to experience the fullness of bringing something from imagination to concrete fulfillment, including performing what they created. This full experience could provide a vision of their potentials as people and dancers and, potentially, act as a vehicle for liberation education. In order to show why this project had liberatory characteristics, I need to describe what I do when I teach dance.

My work comes out of the German Expressionist tradition developed by Mary Wigman in the first part of the twentieth century and carried on by Hanya Holm and Alwin Nikolais (at whose school I studied, including studying with Holm), and Phyllis Lamhut, with whom I studied and in whose company I danced for seven years. The gist of the German Expressionist approach is a focus upon the essence of an idea or event expressed in movement, exploring and revealing the inner state which that idea and/or event produces. The movement that is created is not obviously connected with the idea or event. For example, to make a dance dealing with poverty, one might not costume that dance in ragged clothing or portray hunger in obvious ways. Rather, movement stimulated by cultivating the inner state of "poverty" and "hunger" would become the movement for the dance; the artist is being expressive but not representational. The dance becomes "authentic" in the sense that a more direct human connection is made between inner states and ideas/events than between the idea/event and its external correlates.

In the Expressionist tradition, the dancer/choreographer discovers the authenticity of inner states through cultivating the pure movement potentials of her/his body. Rather than teach to an already established movement vocabulary (ballet, conventional modern dance forms, folkloric style of dances, such as Chuck Davis's work), the dancer/choreographer is taught about the potential for any movement the dancer/

choreographer might wish to make. The teaching focuses on coming to know, experientially, the movement potentials for various body parts (legs, arms, fingers, toes, face, upper body, middle torso, and lower body), how movement occupies space (close to the ground, normal level, moving into the air, and attending to how moving in directions feels), how movement occupies time (slow motion, fast motion, and time as pure duration or how long it takes to perform a movement), and about the body as sculptural shape. As these abilities to know one's moving body are developed, attention is turned to cultivating an understanding of inner states, beginning with more obvious ones related to the emotions, but, eventually, branching out into ideas and events as also having inner state responses that can be made into choreography. It is in this regard that the German Expressionist tradition provides potential for liberation. Once the dancer/choreographer comes to understand abstraction and the process of extracting essences from an experience, s/he has the ability to submit her/his daily life experience to the same process, developing new awareness of life circumstances, including the pain associated with that life. This pain, experienced in this way, might lead the person to seek the sources of the pain and do something about them, perhaps even through sharing the dances with others who can begin to connect with those life experiences. In this way, dance might contribute to social change.

Returning to the project, I worked with the children in this middle school with the basic abstract vocabulary curriculum set out above. My idea was to help them develop a sense of themselves as moving beings who felt and who could, in turn, manifest feelings into movement and organize the movements to express certain states of affairs. For the Friday group, we focused specifically on choreography built around the four "concepts" of body motion, space, time, and shape. Although this may seem purely abstract and disconnected from their daily lives, the "content" of the inner states they explored as they created these so-called abstract dances inevitably expressed their daily lives because whatever movements emerged from their bodies was a direct expression of that life. I did not have time to pursue this connection because the grant ran out and the school wouldn't have considered making this project part of their regular curriculum. However, it was clear to me that they were expressing their daily lives in the kind of energies they employed in their movement explorations as well as in the kinds of movement they chose, albeit abstractly conceptualized and performed. Although they had never seen dance like this (only break dancing and dancing on television), they took to it immediately and strongly. It attracted their sense of inner self and the freedom to create outside of the constraints of commercialized movement vocabulary and brought to them the opportunity to think anew and in ways that amazed them (as they communicated to me). In this I was participating most strongly in the tradition exemplified by Miller and Jones.

The most important "outcome" of this six-week workshop for the school was the final performance of the Friday group. Both the school people (students, teachers, administration, staff) and the young people themselves were overwhelmingly enthused by the final performance. They saw something in themselves of which they had no previous idea; it emanated from a place that was genuine and energized. It was, in fact, so energized that the Friday group asked me if I would approach the school administration about doing the performance again at a local elementary school. I agreed, approached the administration of the school, and secured their permission to do this performance, which we subsequently did two weeks later. This interval required more visits to the school, in order to rehearse for the performance as well as accompanying the students as the "artistic director" of the event to the school and teaching them, in so functioning, what it meant to perform for a public. When we performed at the elementary school, the middle schoolers were again greeted with great enthusiasm and pride by the students, faculty, and administration of that school.

What made this project significant from the point of view of developing an aesthetic consciousness that might be liberating? One way to conceptualize the program is to see it as what Lowe refers to as using the arts to "ameliorate social problems and to promote healthy communities. In particular, . . . to address social issues, . . . a recognition of the power of art to effect individual and social change and its ability to compel changes in individual identity, . . . to develop and express collective identity, to build community, and to address community problems."[11] For a time both the participants in the special workshop designed to produce the performance (which, as I have stated, had not been part of the original project) and the school people not involved in the Friday group began to structure an identity, that was particularly identity-building as African-American young people capable of something new, different, and authentic to themselves as people. The school became a place that could potentially develop an identity through art, and the students were celebrated for the skilled performance of their own movement. In these ways, individual change occurred and collective identity was fostered.

The project was, to some degree, "radical" in that the faculty didn't believe that these children were capable of a high level of professional investment in serious creation, and I was able to show them that they were wrong about these young people. Some teachers, when they brought their classes to study with me for a class period, either ignored what we

were doing by leaving for the class time or stayed and ignored what we were doing. One teacher, in particular, actively attempted to undermine my work with the young people by doing exactly what I asked her not to do: yell at the young people when they were "misbehaving" in her eyes (I didn't see their activity as "misbehavior" but as exuberance that held motional potential and could be channeled into dancing) and stating out loud that this program was a waste of these children's time. With this same teacher, when during one class one young man was becoming very aggressive with another student and I intervened and was attacked, she did nothing but watch. Thus, in general the faculty of the school was not very supportive of the project. So, although we did not enact critically social work of an explicit political type during the six weeks, we moved from a state of near total resistance by some children and faculty, tepid response by others, and active enthusiasm by some, to a place where the project was acknowledged as a great, albeit surprising (except to me) success. A new vision of these children's future was forwarded. To this degree, the work might be characterized as "radical."

In the end, the project was only potentially liberating in that there was no opportunity to pursue it further. However, we can see the potentials for such liberation in the way in which the project was carried out. First, I did not impose a foreign vocabulary upon the students (ballet, modern dance of one sort or another). Rather, I began with the basic facts about all human movement, no matter what its origin or meanings. All human movement is involved with body motion, space, time, and shape. We didn't study a school of dance, but rather a way of dancing. Second, the movements came from the students. As with most liberation-oriented curriculum initiatives, this is crucial: The material for the curriculum can only relate directly to the lives of the students if the lives of the students are at the center of the curriculum. Third, a process for exploring was offered (the German Expressionist tradition), which did not allow for the students to simply bring in prepackaged versions of human movement (in the form of that present-day popular dance), but to explore movement itself as movement. In so doing, break dancing, for instance, might come in but it would be subjected to motional exploration, as would any other movement. It would not be accepted as privileged movement to be learned and well executed if one were to consider oneself a dancer. Fourth, anyone could participate and skill was centered not around athletic ability to perform movement but on dedication to exploration of any movement. This democratized a potentially elitist practice (only those with great, innate physical skill would ordinarily be allowed to participate and perform). Fifth—and this is where the undeveloped potential lies—had we been able to stay together for a long time, I would have taught toward the students exploring their daily lives in a more explicit manner, but with abstraction/essence/expression at the heart of the exploration. In this way, they might have been able to develop dance that, when viewed as well as experienced by them, might have engaged others in conversations about their experiences of the dancing that would lead toward consideration of new ways of living in their community. Additionally, we would have worked to see every movement they made in their daily lives as having aesthetic potential. This is a species of aesthetic consciousness that transforms daily living into a daily creative act. Further, as they became sensitized to movement, they could view movements that they see in a new critical light through an aesthetic analytic lens. Last, in all this, their status as African Americans would be featured, in that the material for their dances would be directly related to deep inner states of being

structured through their lives as African Americans living in the United States. It is this approach to dance, replete with aesthetic consciousness, that I believe holds the greatest opportunity for what I have termed "authenticating" personal and social liberation education through the arts.

NOTES

1. Mautner, T. (Ed.). *Dictionary of philosophy* (p. 8). New York and London: Penguin Books.

2. Wolff, J. (1981). *The social production of art.* New York: St. Martin's Press; Eagleton, T. (1990), *The ideology of the aesthetic.* Oxford, UK: Basil Blackwell.

3. Goffman, E. (1959). *The presentation of self in everyday life.* Garden City, NY: Doubleday.

4. Gans, H. (1974). Popular culture and high culture; an analysis and evaluation of taste. New York: Basic Books.

5. Williams, R. Base and superstructure in Marxist cultural theory. *New Left Review, 82,* 3–16.

6. Bourdieu, P. (1984). Distinction: A social critique of the judgement of taste. Richard Nice, Trans. London: Routledge & Kegan Paul.

7. Bittner, E. (2004, March 13). Sideways ballcap lands Scottsdale teenager in jail. *Arizona Republic*; Bittner, E. (2004, May 20). Saguaro's cap controversy won't die. *Arizona Republic*; Ryman, A., & Bittner, E. (2004, March 16). District will investigate handling of hat incident. *Arizona Republic.*

8. Benjamin, W. (1986). Theses on the philosophy of history. In H. Adams and L. Searle (Eds.), *Critical theory since 1965* (p. 682). Tallahassee: University of Florida Press.

9. Dunham, K., Biography of Katherine Dunham. Retrieved from the John F. Kennedy Center for the Performing Arts Web site: http://www.kennedy-center.org/calendar/index.cfm?fuseaction=showIndividual&entitY_id=3721&source_type=A; Harman, T. (1974). *African rhythm—American dance: A biography of Katherine Dunham.* New York: Knopf.

10. Carman, J. (1999, August). Bebe Miller Company, the Joyce Theater, a review. *Dance Magazine.* Retrieved from http://articles.findarticles.com/p/articles/mim1083/is_8_73/ai_55292594.

11. Lowe, S. (2001, August). The art of community transformation. *Education and Urban Society, 22* (4), 457.

CREATING CONNECTIONS, SHAPING COMMUNITY: ARTISTS/TEACHERS IN URBAN CONTEXTS (URBAN GYPSIES)

Gene Diaz

Artists are people who live across and among various contexts. For the most part, they are multiple-jobbers who engage in work other than their artistic production to pay their bills and meet expenses. They inhabit many worlds, yet they are part of a discursive community that frequently brings them together at meetings and forums, concerts, exhibits, performances, and in some cases, schools and universities.[1] Through the art they create and the collaborative processes they generate, artists create connections that grow across neighborhoods, between communities and cultures, and within and across generations. As the gypsies of urban culture, they travel among us, leaving their creative work of collaborative art building as a kind of glue that holds our sometimes fractured and fragile communities together, fostering continuity and solidarity.

Those artists who are also educators, those that hold school contracts, and those that work as itinerant teachers across schools and districts, or within community arts organizations or galleries, frequently move across the borders and boundaries of their particular neighborhoods and geographic locations when they travel to work. The urban landscape requires this of many of us, since we don't live where we work. Unique to teaching artists, however, is the work that they do in bringing their home along with them. Their home is the art that they inhabit—the incredibly complex array of artifacts, materials, and urban detritus that inhabits the back part of teaching artists' cars or their ever-present backpacks, and the creative impulses they, themselves, exhibit and encourage in their students.

Teaching artists make connections between their art form and all areas of their lives, from their work in schools to their political views and to aspects of other people's lives, students most often. In the inaugural issue of the *Teaching Artist Journal*, Eric Booth suggests that as teaching artists engage people in creating meaning through art, they also create connections between their art experiences and their and others' lives. "They artistically engage participants as meaning makers. Phillip Ying suggests that a good subtitle for the *Teaching Artist Journal* might have been *Art that Connects*."[2]

Debra Holloway and Beth Kensky, as guest editors of *Education and Urban Society* in a special issue in 2001, focused on the importance of arts education in and outside of schools in urban contexts. They suggest that "an increasing number of art educators and educational researchers have found that the arts' effect on personal development influences the social context and has profound implications for social change."[3] Seeing the arts as a vehicle for "communicating ideas, revealing symbols, forging connections, and helping to prepare individuals for social interaction," they support claims that the arts have the power to transform the community and the social context within which the creator and the works exist.

Not all artists are teachers, and not all artists should be in schools. The success of the urban teaching or community artist depends upon their ability to bring people along on their journey of discovery; this journey requires creative exploration and expression of engagement in risk-taking and imagination. Like the contemporary gypsies of Spain or Rumania, these urban gypsies maintain traditions that have evolved over the years of their participation in their respective cultures. For artist/teachers, these traditions combine a sense of commitment to the communities we live in and the people who are our neighbors with a sense of dedication to art-making as social agency. At a forum for community artists in New Orleans years ago in which a panel of successful artists and arts critics spoke to the rag-tag audience of multiple-jobbing artists, one of the questions to the group was, "Why do you make art?" The response from a younger member of the group standing near the rear of the alternative gallery space on Magazine Street was: "Because I can't NOT do it!" I ask the question, "What is it about what we do, that we can't NOT do it?"

This chapter looks at teaching artists and community artists—urban gypsies—in two cities as they create connections, shape community, and build culture. With examples from New Orleans and Philadelphia, the stories come from the perspective of the artists working in schools and communities.

NEW ORLEANS

Arts Connection is a staff development program designed to provide comprehensive discipline-based arts education to students and their teachers in dance, theater, and visual art in the elementary schools of the New Orleans Public School (NOPS) system. Through ongoing collaborative artist/teacher and classroom teacher partnerships, students receive thematic integrated, interdisciplinary lessons focused on arts history, production, aesthetics, and critical analysis. In 1998 I conducted an evaluation of the program based in ethnographic research methods. Many of the artist/teachers were my colleagues in another summer arts program in nearby

Metairie known as Country Day Creative Arts.

Arts Connection emerged as an outgrowth of the Cultural Resources Program through the commitment and dedication of the then cultural arts coordinator in New Orleans, Shirley Trusty-Corey. From writing funding requests for the performing arts, Trusty-Corey moved into writing grants for artist residencies for visual artists. These residencies provided space in the schools and the time for students and artists to work collaboratively. Although artist residencies today are common practice, at that time, in the early 1980s, they were relatively new and untried. Trusty-Corey told me, "I certainly had the concept of artists being residents at schools before there was funding sources that one could tap into, that were called artists-in-residence programs."

The concept that was evolving through these efforts was that of providing students with educational experiences that honored a sense of creativity and aesthetics. Trusty-Corey believed that, despite the existence of a few art and music classes, aesthetic experiences were missing in schools at that time. Certainly theater and creative dramatics were not available to students, and dance. "Heaven forbid!" she exclaimed in mock horror. Itinerant music teachers, like so many traveling troubadours, made the rounds of as many schools as their time and budget permitted. But a coherent, organized arts program was needed to provide students with the challenging experiences of creative expression and to provide a rigorous, consistent curriculum for the arts. This was the goal of *Arts Connection*.

As Trusty-Corey saw that there was a lack of value placed on the arts in education and a lack of resources to sustain a program, her mission became clear. She would develop a program that used the arts resources available in the community and connect them with schools that had a need and a vision. As a problem solver by nature, she found the solution in forming a connection between the artists in the community and the students in the schools. Not all artists are educators; in fact, very few are able to meet the requirements of becoming an artist/teacher. Perhaps recognizing this fact is the most important insight that Trusty-Corey brought to the beginnings of *Arts Connection*.

As classroom teachers participated in the program, they repeatedly emphasized the changes in their practices, their ways of thinking about specific topics, and their development as individuals as a result of working with the artist/teachers. These changes were attributed to the use of discipline-based arts education (DBAE) activities led by the artist/teachers of *Arts Connection*. By definition, DBAE activities must incorporate four elements into the lessons: art production, art history, aesthetics, and art criticism. While each lesson offers a different balance of these elements, together they form a consistent basis for the projects that evolve through a continuous interdisciplinary collaboration between the artist/teachers and the classroom teachers.

The teaching methods and practices that are employed in presenting the program in the schools are based in experiential learning, or learning by doing, and on constructivist learning principles. Constructivist principles are based in the notion that students will construct their own knowledge as they participate in learning activities and are exposed to situations to which they bring their own life experiences. Constructivist classrooms reflect the principle that teachers do not act as knowledge purveyors but as facilitators of learning. Some of the practices employed by artist/teachers in this program include creative expression through art projects and performances, collaborative elaboration of group projects and productions, individual research and analysis, and assisted performance and production. These practices are congruent with the stated aims of the program and offer students opportunities to take responsibility for their own learning experiences.

Because of the structured format of the school day, leaving little unscheduled time available, teachers and artist/teachers find limited opportunities for sharing experiences with one another. Generally, while the artist/teacher is preparing for an art lesson, the teacher is in the classroom with the students. Other than the initial planning session at the beginning of the semester, many artist/teachers have little time for discussing follow-ups with the classroom teacher. The biannual workshops, however, provide more direct interaction between them, although there is not a specific method currently used for them to offer suggestions for each other. The "Regular Classroom Teacher's Survey," which teachers fill out at the end of their time with the program, incorporates questions with answers on a Likert scale, which provides only a glimpse at what the teacher is thinking.

The lessons and activities the artist/teachers bring into the classrooms and the schools in the program are specifically designed by practicing artists, and as such would generally not be activities that could be developed by a nonspecialist classroom teacher alone. However, many teachers found that working side-by-side with an artist enabled them to perceive their students differently, observe the world around them in a new way, and embellish their own work with new visions. It is unlikely that teachers will become artists or arts educators through their involvement of a semester or a year in the program, but it is not unlikely that they will become more aesthetic educators, more creative explorers, and more active learners.

Throughout *Arts Connection* are examples of students and teachers connecting with their own culture through activities that focus on their cultural heritage, their specific environment, and their personal lives. In a predominately African-American population of students, there are many visual arts activities based on the Harlem

Renaissance artists and writers; dance and theater pieces based in the historically significant Underground Railroad; murals of important black historical figures; and studies of the architecture of African peoples. Many activities involve students going out and looking at their neighborhoods, their school communities, and their families. This focus brings to the students, and the teachers, an increased awareness of and sense of responsibility for their own communities and cultures, and the world around them.[4]

It is through this sense of responsibility that students, and teachers, become empowered to make their own choices. Whether writing a script, designing a mural, or developing a dance, students make critical decisions based in creative choices. These decision-making processes and creative endeavors are learning experiences that can transfer to other areas of their lives, both inside and outside of schools. Whereas academic subjects traditionally are based in "getting it right," artistic expression is based in "getting it." Students and teachers relish the ability to succeed through the creative activities in the arts offered through *Arts Connection*. Because they are not pressured to "get it right," the traditional trappings of learning do not constrain the creative experience, suggesting to the casual observer that what they are doing is "just fun." In the words of one artist/teacher:

I really find it a unique experience for the kids. And the thing I've always liked about it is that it's taught in a way that all the kids can feel somehow successful, and be learning without realizing they're learning.

Not only are they learning, but research also indicates that artistic cultural enrichment programs such as *Arts Connection* make a difference in student achievement in other areas. The Partnership Assessment Program, a four-year assessment study by the Texas-based Partnership for Arts, Culture and Education (PACE) found that elementary students in socioeconomically deprived settings, such as the students in many of New Orleans's public schools, benefit academically from exposure to community arts and cultural programming.[5]

There is not enough art in our schools to avail all students of the opportunities for dreaming a future full of possibilities, a future complete with opportunities, and a future, in the words of student April Green, "where there would be no very hopeless people." Art is not a luxury item partaken of during times of prosperity, but an essential component of quality education, without which our students might never gain the dispositions which both Elliot Eisner and James Catterall propose as a particularly important set of outcomes for arts education: the abilities to imagine possibilities, explore ambiguity, and recognize multiple perspectives.[6] Without the arts how can our students contribute to forming a more equitable society, a more just and peaceful world, and their own sense of hope?

Arts Connection offers one example of the connections made across communities by teaching artists. It represents the fostering of what Maxine Greene would call a humane community. In schools where students with the stigma of "lower socioeconomic class" frequently become recipients of mindless training or treatment programs from well-intentioned educators and policy makers, this program considers students and teachers alike to be "capable of imagining, of choosing, and of acting from their own vantage points on perceived possibilities."[7] The teaching artists in this program encourage teachers to explore possibilities for learning through and in the arts, and create yet another connection across this diverse city.

PHILADELPHIA

Center in the Park, a nonprofit community center in Northwest Philadelphia, focuses on the needs of older people by offering academic, leisure, health, and life enrichment courses and activities. The programs are meant to expand the ambitions, capabilities, and creative capacities of older adults.[8] In 1997 several of the visual art course instructors noticed that the elders, predominantly African American, told stories to each other and to the instructors as they created clay sculptures and elaborate paintings. Their stories centered around their experiences of growing up in a severely racialized city, and focused on themes such as: a sense of community; the value of education and persistence; the importance of family lessons and advice; the pain of experiencing prejudice and discrimination; and their hopeful visions for the future.

Together with John Broomhall, the executive director of the Pennsylvania Alliance for Arts Education (PAAE), these artists conceived of a project in which these stories could come alive, through the arts, for children in elementary schools in the area to foster cultural continuity and forge intergenerational understanding. The elders agreed to participate in this project and offered their narratives in order to establish a cultural continuum through the sensitive application of their content to arts activities and lessons. In the words of African-American novelist Paule Marshall:

An oppressed people cannot overcome their oppressors and take control of their lives until they have a clear and truthful picture of all that has gone before, until they begin to use their history creatively.[9]

As an artist/teacher and ethnographer, I was called on to gather the stories that would inform the project. I arranged to meet with the participants in two focus group interview sessions, and subsequently transcribe, sort, and edit the narratives of the elders. I then met with the artists who were working in the schools to discuss the outcome of the group storytelling.

Focus group interviews were specifically indicated for this project because of the emphasis expressed in the project proposal on maintaining and continuing cultural integrity. The research process itself presents an opportunity to explicitly contribute to cultural continuity by respecting the nature of storytelling as a culturally specific activity. Storytelling is a uniquely social practice in which people share their experiences with others for multiple purposes: informing, influencing, effecting change, and sharing communal values. Within the African-American Diaspora, storytelling has traditionally been the specific work of the female members of the community, and has been identified with bonding and folk culture.[10] Thus, conducting focus groups in which a number of members sit and tell stories to one another is in itself an example of fostering cultural continuity.

The narrators in the focus groups participated in an openly friendly discussion that lacked any sense of suspicion or uneasiness. In a group of their peers, they exchanged their tales of growing up and growing old in the pre-Civil Rights era in Philadelphia. They remembered events together, recalled similar incidents in their lives, and corroborated beliefs and values exemplified in the stories. The "Oh, yeahs" and "Um-hmms" peppered throughout the tape recordings of the stories reveal a connection between the narrators' lives deeper than the common meeting place or their current life circumstances. The stories consisted of personal anecdotes, personal reflections, and observations of events or situations in the lives of the narrators, their families, and communities. Those selected and transcribed for the project were representative of the larger group of stories. The criteria for selection of the stories included in the project consisted of the following: They were appropriate for young children; they represented values and beliefs of the culture; they contained detailed description and visual imagery; they reflected the characters of the narrators.

A major aspect of traditional African and African-American cultures is the belief in the continuity of the culture from the ancestors to the descendants. A disintegration of community results when members leave and make no commitment to their culture and its continuity. Thus, traditions such as storytelling can be used to revitalize communities through a recreation of a cultural continuum. In the contemporary urban culture of America's inner-city communities, the fragmentation of daily life disrupts this continuity and leaves little space and time for the practice of traditional methods for maintaining community. This project sought to reopen that space, and revitalize the practice of traditional oral literature in the African-American community in the Germantown area of Philadelphia.

The purpose and function of stories in folktales is to initiate and to instruct; women speak of power and the responsibility to pass on to future generations the stories of their experiences.[11] In the words of Sadie Delany, an African-American centenarian, "Young people need to know their family history, and it's the responsibility of old folks like us to tell them."[12] The stories included in this project represented part of an effort to make the connection between the lives of the elders of the Germantown community and the lives of children in the neighboring elementary schools. As such they are representative not just of this community, but also of the African-American culture born of the struggle to maintain dignity and respect in a society that classified African Americans as second-class citizens. Many of the narrators told of their own or their parents' journeys from the segregated South, yet their focus is not on bitterness derived from discrimination, but on the lessons they learned along the way. They told of the values instilled in them through the support and encouragement of their fami-

lies and communities—values such as integrity, responsibility, cleanliness, persistence, and compassion. They told of the participation of the community, the church, and the schools in forming their ability to overcome the difficulties of poverty and prejudice and "live a good life." Like the Delany sisters, they confirm that "We didn't have one penny—not one penny—when we were growing up, but we had a blessed childhood."[13]

After I compiled the stories and the project directors made the connection to one of the neighborhood schools, we were invited, along with the storytellers themselves, to visit during a school faculty meeting. We were an interesting mix as we arrived at the school library that day, white and black, old and young, professionals and working class, yet we shared the purpose of creating a sense of connection through the arts. As the teachers questioned us about the project, the storytellers dropped into their stories once again, with a visible effect on the teachers gathered in the room. Tentatively at first, and more emphatically as the discussion progressed, the teachers invited the storytellers to become part of the school, to participate in classes, to visit with their students. While they were delighted with the offer of the participation with the artist/teachers and their work with the stories, they were passionate about having the seniors of their community become active participants in their school. The connection was made. The gypsies created magic in this community.

COMMUNITIES OF POSSIBILITY

For the most part we think of community as a place where people reside, or as a group of people who hold a common connection and share a workspace or a purpose for being together. Yet Maxine Greene suggests that in thinking about community, we emphasize process words—words such as making, creating, connecting, weaving, saying. Community is not a mandate, but an achievement we make together.

Community cannot be produced simply through rational formulation, nor through edict. Like freedom, it has to be achieved by persons offered the space in which to discover what they recognize together and appreciate in common; they have to find ways to make intersubjective sense. Again, it ought to be a space infused by the kind of imaginative awareness that enables those involved to imagine alternative possibilities for their own becoming and their group's becoming. Community is not a question of which social contracts are the most reasonable for individuals to enter. It is a question of what might contribute to the pursuit of shared goals: what ways of being together, of attaining mutuality, of reaching toward some common world.[14]

In the case of *Arts Connection*, the shared goals are for students to imagine, and create with their teachers, their own futures, their common world. As with the students, artists, and teachers in the *Center in the Park* project, community comes through connecting their futures with their pasts; learning from the imaginative resilience of the elders who suffered and persevered in their quest for equality. Students learn to imagine alternative possibilities as they actively engage, actively say, create, weave, and build in the projects the teaching artists connect with their lives.

Alternatives to undemocratic schooling and the fractured landscapes described in Karel Rose and Joe Kincheloe's book *Art, Culture, and Education* take shape in many cities across the United States. Those of us who, like Kincheloe, are aware of the transformative effects of the arts are indeed compelled to "use it for most socially just purposes and to connect it to the project of promoting more tantalizing modes of being human."[15] We design learning activities such as those Rose describes in her Arts and Society class for Lesley University, in which teachers become artists who make critical choices about curriculum instead of relying on the manufacturers of textbooks

to determine what is of most worth for students to learn in our schools. We create theatre projects in which teachers engage with students and principals in a dialogue about democratic schools. Democratic schools, where children are "encouraged to study and investigate as a process of discovering the truth for themselves," as Noam Chomsky suggests, can still be found in a few imaginative alternative contexts.[16]

In Durham, North Carolina, in the innovative program *Literacy through Photography*, in which local artists and writers collaborate with teachers in now 14 schools, student photography becomes the catalyst for investigations of self, community, family, and dreams. The artist-in-residence program has four goals: (1) to give students and teachers the opportunity to interact with artists; (2) to give artists the opportunity to develop projects within an educational context; (3) to increase the students' range of visual literacy and written capabilities; and (4) to create models for other Durham public schools.[17]

In Boston, Massachusetts, two collaborations supported by the National Arts and Learning Collaborative have focused on transforming the Marshall School, a community school in Southeastern Boston, into one where the teachers and students actively engage in artistic and aesthetic teaching. Creative arts educators from Lesley University have created professional development workshops for participating teachers; and students from a nearby private arts school offer arts-based afterschool activities with students from the Marshall School.

These few examples of the possibilities to foster connections and create community through the participation of artists in schools and communities illustrate the transformative nature of the arts in our urban environments. Lowe offers additional evidence in her analysis of community art to form "common ties of solidarity and collective identity among participants."[18] The arts are about quality—quality of education and quality of life.

Although many educators make claims about the effects of art experience on academic achievement, such as the above-mentioned PACE assessment, we need not lose sight of the underlying experience. As they move among us, these urban gypsies, the artist teachers, make cultural connections that improve the quality of life and learning for our students and our communities.

NOTES

Pseudonyms have been used for the school and the district throughout the analysis of this project—most commonly, "Pacific Beach High School" and "Pacific Beach School District." Other references are to "James Madison High School."

1. Diaz, G. (1998). *Making connections.* New Orleans Public Schools; Becker, H. (1982). *Art worlds.* Berkeley, CA: University of California Press.

2. Booth, E. (2003). Seeking definition: What is a teaching artist? *Teaching Artist Journal, 1* (1), 7.

3. Holloway, D., & Krensky, B. (2001). Introduction: The arts, urban education, and social change. *Education and Urban Society, 33* (4), 355.

4. Diaz, G. (1998). *Making connections.* New Orleans Public Schools.

5. Tunks, J. (1998). Integrating community arts programming into the curriculum: A case study in Texas. Arts Education Policy Review, *98* (3), 21–27.

6. Eisner, E. (1998, January). Does experience in the arts boost academic achievement? *Art Education*; Catterall, J. (1997, September). Does experience in the arts boost academic achievement? A response to Eisner. Review draft.

7. Greene, M. (1995). *Releasing the imagination: Essays on education, the arts, and social change.* San Francisco: Jossey-Bass, Inc.

8. *Center in the Park.* Retrieved June 10, 2004, from http://www.volunteersolutions.org/volunteerway/org/215646.html.

9. Cited in Wilentz, G. (1992). *Binding cultures.* Bloomington: Indiana University Press.

10. Wilentz, G. (1992). *Binding cultures.* Bloomington: Indiana University Press.

11. Wilentz (1992).

12. Delany, S. (1994). *The Delany sisters' book of everyday wisdom.* New York: Kodansha International.

13. Delany (1994), p. 3.

14. Greene (1995), p. 39.

15. Rose, K., & Kincheloe, J. (2003). *Art, culture, and education: Artful teaching in a fractured landscape* (p. 11). New York: Peter Lang.

16. Chomsky, N. (2000). *Chomsky on MisEducation.* Lanham, MD: Rowman & Littlefield Publishers, Inc.

17. Dixon, D., & Ungemah, L. (1998). *Artists in the classroom: Ten collaborative projects.* Durham, NC: The Center for Documentary Studies at Duke University.

18. Lowe, S. (2001). The art of community transformation. *Education and Urban Society, 33* (4), 457–471.

URBAN ART MUSEUMS AND THE EDUCATION OF TEACHERS AND STUDENTS

Victoria Ramirez

A dedication on the façade of the large, metropolitan art museum where I work, carved in stone, reads, "Erected for the People, By the People, and for Use of the People." Although written more than 100 years ago, this commitment still holds true today, as museums around the country increasingly consider themselves to be institutions that place the needs and interests of their audience at the core of what they do.

But is this commitment unusual? Historically, and perhaps by reputation, museums have not placed such importance on their audience and have not established a place for the people.

It [a community] erects these buildings and collects their contents as it now builds a cathedral. These things reflect and establish a superior cultural status, while their segregation from the common life reflects the fact that they are not part of native and spontaneous culture. They are a kind of counterpart of a holier-than-thou attitude, exhibited not toward persons as such but toward the interests and occupations that absorb most of the community's time and energy.[1]

In 1934, John Dewey observed that museums, by nature of their institutional goals, were not erected for the people, but for and by certain people, a select part of society that defined museums simply as houses of objects. Museums, collections, and their activities were primarily driven by a mission to collect, preserve, and exhibit objects. Prior to the 1960s, consideration of who walks through the museum doors and encouragement of museum participation "by the people" was not a primary goal of many museums.[2]

Museums are changing and are increasingly reconsidering ways to improve the accessibility of their institution as a place of learning for people of diverse backgrounds and levels of understanding of art. Museums are seeking ways to develop deeper relationships with diverse audiences and encourage their participation in museum activities. In 2003, the Urban Network published a book describing how they brought together urban museums from cities throughout the country and explored the ways in which different institutions are developing strategies that "attract, serve, and engage diverse audiences."[3] Focusing on their individual metropolitan communities, this initiative developed goals that sought to cultivate a museum audience that better reflected the demographics of their urban environment and implement a concentrated effort that increased museum participation by people

traditionally underserved by the museum. This focus on museum audience is forward-thinking, as museums strive for change during a time when their communities are quickly changing and becoming more diverse. Keenly recognizing the decades that "popular culture existed outside the walls of most museums,"[4] museums directors are no longer content with institutions that house dusty relics of the past. Institutional goals and interests are evolving and through collecting practices, exhibitions, and educational programming initiatives, museums are demonstrating a committed desire to be institutions that are as vibrant and diverse as the communities they serve.

Audience-focused initiatives must be a museumwide commitment. While education departments are establishing programs and opportunities that seek to bring diverse audiences to the museum, collecting habits and exhibition schedules must also reflect this commitment to better engage the community in museum activities. In this regard, museums are considering their audiences and potential audiences when acquiring a work of art and during the development of their exhibitions. Taking note to feature works of art by more diverse artists and different types of exhibitions in their galleries, today's museum professionals recognize the importance of their visitors making a connection with what they encounter in the galleries. Works by local artists, theme-based exhibitions relevant to the community, and more innovative programming have become an important part of the museum's primary mission. Dispelling Dewey's 1934 vision of museums as "holier-than-thou cathedrals," the museum today is making efforts to appeal to greater and less-traditional audiences. These changes particularly affect schools and students, as the opportunity for their engagement with the museum becomes richer, more diverse, and ultimately more meaningful.

The focus of this chapter is limited to the experience of students and teachers in the museum and their experience as viewers making meaning of what they see. Thus, the term "visitor" implies student and/or teacher. Also, although not specified, the examples shared are the experiences of a large urban museum whose initiatives are efforts that place value and importance on the urban communities in which they live. Specifically, this chapter examines the museum as a place of learning and discovery through vignettes based on three aspects of the museum: the collection, the exhibition, and the educational program. Collecting habits of museums once followed the tastes and interests of the patrons and donors. Now, more museums are taking the visitor and their audience into consideration when acquiring works of art, and collecting, for example, works by local or regional artists. Art that may spark a conversation about a communal or pertinent issue or offer an opportunity for visitors to see themselves in the museum is becoming increasingly commonplace in the galleries.

The same can be said for museum exhibitions. No longer necessarily only about highlighting certain artists or time periods, exhibition schedules now feature theme-based shows that present works of art focused on a particular issue, concept, or idea. In this sense, the exhibition is not simply presented to the visitor for their passive enjoyment, but is displayed in the gallery to empower the visitor to begin a dialogue about the art and make meaning of what they see. The exhibition is not a separate entity, but in some ways reflects or speaks to the community. Art by student artists or exhibitions that are a by-product of a museum/school collaboration, for example, are also becoming important components of a museum's mission, as they open a dialogue between the museum and community and, maybe even more importantly, open a dialogue among the community.

At the heart of the educational mission of most museums is the interpretation of the works of art. Most museums, regardless of size or nature of collection, offer organized staff- or volunteer-led tours of their galleries as one of their primary opportunities for visitors to engage with the art. But museums are forming new approaches to their tour opportunities, especially for school tours, and are emphasizing the importance of students making meaning of art for themselves. In an attempt to erase the attitude that museum experiences are a tangential part of students' education, organized tours are becoming more student-centered in their approach and are focused more than ever on providing students with an individual experience with art. In this regard, educators recognize and capitalize on the difference between learning in a museum and a classroom, and structure more museum experiences that are self-directed in nature.[5]

SPEAKING TO THE COMMUNITY: THE MUSEUM COLLECTION

A few years ago I was leading a group of third-graders around the museum and we stopped at a display containing a group of Greek vases. The students, who had already studied ancient Greece in their classroom, immediately recognized the objects, so we were able to discuss how the objects were used, why certain images were painted on the surface, and the size and shape of the different vessels. I felt the students were really examining the works in critical ways when a young boy asked, "Where's the real one?" With that one question my whole perspective on museums and visitors' experience with objects changed, as I realized that for many who come to the museum there is still a sense of disbelief that they are actually engaging with the *real* thing. For many museum visitors, both adults and the young boy looking at the Greek vase, there is a disconnect from what they are seeing and that they are in the presence of the actual work of art—the real work that was touched by the artist's hands, buried for hundreds of years, or created in a distant place.

After I did my best to explain to the student that they were indeed in the presence of the actual object, our tour of Greek art continued and the students slowly began to see the museum as a place filled with "real things." A new sense of awe and excitement permeated the group. For the rest of our tour, the students were rethinking their definition of the museum, the works of art, and the purpose of their field trip. The students' comments were now reflective and made me think not only about the works of art and the museum, but the ways in which other visitors engage with what they see. These students were not only experiencing art, but were also considering the museum as a construct within which the experience takes place.

The students on my tour were thinking about Greek art within the context of understanding how the museum visitor makes meaning of works of art as individual objects within the construct of the museum. While these students were making meaning of what they were seeing based on their previous experiences and knowledge, they were subscribing to the idea of museums and art as an independent experience. Dewey writes about the intersection of previous experience and an experience with art when he emphasizes the importance of not viewing that experience "as qualitatively apart from the rest of life. Instead, we need to see it as a refinement, a clarification, and an intensification of those qualities of every experience."[6]

Falk and Dierking developed a construct with which to describe such a museum experience, the Contextual Model of Learning. Considering the museum as a unique learning environment, this approach describes learning as embedded in a series of contexts that occur in the physical and sociocultural world. Taking into consideration the museum as an effective force on one's experience, Falk and Dierking include four types of contexts in their model: the personal, sociocultural, the physical, and time, and posit that learning is the process of the interactions between these contexts.[7] The four contexts take into account not only the work of art itself, but the museum as an environment that shapes and influences one's experience with that work of art. Also important in this model is the viewer and what they bring to the museum experience and what they take away with them. The visit is structured by the museum, as the design of the building, layout of the galleries, and presentation of the work influences the experience with art. For the students studying Greek art, their own previous understandings, their interaction with the other students, and the museum environment all combined to shape their experience and understanding of the Greek vase. My open-ended questions may have prompted my group to think about what they were looking at, but their responses were based on their own understanding of what they were seeing and the understandings of others in the group. The experience with the work of art is couched within the context and environment of the museum. Falk and Dierking's Contextual Model of Learning helps define and describe the uniqueness of learning in a museum environment by emphasizing the uniqueness of the environment. Carol Duncan articulates the relationship between visitor and museum by defining the museum as more than a house of objects or architectural structure. She describes the museum as a space that is "marked off and culturally designated as reserved for a special quality of attention—in this case, for contemplation and learning."[8]

Works of art that speak to the needs, concerns, or interests of their visitor or shape and reflect their urban community can challenge one's ideas and opinions and help museum audiences see themselves in the art. Art that engages the viewer on multiple levels, such as an installation work, provides visitors with a unique opportunity to actually become a part of a work and engage with it in ways that cannot be replicated outside the gallery setting. In a Deweyan sense, installation art may be the definitive art experience, as the experience itself often requires some physical participation from the visitor, as they are invited to physically interact with the work by walking into or around the piece. To further engage the viewer, an installation artist may incorporate sound, scent, and even tactile materials, resulting in a multisensory work that participates in a dialogue with the viewer.

Installation art can offer students and teachers some of the most memorable and powerful gallery experiences. While leading a tour of an exhibition of work by African-American artists, I had the opportunity to introduce a group of high school educators to several installation works of art. Engaging with one of the works, I found the usual group chatter lessened as the teachers quietly walked through, read, or were enveloped by the experience. One specific work, an installation by artist Vicki Meek, prompted a variety of responses from my teacher group and generated the most dialogue of all the works in the gallery.

Created in 1992, *The Crying Room: A Memorial to the Ancestors* is a mixed-media installation by artist Vicki Meek. Exhibited in a small gallery, the work combines sight, sound, smell, and an interactive component as visitors are provided with pencils and small slips of paper on which to write an "offering." These offerings are then pinned to one of the walls of the installation. The visitor enters the space, dimly lit in red and white lights, and immediately hears a chanting voice and soft music. A mound of sand, lava rock, and a long trough of cowry shells are arranged on the floor. Candles line the black walls, which contain writing in stark white lettering and

an African Yoruba design. The wall reads: "400 years of slavery, 15 million enslaved, 30 million died." Also on the wall, arranged in the shape of Gothic church windows, are tiny coffin-like unopened sardine cans, adorned with the name and age of a deceased individual.

In her installations and assemblages, Meek analyzes major aspects of African-American history. *The Crying Room: A Memorial to the Ancestors* is a powerful commemorative statement, a celebration of the survival of the human spirit in the face of adversity. But Meek is not creating the work alone. In this piece, she includes an opportunity for visitors to participate by providing paper and pencils on the back wall where one can write an "offering." Reflecting on this work and my tour for the high school educators, I found myself intrigued by how each teacher made sense of Vicki Meek's work and contributed to the wall of "offerings." While some hesitated and simply read the slips of paper contributed by others, other teachers carefully composed personal messages or responses to existing messages. As the offerings were not really organized on the wall in any particular fashion, some visitors responded to one another with their messages through the placement of their paper within the wall of other offerings. As was intended by the artist, the teachers were participating in the work by taking part in a written and a silent dialogue with both themselves and others who chose to leave their comments.

The participatory component of the piece represents the community, as visitors express their ideas, thoughts, and opinions through their offerings. One does not have to include an offering to participate in the dialogue, as visitors—such as the teachers on my tour—can read the wall of offerings and silently participate. Offerings on the wall are in many different languages and are written to deceased relatives, friends, and even pets. Messages were written by young and old—

"freedom" in young-handed letters; "Where is the love?" and "Viva Venezuela" in more elegant script. Because the offerings are anonymous, many visitors feel more comfortable expressing themselves. One visitor wrote: "Dear Ms Art, The light shines in this work like a beacon of hope wrapped around my future." In this work not only are visitors having an experience with the art, but an opportunity to share with the community. One can visit the installation alone, as I have many times, and be a part of the community just by reading the offerings. For the high school teachers on my tour, the museum visit was no longer confined to the participants in the group, but included the community who had previously left offerings. The museum was part of a community and the group was part of that community outside the museum doors.

With works of art such as the Vicki Meek installation, the museum has redefined itself as a communal place for dialogue and a public forum where people can come together to create new knowledge and think about their world in new ways. The museum is a living and breathing, dynamic place where different ideas and perspectives are reflected and expressed. Speaking to our senses and requiring our participation through writings on slips of paper, the Meek installation emphasizes the importance of our experience being connected to something outside of ourselves.

Instead of signifying being shut up within one's own private feelings and sensations, experience signifies active and alert commerce with the world; at its height it signifies complete interpenetration of self and the world of objects and events.[9]

In this respect, experience within the museum involves more than just our own selves and our past experiences, but is an exchange between the art, the artist, other visitors, and the museum itself. Thus experience is not a purely cognitive, insular interaction, but it involves all of our connectors to the world—our senses. According to Dewey, the senses are our greatest connections to that which is outside of our private selves; sight, sound, smell, touch, and taste are entryways to our inner selves. Experience in a museum setting requires the alertness of our entire body, as we are not passively viewing works of art as mere spectators, but we are part of the experience as we maneuver ourselves through the museum. Body, museum, and experience are intertwined in the way Falk and Dierking's Social Contextual Model takes into consideration the components that define an experience with art in a museum. Dewey describes this interaction as a "rhythm" which takes place between viewer and surroundings.[10] With a developing rhythm, the viewer builds a relationship with the art and the museum just like the third-grade students discovered the realness of the Greek art and the teachers engaged with *The Crying Room*. Both of these groups engaged in a rhythm of understanding between themselves and the art. But, experience does not happen instantaneously. It unfolds over time in a flow of understanding about an object, situation, or place. Art is a part of life and the intersection of art and life is the experience. Dewey defines great art not as those works that have specific indefinable qualities, but those works that, throughout time, can be valued and experienced in new ways by different people.[11] Art is an imaginative and emotional experience, and the most meaningful art and aesthetic experiences can only take place with the *real* work of art.

The ideas of Dewey, Falk, and Dierking prompt me to reconsider the museum experience of my third-grade tour group, who had been studying ancient Greece in their classroom. The students visited the museum with an understanding of the context of Greek vessels, but did not truly understand the function of the museum until one brave boy asked where the real Greek vase was located. After that realization, the students' interaction with the art and experience in the museum changed. Each student's excitement played off of one another as they saw new works of art and imagined the life of that work and other visitors coming to the museum with the same sense of wonder and excitement as they had that day. The same can be said about the high school teachers' interaction with the Meek installation. The physical and emotional experience of the art combined with the interaction of writing or reading the "offerings" resulted in a complex conversation between the teachers and the work. For both of these examples, the visit to the museum and the experience with the art was not a passive activity, but one that, consciously or not, prompted the students and teachers to begin to think about themselves, their community, and the world in a new way. Art, and their experience with the museum, is not a segregated activity but a part of life.

MUSEUM EXHIBITIONS: A REFLECTION OF THE COMMUNITY

For many visitors, especially students, *experiencing* the museum can be especially challenging as they tend to have either negative perceptions of the museum or they feel that the museum is not a place where they can see or discover themselves. A look at an in-gallery visitor comment book provides an opportunity for visitors to anonymously speak to the museum and express their thoughts and opinions about their experience. "This is boring" is written too frequently in several museum visitor comment books. In another example, to further emphasize the disconnect between the museum and their student visitors, Therese Quinn of the Art Institute of Chicago developed a museum class in which local high school students visited various museums throughout Chicago and reflected on their impressions and experiences. The overall consensus of the high school students was that museums are "boring" and the collections "stale." In Quinn's experience, the stu-

dents expressed a disconnect between themselves and the museums by explaining that they could not see why they should visit them in the first place.[12]

Experiences such as Quinn's reveal that if museums truly want to be places where students can see themselves and if they want to create experiences for schools in their community, they must consider their visitors in what they do—including the creation and presentation of exhibitions. There are a variety of different types of museum exhibitions. Some are more academic in nature, speaking more to the field than the average museum visitor. Others are more sweeping views that provide the visitor with a broader look at a topic—a selection of masterpieces or highlights from a collection, for example. But exhibitions can also demonstrate a commitment to their audience by presenting works that speak to or reflect the needs and interests of their specific community.

As museums seek to become institutions more like the community of which they are a part, the types of exhibitions they host are changing. More and more museums are devoting specific galleries or spaces to student work. My own institution has an almost ten-year relationship with a local high school photography teacher who creates an assignment for his students that culminates in an annual exhibition of student work at the museum. The students are assigned to walk their neighborhood streets and photograph the people and places that define their community. The images created are personal statements that reveal the students' perceptions and the physical features and spirit that define their neighborhood. Students are instructed to shoot dozens of images and choose the strongest photographs they feel best reflect their vision. The images chosen are submitted to the museum for consideration in the final exhibition, which consists of approximately thirty photographs. The exhibition is titled *Eye on Third Ward*, a reference to the part of the city where the images were taken.

Eye on Third Ward is a look at a community through the eyes of high school students. The most popular subject matter of the work is family, neighbors, and friends, followed by photographs of homes, buildings, and various city landmarks. As individual photographs, these images speak to issues of hope, poverty, and the people that comprise the community. As a collective exhibition, they offer a look at one of the oldest historically African-American neighborhoods in the city through the eyes of students who call it home.

An integral part of the exhibition is the opening reception, which invites friends, family, and the media to the museum to meet the student artists and celebrate the exhibition. Unlike opening receptions offered for other museum exhibitions, this event attracts more families and is typically held on a Sunday afternoon to accommodate the after-church crowd. The celebration attracts upward of 300 people who typically do not visit the museum. But for this event the museum is a part of the community, and the community can see themselves in a new way—through the eyes of the students.

There is a sense of pride in the exhibition, and students feel empowered to talk about their photographs. Museum visitors recognize community landmarks, popular stores, and even people from the neighborhood. But, the museum benefits equally from the collaboration by recognizing that it is when students and communities see themselves in the art that they find the most meaning in both the art and the museum. Erasing the reputation Dewey spoke of in 1934 of the museum as an isolated institution that simply collects and preserves objects, the museum is striving to be a vital part of the community. Through exhibitions such as *Eye on Third Ward,* students have the opportunity to discover works of art in the museum and, most importantly, see the connection between art and their lives.

Visitor responses from the in-gallery comment book emphasize the importance for the community making connections to the art in the gallery. Consisting of mostly comments of praise, some visitors contribute their opinions, others scribble drawings, and some pages of the book include actual dialogue where visitors are responding to the comments of others. Interestingly, messages in comment books in galleries with student art tend to speak more of the artists than of the work itself. Comments include: "Children are our future artists;" "Love the children's work;" and "This place is s-o-o-o boring, except for this kid art." Other comments include actual sketches appearing to be from the hands of children. Here, the child viewer is relating to the student art by creating their own sketch, as if to say, "These students are artists, and I am one too." The students are inspired by the art, and they interact with it by creating work of their own. Adult comments also express support for student work in the museum and ask for more student art in more museum galleries. Comments include: "Better than the pieces in the rest of the museum" and "Life is always more refreshing when seen through the eyes of others." One visitor even commented, "It was nice to see a good exhibit in such a white museum."

The number of comments in the comment books and the time visitors take to include their thoughts indicates that visitors are positively responding to the work and respond favorably to the museum presenting exhibitions of student work. But for museums in urban environments, community-based initiatives, such as *Eye on Third Ward*, demonstrate their commitment to the place in which they live. Urban environments such as the one in which I am situated are marked with a dense population of diverse people who desire and seek experiences that connect their community. In this sense, it is the urban museum's obligation to offer such opportunities for its community.

For museums to truly connect and expand their audience, including community-based exhibitions in their schedule is a critical step. Museum visitors need the opportunity to see themselves in the museum and make connections between their lives and art. Our compartmentalized classrooms separate the arts from other disciplines so much so that it is challenging for students to see how integrated and tightly woven art is to our everyday lives as people. Advocates, such as Maxine Greene, write of the importance of the arts in a public school education as a means for reshaping imagination and "developing a dialogue to becoming more wide-awake to the world."[13] Greene clarifies her position by challenging teachers to encourage learners to "name their own worlds."[14] Art and the museum can help students find and develop their own voice that will shape and define their own worlds.

For the students, whether their work is featured in the exhibition or not, it is their experience with student-based exhibitions that can yield some of the most powerful museum experiences. Seeing artists just like themselves and thinking about the work within the context of the museum can empower students to believe they have a voice and that their opinions, thoughts, and ideas have value. Offering students an opportunity to engage with other student work can be reflective and prompt them to organize and articulate their ideas and consider what and why they think of the world the way that they do.[15]

Engaging with art made by other students provides another context for students to create and engage in dialogue about their own thoughts, concerns, interests, and motivations. This interaction allows students to make meaning of their world and provides educators an opportunity to understand how surroundings affect the ways in which students construct knowledge, make meaning, and come to an understanding about what is around them.[16] For *Eye on Third Ward*, sometimes students visiting the exhibition enter the gallery and do not initially realize they are looking at photographs made by their contemporaries. This realization prompts another look and intrigues them enough to look at each work and see what the student photographers have to say. Museums can learn from these experiences and develop a better sense of how these discoveries are made and how future museum programs, resources, and experiences can be crafted so they are more meaningful for the student.

EDUCATIONAL PROGRAMMING: MAKING THE MUSEUM ONE'S OWN

Most students visit the museum as part of a field trip experience. Typically lasting about one hour, the field trip is usually led by a volunteer docent or museum educator who has a predetermined plan for the students' visit. Carefully mapping the travel routes through the museum and choosing the works of art for focus, the field trip experience is literally a prescribed lesson plan in the museum. The tour leader knows what the tour will cover and which works of art the students will see before ever meeting the group. The ideas of social interaction and group learning and discovery are secondary, as students need to quickly assimilate to their new environment, meet their new museum teacher, and participate in the experience that has already been structured for them.

But some museums are changing and have initiated a new type of tour called Open Space in which the students take the lead in creating their own experience by determining which works of art are discussed on their museum visit. Based on an approach more typically utilized in business meetings, Open Space allows the participants to guide the activities and goals of the activity with the help of a museum facilitator. In the Open Space tour approach, the museum docent or tour leader does not predetermine the focus works of art, but allows the students to browse the gallery at their leisure and choose the works for discussion. Students are prompted by the facilitator to consider which works of art strike them or which intrigue them. The student leads their own experience with the art, as they choose the works of interest to them individually and as a group. Falk and Dierking define this personal context as one's "reservoir of knowledge, attitudes, and experience, influenced by the physical characteristics of the museum."[17]

Questions are raised, and discussions are sparked by the students' own curiosities and interests. This approach is particularly successful, as museums are better able to craft a more meaningful and memorable experience for students. Utilizing the Open Space approach also respects the students as individuals with thoughts, ideas, experiences, and opinions. In this approach, students and their chaperones are discovering the work together—by asking questions, making connections, and coming to a better understanding of what art meant to them and their lives. The Open Space tour emphasizes discussion and participation and thus the museum visit is social, emphasizing the importance of group learning.

With Open Space, art becomes an object requiring discussion and discovery. During the tour, the docent or tour leader does not stand next to the work of art being discussed while the rest of the group look at the work. Instead the entire group walks around the gallery together. In this format, no one person has a better relationship or understanding of any work of art. Each work belongs to everyone equally. This approach also emphasizes the importance of Falk and Dierking's Contextual Model of Learning, where the physical space of the museum is factored into the experience; as students are encouraged to pursue their own interests, they are making sense of the museum as a construct.[18] Museums as non-traditional learning environments offer the opportunity for students to openly discuss and reflect outside the confines of the classroom. Studies by museums and universities, including one by Bank Street College in New York City, have examined student field trip experiences and discovered that visits in which students could exercise choice and personalize the experience were some of the most effective and remembered experiences. The docent, or museum educator, learns as well by gaining a sense of which works of art the students are interested in, and what makes them question, curious, or speaks to them. In a Freirean sense, the student, tour guide, and chaperones are learning and discovering the works of art in the galleries together. All are encouraged to share their ideas, interests, and opinions and thus the visitors are not reduced to objects who have been alienated from their own decision making.[19] With Open Space, the students are in control, and their experience is shaped by their own decision making.

In my experience, at the start of a museum tour when I have asked students what they expect to see and discover during their museum visit, I have heard "we are going to see a bunch of old stuff" and "art is only made by dead people." Given these beginnings, the question remains, "How do you meaningfully contextualize this work for students and dispel the myth that art is for and about someone else?" Open Space allows meaningful connections to be made with works of art by building on the social aspects of the experience and allowing students to discover on their own and at their own pace. Students who are talking amongst themselves about art or those who wander off because another work of art has caught their eye are not told to be quiet or join the group, but rather this type of interaction between student and the art is welcomed and encouraged.

Museums are social institutions. Experiences are social. By promoting social engagement in the galleries, the experiences are more meaningful and are memorable for the students. Open Space tours advocate this type of learning and interaction and place the role of "tour guide" in the hands of the student.

CONCLUSION

Once again I consider Dewey's 1934 description of a museum and its collection as an institution that "reflect(s) and establish(es) a superior culture."[20] But I believe through collections, exhibitions, and educational programming opportunities, museums are slowly changing their attitudes and practices and doing what they can to erase that reputation. Museums are playing an increasingly important role in their communities, and more and more audiences are engaging with art and viewing their local museum as a place "Erected for the People, By the People, and for Use of the People."

NOTES

1. Dewey, J. (1934). *Art as experience* (p. 9). New York: Perigee Books.

2. Alexander, E. (1993). *Museums in motion*. Nashville: American Association for State and Local History.

3. Amdur Sptiz, J., & Thom, M. (2003). *Urban network: Museums embracing communities* (p. 3). Chicago: The Field Museum.

4. Amdur Sptiz & Thom (2003), p. 11.

5. Falk, J., & Dierking, L. (1992). *The museum experience*. Washington, DC: Whalesback Books.

6. Jackson, P. (1998). *John Dewey and the lessons of art* (p. 8). New Haven: Yale University Press.

7. Falk, J., & Dierking, L. (2000). *Learning from museums*. New York: AltaMira Press.

8. Duncan, C. (1995). *Civilizing rituals: Inside public art museums* (p. 10). New York: Routledge.

9. Dewey (1934), p. 19.

10. Dewey (1934).

11. Dewey (1934).

12. Quinn, T. (2001). Where we can see ourselves? *Rethinking Schools*, 16 (2).

13. Greene, M. (1995). *Releasing the imagination*. San Francisco: Jossey-Bass.

14. Greene (1995), p. 11.

15. Greene (1995).

16. Kincheloe, J., Steinberg, S., Rodriguez, N., & Chennault, R. (1998). *White reign: Deploying whiteness in America*. New York: St. Martin's Press.

17. Falk & Dierking (1992), p. 25.

18. Falk & Dierking (2000).

19. Freire, P. (1970). *Pedagogy of the oppressed*. New York: Continuum.

20. Dewey (1934).

THE ARTS IN URBAN EDUCATION

Merryl Goldberg

To live, we hope; To hope, we dream; To dream, we imagine our improved future. To imagine, we act; We make constant our effort to realize our dream. To realize our dream, we improvise our realities.

Improvisation is ancient and modern; It is arts; It is philosophy; It is life. To live, we improvise.

—Xin Li
The Tao of Life Stories[1]

This chapter discusses the improvisations of several individuals as they enact projects and programs in the arts in urban school settings. It is about people who are dedicated teachers, community members, artists, principals, and parents who have a dual role of warrior, fighting for what they perceive is an excellent education for their children. It is about finding ways to realize what is possible while working within large systems that all too often are more of a barrier than an opening.

By federal law, a comprehensive and equitable schooling for all children includes an education in and through the arts. In this chapter I raise issues specific to urban schools in California, such as English language learners mainstreamed throughout classes and how the arts open important learning opportunities. I look at how schools within urban settings can subvert the system to include the arts as central to the curriculum despite top-down directives to teach only to reading and math, and how arts-rich school environments can bring diverse groups within the community together.

Artists and arts institutions working with schools and school districts have a unique and important role in subverting the system. As Judith Hill writes:

We have a rich and deep presence in the public schools, and we work with classroom teachers and students daily, yet we are also free of the many strictures and structures that commandeer public school life. We mediate our students' lives by creating intentionally educative experiences rather than by executing somebody else's ideas of what and how to teach; the power of the curriculum and the nature of instruction is in our hands. . . . It is our own educational ideals and our school partners to whom we must hold ourselves accountable. This makes for delicious dangers and opportunities.[2]

Although Hill was discussing urban education and the arts in general, her point is right on the money for our situation in southern California. My work in California is in several districts where the arts play a significant part in the culture of schools through partnerships with artists and arts institutions. Although I have worked in and with schools for more than ten years now, I am continually amazed to witness kids' and teachers' sense of purpose, inten-

sity, and motivation as they work in and through the arts. Children are not only capable of amazingly creative and complex undertakings, but such undertakings come to them naturally. They are eager to take risks and work toward a goal. One look at any one of the settings I will describe in this chapter is a reminder of what an opportunity we all have to believe in kids and their often amazing ability to understand their world through arts.

Through the arts, children can dream, hope, imagine, escape, reflect, try on a new identity, or make visible an identity that they had hidden. In the urban settings where I work, we find children with very limited English skills confidently exploring Newton's physics through mime. We find a student who is completely alienated to science until his teacher discovers that enabling him to draw during class completely opens him to the world of science. We find students, who, "against all odds" have an inner urge to express themselves, not necessarily thinking of what they do as art.[3] We find children with hidden talents—kept hidden until the opportunity and encouragement of a particular teacher embraced them.

Children in urban settings often lack the financial means of their counterparts in suburban settings, and thus have had less opportunity to have their artistic talents "discovered" through an afterschool art program or by an art teacher. However, children in urban settings are no less creative and artistic than those in more wealthy districts. In some instances, the lack of formal arts activities gives rise to the blossoming of creativity. As well, urban landscapes are often glorious canvases of artwork and performing arts. For example, in San Diego we have Chicano Park, an important and historical park with mural after mural depicting Chicano culture. To embrace the creative urge in children and encourage it in urban settings is a fundamentally humane way to support our collective future.

IT IS THE LAW

All children are entitled to an equitable and comprehensive education and that education includes the arts as a core academic subject. Under the No Child Left Behind Act, all four arts disciplines—music, visual arts, dance, and theater—are defined as "core academic subjects" on equal footing with math, science, language arts, and social studies. In addition, there are national standards in arts education to guide the K–12 curriculum, and here in California we have a mandate in the visual and performing arts, with a framework that spans all four disciplines and all grades, pre-kindergarten through grade 12.

I would also like to shatter two myths about the arts and their role in education as a way to contextualize the discussion in this chapter.

Myth Number 1: The arts are not economically important. They do not hold the promise of a good job.

Education in the arts prepares the U.S. workforce for jobs in the robust arts industry, as well as in numerous other industries. For example, California alone has 89,710 arts-related businesses, including jobs related to animation, movies, television production, lighting technicians, recording artists, gallery owners, and so on. According to the 2004-updated study, *The Arts: A Competitive Advantage for California II*, these businesses employ 516,054 individuals (California Arts Council). That is more people than all the students and faculty currently enrolled throughout the entire California State University system. These jobs do not take into account all the individuals who work in arts-related jobs outside of arts businesses, such as Web masters, brochure designers, self-employed local artists, and arts teachers in schools. Nor do they account for the artistic skills essential to fields such as architecture.

Sadly, many of the arts jobs in California go to individuals from outside the state and even outside the country because our students are inadequately trained for arts work. For example, although individuals can learn computer techniques quickly for jobs that rely on computer animation, these techniques cannot make up for the lack of arts training needed to create the original artwork or storyboards.

Myth Number 2: The arts are nice—but they are far less important than a child's ability to read and write and do arithmetic.

Research has shown (and continues to show) that schools in which the arts are present have higher test scores in all areas; more motivation and participation among students, teachers, and parents; and more success among exceptional students, gifted and talented learners, and English language learners.[4] High school students who have taken arts classes consistently score higher on the SAT.[5] Further, the arts teach students important lessons in discipline, perseverance, creativity, and risk taking. These skills are becoming more and more prevalent in a transforming workforce where employment in areas that demand imagination and creativity are seeing great gains.[6]

Every parent wishes for the best education for their children. Most would agree that an education that includes the arts, science labs, up-to-date technology, and well-trained teachers and staff is what all children deserve. Unfortunately, in urban education, school budgets rarely can begin to provide even a small piece of the ideal. Systemwide decision making often makes it challenging to fund the arts, even in the best of circumstances, and those individuals who believe in the arts need to find ways to circumvent the system in order to succeed.

Obviously, one way to change the system would be to change the reality of the budget. Although school districts within suburban locations can raise funds to support an excellent education through their tax base and the establishment of educational foundations, urban schools are often lacking in this area. Thus, schools wanting to include the arts often need to find a way to circumvent the challenge of the budget by changing their status to have more autonomy from the system, partnering with arts institutions, writing for grants, or independently raising funds for projects.

The more realistic potential for systematic change would be to lobby at the local and state political level for general funding for the arts. For example, a community outside of Boston recently voted to override a tax cap for school funding so that art and music teachers could be restored to school funding. Unfortunately, despite the glimmers of hope, such as with the previous example, arts programming whether in the public schools or in the general public (museums, concert halls, etc.) has been under attack for quite some time. Some would argue that the arts have little purpose in education, maybe even in society. This is not the case historically or culturally if we look around the globe. The arts were so important to the Greeks, for example, that they were indistinguishable from basic activities associated with the pursuit of truth or beauty.

In many cultures, the arts have been inseparable from everyday activity, and do not even have names associated with specific acts (such as singing or visual art). However, when the arts were first introduced to public school education, they had specific purposes. Music was first introduced into the public schools in an urban setting—Boston, 1838—to promote hymn singing. Boston was also home to the first drawing program, which was introduced as a result of the Industrial Drawing Act of 1870 (adopted by legislators, composed and signed by manufacturers). The Industrial Drawing Act was designed to introduce drawing to children for the purpose of training individuals for work related to design in manufacturing.

Arts remained a significant aspect of an integrated curriculum within schools until the 1950s when, in direct response to events surrounding the launching of Sputnik, discipline-based study became the norm. The purpose of a new discipline-based education with special emphasis on science and mathematics was intended as a method to create a cadre of citizens who could effectively compete with the Soviets, especially in science.

Arts educators joined the discipline-specific frenzy of the late fifties and moved forward with curriculum that focused on the study of arts for their own sake. By that I mean study of great works or art, or studying the technique involved in creating art. Individuals associated with the Getty Foundation in the late 1970s and 1980s broadened the definition of discipline-based education in the arts to include the study of historical and aesthetic contexts. Many people bought into this discipline-based arts education, and for good reason; it was thorough and very well thought out. It was adopted as a basis for many arts education programs, including the California Frameworks for elementary education. It was challenged in terms of what some perceived as a narrow Western focus, and to the Getty Foundation's credit, they expanded their focus and materials to become more multicultural. However, as education budgets dwindled, the fight for arts became tougher and tougher.

By the 1980s another challenge to U.S. education emerged: the education of an increasingly multilingual and multicultural student body in the context of a society immersed in technology. In response to these challenges, several theories emerged and blossomed onto the education scene, including Howard Gardner's theory of Multiple Intelligences. Gardner's theory had a tremendous impact on education, broadening teachers' views on how to teach and reach students. Soon after, the arts started playing another role, an additional one to the discipline-based roles outlined by Getty. The arts began to play an important role in interdisciplinary learning, providing learners with strategies to express subject matter through arts-based methods. For example, students learning about metamorphosis might dramatize the life cycle of a butterfly to understand it, or draw from nature as a method to study ecology. Often this is referred to as "learning through the arts."[7] In the 1997 California Department of Education publication of *Artswork*, "Literacy in and through the arts," was recognized as a core principle. Art was deemed as not only a discipline to be studied, but as a guiding force for the study of other subjects.

THE CHALLENGE OF ARTS EDUCATION IN URBAN SETTINGS

Education in the arts has challenges in most settings, and some more specific to urban settings. To frame these challenges, I discuss two urban school districts in southern California, each with its own unique set of circumstances: Escondido Elementary School District (about 45 miles north of San Diego), and San Diego City Schools. I also touch upon a charter school for the arts in Oakland to provide an example of what is possible for children who wish to pursue a career in the arts.

Community involvement and creating partnerships can be key to success in building capacity to support arts in urban schools. In my examples, the community plays a significant role in the success of a program, as does the presence of artists in schools representing arts institutions. By community I mean the local community including parents, artists, politicians, and donors, as well as the school community itself comprised of the children, teachers, staff, and administration. By artists, I am referring to professional artists of many backgrounds and cultures working in classrooms as part of their daily experience.

SUAVE

Escondido, California, is roughly 45 miles north of the border with Tijuana, Mexico. It is a moderate-sized city of approximately 133,000 with a significant Mexican-American population. Many of the children entering the elementary schools are native Spanish speakers, and in some schools the majority of the population are English language learners. Since 1994, a program called SUAVE (*Socios Unidos para Artes Via Educación* [transl. United Community for Arts in Education]) has been part of the school district's professional development. It is a relatively poor district in terms of funding. At the time of this writing, they are forming a foundation to begin finding outside funds to supplement their budget.

SUAVE came into existence to serve several needs of the local community. In 1993, a newly built (and city-owned) Center for the Arts needed to create an educational program in order to fulfill its agreed-upon mission. Funding for new schools was delayed in an agreement that the arts center would provide arts education for tax-sharing partners. I was new to the area at the time, having been hired as faculty at Cal State–San Marcos in the neighboring city, which was part of the tax-sharing partnership. At that time, budgets were fairly robust, and the school districts, arts center, and university were able to create ideal programs. In that culture, we were able to build a partnership, share costs, and implement a joint program.

I developed SUAVE in collaboration with several local teachers, principals, and community members. In choosing where to begin the program (within the tax-sharing partnership), we identified three principals who were not only inclined toward the arts, but had either backgrounds in the arts or professional associations with the arts. The original principals were thrilled to pilot the program. Thus, we began with grassroots support and built community buy-in. The principals set the tone for their teachers, and we were off to an exciting beginning.

I realized rather quickly that even though budgets were decent in the early nineties, arts specialists were absent from the district. Classroom teachers were responsible for arts education if the children were to receive any training in the arts at all. However, most teachers, having grown up in California, were themselves not trained in the arts, having gone through schooling with very little arts education due to Proposition 13, which dramatically changed the funding for public education in the late 1970s. The classroom teachers, although interested in the arts, did not feel at all competent to teach the arts. I decided on another approach—the teaching through the arts approach. In other words, train teachers to use the arts to teach content: using drama to enact the life cycles of insects, creating puppets to act out periods of history, using dance to understand mathematical concepts such as complex patterning, and using visual arts to study nature.

This technique of learning through the arts by pairing professional artists with classroom teachers brings life to classrooms, and students began to shine in significant ways. Teachers have expanded their methods of reaching their students. One teacher put it this way:[8]

Until (the artist) started having us do movement to poems and things like that I hadn't thought of doing a social studies lesson this way. We teach about the land bridge, people coming across the land bridge to North America and becoming Native Americans. So I took a section of the playground . . . [and] had them act out the whole thing. And we slowly crossed the land bridge and moved down toward North America and then down to South America. We were chasing herds of animals and some of the kids were the mammoths. As we moved toward the equator we noticed it was getting warmer. I know that they are going to remember that. It wasn't just the two-page spread in the social studies book with a picture . . . of an Eskimo or whatever in furs and a bunch of words. . . . They acted it out, they moved, they walked, I talked to them the whole time.

Another significant impact of the program was its effectiveness in gaining skills to help English language learners succeed:

When working in dual language instruction, [teaching through the arts] made it very visual and concrete for the kids. Kids have benefited from it, bilingual kids learning a second language—I mean it is just so visual, so tangible for them to acquire and have access to the curriculum that it has made such a big difference in the way I teach. Everything is so tangible across the curriculum. I mean they can understand; they can see it, they can feel it, they can act it, they can say it.

In a three-year research project sponsored by the Spencer and MacArthur Foundations, SUAVE's success and limitations were looked at very closely. In documenting and analyzing curriculum jointly developed by teacher/artist pairs, my team found the arts often are used in interesting ways, including as a tool for assessing student learning, and as an effective tool for reaching English language learners.[9]

The discovery of the potential of the arts in reaching English language learners became a significant highlight of the program over the last ten years. So much so, that the program became a recipient of a Department of Education Model Arts Grant (No Child Left Behind Act) to look specifically at the impact of the arts in teaching English language learners. The role of arts within the district began shifting from an arts education and professional development emphasis to the arts' role in teaching students English.

As a surprising side result to our studies, we found that teachers, after having been trained in using the arts in the ways that artists use the arts, have become more interested in the arts in and of themselves as important disciplines in their own rights. Teachers have taken art classes, are attending more performances, and are in effect, introducing discipline-based arts education into their classrooms. In other words, the teachers themselves are finding an importance or purposefulness of arts as a discrete subject on their own, and are incorporating the study of arts into their curriculum. Thus, although it may be a backdoor approach to invigorating arts education, learning through the arts is important as an educational strategy, and also creates a stage for the discipline of arts to be studied.

Often, artists in residence are left to their own devices. In the SUAVE program, artists meet weekly and have formed a strong community. In our "coaches' meetings" we discuss what is going on in classrooms, and brainstorm effective ways to reach teachers and support them in their efforts to teach curriculum through the arts. Classroom teachers know we meet every week and will on occasion attend the coaches' meeting, or send along questions or ideas to share. A typical coaches' meeting entails coaches bringing challenges to the table, such as, "one of my fourth-grade teachers wants to focus on division and movement; do you have any ideas on what I could do?"

Another significant aspect of the program is writing for grants to support teachers and artists to attend workshops together. We have been successful in this arena, and teachers and artists have been able to learn side by side on trips to India to study puppetry, to Mexico to study fandango, and in mini workshops held at the Center for the Arts, Escondido, with visiting artists such as Marcel Marceau, Bella Lewitsky, Ballet Hispanico, Missoula Children's Theater, and the Shakespeare Company.

At the time of this writing, the state of the school district's budget is about as dismal as ever. Even though the program is jointly funded by the university, arts center, and grants, the district was to provide its share, which came to $50,000 (a reduction from its contributions of the past). However, the program went on the cut list for the district. Not surprisingly, and due to the grassroots formation of the program and community buy-in, numerous parents, teachers, artists, and community arts organizations began to protest. While the district did not come up with the funds, a private foundation dedicated to improving the lives and education of Latino families stepped up to the plate to fill in the gap. Hence the program continues in full force for at least another year while the district tries to find the money for the future.

Several school board members as well as the superintendent have publicly stated support for the SUAVE program; however, when push comes to shove, they have relied on the generosity of the community. Fortunately, the community has been able to come through and support the children. This is not always the case. This is especially difficult in urban settings unless the city has a dedicated community donor or individuals who will consistently come forward for children.

FREESE ELEMENTARY

Like many big school districts, a challenge for any individual school is to work within the district and still hang on to some autonomy. Individual schools have less freedom in larger districts than in small districts, because decisions such as whether or not to hire arts specialists, are made at the district level and not at the school site level. In smaller school districts, there is more freedom site to site— and in middle-class and wealthier communities, school sites in collaboration with PTAs often can raise enough money to hire arts specialists.

In San Diego City Schools, a vibrant special educator took another approach to arts education. Freese Elementary is a city school in southeast San Diego. The neighborhood has changed over time—in the past it was a primarily African-American community and has evolved to a community that is roughly one-third African American, one-third Latino, and one-third Filipino. It is a poor neighborhood, and San Diego City Schools, like most city schools is California, is a poorly funded district. For the last several years it has been run from a top-down administration. However, at the time of this publication, a new administration is in charge and it is hoped that change will be in the air. Even more than Escondido, schools within the San Diego City Schools have very little autonomy.

Freese Elementary took another approach, and a very successful one. They applied for magnet status to become a culture and arts school. They were granted that status, which provided them the freedom to set up curriculum differently from the mandated math and reading blocks at all other schools. Mary Pat Hutt, the special education teacher now in charge of arts coordination at Freese, began networking like crazy with the arts institutions in San Diego. Unabashedly, she would call the opera, museums, symphony, playhouses, and pull on the heartstrings of whomever she could at each institution and ask for tickets for her kids who had never experienced live performances. She was so successful that the school attracted more than thirty arts partners; won grants from a number of agencies, including National Geographic; and has a teaching staff that is quite stable (not so common for city schools). Family nights are arts-centered and bring families from the community together.

Hutt, her principal, and teachers—like those individuals involved in SUAVE—have taken a decidedly grassroots approach to their school in the midst of a system that is top-down. The students are brought into curriculum decisions and given "release time" to discuss and critique projects and programs at their school. Their input is part of the decision-making process at the school. All artists who work in the schools also engage in reflective thinking concerning their work at the school. A sense of ownership in learning is created and valued.

OAKLAND ACADEMY OF THE ARTS— A CHARTER SCHOOL

I would like to briefly mention another important way to provide arts experiences to children in urban settings by briefly highlighting the Oakland Arts Academy. Jerry Brown, the mayor of Oakland (at the time of this writing), decided to embark on opening a charter high school for the arts with its mission being pre-professional training in the arts within a college-preparatory curriculum. This is an approach to education that directly benefits children who wish to pursue an arts career. Charter schools are public schools that receive the same funding as other schools, but have autonomy when it comes to decision making and approaches to the curriculum. The charter school is a way to "work the system" rather than subvert it, to achieve an arts education goal.

The Oakland Academy of the Arts became a reality in 2002 under the direction of Loni Berry, when it opened its doors at the Alice Arts Center with 100 ninth-graders. The school was created to provide an opportunity for teens talented in the arts to receive a college-preparatory education with training in the arts. The school attracted many more students than could be admitted. Admittance was by audition. Students attending this school begin their studies at 8:30 AM and conclude at 5:30 PM. Often they stay even later to rehearse shows or put up a gallery of original artwork. Students have access to formal dance classes, animation, arts, music, theater, and arts technology.

They have a community of teachers, arts and non-arts, who work together and coordinate the curriculum across disciplines. Teachers have created a "windows" approach to the curriculum, whereby a period and culture in history, such as Leningrad, 1914, becomes a window through which each teacher and his or her students approach their discipline. Several windows are approached each semester. Even in its infancy (the school will serve 400 students by 2005), the school is achieving the highest test scores in the district, has a 97 percent attendance rate, and is a vibrant school full of inspirational and motivated kids.

THE ARTS AND RISK TAKING

Significant in all of these examples is an attention to taking risks, to working outside of systems, working within systems, and working despite systems. It is not so surprising that risk taking would be a significant factor in the success of arts in urban settings.

The *American Heritage Dictionary* defines risk as "the possibility of suffering harm or loss, danger."[10] Artists, however, are drawn to risk, and more often than not, risk is defined as perceiving or exploring the possible. One SUAVE artist put it this way: "Attempting something beyond the realm of what is known to the person taking the risk." Another put it this way: "That which calls to be . . . a journeyer into the unknown."

Shirley Brice Heath,[11] in describing arts-based afterschool programs, writes this of risk:

Risk heightens learning at effective youth-based organizations. While public rhetoric laments the fate of 'at-risk youth,' our research reveals how youth depend on certain kinds of risk for development. Rather than live at its mercy, youth in arts organizations use the predictability of risks in the arts to intensify the quality of their interactions, products, performances.

Risk taking within teaching has been identified as a positive and essential ingredient for successful teacher learning and growth.[12] It requires individuals to engage in uncertain behaviors with a potential for negative consequences.[13]

Part of my interest in risk is in uncovering the positive role of risk taking in teaching and learning, not only for teachers, but also for students. Risk taking is familiar to the artists as it underlies the nature of artistry. In describing "risk," the artists of the SUAVE program have offered the following definitions:[14]

- Trying something new without certainty of the results
- Attempting something beyond the realm of what is known to the person taking the risk

- Reveal, ignite, shape, know, kindle
- That which calls to be, to be accomplished and seems beyond usually connected with fear and failing, or exhilaration to jump and dive in and try

When asked about their definition of themselves as artists, it was no surprise to uncover that risk also defined their view of themselves as artists. For example, an artist is:

- One who takes risks in society to speak their truth through the media of dance, visual arts, performance, and poetry.
- One who ardently "arts," a way of being, seeing, and hearing—using all the senses to perceive dreams and realities.
- Someone who takes risks at making people feel and see their own lives.
- A creator, transformer, innovator, and interpreter; a person who colors life, redefines and recreates reality, crosses established boundaries, speaks universal languages, and reaches the soul

Rather than focus on prevention and detention for "at-risk" youth, the organizations Heath examined urge creativity and invention with young people as "competent risk-takers across a range of media and situations" (p. 21). She continues, "The high risk embedded in the performances and exhibitions of these organizations creates an atmosphere in which students know how to solicit support, challenge themselves and others, and share work and resources whenever possible. Critique, as an *improvisational* and reciprocal process, amplifies practice gained during project planning. . ." (p. 26) [italics added].

COMING FULL CIRCLE

To live, we hope;
To hope, we dream;
To dream, we imagine our improved future.
To imagine, we act;
We make constant our effort to realize our dream.
To realize our dream, we improvise our realities.[15]

—*Xin Li*

The programs and individuals I have described and discussed in this chapter are improvisers, dreamers, and risk-takers. The teachers, artists, parents, and administrators involved with SUAVE, Freese Elementary, and the Oakland Academy for the Arts have worked relentlessly to bring arts into the lives of the children in their community. They are ardent arts activists in addition to their roles as teachers, artists in the schools, administrators, or parents. They have realized their dreams into realities. The realities do not come without their price of constant advocacy and continual action toward attaining public support. The community of artists, teachers, parents, students, and administrators described in this chapter know how to work in and through systems, and ultimately, how to subvert systems through attaining grants, speaking at school board meetings, creating status within schools that provide for more autonomy, such as magnet or charter school status. They realize dreams through constant and dedicated effort—and more often than not, go to bed completely exhausted.

The challenge and creativity of working inside and outside of the urban school systems is possible, if not exhilarating. Efforts to integrate the arts into urban education often provide the opening that can uncover children's arts talents. The potential and talents of children who engage in the arts is limitless. Their improved futures are no doubt enhanced by the folks who are willing to improvise school realities and create the opportunity to dream.

NOTES

1. Li, X. (2002). *The Tao of life stories: Chinese language, poetry, and culture in education*. New York: Peter Lang Publishers.

2. Hill, J. (2004). What is urban education in an age of standardization and scripted learning? In S. Steinberg & J. Kincheloe (Eds.), *19 urban questions: Teaching in the city* (p. 124). New York: Peter Lang Publishers.

3. Rubin, S. (2004). *Art against the odds: From slave quilts to prison paintings*. New York: Crown Publishers.

4. Goldberg, M. (2001). *Arts and learning: An integrated approach to teaching and learning in multicultural and multilingual settings, 2nd edition*. New York: Addison Wesley/Longman; Goldberg, M. (2004). *Teaching English language learners through the arts: A SUAVE experience*. New York: Pearson/Allyn and Bacon.

5. Catterall, J., Chapleau, R., & Iwanaga, J. (1999). Involvement in the arts and human development: General involvement and intensive involvement in music and theater arts. In *Champion of change: The impact of the arts on learning*. The Arts Education Partnership and the President's Committee on the Arts and Humanities.

6. Cox, W., Alm, R., & Holmes, N. (2004, May 13). Where the jobs are [Op-Chart]. *New York Times Op-Ed*.

7. Goldberg (2001); Gallas, K. (1994). *The languages of learning: How children talk, write, dance, draw, and sing their understanding of the world*. New York: Teachers College Press.

8. Goldberg (2004).

9. Goldberg (2004).

10. *American Heritage Dictionary* (second college edition, p. 1065). (1985). Boston: Houghton Mifflin Company.

11. Heath, S. (1999). Imaginative actuality: Learning in the arts during nonschool hours (p. 27). In *Champion of change: The impact of the arts learning*. The Arts Education Partnership and the President's Committee on the Arts and Humanities.

12. Cohen, D., & Barnes, C. (1993). Conclusion: A new pedagogy for policy. In D. Cohen, M. McLaughlin, & J. Talbert (Eds.), *Teaching for understanding: Challenges for policy and practice* (pp. 240–275). San Francisco: Jossey-Bass Publishers; Darling-Hammond, L., & McLaughlin, M. (1996). Policies that support professional development in an era of reform. In M. McLaughlin & I. Oberman (Eds.), *Teacher learning: New policies, new practices* (pp. 202–218). New York: Teachers College Press; Fullan, M., & Miles, M. (1996). Getting reform right: What works and what doesn't. *Phi Delta Kappan, 7* (10), 744–752; Fullan, M., & Miles, M. (1996). Getting reform right: What works and what doesn't. *Phi Delta Kappan, 7* (10), 744–752.

13. Fullan, M. (1995). The limits and the potential of professional development. In T.

Guskey & M. Huberman (Eds.), *Professional development in education: New paradigms and practices*. New York: Teachers College Press.

14. Goldberg (2004).
15. Li (2002).

CITIES: CONTESTED AESTHETIC SPACES

Karel Rose

My father had a boundless, indiscriminate love for New York City. One of his favorite songs was "East Side, West Side." I remember his body swaying and singing the words as if they were a hymn, a paean to his birthplace. Since he never went beyond the sixth grade in school, the streets were his teachers. The city was an extension of his body. It was in his strong muscular arms and his heavily calloused hands. He was permanently anchored to the rhythms, the sights, sound, and smells of uptown and downtown. He had an ever-expanding collection of postcards: Grand Central Terminal, the Flatiron Building, the Washington Market, The Empire State Building. My favorite was the one of a crowded street on the lower east side, an exotic place that gave me a new version of my world. The picture showed people of different ethnicities selling brooms, pickles, wooden bowls, and shoes. A young girl peddled strawberries. I could just about hear the foreign-accented street cries and smell the knishes. The people wore the clothes from the pushcarts.

My father did hard labor in the city every night. He would deliver newspapers, tying them up and then hoisting them onto his truck. I can still see the metal ring that he wore on his pinky finger for cutting the heavy rope that bound the stacks of papers. I used to beg to be taken along but that never came to be. I wanted to experience the city at night, see it go to sleep and awaken with the dawn. The windshield of the truck would be my lens. I wanted to be the first to read tomorrow's headlines.

When my father's coworkers would have a beer at my house, they would tell me that he was always smiling, engaged everyone in conversation, eager to hear their stories. He told me about the Italian newspaper dealer on the corner of Delancey and Essex Streets who gave him comic books for the "kids," his nightly coffee break with the black truck driver from Alabama to whom he loaned money and the Asian hunchback who serviced his truck. When he became a foreman, he hired workers who differed as much in appearance as they did in cultural commitments. This was his urban pool. They were all his friends. He didn't seem to see the diversity, and if he did, it only enriched his life. My father's response to difference contradicted the negative conceptions about the "other," which I learned from my silk-stocking school and an assortment of friends and relatives. When I got older and unpacked my metaphoric suitcase, I gladly discarded many of these attitudes. I am grateful that my father's generous perceptions of people and his embrace of difference prevailed.

My father's love of the city extended to places where he never went. When he was in his seventies, I took him to the Metropolitan Opera House for a performance of "Madame Butterfly." The story resonated for him and he was completely comfortable with the crowds and the glamour. He had amassed a wealth of information from living and working in the city. Although his experiences outdistanced his ability to reflect on them, they made his life rich.

As a white woman teaching at The City University of New York, a working-class uni-

versity, I often reflect back upon my early years with my father and try to analyze why those boundary crossings came so easily to him. Out of necessity and a genuine impulse of care, he never put up walls or feared difference. I slowly learned to appreciate his multiple versions of the world. I am deeply connected to those memories, reinventing them and changing myself in the process. As all children should, I now have the freedom to honor his memory in my own way, if only in the default mode. My father's version of "East Side, West Side" has embellished my own understandings and desires to continually cross my own borders. What better place than a large, diverse city for this teacher to challenge her preconceptions and work for social justice.

In this chapter, I want to explore how urban teachers can heighten their artistic and moral sensibilities through more profound emotional and intellectual engagements with the city that surrounds them. One of my major objectives is to heighten awareness of the many aesthetic opportunities that suffuse city life and wedge cracks in the safe of narrow-mindedness and parochialism. Building on issues Joe Kincheloe and I raise in our book, *Art, Culture and Education*,[1] I want to continue to explore the relationships between teaching and aesthetic experience. The following list of questions drives this chapter:

- How does the discourse of art help us to analyze teaching?
- How are teaching and art hermeneutical activities?
- How do context, cultural climate, time, and place influence teaching and art?
- How does aesthetic experience conflate with knowing?
- How do urban ceremonies, rituals, and events raise questions that connect to the discourses of art and teaching?

Some more difficult questions:

- How might experiences with the arts assist students and teachers to engage with critical social issues?
- How are the arts catalysts for social change?

PRIVATE AND PUBLIC WORLDS

My life prepares me for my life. As a teacher and writer, my private and public worlds merge. I cannot easily separate teaching from traveling, a good play from a good class, dancing at a wedding from choreographing a class presentation. Similarly, curriculum and pedagogy are conflated as is education and democracy. I'm not sure that I agree with those Buddhists who speak about the distinction between being and doing. The preparation of teachers, from my perspective, is all about developing independent, empowered thinkers who do not live their own lives in discrete curriculum areas. I fantasize that on Saturday nights, over a glass of wine, my students will have grand conversations and argue passionately about the issues that we discussed in Wednesday's philosophy class. I want them to connect their private worlds to the compelling concerns of our time. They need to confront what enrages them. Is it homelessness, racism, child abuse, poverty, war? The synergy with others will come when it connects to their own humanity.

The rich artistic and often chaotic world of urban life helps to reframe crucial issues. A reflective classroom can be the scrim, the mediation center, or the place where the intellectual and artistic merge and where concerns can be safely negotiated. In an earlier book, I noted that the artistic tone, however, is not moral; it is ironic. The artist in control of the art form maintains an aesthetic distance, struggling between his or her own passions and the subject matter.[2] The things of art stand away from the world and invite perception. The frame is real.[3] But the frame may be enlarged to include even those things that cannot be placed between the covers of a book, a gilt frame, or on a stage. Sometimes, it remains the task of the perceiver to imagine the framing and personally discover the aesthetic moments. Although greeted with mixed emotions,

"The Gates Project," in which Christo and Jeanne-Claude created a blaze of saffron fabric throughout Central Park for 16 days, was an opportunity for people to create their own framing and rely upon their own definitions of art.

TEACHERS AS ARTISTS

Teachers who do not have a rich background in the arts may not always acknowledge the many informal aesthetic encounters in their lives. Mimicking the way they were taught, they create spatial and temporal boundaries that organize knowledge into discrete boxes. This reification of old epistemologies with their convenient categories may be initially comforting, but too often this compartmentalization provides a false sense of finality and discourages creative thinking. Deferring completion, retaining the element of surprise and focusing on the process that Picasso has described as "a sum of destructions" heightens interest and mitigates against boredom.[4] Just as a good Scrabble player finds a way to build new words from old ones, so the artful teacher improvises and revises the extant categories. No version is final. Teaching is a constant negotiation among the students, the content, and the teacher. At its best, it is an articulate, informed argument.

Curricular and pedagogy are enlivened when the multiple languages and conceits of the arts are celebrated. Color, rhythm, texture, form, image, and improvisation are not bound to individual disciplines but inform perception across curricular boundaries. The arts are not just clarifiers for something else but significant ways of knowing unto themselves. Pasting the "Battle Hymn of the Republic" onto the study of the Civil War illuminates neither the history nor the music. Each must stand alone and be appreciated for its particular attributes; each way of knowing contributes to understanding the other but on its own terms.

Joe Kincheloe argues that U.S. society is not generally aware of the relationships connecting art, politics, culture, and education. I agree. One of the goals of teacher education should be to highlight these connections. Teachers need both art and didactic texts to address these complex interactions. Aesthetic experience is a way of knowing that articulates feeling facts. For it is the safe remove of art in its address to the emotions that inspires concern, invites questions, and democratizes the classroom. A cry of pain aesthetically rendered may be more persuasive than the essay, but it has limitations. Resistance may occur if there is an emotional unwillingness to confront that which illuminates life in a painful way. The reciprocal relationship between aesthetics and thinking, the rigorousness and intellectual content of the arts, and the concept of multiple intelligences as mutually reinforcing thought processes provide considerable support for educators.[5]

THE CITY AS AESTHETIC LABORATORY

The artistry of the city may elude us as we rush to catch the bus and dodge the cars. But the crowds, the first snowfall, the textures, the changing reflections, and the tender human street encounters are worthy of notice. A keen observer, a determined voyeur raises many hermeneutical questions. Teachers wandering the city in search of the artful will ask: "What is art?" Who decides?" "Does location count?" Variants of these questions continue to haunt teachers when they reflect on their pedagogy, the prescribed curricula, and standardized testing. It may be a tenuous situation to encourage students to interpret, criticize, and interact with controversial issues. Urban teachers often feel that they are in the eye of a hurricane and need support. Acknowledging the uniqueness of each voice is what John Dewey meant when he implored us not to create a rift between art and ordinary experience.

Democracy is perhaps the most compelling argument when students are encouraged to be rigorous questioners.

"High Art: Low Art" was a course that Joe Kincheloe and I designed. We were determined to help our students recognize art as an agent for social change. It would be necessary to expose them to the social complexities and fallout when aesthetic expression crosses traditional boundaries. Not wishing to "throw the baby out with the bath water," we acknowledged that all art enriches lives, but the focus in our class would be the role of transgressive art in a democracy. Throughout history, the distinction between high and low art has been carefully monitored except for a few spurts when art forms from different domains nourished each other. Think about the way Negro spirituals and jazz infuse contemporary music and opera.

Urban teachers—all teachers—need to know that there is not one single story. The aesthetic perspectives of feminists, non-Westerners, and outsiders are critical to our understanding of contemporary issues. Their voices belong in our classrooms and teachers as the storytellers of the culture need to present and transform these stories for their students. The arts challenge our intellect and our deepest emotions and as a result are significant catalysts for social change. The issue is not only about standards or which art has most value (all art has value) or appreciating art on its own terms, but it is also the recognition that aesthetic experiences foster intellectual consciousness of significant social issues. Historically, great artists have expressed their deep concern for social issues, hoping that their work might have political impact. Centuries ago, Breugel and Goya, among others, did so before their time was ready to accept their ideas. Today, with greater freedom, many contemporary artists create their own "Sensation," when they address the social crises of the day in their works, seeking not necessarily to beautify the world but to reflect it. The 2000 Brooklyn Museum "Sensation" exhibit became the final subject of our course.

Our class used the city as aesthetic laboratory. We wandered the city streets, visited museums, and interviewed artists, curators, and community people. There was heated discussion about what art should do for people. How did culture determine preferences? Should art be beautiful, consoling, disturbing, truthful? It may not be necessary to respond to these dichotomies. There are serious problems attending art's selective value. There is a need to acknowledge people's dependence on cultural frameworks and the admissibility of a simultaneous plurality of truths and realities for all.[6] For almost as long as there has been art, there has been iconoclasm and "art rage." Why the concern? All artworks aspire to be arguments for arguments' sake.[7] Aesthetic experiences foster engagement by speaking to our emotions. That may be why some view the arts as dangerous whereas others appreciate the aroused feelings that connect us to the world. Teachers need to be aware of this complicated schism and openly explore with their students ideas about what is beautiful. The urban setting raises many social and political questions; the context is often artful, the process is often artful, the product may not be "beautiful."

DIVERSITY IN AN AESTHETIC CONTEXT

Cities are ecotones, environmental edges that teem with diversity. Given their size, imposing order, and constant movement, cities can be liberating or constricting, thrilling or terrifying, The museums, the concert halls, those grand and imposing institutions, formally and cautiously honor diversity and influence our artistic perceptions. But aesthetic preferences have a way of "outing." They come outdoors, making visible an ecotone that often escapes the imprimateur of the museum.

It is 8:30 AM on a summer day in New York City. The city is already awake. A hand truck laden with clothes is pushed by an immigrant man. A Calvin Klein commercial shoot halts as an ambulance with sirens blaring races down the street. Everyone is an original. Skin tone, hairstyle, jewelry, age, and ethnicity change even before I turn the corner. Hats piled high on the corner wagon are reminiscent of the children's book, Caps for Sale. *The colors stir up their own exquisite sensations. There are music, hawkers screaming incomprehensibly, people talking into their cell phones. Max Beerbohm said that a quiet city is a contradiction in terms. The smell of hot dogs, a Proustian moment, reminds me of my youth. I realize that I didn't have breakfast but the walk is its own sensual feast. I'm satisfied, not hungry.*

My walk bears eloquent testimony to what Rachel Carson called the "lifelong durability of the sense of wonder."[8] I am completely engaged; I can't stop looking. I feel pleasure and satisfaction. What is artistically good is whatever articulates and presents feeling to our understanding.[9] But not being in a museum or gallery, no one but me has decided that I am having an aesthetic experience. What freedom! I simultaneously read many visual languages; the group waiting on line at the Social Security Office, the skinny models rushing to work, the mother carrying a baby and clutching the hand of a crying toddler. I get to Times Square. The billboards scream their seductions. The news of another tragedy appears on the marquis of a building. I need a vocabulary to write about these visual experiences. So will my students. The languages of the arts will work. We'll speak of shape, color, texture, plot, form, design, and balance. We'll interchange languages as we choreograph the visual and write poetry about urban sounds. The diversity resides not only in the people. The buildings, the open spaces, the fruit stands, the billboards, all speak to differences. I know now what Diane Ackerman means when she revels in synesthesia, the stimulation of one sense stimulating the other. The senses correspond to each other; a sound can be translated through perfume and a perfume through vision.[10] It is all so seamless; the sensory blending never ends.

On a summer weekend, fairs and festivals are everywhere. Ethnic groups from around the world accustomed to a rich street life bring their culture outside. At these urban rituals, everyone shares the same space. The exuberance is infectious. I see a large group surrounding a street singer. He and the audience sway to the music. In Street Theater, no fourth wall separates actors from audience; we are all part of the play. I must not separate myself either. I know that I am getting ready for tomorrow's class. They, too, must experience the wonder and beauty of the streets and carefully observe:

- *The commonplace (a woman in a babushka peeling potatoes)*
- *The contradictions (a display of African masks juxtaposed against an art deco building)*
- *The close-up wonder of the ordinary (an Asian woman's long black hair shining in the sun.)*

Cities are the stews of the world. Exotic foods are constantly being added to the pot as recently transplanted people try to make sense of their new world. They write their stories, visually depict their longings on canvases and the walls of buildings. They newcomers open stores and perform their music and rituals out of doors. As if by spontaneous combustion, street graphics appear and the streets become a giant storyboard. I help my students to read the world by taking a walk in the city. I ask them to "read" the architecture that frames our private and public spaces. What do they tell about the values of the architect? About the powers that financed the buildings? Why do buildings such as the White House, Big Ben, and Eiffel Tower become synonymous with the city itself? The Forum (Pompeii), the Brandenburg Gate (Berlin), the Parthenon (Athens), and the World Trade Center (New York) are drenched with symbolic meaning. These structures overwhelm us as a flood of emotions and ideas link the concrete and the abstract. Teachers need to clarify the relationships between abstract thinking and tangible forms. Learning to read between the words, the signs, and the objects is a skill that needs practice. Symbolic and abstract thinking encourage students to extend their range beyond the anecdotal, escape their particular frame of reference, and see beyond the materialism that suffuses them.

Students at The City University of New York understand diversity. Many have scaled unfamiliar walls, discarded metaphoric clothes from their suitcases, and broken the mold by being the first in their families to go to college. But like all of us, their boundaries always need revision. A walk in the city will help. There's a white father with his Asian son, a West Indian woman wheeling a sleeping white baby, two men holding hands, a young woman with her much older lover sipping wine at an outdoor café, and a man in a motorized wheelchair zigzagging through the crowd. It's a tableau that I want to freeze. I will show my students the work of the Ashcan School artists, Reginald Marsh and John Sloan, who, striving to counter social injustice, depicted workers in the city. Joseph Stella spent many nights under the Brooklyn Bridge before he painted his eponymous work. The bridge for him was the place where you faced nature, diversity, and the many wonders of the city. Today, there is general agreement that the Brooklyn Bridge is one of the classic and most beautiful walks in the world.

DISLOCATION AND OUTSIDERNESS

People who migrate within their own country or across international borders yearn for a better life. Some are disappointed and exchange their old chains for new shackles. They adjust in different ways: Some live in ghettos to maintain a sense of security and others reach out to new frontiers. In the United States, it is very difficult for people of color. Black Americans, in particular, have been denied access whether in the north or the south to the detriment of their quality of life. Jacob Lawrence painted his "Great Migration" series poignantly showing the conflicts, struggles, and outsiderness of black Americans in their own country. Fortunately, for him, "Out of the struggle came a kind of power and even beauty."[11] The arts, for some, are a means of making sense of a hostile and often lonely world.

My students spent time at "Crossing the Boulevard,"[12] an exhibit at the Queens Museum of Art in 2003, by documentary artists Warren Lehrer and Judith Sloan. The exhibit is an example of how the arts enable newcomers to respond to the dislocations they feel between their country of origin and their new home. The artists interviewed hundreds of people in Queens, a New York City borough where 138 different languages are spoken— probably the most ethnically diverse locality in the United States. The exhibition includes striking photographs, stories both in text and on audio, and original music. It is a testimony to people from around the world who have recreated their artistic roots to relieve the sense of outsiderness. A group of Nigerian women who started a church sang prayer songs. A Nepalese man honoring the Charya Buddhist tradition told his story in dance. A woman from Kabul wrote about the cosmopolitan city that she left and the mother she hasn't seen in 22 years. An Egyptian man proudly exclaimed that he was the first to start a café on the block. The arts granted professors, students, film makers, members of the Falun Gong, factory workers, dishwashers, security guards, and lawyers a means of expression to balance the world of their forebears with the realities of life in New York City. This richness just outside the walls of urban schools and universities just waits to be discovered.

The students returned to class connected to the ways in which the arts through multiple symbol systems can dispel dislocation and open doors to insiderness. Words, music, movement, and theater illuminated our understanding of complex concepts. The stories resonated as we looked at difference, rather than sameness, and inspired connections rather than dislocations. How instructive for teachers who have to take a curriculum and transform it into another symbol system. Truth and beauty, artfulness and interpretation are not limited to what is already between the covers of published books or on the walls of museums. It begins with personal experience and the awareness that philosopher-kings live in our own backyards. The search for authenticity, so gracefully revealed at the Queens exhibition, was empowering. Reinvention of the self is a life's work for all of us. The great thinkers who preceded and who live with us are better accessed when we acknowledge our own understandings.

PRAXIS FOR SOCIAL JUSTICE

The deep chasm between social classes, the unfair treatment of racial minorities, and the continuing marginalization of women demand and inspire aesthetic responses. The power of the arts to alter perceptions for good and noble reasons cannot be assumed. The arts may be used to support brutal repression as in Nazi Germany or the development of justice, equality, and democracy. Tyrants and saviors have recognized the power of the aesthetic for reaching the emotions and concentrating attention. The arts have been labeled filthy, ugly, sick, and dangerous. Why else burn books; outlaw "degenerate" art; or censor adult films, plays, and exhibitions? From the educator's perspective, the capacity of the arts to speak to both the emotions and the intellect is a powerful pedagogical tool for praxis in social justice. Teachers

always search for ways to prepare students for the unfamiliar and extend their reservoir of experiences. The "safe remove" of the art work helps students integrate powerful contradictory and disturbing feelings and imagine themselves in another's world. They stumble on discoveries. In the classroom, the exchange of ideas increases and students not only show up but are in the moment. As the terms that define outsider/insider art become blurred and art that addresses social issues is more visible in mainstream venues, new ways of thinking emerge. The need to confront inequality and domination is the work of many artists and provides direction to hospitable teachers who want to find new ways to question the canon and prescriptive "truths." Artists raise moral questions about what the world should and could be like. What follows are some examples of public art in urban areas and discussion of some sad cities that rigorously and critically ask us to examine issues of social justice.

PUBLIC ART

The artist is Judy Baca who designed "World Wall: A Vision of the Future Without Fear." This 210-foot mural in seven parts, first displayed in Los Angeles, addresses the contemporary issues of global importance: war, peace, and interdependence. Executed with the support of ethnic scholars, multicultural neighborhood youth, and hundreds of local support staff, the process was as important as the product. Different parts of this mural are now touring the world. Baca has produced more than 73 murals in almost every ethnic community in Los Angeles that address the needs of different groups. A video of her work has been produced by PBS and is part of the Annenberg series, "A World of Art."

On Avenue C in Manhattan, Hispanics have painted a large mural whose large letters read "Loisada," the Hispanic phonetic spelling of "Lower East Side."

Sue Coe, the activist artist, designs such public art as murals or billboards that encourage social action. Her themes address AIDS, animal rights, and workers. In Chicago and in Pittsfield, Massachusetts, billboards featured horrific images of animals being slaughtered.

SHRINES AND HOMAGE TO THE DEAD

Public mourning may take the form of makeshift shrines. Sacred spaces spontaneously spring up providing clues about the dead and the living. The deaths at Columbine High School, for example, called forth their own responses. The small and the grandiose, side by side, assumed their own idiosyncratic aesthetic as people mourned the deaths and their own disbelief. Transformations of private grief into public statements are seen in cities and towns in response to world events, the death of revered individuals, or outrage at injustice. Whether mourning ethnic cleansing in Bosnia, starvation in Somalia, the deaths in the Iraq War, the stoning of Islamic women, or the abusive death of a child, shrines are statements. Heightening consciousness of the issues behind the tragedies, they may encourage praxis. Whether people mourn Martin Luther King or Jimi Hendrix, they are marking their support for the person as well as for their belief systems.

NINE/ELEVEN

Nine/eleven was a watershed. After 9/11, the memorials spoke not only to the dead but also to the political issues that burst into flame on that fateful day. The deluge of patriotic responses was everywhere in evidence across America. There were trucks covered with dozens of flags, buildings and artifacts painted with the Stars and Stripes. Commemorative murals were all over honoring the firefighters, police, and others who bravely responded to the tragedy. One Harlem mural showed the Statue of Liberty crying blood. A photograph by Robert Rauschenberg also depicted a solemn Statue of Liberty cradling the Twin Towers in her arms. But there were also "flag" clothing, toys, backpacks, and "We're Proud to Be American" bumper stickers. The conflation of commodification and patriotism is a slippery slope, for this was a difficult time to question patriotism. But there were displays that raised issues about U.S. policies on billboards, door fronts, and walls, and in stenciled statements around the country. Barry Dawson's keen photographic eye captured many of the varied responses at this time.[13]

SAD CITIES

Sometimes cities make aesthetic statements without consciously meaning to do so. Their cry of pain resonates with us and although the scene is not beautiful (who said art has to be beautiful?), they remind us that we are all part of the music.

Not all cities can hide their warts. They literally wash their laundry in public. Without calling for social action, their very existence cries out for response. Poverty and racism, the roots of urban deprivation abound. It is hard to forget the images of the squatter settlements outside Johannesburg or the tents in the cemeteries of New Delhi. The necessity for a life lived on the streets is a given in the sad cities. Colorful as the daily functions of washing, shaving, and hair cutting may be for the tourist, they are not so for the residents. Commercial enterprises such as dyeing fabrics or baking tortillas, which may seem exotic, exist out of necessity. Means of transportation may provide local color, but they are lessons in ingenuity and the remnants of a past that remains a necessity in the present. In Cuzco, Luxor, and Lahore, as in hundreds of other places around the world, carts and bicycles pulled by people as well as animals are the reminders of the daily struggle to survive.

Ghettos, in most large cities, are often sad places reminding us of the pervasive discrimination and economic deprivation. In some cases, a former president may decide to make a statement and buy an office in a ghetto, but the world outside remains a grim place. There are the street people, many who are homeless, neglected children, and the unemployed just waiting for something to happen. The garbage-littered streets, junked cars, and ramshackle housing testify to the misery. Most often the schools in the ghettos reflect the absence of social responsibility.

Despite many signs of social decay, racism, the growing gaps between rich and poor, and environmental destruction, there is much hope. Jane Jacobs, the author of the great American classic *The Death and Life of Great American Cities*, identifies in her new but discouraging book *Dark Age Ahead* the promise of higher education for changing the world.[14] The tragedies that are reflected in sad cities and ghettos may mirror our own feelings about being disconnected from a more complete life. But in these lost places, we see courage, the willingness to work through the darker side, and the terrors of annihilation. As educators, we have to teach hope even when we, ourselves, may feel hopeless.

THESIS

A thesis belongs at the beginning. Because many of the ideas that follow have already been expressed in this chapter, I beg your indulgence for this transgression. I believe:

- The arts possess an exceptional capacity to inspire concern through the release of energy and passion.
- The "safe remove" of art helps us to integrate powerful contradictory and disturbing feelings, as we see ourselves in others' experiences, and increases our capacity for caring.
- Art encourages the imagination, and all learning requires imaginative thinking.

- Art can exist for its own sake. It can also exist for social praxis without compromising the artistic process.
- Both teachers and artists bring new forms into existence.

EPILOGUE

I wish my father could have read this chapter. We could communicate about something that bridged our differences. Telling our story and thinking about our thoughts in another context is a beginning. This is the meaning of reflection and the purpose of this chapter. I know that I'll keep looking at those old postcards of New York City.

NOTES

1. Rose, K., & Kincheloe, J. (2003). *Art, culture and education: Artful teaching in a fractured landscape.* New York: Peter Lang.

2. Rose, K. (1971). *A gift of the spirit.* New York: Holt, Rinehart & Winston.

3. Grumet, M. (1988). Where the line is drawn. In *Bitter milk.* Amherst, MA: University of Massachusetts Press.

4. Bruner, J. (1973). *Beyond the information given: Studies in the psychology of knowing.* New York: Norton.

5. Stewart, M. (1997). *Thinking through aesthetics.* Worcester, MA: Davis; Gardner, H. (1983). *Frames of mind.* New York: Basic Books.

6. Dissanayake, E. (1988). *What is art for?* Seattle: University of Washington Press.

7. Smith, R. (2003, May 13). Why attack art? *New York Times*, p. E1.

8. Carson, R. (1956). *The sense of wonder.* New York: Harper & Row.

9. Langer, S. (1956). *Problems of art.* New York: Scribners.

10. Ackerman, D. (1990). *A natural history of the senses.* New York: Vintage Books.

11. Lawrence, J. (1995). *The great migration: An American story.* New York: HarperCollins.

12. Lehrer, W., & Sloan, J. (2003). *Crossing the boulevard: Strangers, neighbors, and aliens in a new America.* New York: Norton.

13. Dawson, B. (2003). *Street graphics.* New York: Thames & Hudson.

14. Jacobs, J. (2004). *Dark age ahead.* New York: Random House.

Education Policy and Urban Education

SYSTEM-TO-SYSTEM PARTNERSHIP AS A REFORM STRATEGY FOR URBAN SCHOOLS

Marleen C. Pugach, Linda Post, Christine Anderson,
Robert Lehmann, and Daniel J. Donder

Partnerships for reforming urban schools are often short-lived, dependent on a single strong leader in one or more of the partner organizations, and involve only a small number of targeted schools. As such, partnerships tend not to be successful in achieving *systemic* reform in urban schools. Many stakeholders and constituencies within urban communities are committed to improving education in their public schools and make significant contributions to this end. Often, however, these represent only limited partnerships—between one business and one school, between one agency and a small number of schools, between a university's teacher education program and one or two specific schools, or short-term grants to a several schools. Individual schools may get a boost—and much needed additional resources—by partnering, for example, with a university as a professional development school, with a health organization to install a school-based clinic, or with a Boys and Girls Club

of YMCA to provide after-school programming. Partnerships like these certainly may be critical to the success of the individual schools that are fortunate enough to participate. But taken together, such efforts do not have the cumulative effect of addressing the full scale of challenges that exist within urban school districts as a whole.

The challenges facing urban schools are systemic, and although each individual school must certainly engage in its own improvement, reforming urban education school by school will simply not get the job done when individual schools exist within a larger educational system that itself requires reform. Done in isolation, small-scale partnership efforts do not span the central players and constituencies that are fundamental to the operation of the schools. Therefore, they cannot hope to have a sustained effect on closing the persistent achievement gap. To attain success in reform and to close the achievement gap that continues to challenge urban schools, it will take a carefully coordinated effort on the part of the community as a whole, a partnership that engages education, community and business leaders, and marshals a collective commitment to the public schools. Partnerships have the potential to support widespread, systemic reform if the partnership itself is designed and implemented as a rigorous reform strategy that is squarely focused on improving the quality of teaching and learning for children and youth in urban schools.

The Milwaukee Partnership Academy (MPA) represents a sustained attempt to reform urban schools by engaging multiple education, community, and business partners in a *system-to-system* reform. It is based on the belief that improving the quality of teaching and learning in the Milwaukee Public Schools (MPS) is the joint business of the universities and colleges, the public schools, and the community at large. These stakeholders must join together to form a serious, long-term, action-oriented partnership—and be willing to support change within and across the partner organizations that all make up the system that currently is failing urban schools—for serious reform to have a chance of succeeding.[1] The stakes for the economic and social well-being of the community and its current and future citizens are the foundation for the sense of urgency that should drive institutions and organizations within urban communities to join together to plan and implement coordinated, aligned initiatives that are needed to improve the educational experience and success of students in all urban schools—not only to those in a few schools.

WHO ARE THE PARTNERS AND WHAT ARE THE PARTNERSHIP'S PRIORITIES?

The MPA is an urban P–16 council made up of three interrelated groups that form its governing structure: (1) the Executive Partners, (2) the Partners, which represent wide community constituencies, and (3) the Implementation Team, which is the action arm of the MPA. These three groups interact on a regular basis. The partnership's priorities are set by the Executive Partners and are carried out by an Executive Director.

The Executive Partners

The ten-member Executive Partners group is made up of leaders of major organizations within the community. They include:

1. The Chancellor of the University of Wisconsin-Milwaukee
2. The Superintendent of the Milwaukee Public Schools
3. The Executive Director of the Milwaukee Teachers' Education Association, the local teachers' union
4. The President of the MPS Board of School Directors
5. The President of the Milwaukee Area Technical College (MATC)
6. The President of the Milwaukee Metropolitan Association of Commerce, the local chamber of commerce
7. The Chair of the Education Committee of the Greater Milwaukee Committee, a group of business leaders
8. The President of the Private Industry Council
9. The Mayor of the City of Milwaukee
10. The President the Helen Bader Foundation, a local foundation with historical ties to the education community.

Once a month the Executive Partners meet to discuss the MPA's progress and to make decisions regarding the policies and priorities of the partnership. An additional meeting that is held quarterly is a meeting of the full group of partners from across the community. One of the members of the Executive Partners group leads the quarterly meeting, which is a public, two-hour meeting of the full MPA.

These leaders command attention, control resources, and hold power in their organizations and in the community, and their presence is fundamental to the joint commitment to institutionalize, stabilize, and sustain the partnership and, thus, provide stability to education reform in Milwaukee's urban schools. The visible participation of high level leaders—they do not send representatives to meetings but rather have made a commitment to attend themselves—provides credibility to the importance of the MPA. The culture of the partnership has created the expectation that the leaders of these organizations are present at each meeting themselves, with no substitutes, to work together on the goal of improving education in the community.

To focus its work, the Executive Partners identify a set of priorities that address the overall mission of the partnership, namely, to ensure that every child is on grade level in reading, writing, and mathematics. These priorities are essential to the work of the MPA because they provide a common understanding of where and how resources and efforts are to be aligned. In this way, they can begin to counteract the cycle that typically prevails in urban schools, namely, generating and then discarding new, often unrelated, initiatives every year. These priorities are revisited each summer, not to change direction, but rather to fine-tune the work and to respond to conditions that may have changed and that affect their implementation. The current MPA priorities include:

1. Districtwide implementation of a comprehensive literacy and mathematics framework
2. Tutoring and family literacy
3. Teacher and principal quality (with an emphasis on coaching and embedded professional development)
4. Research and evaluation
5. Skunkworks (a group that thinks "out of the box" about educational issues)
6. Community partners (to align the work of informal educational agencies and foundations with the MPA)

The MPA Partners

Participation in the MPA exists laterally across the community, and vertically within partner organizations through its extensive group of Partners. Partners include broad representation from the metropolitan community. Leaders from the public library, the YMCA, the museum, and the zoo, for example, participate regularly in the MPA. Membership also includes the deans of the School of Education, College of Letters and Sciences, and Peck School of the Arts at UWM, as well as the Chairperson of the Department of Curriculum and Instruction. The broad range of affiliates extends as well to the local foundation and donor community, private colleges and universities, as well as to the ongoing, consistent presence of government officials—for example, the state Superintendent of Public Instruction, who regularly attends each meeting with staff.

These quarterly Partner meetings serve an important public function for the partnership. It is here that the Executive Partners report on their work, workgroups report on their progress, and the input of community stakeholders is solicited on MPA initiatives. These meetings provide ongoing momentum for the work of the partnership at the community level. In addition, they function to create a common understanding of the activities that are being implemented to address the priorities and to align the language and concepts that undergird the collective efforts of the partners. Quarterly meetings begin with a report from the superintendent of schools and from the partnership's Executive Director. Discussions about critical issues in the district and the community take place. Each meeting is an important opportunity both to honor accomplishments and to refocus and recommit the partnership to its goal of improving the quality of education for the children of Milwaukee. Ultimately, the dialogue is focused on the well-being of the children of the community, and there is a high level of awareness that collective leadership across the full complement of partners is unique and, as such, provides a unique and unusual opportunity to make a difference for the entire local urban community.

The Implementation Team

Partnerships that are serious about reforming urban education cannot merely meet to discuss the issues. The Implementation Team is the action arm of the MPA and is charged with creating and carrying out action plans to support the MPA's priorities. This team was appointed in 2001 and includes multiple representatives from the partner organizations. The Executive Director of the MPA chairs the team, sets the agenda, and keeps the work of the group on track. For each priority there is a workgroup that reports to the full Implementation Team, which meets on a biweekly basis. The Implementation Team's workgroups extend participation to include any interested stakeholders, and it is not uncommon for the Executive Director to get calls from individuals who wish to participate; participation is entirely voluntary.

From an initial schedule of weekly meetings for two full years (2001–03), the team now meets one half-day per week on a biweekly basis, 12 months of the year. The full team meets for two hours, during which workgroups report on their progress. This helps to avoid duplication of effort and also enables workgroups to combine their meetings and short-term goals appropriately. This is followed by a two-hour meeting of each of the workgroups (although some workgroups meet on a different schedule). Periodically representatives of specific programs that are relevant to the workgroups make brief presentations to the team.

The Implementation Team is commonly referred to as the place where the "real work" of the MPA gets done. The goal of its work is to keep focused on the critical priorities of the partnership and resist having efforts be diffused across a broad range of unrelated initiatives. This team keeps it focus on aligning initiatives, realigning resources for the priorities, garnering new resources in an aligned manner, and streamlining the work of the schools—in short, to change the way "business is done" within and across the partners to improve the quality of teaching and learning. If the Executive Partners are thought of as having responsibility to work "on the system," the Implementation Team has the responsibility of working "in the systems," that is, in the various systems within each of the partner organizations themselves.

Key related activities of the district flow through the Implementation Team for ongoing direction and feedback. Early in its first year, this team directly addressed the long-standing skepticism of local teachers that any initiative could be sustained over time or that enough people in charge had the big picture in mind. As the team planned for introducing the priorities, the question of how to gain the teachers' "buy in" and the seriousness of purpose were central considerations. The direct participation of the teachers union in all levels of the partnership helped ensure that from the outset of the partnership, there was a shared understanding of the teachers' concerns and how to address them. The existence of the partnership as a whole, and the Implementation Team in particular, have begun to permeate the vocabulary of all partners and it is becoming common knowledge that if one wishes to interact with senior people from the partner organizations regularly, every other Monday afternoon, which is when the team meets, is the time and place to find them.

Although there are official voting members of this team representing the principal organizations in the partnership, the work that has been accomplished to date has been accomplished by consensus. Membership on the Implementation Team remains constant and includes representatives from the district, the local public university, the community college, the teachers' union (including its president), parents, community organizations, and two representatives from the five private colleges and universities in the area. The three university and college representatives are all senior faculty members who carry a high degree of status on campus. Leaders of the major departments in the school district, including the Director of Teaching and Learning, the Chief Academic Officer, the Director of Assessment and Accountability, and the Director of Leadership Support, are part of the district's membership. Stability of membership is required because this team must deal with complex issues that challenge the status quo directly; this requires a high degree of trust among members.

The Implementation Team is a labor-intensive effort, which has become a critical source of brainstorming, action, and consensus building around the work of the partnership. This team is evidence of an important principle of the partnership—namely, that it takes *both* senior-level leadership on a communitywide basis and leadership at the level of those who take daily action to be successful in achieving system-wide change. Implementation Team members are asked to participate in the quarterly MPA Partner meetings, and several do; workgroup chairs must be present to report on the progress of their group's goals. A substantial portion of the agenda for the quarterly meetings evolves directly from the work of the Implementation Team, and the agenda for the team is directed by the decisions of the Executive Committee.

HOW DOES AN URBAN PARTNERSHIP ALIGN ITS WORK?

The MPA provides the Milwaukee community with a broad-based infrastructure to promote sustained engagement in aligning the educational efforts of all partners to produce a shared educational framework within which to improve student learning. Unlike the situation in many other urban communities, the infrastructure provided by the MPA creates a local policy environment that is focused on mobilizing the various strengths and resources of the urban community toward collaborative and shared responsibility in ensuring student success in the Milwaukee Public Schools. It provides a structure for the regular presence of leaders from various constituencies to demonstrate their commitment to education in the community, with a common interest in the quality of learning for Milwaukee's youth and a commitment to shared responsibility to provide stability and sustainability in reforming education.

The MPA not only allows multiple stakeholders and key constituents to come together to make the changes that will ensure student success in the educational system, but by providing shared identity and visibility to this collaborative relationship, it has also compelled a more consistent commitment and greater accountability on the part of all the partners. The breadth and range of this constantly growing partnership indicates an increasing public awareness that reforming urban education is a collective responsibility and that this change must be systemic. As such, all participating partners realize their role in contributing to a collective vision of school success, and consider how their organization may need to change to maximize its contribution to local educational reform. How resources and activities are aligned is central to this effort. With the concept of alignment firmly established, local leaders look toward deliberately creating opportunities for alignment across the regular range of activities, requirements, and resources that exist both within the school district and across the partners, and consider new ways of thinking about their own organization's commitment to the education community.

One important example of alignment relates to one of the strategic priorities of the MPA—*teacher and principal quality.* The ongoing professional development of teachers is a critical component in reaching the goal of having all children on grade level in reading, writing, and mathematics. Like the other priorities of the MPA, the teacher and principal quality priority has as one of its goals the coordination and alignment of resources to improve the district's capacity to offer high quality professional development opportunities that are squarely focused on the goals of the district. Typically, especially in a decentralized system of schools, principals and teacher committees seek professional development opportunities wherever they can. Many high-quality opportunities for professional development are offered across several departments of the district, but as is the case in many large urban districts, they have not been well aligned. The development of the MPA has provided an entity that can shape, broker, align, assess, and evaluate professional development opportunities for teachers in MPS to help improve classroom practice specifically for urban schools. Working in a highly coordinated fashion through the Implementation Team, the ongoing development of teachers is seen as a community-wide responsibility in Milwaukee; which is a fundamental assumption of the MPA itself.

Related to professional development is the role of the local institutions of higher education, the relationship of their goals to the priorities of the MPA, and reforms needed within these institutions. As state requirements for teacher education shift, the intersection of those changes with the goals of the partnership has become extended territory for discussions about alignment. For example, when the state shifted to a standards-based approach to initial teacher certification and a career ladder for moving to permanent licensure,

the MPA viewed this as an opportunity to create—with these institutions, the district, and the teachers union—a conceptual framework for what those standards mean, specifically for teachers in urban schools, that would guide the career-long professional development of MPS teachers as they move from initial to permanent status. This document, *Characteristics of a High-Performing Urban Classroom,* provides a common language for dialogue about instruction in several critical areas. A final example of alignment as regards teacher and principal quality is the development of a comprehensive induction system for new teachers, which is aligned to the new state career ladder.

Another area in which the MPA is building a commitment to alignment is through grant writing. Partners seek grants to support the priorities of the MPA and work across institutions within the partnership to develop proposals. Grants are seen as opportunities to support various aspects of the MPA priorities and these priorities shape how grants are written and which partners are included. As grants are being prepared, progress is reported out to both the Implementation Team and at quarterly MPA meetings. As the MPA has grown in stature in the community, grant writers from various institutions, not limited to Milwaukee, are increasingly interested in drawing on the partnership as part of the rationale for their proposals. To ensure alignment, individuals or groups that wish to submit a grant that references the MPA as part of the rationale must present the proposal to the Implementation Team. The Research and Evaluation Workgroup co-chairs review the proposal and bring it to the full Implementation Team for approval; only then will the grant writers receive a letter of support from the MPA. In addition, those who staff the grant in question must contribute directly to the work of the MPA. If this has not occurred before the grant is written, it becomes a condition of MPA approval that participation in the MPA take place. In addition, the Director of the Division of Assessment and Accountability often receives grant proposals directly and, if they are related to the priorities of the MPA, brings those to the Implementation Team for approval as well. These are all efforts to align the work to the priorities of the MPA, maximize resources, widen the scope of participation in the community, and reshape the view and practice of research from an individual to a collective purpose. This requires changes—especially for the colleges and universities—in the way grant writing is conducted. The regular meetings of the Implementation Team assure that grant writers have frequent, easy access to the MPA to support grant preparation in a timely manner. Further, the MPA has worked with local donors to provide direct support to strategic organizational strategies, for example, to support school-based leadership teams, known locally as Learning Teams, as the agents of organizational change in the schools.

A third example is the concerted effort to increase the number of school nurses in MPS. The number is markedly low in Milwaukee, compared to the rest of the state, which directly affects the ability of the children in MPS to focus on their studies. This effort began at the district superintendent's office. The partnership became a focal point for this effort by educating the partners about this problem and by bringing together the deans of nursing and education from area institutions to support the effort and to rethink their preparation programs in relationship to the schools.

Alignment, focus, and keeping on message continue to be critical to the success of this partnership. The process of shaping the actions of the partners around the priorities and goals of the partnership—as a mutual and reciprocal activity—is never a completed task, but requires constant attention if the alignment process is to result in the level and scope of improvements that are needed.

BUILDING TRUST ACROSS LARGE URBAN BUREAUCRACIES

Whether it is entering into a joint business venture, embarking on a long-term personal relationship, or developing a complex partnership with multiple organizations, the concept of trust building is essential if there is to be meaningful involvement and mutual benefit. In many ways, the first two examples cited are far easier to develop and sustain than the latter. Individuals seeking to join resources and expertise in a business climate usually have had previous knowledge of each other's work and experience in a professional environment that helps them decide whether or not entering into a working partnership is in their mutual interests. And certainly those who are making decisions concerning life partnerships often have developed close relationships that start with an opening of self and continue by nurturing an ongoing commitment.

Organizational partnerships, on the other hand, often begin with certain stressors already in place and are faced with the challenges of not only overcoming past histories, but also reversing relationships that may have been founded on diametrically opposed philosophies. For example, in a complex structure such as the Milwaukee Partnership Academy, partners who are firmly planted on opposite sides of the school voucher issue work together in concert around a framework for improving Milwaukee Public Schools. One has to ask how organizations that are so polarized ideologically on such a fundamental level can even be at the same table, let alone develop and sustain a trusting relationship. The answer, although quite basic in theory, is far more complex in practice. The fact is that, unlike business partners or married couples who enter into long-term relationships from a base that may already be strong, with the desire to make it even better, organizational partnerships are often begun in an environment that may be less than ideal, but may risk even further peril without systemic change. In other words, all parties must believe it is in their individual and collective best interests to work together for the greater good.

The real challenge then is to get the parties to realize that, if there is to be an end product that is beneficial to all, they must set aside their personal agendas and trust that others will do the same. This should not require a compromise of values or an expectation that others should cede their fundamental beliefs in an effort to make the partnership work. To do so would most assuredly guarantee failure. Rather, the partners must develop a level of trust that says, "This is where we stand when it comes to this issue. We understand that while we are both working toward a common goal, we can respectfully disagree on this issue and trust that neither party will use its influence to try to leverage the other partners in this area." This can only work if several key pieces are in play.

First, issues about which disagreement exists cannot be so fundamentally opposed to the very reason for the partnership that parties cannot function within their common agenda. Given the voucher example previously cited, both the teachers union and the chamber of commerce can stand solidly on opposite sides of this issue. As long as their common agenda recognizes that a strong public school system benefits the entire community, they can work together through the MPA to improve student achievement within Milwaukee Public Schools and continue to support their positions on vouchers outside of the partnership. This relationship can only work if there is a level of trust between partners that is open and honest about issues of disagreement, and if the partners remain

true to their commitment to the common goal of improving education for all of Milwaukee's students.

A second important aspect in the success of such an arrangement is the role of the other partners in helping strengthen relationships between parties, especially in instances where day-to-day operations can put a strain on the partnership. Several examples may clarify this point. During a time of intense collective bargaining between the union and the district, for example, it is imperative that the other partners are sensitive to this dynamic and keep both parties focused on the bigger picture. Similarly, when staffing concerns arise between the university and the district's human resources department, the other partners need to be sensitive to such potential problems and refocus energy toward the larger goal. Approaching problems as an expected part of the process enables the partners to address them less as crises or adversarial events and more as barriers that require the best thinking of all of the partners, as well as timely interventions and solutions. A strong partnership can actually enhance these working relationships and help to mitigate otherwise damaging situations.

The third, and probably most important, component to a successful partnership is that the reason for its very existence has to be of such significance that the partners would be negatively impacted if the partnership were to dissolve. In other words, the stakes must be so high for the success of the partnership that each of the parties must commit to a positive outcome—because failure is not a viable option for the students in MPS and for the community. This last point emphasizes the necessity for a relationship among all partners built on trust. As trust builds across the partners, honest feedback and criticism can take place relative to all of the partners. Each partner serves as a friendly critic of the others in a context of trust and a shared focus. Each partner must be daring enough to bring to its constituency the work of the partnership, and each must honor the trust that the other partners place in it. To do otherwise could destroy the partnership.

SUSTAINING THE PARTNERSHIP FOR LONG-TERM EFFECTIVENESS

This then leads us to a brief discussion on sustainability. For any partnership to be effective it must stand the test of time. There are most certainly no guarantees to the longevity of any relationship, even those that are founded on mutual respect and understanding, borne out by the high divorce rate and equally high number of business failures reported in this country every year. Several tenets in establishing organizational partnerships can help to maintain the relationship. Especially important is the realization that, although strong individuals are necessary to any working relationship, particularly in the establishment phase, solid structures are far more important.

Most assuredly, with time, individuals will come and go, but if the partnership is to sustain and grow, it must be able to withstand such mobility, and consequently structures must be in place early on to make this happen. This partnership has sustained three major leadership changes—the local superintendent, the chancellor of the local university, and the teachers union—indicating that it is becoming institutionalized as a way of approaching educational reform in Milwaukee's urban community and in its urban schools. During these transitions, key leaders—both formally and behind the scenes—worked assiduously to communicate the goals and benefits of the partnership to the new leaders. As the MPA is increasingly established as a force in the community, its visibility, existence, and success can create the expectation that new leaders will sustain active participation.

Another key factor in the sustainability of organizational partnerships is the development of mechanisms to deal with surfacing problems, as well as intermittent crises, quickly and effectively. At the outset, the partners need to identify individuals who are given the authority to make decisions for their respective organizations, and this group needs to meet on a regular basis to identify and address issues as they arise. Trust is strengthened and nourished with each successful resolution to such situations, and as trust grows, the chances of sustaining the partnership increase. And probably the single most important factor in the success of any partnership is communication. Structures need to be in place not only for a regular sharing of ideas and concerns, but also for periodic retreats of a more substantive nature that allow for midcourse assessment and directional adjustments.

In terms of meeting the challenges facing urban schools, there is perhaps no single reform effort that holds such promise as the forming and forging of such partnerships. Because the potential is so great and the desired outcomes equally promising, the risks of such endeavors are certainly worth exploring. If the parties are so inclined, however, they must be willing to travel outside of their normal operational comfort zone and be willing to place their organizational trust in each other and, more importantly, in the newly formed entity that is the partnership.

HOW CAN SYSTEMIC PARTNERSHIPS BENEFIT URBAN SCHOOLS?

What are the specific benefits that can accrue to urban schools within a systemic urban partnership? What results have been attained thus far?

Urban partnerships uncover the complexity within the array of institutions and organizations that are responsible for P-16 education. Each education partner learns the complexity of each other's institutions and bureaucracies and provides a realistic understanding regarding how business gets done—and how business needs to change to better support the schools.

Further, the partnership provides a structure within which all of the local area institutions that prepare teachers come together regularly to discuss relevant issues, raise concerns, and interact collectively with school district personnel. This occurs through the regular structures of the partnership. It also takes place through a new local organization, the Metropolitan Milwaukee Area Deans of Education, which is convened by the Dean of the School of Education at the University of Wisconsin-Milwaukee and includes all the education deans from the local public and private institutions as well as the Executive Director of the MPA. Because the partnership's priorities—and not the priorities of any individual institution of higher education—drive the MPA, each institution has to rethink its relationship to the district and how best to contribute to it. For example, this is the group that convened the joint meeting of the deans of nursing and education to address the shortage of school nurses in the district.

Next, there is a joint sense of accountability across partner institutions, which shifts the conversation from blaming the school district in an isolated fashion for problems and challenges to a conversation based on joint responsibility for its improvement. The structure and membership of the MPA enable the tone of local discourse about education to be a discourse of mutual learning and action across education and economic forces and institutions within the community.

The partnership also enables regular discussions to take place regarding teachers' content preparation by having school district and partnership personnel interact with deans and faculty in the arts and sciences on a regular basis. The resources of the institutions of higher education are not limited to education departments, but extend campus-wide as a way of beginning to rethink the relationship between the academic disciplines, the preparation of teachers, and the school district's curriculum. Further, the relationship between academic preparation at the community college and the four-year institutions is also facilitated through the partnership.

Finally, because the partnership is committed to using evidence to drive its work, data regarding the academic performance of students are being looked at and disaggregated in new ways. For example, a new reporting structure instituted in the first set of priorities provided data on individual students, classroom progress, and school-wide progress in a formal report that was never before available. This also enabled a discussion of how data are collected and what data are needed. These data were never before collected, with the result that district teachers, administrators, and families were not well informed about student progress.

In terms of student learning, the MPA is starting to see the results of its work in improved student achievement in the elementary grades that has been sustained over a three-year period, although challenges still exist at the secondary level. The comprehensive literacy and mathematics frameworks have resulted in a sustained commitment to job-embedded professional development in each local school site. School-based learning teams that require the membership of teacher leaders in literacy (literacy coaches) and mathematics (mathematics teacher leaders), as well as the building principal, have been developed and implemented to take responsibility for creating professional learning communities in each school and to use local evidence to inform its decision making. A coaching model for principals and teachers sustains the focus on teacher development. These early accomplishments enable the partnership to renew its commitment to sustaining its work for long-term gains—rather than changing course because the gains are not broad enough or deep enough in the short term, which is typically how urban districts have functioned in the past.

CONCLUSION

Why are systemic partnerships so crucial to the improvement of urban schools? The various institutional bureaucracies that affect education are larger, more numerous, and perhaps more intractable in urban communities. Often they cloud the issues rather than clarify them. Through its structure of distributed and shared leadership, the MPA not only allows its members to cut across institutional and organizational boundaries to work collaboratively toward improving the quality of urban education, but also lets the partners engage with each other to envision and plan for education reform without being limited as much as usual by existing bureaucratic governance structures. The mission of the MPA—shared responsibility and accountability for student success—is echoed by other P-16 councils across the nation. By joining together, the entire community takes responsibility for the education of its students and serves as a counterweight to the long-standing practice of blaming either the school district or the teachers union for the problems that exist.

What is unique and groundbreaking about the MPA is the manner in which the partners have embraced the challenge of aligning efforts to improving the education of all children through better preparation, recruitment, and retention of teachers in an urban setting. The MPA presents a bold move on the part of various institutions and organizations in Milwaukee. It is not the "initiative of the week." Rather, this work represents a collective commitment to accept the challenge that improvement means staying the course, while also maintaining a sense of urgency as a driving force to improve the education—and the future—of students in urban schools.

NOTES

The authors would like to acknowledge each of their colleagues who work on and contribute to the Milwaukee Partnership Academy, as well as Nancy Zimpher and Kenneth Howey, who were instrumental in establishing the partnership and supporting it in its early years.

1. Pugach, M., Post, L., & Thurman, A. (2006). All-university engagement in education reform: The Milwaukee partnership academy. In S. Percy, N. Zimpher, & M. Brukhardt (Eds.), *Creating a new kind of university*. Bolton, MA: Anker Publishing.

DIVERSITY AND SECURITY CHALLENGES FOR URBAN SCHOOL PLANNING AND CHANGE

Carol A. Mullen

What are some of the major challenges in preparing teachers for their future roles as leaders of urban schools? Specifically, what roles do security and diversity play in relation to one another as educational reform goals? This chapter addresses these two questions.

The potential impact of terrorism attacks on schools has necessitated a new role for leadership teams at the school and district level. Although learning how to deal with terrorism has become central to U.S. foreign policy, transference has only just begun: Principals and superintendents have been called upon to guide action for preventing catastrophe and simultaneously to promote the health of school populations. In this picture health has two central meanings—safety and inclusion—and involves crisis awareness and diversity awareness.

CLIMATE OF CRISIS AND UNCERTAINTY

The responsibility for security will need to be shaped in accordance with cultural diversity goals and a democratic commitment to safe and inclusive schools. Importantly, although efforts to counter escalated violence can create safer schools, goals of diversity and democracy have yet to be mindfully integrated as part of this vision.

Violence prevention at the school community level is a timely topic for both scholarship and practice, which researchers and practitioners have only begun to address. Leaders engaged in planning (bio)terrorism prevention have before them the challenge to promote diversity and security consciousness in crisis emergency preparedness. Any planning that addresses making schools safe without taking into account diversity issues will create an unbalanced coordination effort, even unintentionally permitting racial acts. As recognized by the co-editors of this publication, "The crisis atmosphere and the uncertainty of the continuity of urban educational governance structures make it difficult for urban school administrators and teachers to focus on long term projects."[1] The climate of crisis in America tends to thwart long-term planning within its urban schools, which ironically diverts attention away from the responsibility of forging communities out of ethically and economically diverse cultures that are free of "hidden interpersonal violence (bullying, harassment, and sexual violence)."[2]

School principal teams face the challenge of guiding action at all K–12 levels in order to demonstrate the cultural awareness and problem-solving required for developing emergency preparedness and response systems consistent with expectations for homeland security. Although efforts to counter the threat of new forms of violence can create safer schools, the national goals of diversity and democracy cannot be sacrificed in the process. Indeed, with the tightening of security, the country has been witnessing an escalation in the scapegoating of particular ethnic groups.[3] The protection of schools through emergency preparedness therefore demands vigilance against racial profiling.

Stories about racially motivated acts have abounded since 9/11/2001. For example, a Middle-Eastern university student experienced blatant mistreatment by national authorities. Handcuffed and detained after he registered, as required, by the U.S. Citizenship and Immigration Services (USCIS) for having aroused suspicion, he was later discovered to have been "guilty" only of registering for less than a full load of courses that semester—a course load that his advisor had approved.[4] It appears that even when communities of color access what K.S. Berry refers to as "institutionalized sites of whiteness," that "signs of racial superiority and cultural hegemony" remain hidden, obscuring "the violence of power and privilege."[5] Once triggered, racially motivated assaults guised as security, protection, and patriotism rise with grave consequences for schools and society.

School leaders need to learn to deal productively with what on the surface appears to be a contradiction between emergency prevention and diversity awareness. This requires more than sensitivity to the complex issues involved, perhaps even the recognition of a new leadership disposition expressed as a whole-community attitude that envisions stakeholder groups as collaborators in fostering safety, tolerance, and inclusion while vigilantly monitoring inhumane incidents.

PIVOTAL TERMS AND DEFINITIONS

Key definitions herein include *diversity awareness*, which refers to the capacity of school leaders to demonstrate "democratic fairness and justice" in identifying and changing "systemic racism" as well as the "inequitable treatment of children of color in our schools."[6]

Next, the term *rationalized racism* may be original: it denotes the opposite of social justice, meaning those values and behaviors that violate the fundamental premise of democracy and the right of every citizen to be treated equally in all public spheres, including schools.

Racial profiling, which is pervasive in society and ranges from employment and promotion contexts to policing and arrests,[7] underscores the escalated stereotyping of outsiders, internationals, and persons of color as potential sources of threat within the context of violence prevention.

Finally, *terrorism* means repressing or domineering by means of panic and fear. And *bioterrorism* is "the intentional use of infectious biological agents, or germs, to cause illness."[8] The author will use "(bio)terrorism" throughout this chapter to represent both terms.

TRENDS IN THE RELEVANT LITERATURE

This section spans terrorism and policy, school safety trends in the literature, and leadership standards for school administrators.

Terrorism and Learning

Terrorism and learning how to deal with inherent perpetual threats at the national and global level have become central to U.S. foreign policy. However, this transference has yet to occur locally, at the organizational level of schools and universities.[9] At this time, curriculum remains almost unaffected while major universities throughout the country conduct "national security research" that addresses "the federal government's homeland security priorities." For example, the state of Florida recently awarded $5 million to the University of South Florida to build a Center for Biodefense.[10]

Given that the nation's security concerns have changed so dramatically since the tragedy of 9/11 and the war with Iraq, schools are being called upon to think and act differently. Activism is needed at the action-oriented preventive level, as well as at the more abstract level of conceptualizing violence (e.g., terrorism, (bio)terrorism, and war) and its potential impact on schools. Specialized types of curricula have begun emerging to help children and adolescents understand racially-sensitive issues resulting from terrorism, particularly that of "wrongful attribution," and also to help them process powerful feelings of fear, hatred, and anger.[11]

Innovative programs that comprehensively address the issue of building skills and awareness in diversity–security planning have sporadically appeared. The Texas School Safety Center claims to prepare school administrators to address cultural sensitivity in developing more secure school environments.[12] A significant challenge for leadership teams and university educators is to resist avoiding diversity–security planning while engaged in the process of crisis prevention and change. A surface approach to whole-school change would separate diversity from security awareness-building or simply pay homage to the former. As a solution, diversity training can be carried out simultaneously with emergency planning to reinforce their interrelatedness in achieving safer schools. However, beyond sketchy programmatic descriptions, an understanding of this change process has yet to be illuminated in the literature.

In some educational and societal circles it appears that commitment to social justice has been reinvigorated. On the other hand, some curriculum theorists and policy analysts have described what they see as a "new security regime" coming to life, one that is "dangerous" and that goes beyond the attempt to protect U.S. citizens in order to promote "a new political order."[13] The vigilant activity of the FBI has apparently "increased at colleges and universities since the 9/11 attacks and the passage of the USA Patriot Act in 2001."[14] This act gives the FBI and other national and state authorities the freedom to conduct surveillance and intelligence work without hindrance, in effect suspending the civil rights of students and faculty at college campuses.[15] International students and faculty have been targeted during such campaigns, and some have been subject to detainment and imprisonment, even where terrorist connections have been alleged but not proven. It becomes obvious, then, why emergency procedures must not be developed and enforced independent of a school's diversity mission.

In the following section I describe a master's-level course that I taught in my role as university professor, in which an anonymous FBI agent and sheriff participated as guest lecturers. These individuals were identified by class members as knowledgeable community-based partners. The group of practicing K–12 teachers and aspiring school leaders had interacted with the guest lecturers in their respective K–12 school settings, and had recommended them as potential speakers.

On a related topic, the threat of terrorism for school communities throughout our nation occupies a space between reality and fantasy, or between the here-and-now and the imagined future. Given that acts of violence within school environments typically involve explosives and weaponry brought onto campuses by students,[16] the attention terrorism receives in school planning is understandably less immediate. Also, the threat experienced by schools is typically from students and employees, members of the internal population, rather than from outside forces.[17] Having established the source of most threats launched against U.S. schools, it is also believed by some that schools increasingly constitute soft targets that could attract terrorist attacks.[18]

Children and schools represent national icons that may be in preeminent danger, much like renowned buildings, as demonstrated by 9/11. As Kenneth S. Trump, president of National School Safety and Security Services, claims, "Al Qaeda has reportedly made a direct threat to kill one million of America's children…and schools and school buses with children aboard have been victims of terrorist violence abroad."[19] According to safety and legal specialists, schools must be more protected than ever, as they house innocent citizens and signify the future.

The American Red Cross warns that institutions should prepare for the unthinkable. Under the Homeland Security Advisory System, Code Orange (high threat condition) dictates that school leaders become "alert to suspicious activity and report it to proper authorities" and "review emergency plans," as well as "discuss children's fears concerning possible terrorist attacks." Code Red (severe threat condition) means that such vigilant activities are to be escalated; also, lessons are to be taught on fear and terrorism with mental health counselors available on site.[20]

School Safety Trends in the Literature

Procedural information has rapidly become increasingly available for facilitating the development of whole-school coordination plans and safer contexts for learning. These articles and news updates pertaining to security and terrorism precautions, accessible via the Internet, tend to emphasize the value of particular interventions. Among the most popular elements are student-run, anti-violence organizations; ongoing communication with local experts in emergency operating systems;

partnerships with mental health services, emergency personnel, and other agencies; regular whole-school drills that include and extend beyond bomb threats; security improvement through surveillance measures and increased awareness; and student-staff assemblies that focus on resolving conflict and identifying violent behaviors.[21]

Another literature base emphasizes that emergency plans be developed on site by administrators, teachers, and other partners in order to satisfy the needs of particular situations and entire schools. Context supercedes the value of adopting templates developed by others, as "no single strategy" or set of change strategies fits all school contexts.[22] However, school teams may find available templates useful as starting points for creating and enforcing their own security plans.

In contrast, few research-based case studies have been published that provide living accounts of emergency preparedness, especially from the school practitioner's perspective. In one such account, a teacher leader in Florida explores unresolved questions concerning violence prevention.[23] For this case investigation, a lockdown drill is the basis of the featured scenario. Author P.E. Llewellyn deconstructs this event from the reactions of the assistant principals and principals involved, real "actors" whom she interviewed in her quest to learn to what extent her own district was safety-conscious. However, Llewellyn does not raise the issue of diversity, and particularly of racial awareness.

In another case study, a principal's story about change illustrates a local school process—in Israel. Chen Schechter's narrative features a principal, a former military leader, who successfully led a communal process during a crisis after conducting a self-study assessment of violence. Both personal and cultural levels of instability at the school were investigated, and key stakeholders participated in shared decision-making and action. "Process-orientation learning, as opposed to a quick-fix orientation," was modeled, despite the pressure from faculty to rush the change process.[24]

LEADERSHIP STANDARDS FOR SCHOOL ADMINISTRATORS

Professors in leadership studies are currently expected to follow Educational Leadership Constituent Council (ELCC) standards for developing and teaching courses. However, meeting the ELCC standards implies a certain readiness that is not easily conceptualized, taught, or measured by school leaders, university researchers, and policymakers. Only one mention of safety appears in the ELCC standards: "Develop and administer policies that provide a safe school environment and promote student health and welfare."[25] While one could counter that emergency (e.g., bioterrorism) preparation is an example of this standard, this position overlooks contextual issues and how dramatically the world is changing. Instead, the standards give the impression that issues of safety are what they have always been for schools, a myth that promotes complacency or even denial.[26] Managerial-oriented principals (such as those envisioned by the ELCC standards) protect the status quo instead of forging productive change, which some view as endangering the health of schools.[27]

The teaching of the university curriculum that this chaper reports involved risk. A course that deals with (bio)terrorism planning may not be in keeping with the standards or indicators governing those aspects of leadership that a faculty member is supposed to teach. With the adoption of national standards by which to judge university preparation programs that are accredited by the National Council for Accreditation of Teacher Education (NCATE), unresolved issues are evident.

EMPIRICAL CASE STUDY CONTEXT

This empirical case study uses as data the emergency preparation reports that a group of school practitioners collaboratively wrote.[28] The six coauthored case studies were compiled as a course book, and references throughout this chapter will be made to the compilation of student papers that were published internally as a course book.[29] As will be revealed, the treatment of diversity awareness, rationalized racism, and racial profiling was out of step with the expectations for the assignment, and the expectations themselves were less explicit than they should have been. These outcomes serve to emphasize just how difficult it seems to be, even for experienced educators, to integrate emergency preparation with diversity awareness for today's urban schools.[30]

The exercise in diversity–security awareness-building was launched with a challenge put to the teacher group to think "out of the box." On the one hand, individuals were to learn about the impact of biological, chemical, and nuclear terrorism on schools while generating possibilities for aiding prevention and facilitating coordination responsibility. On the other hand, they were to integrate diversity awareness and balance the overall agenda by finding ways to support a new climate of school reform: "Violence prevention and humanitarian values must go hand-in-hand."

Participant Profile and Pedagogical Innovation

A group of 25 master's degree students in an educational leadership program at the University of South Florida, a doctoral, research-extensive institution, participated in a course titled Case Studies in School Administration. The class included only five males, two African Americans, and one Latina. As is typical of this particular graduate context, the majority were U.S. white female students, ranging from 30 to 55 years of age. All were K–12 teachers at the elementary, middle, and high school levels. Four had assumed the dual role of acting assistant principal, and most aspired to be building administrators.

The author had been redesigning the course for increased relevance and contemporary appeal over a five-year period. The spring, 2003, semester in question was no exception and, in fact, represented a culminating effort. The student evaluations portrayed it as a high-risk, cutting-edge experiment in diversity–security preparedness that was timely and important for administrators and teachers alike.

BIOTERRORISM REPORTS

(Bio)terrorism Project Guidelines

The students' crisis management case studies–part fiction, part factual–contained stories and research illustrating the threat of (bio)terrorism and preparedness at the local school-district-community level. Because this topic is new for most students, especially as related to school community awareness and preparation, the goal for the assignment was to gather information from as many sources as possible (e.g., published reports, Internet sites, and experts). This public health issue was presented as one that should concern everyone, not just emergency personnel, policymakers, and media journalists. In an effort to think collectively about the emerging role of leadership as related to crisis prevention and community participation, information about terrorism and bioterrorism was discussed. Guest speakers shared specialized knowledge. Additionally, documented accounts of racial profiling and its recent escalation in the lives of students across the country were also furnished.[31]

The level of discussion was in concert with the pedagogical goal of shedding light on the current realities of what I referred to as rationalized racism at all levels of the educational system. The thought-provoking constructs of "cultural hegemony" and "white privilege"[32] were not used during the discourse. The serious time constraints imposed by the nontraditional academic calendar of eight sessions meant that accessibility was essential, so stories of racism had priority—particularly those documented following 9/11.

The objectives for class members were to explore the issues of (bio)terrorism and racism that confront school leadership today by writing case studies, and to express creativity. The syllabus identified the case study components to be incorporated into the report, ranging from scenario development to planning to tentative solutions. The written instructions were as follows:

Write a case study in (bio)terrorism preparedness that fits your school context(s) and that includes the key stakeholders involved (e.g., superintendent, principal, lead teacher, parent, student, expert, community agency). This is not an isolated problem, but rather one that grows out of the new national standards for violence prevention and expectations for consciousness-raising. Develop a specific scenario and examples that fit this context (e.g., anthrax and contagious disease [e.g., smallpox] threats).

Questions for consideration in your report include:

1. Do you know how to best educate your faculty and school about terrorism and biochemical prevention?
2. Specifically, do you know how and what data to gather and analyze, in order to promote awareness about protection, survival, and future concerns?
   - As examples, do you know which agencies can help with increasing awareness, and do you know their specific areas of expertise and functions (e.g., public health and community medical care centers)?
   - Do you know what you can do to protect yourself and your school relative to different kinds of attack, such as one involving a biochemical agent?
   - Finally, if relevant, identify the most likely biochemical agents and their properties and effects, as well as the

treatments for infectious and/or contaminating agents.

In your case study, provide preventive guidelines or coordination plans for bioterrorism attacks. Specify any staff or school training that may be needed, *identify tensions and deep cultural issues* [emphasis added], and keep recommendations or solutions open. Involve key agencies and stakeholders in the assessment of the problem, and interview knowledgeable leaders and specialists in the state and/or at your school and county. Locate and incorporate relevant sources (at least 10) in your report.

Case Study Results: Overview

A comprehensive, analytical reading of the six case studies, yielding five major themes, will now be briefly discussed. In all instances, the case studies reflect the assignment components, with one consistent and significant omission: implications for monitoring racial profiling and increasing diversity awareness. This language, although not specified in the syllabus, was used and illustrated in the class during all meetings. The reports introduced creative elements, including appropriate uses of humor in the development of scenarios and characters (e.g., Dr. Spores, a hospital physician). In no specific order, the case writers developed these six scenarios:

1. Anthrax scare and contamination via flower delivery to a school.
2. A school's exposure to smallpox and the threat of contagious disease.
3. Dispersal of lethal gases from small airplanes flying over a school.
4. Radiological attack on a school via a missile launch into a nuclear power plant.
5. Takeover of the local nuclear power plant in the vicinity of a school.
6. Invasion of a school through contamination of its water supply.

Thematic Patterns in the Reports

Identifying high-risk, (bio)terrorist targets. The writers identified areas within schools as well as markers surrounding them as potentially high-risk terrorist targets.

These included widespread exposure to anthrax through an everyday delivery of flowers to the school office. Similarly, another group constructed a building-level terrorism attack through the spread of smallpox, in the innocuous form of a kindergarten boy who had gone on a cruise on an infected ship. A third case featured the deliberate and widespread contamination of a school's water supply, originating from its own food service facilities. Other cases staged terrorism targets in the immediate communities, but with direct effects on particular schools in the area, through such methods as an air strike using a nearby airport landing strip and a missile launch at a nuclear power plant, as well as the hostile takeover of a nuclear plant.

The imaginary scenarios described had realistic dimensions. Notably, one of the class members' schools was situated directly beside an airplane landing strip, and two others were within a few miles of a nuclear power plant.

Locating the necessary resources. All the emergency prevention reports highlighted resources where (bio)terrorism had erupted within the school communities. The students viewed expert advice, clear procedures, reports, and school funding as indispensable resources for emergency planning. Funding from state and federal governments was recommended to obtain expert consultation and cover the costs of staff training and bioterrorism crisis management. Existing publications from knowledgeable sources were thought essential for educating teachers on how to enhance school security, and so guidelines were incorporated from practical reports.[33]

The case studies encouraged ongoing research for local emergency and other officials to stay current, and stressed the need to update school emergency policies and available expertise. Being able to readily access the necessary information at one's school was highlighted. Some groups believed that a critical resource was information that had already been memorized by staff concerning procedures to be followed for every conceivable emergency, and even names and phone numbers of key agencies.

Given that official plans for addressing (bio)terrorism were not yet underway in any of the students' actual K–12 schools, one significant resource was the insight shared by local agencies and state experts in the class I taught. To this end, updates were incorporated into the reports to reflect surveillance tips (e.g., maintaining highly visible, well-lit school buildings so that intruders and objects cannot be concealed) from the FBI agent, county sheriff, and other guest speakers.

Partnering with external agencies. Class member reports recognized partnership development as a solution for resolving the relative isolation, complacency, and even deficiencies of schools. One case study portrayed the local emergency ward of a hospital as an avenue for both immediate treatment and a sustained relationship. Better relations with one's own school district personnel and board members were also generally perceived as valuable. Also, reports maintained that any specialist at the school, district, or community level involved in crisis management, such as supervisors and coordinators, should become immediate allies in the coordination of emergency plans at the building level.

All groups saw the necessity for creating and sustaining new unions with existing agencies. These included law enforcement and public health, as well as disease, poison control, and bioterrorism alert centers. Even school weather stations were mentioned in one report, in which the student writers hypothesized that schools across the nation could help save lives in the event of a chemical or biological attack by participating in a national weather monitoring network.

These results fit with the National Public Health Leadership Institute's recommendation that critical relationships be built and reinforced at the school level, beyond skills-based training that prepares leaders for emergencies and bioterrorism.[34] Developing multi-institutional partnerships that link schools, universities, and businesses, particularly in impoverished urban and rural areas of the country, can bring strength and power to each school entity.

Developing a preventive plan for bioterrorism. Every group's case study offered a preventive emergency plan for their schools and school districts; however, the execution of this process seemed to suggest that two somewhat different approaches involving grassroots engagement had been used, probably unwittingly.

For example, in "The Delivery: A Case Study in Bioterrorism Preparedness," the emergency coordination planning process was portrayed as a community partnership endeavor. However, it was the district officials who created the context for input from stakeholder representatives, such as medical experts and law enforcement as well as university and government specialists. It seems disconcerting, even disempowering, that the writers, who are teachers, did not include school representatives—persons like themselves—in their own district planning scenarios. Lines of power and authority are covert bureaucratic structures throughout this case study, even at the point where school personnel finally enter the scene–as recipients of the school district's crisis prevention training for onsite implementation. Here, at the school level, the two components emphasized were: (1) notification of the district supervisor, and (2) containment, following the directions provided, of the bioterrorism agent. Thus, the expectation in this overview of who assumes leadership and who follows seems self-evident, or not subject to question and the opportunity for transformation.

A second approach, representing the middle ground, is reflected in "Case Study: The Cruise to Smallpox, a Week of More than Sun Exposure." Here, the local school context is understood as having agency in the development of coordination plans. However, the role of the school, and specifically that of teachers and administrators, is not actually stated per se. For example, the sentences in this section of the report were constructed with the presumed referents of school, teacher, and administrator, as in "planned coordination with the county and local government emergency management agencies." It can probably be assumed from this semantic construction that some group at the school site is fulfilling the action; however, the nouns are not provided and so must be inferred.

None of the case studies provided a view of teachers and administrators grappling with change together, or of one group channeling genuine support to the other to do so. One explanation might be that class members seemed unaware of the status of the emergency plans in their own schools and district. Anticipating this possibility, the instructor recommended that the groups interview knowledgeable leaders in the state. From this encounter with others, the writers typically learned that, as one group wrote, "All schools in our Florida county have evacuation plans for inclement weather, bomb threats, etc., but no official plans to specifically address terrorism."[35]

Coping with the effects of (bio)terrorism. Although coping with the effects of (bio)terrorism was the least developed theme across the case studies, it nevertheless provided a convergent point of reflection on a critical topic. Several reports mentioned post-traumatic stress syndrome and the various agencies that are prepared to assist with trauma disorder at the school level.[36] The student writers saw the need for preventive care in this context as a rationale for school leaders to develop partnerships with outside agencies.

For all groups, the theme of coping was an outgrowth of the coordination plans they had developed. They emphasized strong bonds with students, families, faculty, government workers, and community agencies. Another recommendation aimed at emotions management and school preparation involved the ongoing training of staff at all educational levels in the acceptance of this new reality. One group strongly suggested that local communities sponsor Neighborhood Watch groups to look out not only for suspicious persons but also for "possible terrorists." This recommendation did not include a reflection on the consequences for racial profiling. Finally, school evacuation drills related to terrorism and bioterrorism threats were endorsed, with support for involving community emergency officials in rehearsals.

DISCUSSION AND REFLECTION

Analysis of the crisis management case studies suggests that, although the master's class experienced a breakthrough in crisis planning, the students insufficiently considered democratic concerns. Related to this, a critical reading of the papers highlights the limited imagined roles of teachers in urban schools. The case studies generally define teachers and even building leaders as passive recipients of orders, not as empowered decision makers. It was disturbing to learn the extent to which dynamics of bureaucratic control were not only implicitly communicated but also presumed to be the natural order and self-evident. These were presented as narrative ideas and actions that supported the plots described rather than as sources of critique. The change agentry of school persons was contingent on the permission granted by school districts, in accordance with decisions endorsed from the top down.

Beyond this experienced K–12 group there appears to be a reified, paternalistic view of school and central administration for many teachers.[37] This "follower mentality" probably reinforces an unconscious

acceptance of one's lesser role in the hierarchy, consequently harnessing opportunities for change. One of the new conceptual frames of the master's course features critical philosophical introspection as applied to the worldviews of educators. Teachers who aspire to lead schools may find it empowering to have a profound understanding of the worldview they embody and, where necessary, alternatives that offer not transitory substitutes but a higher threshold for democratic participation.

Reflection on the pedagogical experiment itself brought to light the need for explicit writing direction and reinforcement. School practitioners may require oral and verbal support in order to confront the difficult topic of rationalized racism and its effects on emergency planning, particularly involving (bio)terrorism and the fears this ignites. They also need time for reflection and experimentation, as well as opportunities for collaboration and critique. School practitioners are not alone in the need to collectively bring cultural sensitivity to the forefront of institutional reform. Professors and policymakers also may find it crucial to grapple with more profound understandings of cultural diversity, teacher empowerment, and crisis planning in urban education.

The case-study exercise discussed above provides only a beginning step in this direction; the small sample used (of one group at a single university) makes it difficult to know what can be generalized. However, the questions raised and the results shared should have relevance for anyone inspired to enact social justice agendas where power inequities and personal truths are acknowledged. Also, the broader issues of balancing concerns regarding the appropriate responses to the threats of terrorism are, undoubtedly, of wide interest.

The revised syllabus for this course now expands upon and deepens the original statement, "identify tensions and deep cultural issues." The new instructions for case studies guide the writers to probe relevant issues in readings on racism, diversity, and learning. The groups have since built into their school scenarios and coordination plans practical ideas related to racial interrogation, social justice, and tolerance. Greater balance has been afforded, but the security issue still tends to overshadow the diversity issue, and their interrelationship is not as well understood as it could be. By continuing their own research, these students can return to their workplaces with new possibilities for developing guidelines for healthy school communities that manifest democracy as a condition of security. The effort to produce a more fully-awakened consciousness through emergency planning, whether at the university or school level, necessitates deliberate intervention. Peter N. Stearns, a university provost, claims that any such attempt at transformation is a form of "culture management" where cultural factors are intentionally altered in order to bring about changes in human and social behavior.[38]

Finally, the extent to which crises in terrorism have been manufactured in the United States is not addressed here, but is nonetheless a recognized debate. Legislative mandates involving safety and liability issues for schools have spawned marketers in the form of consulting firms that target crisis preparedness training.[39] Such coalescing realities make it difficult to ascertain how much emergency school responsiveness is rational and authentic apart from media capitalists' own motives. Terrorism cannot escape scrutiny, then, as a marketing and media extravaganza that strategically garners material for both profit and headlines. In their book, *Kinderculture: The Corporate Construction of Childhood*, Steinberg and Kincheloe explore myriad ways in which corporate America shapes childhood identity through a supersaturated, media-frenzied world.[40] This version of reality exhumes the subtext of terrorism and questions the political forces behind the creation of high-scrutiny institutions that promote collective fear and restrict human freedom.

POSTSCRIPT

The road to leadership necessitates a steep climb in today's postmodern urban context. Activism forces change through the confrontation of profound contradictions not only in our immediate environments, but also within our own learning and leading. Through deliberate intervention and reflective inquiry, practitioners can imagine anew while questioning what is taken for granted, and can thereby enact change.

NOTES

In accordance with the University of South Florida's rule 6C4-10.109.B-6, the author confirms that the opinions stated in this publication are her own.

The author, a university professor, is grateful to her graduate students for their participation in this pedagogical experiment, and for their permission to quote from their materials without attribution. The author presented an earlier version of this chapter at the 2003 annual meeting of the University Council for Educational Administration, Portland, OR, and has published a more detailed version in Chapter 10 of her book, *Fire and ice: Igniting and channeling passion in new qualitative researchers* (New York: Peter Lang).

1. Kincheloe, J., Anderson, P., Rose, K., Griffith, D., & Hayes, K. (2003). *Prospectus: Urban education: An encyclopedia*, p. 2. Westport, CT: Greenwood Publishing Group.

2. Lucas, P. (2003, March). Being down: Challenging violence in urban schools. *Teachers College Record, 105* (1), pp. 1–3. Retrieved May 8, 2005, from http://www.tcrecord.org/PrintContent. asp? ContentID=10909.

3. Hoover, E. (2003, April 11). Closing the gates: A student under suspicion. Special report. *Chronicle of Higher Education, 49* (31), p. A12.

4. Hoover (2003).

5. Berry, K. (2002). Color me white: Dismantling white privilege with young students.

Taboo: Journal of Culture and Education, 6 (10), pp. 85–96.

6. Skrla, L., Scheurich, J., Johnson, Jr., J., & Koschoreck, J. (2001). Accountability for equity: Can state policy leverage social justice? *International Journal of Leadership in Education, 4* (3), pp. 237–260.

7. Hoover (2003).

8. Connecticut Department of Public Health. (2003, February). Bioterriorism preparedness fact sheet, pp. 1-4. Retrieved March 10, 2005, from http://www.dph.state.ct.us/Agency_News/FCT_bioterror.

9. National School Safety and Security Services. (2001). Terrorism & school safety: School safety issues related to the terrorist attacks on the United States, pp. 1–8. Retrieved June 15, 2005, from http://www.schoolsecurity.org/resources/nasro_survey_2002.html.

10. Borrego, A. (2003, April 11). The money scramble: Colleges rush to capitalize on the government's push for homeland security. Special report. *Chronicle of Higher Education, 49* (31), p. A22.

11. Jolly, E., Malloy, S., & Felt, M. (2001). Beyond blame: Reacting to the terrorist attack. A curriculum for middle and high school students, pp. 1–25. Newton, MA: Education Development Center. Retrieved July 3, 2005, from http://www.edc.org/spotlight/schools/beyondblame.htm.

12. Texas School Safety Center (2003). Resources online. Retrieved July 18, 2005, from http://www.txssc.swt.edu/resources.htm.

13. Rizvi, F. (2003). Democracy and education after September 11. *Globalisation, Societies and Education, 1* (1), pp. 25–40.

14. Arnone, M. (2003, April 11). Watchful eyes: The FBI steps up its work on campuses, spurring fear and anger among many academics. Special report. *Chronicle of Higher Education, 49* (31), p. A14.

15. Arnone (2003).

16. Sheriff (anonymous), guest lecture. (2003, March).

17. FBI agent (anonymous), guest lecture. (2003, March).

18. FBI agent (anonymous), guest lecture. (2003, March).

19. Trump, K. (2002, July). The impact of terrorism on school safety planning. *School Planning & Management*, pp. 22–26.

20. American Red Cross. (2003, February). Homeland security advisory system recommendations. Retrieved March 1, 2005, from http://www.tallytown.com/redcross/hsas.

21. Della-Giustina, D., Kerr, S., & Georgevich, D. (2000). Terrorism & violence in our schools. *Professional Safety, 45* (3), pp. 16–21.

22. Fullan, M. (1999). *Change forces: The sequel.* London: Sage.

23. Llewellyn, P. (2004, Spring). Will I be ready as an administrator for school emergencies? *International Journal of Educational Reform, 13* (2), pp. 118–125.

24. Schechter, C. (2002, April-June). Marching in the land of uncertainty: Transforming school culture through communal deliberative process. *International Journal of Leadership in Education, 5* (2), pp. 105–128.

25. Educational Leadership Constituent Council (ELCC). (2002). Educational Leadership Constituent Standards. Arlington, VA: National Policy Board for Educational Administration. Retrieved May 18, 2005, from http://www.npbea.org.

26. Mullen, C. (2003). (Bio)terrorism prevention and rationalized racism: Contradictions in homeland security for schools. Paper presented November 23, 2003, at the annual meeting of the University Council for Educational Administration, Portland, OR.

27. Riehl, C. (2000). The principal's role in creating inclusive schools for diverse students: A review of normative, empirical, and critical literature on the practice of educational administration. *Review of Educational Research, 70* (1), pp. 55–81.

28. Mullen, C. (2005). *Fire and ice: Igniting and channeling passion in new qualitative researchers.* New York: Peter Lang.

29. Mullen, C. (2003, April). *Top secret! School crisis management case studies.* Internally published as Case Studies in School Administration at the University of South Florida, Tampa, FL.

30. Mullen (2005).

31. Hoover (2003, April).

32. Berry (2002).

33. Federal Emergency Management Agency. (n.d.). Emergency management guide for business and industry. Retrieved from http://www.fema.gov/library/biz2.shtm. U.S. Department of Justice. (2001, September). OVC handbook for coping after terrorism. Retrieved June 8, 2005, from http://www.ojp.usdoj.gov/ovc/publications/infores/cat_hndbk.

34. National Public Health Leadership Institute. (2003, April). Public health grand rounds,

bioterrorism revisited—Leadership lessons learned?! pp. 1–4. Retrieved July 19, 2005, from http://www.phli.org/.

35. Mullen (2003, April), p. 7. Interview with unnamed county director of transportation.

36. American Red Cross. (2003, February.) Homeland security advisory system recommendations. Retrieved June 13, 2005, from http://www.tallytown.com/redcross/hsas.

37. Mullen, C. (2002). Teacher activism in education reform. *Teacher Development, 6* (1), pp. 1–128.

38. Stearns, P. (2003, May 2). Expanding the agenda of cultural research, pp. B7–B9. *Chronicle of Higher Education, 49* (34).

39. National Policy Board for Educational Administration. (2002). *Instructions to implement standards for advanced programs in educational leadership*. Arlington, VA: NPBEA.

40. Steinberg, S., & Kincheloe, J. (1997). *Kinderculture: The corporate construction of childhood*. Boulder, CO: Westview Press.

Bibliography

AAM/American Association of Museums. (2003). *Museums working in the public interest.* Retrieved May 27, 2004, from http://www.aam-us.org/resources/general/publicinterest.cfm.

Adams, W. (1995). Education for extinction: American Indians and the boarding school *experience.* Lawrence: University Press of Kansas.

Alexander, C., & Langer, E. (Eds.). (1990). Higher stages of human development: Perspectives on adult growth. New York: Oxford.

Anderson, J. (1988). *The education of blacks in the south, 1860–1935.* Chapel Hill: University of North Carolina Press.

Anderson, P., & Summerfield, J. (2004). In S. Steinberg & J. Kincheloe (Eds.). *19 urban questions: Teaching in the city.* New York: Peter Lang.

Anzaldúa, G. (1987). *Borderlands: The new mestiza = La frontera* (1st ed.). San Francisco: Spinsters/Aunt Lute.

Appadurai, A. (1996). *Modernity at large: Cultural dimensions of globalization.* Minneapolis: University of Minnesota Press.

Apple, M. (1993). The politics of official knowledge: Does a national curriculum make sense? *Teachers College Record, 95* (2), 222–241.

———. (1996). *Cultural politics and education.* New York: Teachers College Press.

———. (1996). Dominance and dependency: Situating *The Bell Curve* within the conservative restoration. In J. Kincheloe, S. Steinberg, & A. Gresson (Eds.), *Measured lies: The bell curve examined.* New York: St. Martin's Press.

———. (1999). Power, meaning, and identity: Essays in critical educational studies. New York: Peter Lang.

Aptheker, H. (1989). *The literary legacy of W.E.B. DuBois.* New York: Kraus International.

Arguelles, L. (2002). How do we live, learn and die: A teacher and some of her students meditate and walk on an engaged Buddhist path. In J. Miller & Y. Nakagawa (Eds.), *Nurturing our wholeness: Perspectives on spirituality in education* (pp. 285–303). Brandon, VT: Foundation for Educational Renewal.

Ark, T. (2002). The case for small high schools. *Educational Leadership, 59* (5), 55–59.

Aronowitz, S., & Giroux, H. (1993). *Education still under siege* (2nd ed.). Westport, CT: Bergan & Garvey.

Arrien, A. (2001). The way of the teacher: Principles of deep engagement. In L. Lantieri (Ed.), *Schools with spirit: Nurturing the inner lives of children and teachers* (pp. 148–157). Boston: Beacon Press.

Asgharzadeh, A., & Sefa Dei, G. (2001). The power of social theory: The anticolonial discursive framework. *Journal of Education Thought, 35* (3), 297–323.

Associated Press. (2003). *White teachers fleeing black schools!* Monday, January 13, 2003: CNN.com/education. Retrieved July 7, 2004, from http://www.cnn.com/2003/EDUCATION/01/13/resegregation. teachers.ap/.

Aveling, N. (2002). Student teachers' resistance to exploring racism: Reflections on "doing" border pedagogy. *Asia-Pacific Journal of Teacher Education, 30* (2), 119–130.

Ayers, W. (2000). Simple justice: Thinking about teaching and learning, equity and the fight for small schools. In W. Akers, M. Klonsky, & G. Lyon (Eds.), *A simple justice: The challenge of small schools.* New York: Teachers College Press.

Babb, F. (1989). *Between the field and the cooking pot: The political economy of marketwomen in Peru.* Austin: University of Texas Press.

Ball, A., & Heath, S. (1993). Dances of identity: Finding an ethnic self in the arts. In S. Heath & M. McLaughlin (Eds.), *Identity and inner-city youth: Beyond ethnicity and gender* (pp. 69–93). New York: Teachers College Press.

Bamburg, J. (1994). *Raising expectations to improve student learning.* Retrieved March, 2003, from http://www.ncrel.org/sdrs/areas/issues/educatrs/leadrshp/ie0bam.htm.

Bartky, J. (1955). The school of education and the university. *Journal of Higher Education, 26* (5), 254–260.

Bennett de Marrais, K., & LeCompte, M. (1995). *The way schools work: A sociological analysis of education.* White Plains, NY: Longman.

Bey, H. (2002). TAZ: The temporary autonomous zone. In S. Duncombe (Ed.), *Cultural resistance reader.* London: Verso.

Beyer, L., & Apple, M. (1998). *The curriculum: Problems, politics, and possibilities.* Albany: State University of New York Press.

Blau, P., & Dudley, O. (1967). *The American occupational structure.* New York: John Wiley & Sons.

Bloom, S. (1997). *Creating sanctuary: Toward the evolution of sane societies.* New York: Routledge.

Blush, S. (2001). *American hardcore: A tribal history.* Los Angeles, CA: Feral House.

Bodeau, D. (1999). *Metabeings and individuals: Aids and obstacles to growth.* Retrieved March, 2003, from http://www.gurus.com/dugdeb/essays/metabeings.html.

Borden, L. (2001). *Skateboarding, space, and the city: Architecture and the body.* New York: Berg.

Boudon, R. (1974). *Education, opportunity, and social inequality: Changing prospects in Western society.* New York: John Wiley & Sons.

Bourdieu, P., & Passeron, J. (1977). *Reproduction in education, society and culture.* London: Sage.

Bransford, J., Brown, A., & Cocking, R. (Eds.). (2000). *How people learn: Brain, mind, experience, and school (expanded edition).* Washington, DC: National Academy Press.

Brecht, B. (1964). A short description of a new technique of acting which produces an alienation effect. In *Brecht on Theatre.* John Willet, Trans. New York: Hill and Wang (pp. 136–147).

Brown, F. (1975). Assessment and evaluation of urban schools. *Journal of Negro Education,* (3), 377–384.

Brown, P. (2002, March 24). Latest way to cut grade school stress: Yoga. *New York Times,* p. 33.

Brown, R. (2002). Taming our emotions: Tibetan Buddhism and teacher education. In J. Miller & Y. Nakagawa (Eds.), *Nurturing our wholeness: Perspectives on spirituality in education* (pp. 3–12). Brandon, VT: Foundation for Educational Renewal.

Brown, W. (1995). *States of injury: Power and freedom in late modernity.* Princeton, NJ: Princeton University Press.

Bruner, J. (1996). *The culture of education.* Cambridge, MA: Harvard University Press.

Brunner, C., & Tally, W. (1999). *The new media literacy handbook: An educator's guide to bringing new media into the classroom.* New York: Doubleday.

Buckingham, D. (1993). *Children talking television: The making of television literacy.* London: Falmer Press.

———. (1996). *Moving images: Understanding children's emotional responses to television.* Manchester, UK: Manchester University Press.

——— (Ed.). (1998). *Teaching popular culture: Beyond radical pedagogy.* London: UCL Press.

———, & Sefton-Green, J. (1995). *Cultural studies goes to school: Reading and teaching popular media.* London: Taylor & Francis.

Bullock, H. (1967). *A history of negro education in the south: From 1619 to the present.* Cambridge, MA: Harvard University Press.

Burack, C. (1999, September). Returning meditation to education. *Tikkun.* Retrieved August 18, 2002, from http://www.findarticles.com/cf_)/m1548/5_14/56065507.

Burawoy, M., Blum, J., George, S., Gille, Z., Gowan, T., Haney, L., et al. (2000). *Global ethnography.* Berkeley: University of California Press.

Busch, C. (2003, July/August). It's cool to be grounded. *Yoga Journal,* 94–99, 154–156.

Bush, G.W. (2001, January 29). *No child left behind.* U.S. Department of Education. Retrieved February 18, 2002, from http://www.ed.gov/inits/nclb/index.html.

Bynoe, Y. (2004). *Stand & deliver: Political activism, leadership, and hip hop culture* (p. 158). New York: Soft Skull Press.

Cain, G. (1974). Socioeconomic background and achievement. *American Journal of Sociology, 79* (6), 1497–1509.

Callinicos, A. (1993). *Race and class.* London: Bookmarks.

Carvan, M., Nolen, A., & Yinger, R. (2002). *Power through partnership: The urban network for the improvement of teacher education.* Retrieved March, 2003, from http://www.urbannetworks.net/documents/tacte%20article,%20final%20revision%201-14-02.pdf.

Castañeda, I., & Zorn, D. (2001). *AAAE Arts Connections longitudinal study: A technical report.* Cincinnati, OH: University of Cincinnati Evaluation Services Center.

———, Zorn, D., Ray, G., Pangallo, M., Geresy, S., & Taylor, G. (2002). *An in-depth study to document how the arts make a difference in student learning.* Paper presented at the annual meeting of the American Educational Research Association, New Orleans, April 2002.

Catterall, J., Chapleau, R., & Iwanaga, J. (1999). Involvement in the arts and human development: General involvement and intensive involvement in music and theater arts. In E. Fiske (Ed.), *Champions of change* (pp. 1–18). Washington, DC: Arts Education Partnership.

———, & Waldorf, L. (1999). Chicago Arts Partnership in Education: Summary evaluation. In E. Fiske (Ed.), *Champions of change* (pp. 38–62). Washington, DC: Arts Education Partnership.

Chizhik, E. (2003). Reflecting on the challenges of preparing suburban teachers for urban schools. *Education and Urban Society, 35* (4), 443–461.

Chomsky, N. (2000). *Chomsky on miseducation.* New York: Rowman & Littlefield.

Churchill, W. (1996). *From a native son.* Boston: South End.

Clarke, J. (2002). The skinheads and the magical recovery of community. In Duncombe, S. (Ed.), *Cultural resistance reader.* London: Verso.

Cochran-Smith, M. (1995). Uncertain allies: Understanding the boundaries of race and teaching. *Harvard Educational Review, 65* (4), 541–570.

Coleman, J. (1966). *Equality of educational opportunity.* Washington, DC: U.S. Government Printing Office.

———. (1973). Review of *Inequality: A reassessment of the effect of family and schooling in America* by C. Jencks, M. Smith, H. Acland, M. Bane, D. Cohen, H. Gintis, et al. *American Journal of Sociology, 78* (6), 1523–1544.

———, et al. (1966). *Equality of educational opportunity.* U.S. Dept. of Health, Education, and Welfare, Office of Education. Washington, DC: U.S. Government Printing Office.

Cross, J. (1998). *Informal politics: Street vendors and the state in Mexico City.* Stanford, CA: Stanford University Press.

Crowell, S. (n.d.). *Case studies.* Center for Contemplative Mind. Retrieved May 30, 2004, from http://www. contemplativemind.org/resources/pubs/case_studies.pdf.

Csikszentmihalyi, M. (1996). *Creativity: Flow and the psychology of discovery and invention.* New York: HarperCollins.

Cuello, J. (1999). *Reconstructing the paradigm for teaching and learning at the university: Lessons from the field of an urban campus.* Retrieved March, 2003, from http://www.culma.wayne.edu/obs/reconstructing.htm.

DanceUSA. (2004). *Facts and figures.* Retrieved May 27, 2004, from http://www. danceusa.org.

Darling-Hammond, L. (1997). *The right to learn: A blueprint for creating schools that work.* San Franscisco: Jossey-Bass.

————, Ancess, J., & Ort, S. (2002). Reinventing high school: Outcomes of the coalition campus schools project. *American Educational Research Journal, 39* (3), 639–673.

Daspit, T. (2000). Rap pedagogies: "Bring(ing) the noise" of "knowledge born on the microphone" to radical education. In T. Daspit & J. Weaver (Eds.), *Popular culture and critical pedagogy: Reading, constructing, connecting.* New York: Falmer Press.

Deasy, R. (Ed.). (2002). *Critical links: Learning in the arts and student academic and social development.* Washington, DC: Arts Education Partnership.

DeChillo, S. (2002, December 14). Stretch. Pose. Rest. It's kindergarten yoga. *New York Times,* B1.

Delgado Bernal, D. (1998). Using a Chicana feminist epistemology in educational research. *Harvard Educational Review, 68* (4), 555–582.

Delpit, L. (1988). The silenced dialogue: Power and pedagogy in educating other people's children. *Harvard Educational Review, 58* (3), 280–298.

Denzin, N., & Lincoln, Y. (Eds.). (2000). *Handbook of qualitative research.* Thousand Oaks, CA: Sage.

De Soto, H. (1989). *The other path of development: The invisible revolution in the third world.* New York: Harper and Row.

Dewey, J. (1916). *Democracy and education.* New York: Free Press.

Dignard, L., & Havet, J. (1995). *Women in micro- and small-scale enterprise development.* Boulder, CO: Westview Press.

Dimitriadis, G. (2001). *Performing identity/performing culture: Hip hop as text, pedagogy, and lived practice.* New York: Peter Lang.

————, & McCarthy, C. (2001). *Reading and teaching the postcolonial: From Baldwin to Basquiat and beyond.* New York: Teachers College Press.

————, & Weis, L. (2001). Imagining possibilities with and for contemporary youth: (Re)writing and (re)visioning education today. *Qualitative Research, 1* (2), 223–240.

Dolby, N. (2000). Changing selves: Multicultural education and the challenge of new identities. *Teachers College Record, 102* (5), 898–912.

————. (2001). *Constructing race: Youth, identity, and popular culture in South Africa.* Albany: SUNY Press.

Doll, W. (1993). *A postmodern perspective on curriculum.* New York: Teachers College Press.

Dresch, S. (1975). A critique of planning models for postsecondary education: Current feasibility, potential relevance, and a prospectus for further research. *Journal of Higher Education, 46* (3), 245–286.

Dropkick Murphys. (2000). *Sing loud, sing proud* [CD]. Los Angeles: Hellcat Records.

Du Bois, W. (1920). Latin. *Crisis Magazine, 20* (3), 120.

————. (1961). *The souls of black folk.* Greenwich, CT: Fawcett Publications.

————. (1973). *The education of black people: Ten critiques, 1906–1960.* New York: Monthly Review Press.

———. (1986). *The souls of black folk.* New York: First Vintage Books/The Library of America Edition.

———. (1992). *Black reconstruction in America 1860–1880* (p. 184). New York: Free Press.

———. (1996). *The Philadelphia negro* (p. 388). Philadelphia: University of Pennsylvania Press.

———. (2002). *Dusk of dawn: An essay toward an autobiography of a race concept.* Piscataway, NJ: Transaction Publishers.

Duneier, M. (1999). *Sidewalk.* New York: Farrar, Strauss, & Giroux.

Edward, S. (1979). *Orientalism.* New York: Vintage Books.

———. (1993). *Culture and imperialism.* New York: Vintage Books.

Eisenhart, M. (2001). Educational ethnography past, present, and future: Ideas to think with. *Educational Researcher, 30* (8), 16–27.

———, & Finkel, E. (1998). *Women's science: Learning and succeeding from the margins.* Chicago: University of Chicago Press.

Eisner, E. (1994). *The educational imagination of the design and evaluation of school* (3rd ed.). New York: Macmillan.

Ellsworth, E. (1989). Why doesn't this feel empowering? Working through the repressive myths of critical pedagogy. *Harvard Education Review, 59* (3), 297–324.

Elmore, R. (1997). *Education policy and practice in the aftermath of TIMSS.* Retrieved March, 2003, from http://www.enc.org/TIMSS/addtools/pubs/symp/cd163/cd163.htm.

Evans, P., & Timberlake, M. (1980). Dependence, inequality, and the growth of tertiary: A comparative analysis of less developed countries. *American Sociological Review, 45,* 532–552.

Eyerman, R., & Jamison, A. (1998). *Music and social movements: Mobilizing traditions in the twentieth century.* Cambridge, UK: Cambridge University Press.

Fanon, F. (1991). *The wretched of the earth* (C. Farrington, Trans.). New York: Grove Press.

Fenwick, T. (2000). *Experiential learning in adult education: A comparative framework.* Retrieved March, 2003, from http://www.ualberta.ca/~tfenwick/ext/aeq.htm.

Fine, M. (2000). A small price to pay for justice. In W. Akers, M. Klonsky, & G. Lyon (Eds.), *A simple justice: The challenge of small schools.* New York: Teachers College Press.

———, & Weis, L. (1998). *The unknown city: Lives of poor and working-class young adults.* Boston: Beacon Press.

———, Centrie, C., & Roberts, R. (2000). Educating beyond the borders of schooling. *Anthropology & Education Quarterly, 31* (2), 131–151.

Fischer, N. (1998, Fall). Teaching meditation to young people. *Turning Wheel: Journal of the Buddhist Peace Fellowship,* 29–31.

Fiske, E. (Ed.). (1999). *Champions of change: The impact of the arts on learning.* Washington, DC: Arts Education Partnership and the President's Committee on the Arts and Humanities.

Fontana, D., & Slack, I. (1997). *Teaching meditation to children: Simple steps to relaxation and well-being.* London: Thorsons/HarperCollins.

Forbes, D. (2004). *Boyz 2 Buddhas: Counseling urban high school male athletes in the zone.* New York: Peter Lang.

———. (2004). What is the role of counseling in urban schools? In S. Steinberg & J. Kincheloe (Eds.), *Nineteen urban questions: Teaching in the city* (pp. 69–83). New York: Peter Lang.

Fordham, S. (1996) *Blacked out: Dilemmas of race, identity, and success at capital high.* Chicago: University of Chicago Press.

Frankenberg, R. (1993). *White women, race matters; the social construction of whiteness.* Minneapolis: University of Minnesota Press.

Frechtling, J., Killeen, D., & Perone, D. (2002). *Transforming education through the arts challenge.* Final evaluation report. Rockville, MD: Westat.

Freire, P. (1970). *Pedagogy of the oppressed.* New York: Continuum.

———. (1996). *Pedagogy of hope.* New York: Continuum.

———. (1996). *Pedagogy of the oppressed.* New York: Continuum.

———. (1998). *Pedagogy of freedom.* Lanham, MD: Rowman & Littlefield.

———. (1998). *Teacher as cultural workers: Letters to those who dare to teach.* Boulder, CO: Westview Press.

Fuhrman, S. (2002). *Urban education: Is reform the answer?* Retrieved March, 2003, from http://www.urbanedjournal.org/archive/issue%201/featurearticles/article0004.html.

Fukuyama, M., & Sevig, T. (1999). *Integrating spirituality into multicultural counseling.* Thousand Oaks, CA: Sage.

Gallagher, C. (1995). White reconstruction in the university. *Socialist Review, 94* (1 & 2), 165–187.

Garbarino, J. (2000). *Lost boys: Why our sons turn violent and how we can save them.* New York: Anchor.

Gardner, H. (1999). *The disciplined mind: What all students should understand.* New York: Simon & Schuster.

Gardner, P., Ritblatt, S., & Beatty, J. (2000). Academic achievement and parental involvement as a function of high school size. *The High School Journal, 83* (2), 21–27.

Gay, G., & Howard, T. (2000). Multicultural teacher education for the 21st century. *The Teacher Educator, 36* (Pt. 1), 1–16.

Geertz, C. (1963). *Peddlers and princes, social change and economic modernization in two Indonesian towns.* Chicago: University of Chicago Press.

Geneva, G. (2000). *Culturally responsive teaching.* New York: Teachers College Press.

Getz, A., & Gordhamer, S. (n.d.). *Interview on mindfulness and violent youth.* Retrieved November 4, 2003, from http://www.youthhorizons.org/interview/James/html.

Gilmore, P., & Glatthorn, A. (Eds.). (1982). *Children in and out of school: Ethnography and education.* Washington, DC: Center for Applied Linguistics.

Gilroy, P. (1993). *The black Atlantic: Modernity and double consciousness.* Cambridge, MA: Harvard University Press.

Giroux, H. (1994). *Disturbing pleasures: Learning popular culture.* New York: Routledge.

———. (1997). Rewriting the discourse of racial identity: Towards a pedagogy and politics of whiteness. *Harvard Educational Review, 67* (2), 285–320.

———, & McLaren, P. (1986). Teacher education and the politics of engagement: The case for democratic schooling. *Harvard Educational Review, 56* (2), 213–238.

Glazer, S. (1999). Conclusion: The heart of learning. In S. Glazer (Ed.), *The heart of learning: Spirituality in education* (pp. 247–250). New York: Tarcher.

Glickman, C. (2003). *Holding sacred ground: Courageous leadership for democratic schools.* San Francisco: Jossey-Bass.

Goodwin, L. (Ed.). (1997). *Assessment for equity and inclusion: Embracing all our children.* New York: Routledge.

Greene, M. (1995). *Releasing the imagination: Essays on education, the arts, and social change.* San Francisco: Jossey-Bass.

Gursky, D. (2002). Recruiting minority teachers. [Electronic version]. *American Teacher, 86* (February), 28–34. Retrieved July 8, 2004, from http://www.aft.org/pubsreports/american_teacher/feb02/feature.html.

Gutierrez, J. (2001). *Critical race narratives.* New York: New York University Press.

Haberman, M. (2002). *Achieving "high quality" in the selection, preparation, and retention of teachers.* EducationNews.org. Retrieved March, 2003, from http://www.educationnews.org.

———. (2004). *Urban education: The state of urban schooling at the start of the twenty-first century*. EducationNews.org. Retrieved March, 2003, from http://www.education news.org.

Halford, J. (1996). *Urban education: Policies of promise*. Retrieved March, 2003, from http://www.ascd.org/publications/infobrief/issue5.html.

Hall, J. (2001). *Canal town youth: Community organization and the development of adolescent identity*. Albany: SUNY Press.

Hall, P. (1999). The effects of meditation on the academic performance of African American college students. *Journal of Black Studies, 29* (3), 408–415.

Hamann, D., & Walker, L. (1993). Music teachers as role models for African-American students. *Journal of Research in Music Education, 41* (Winter), 303–314.

Hampel, R. (2002). Historical perspectives on small schools. *Phi Delta Kappan, 83* (5), 357–363.

Hanna, K. (2002). Interview in punk planet. In S. Duncombe (Ed.), *Cultural resistance reader*. London: Verso.

Hanrahan, M. (1998). *A legitimate place for intuition and other a-logical processes in research and hence in reports of research*. Paper Presented at 1998 Conference of Australian Association of Research in Education. Retrieved March, 2003, from http://www.aare.edu.au/98pap/han98331.htm.

Harding, S. (1998). *Is science multicultural? Postcolonialisms, feminisms, and epistemologies*. Bloomington: Indiana University Press.

Harland, J., Kinder, K., Lord, P., Stott, A., Schagen, I., & Haynes, J. (2000). *Arts education in secondary schools: Effects and effectiveness*. Berkshire, UK: National Foundation for Educational Research.

Harrison, F. (1991). Women in Jamaica's urban informal economy. In Mohanty, C., Russo, A., & Torres, L. (Eds.), *Third world women and the politics of feminism* (pp. 173–196). Bloomington: Indiana University Press.

Hart, T. (n.d.). *Case studies*. Center for Contemplative Mind. Retrieved May 30, 2004, from http://www.contemplativemind.org/resources/pubs/case_studies. pdf.

Heath, S. (1983). *Ways with words: Language, life, and work in communities and classrooms*. Cambridge, UK: Cambridge University Press.

———. (1991). Inner-city life to literature: Drama in language learning. *TESOL Quarterly, 27* (2), 177–192.

———. (1996). Ruling places: Adaptation in development by inner-city youth. In R. Jessor, A. Colby, & R. Schweder (Eds.), *Ethnography and human development: Context and meaning in social inquiry* (pp. 225–251). Chicago: University of Chicago Press.

———. (1999). Imaginative actuality: Learning in the arts during the nonschool hours. In E. Fiske (Ed.), *Champions of change* (pp. 19–34). Washington, DC: Arts Education Partnership.

———. (2001). Three's not a crowd: Plans, roles, and focus in the arts. *Educational Researcher, 30* (7), 10–17.

———, & McLaughlin, M. (Eds.). (1993). *Identity and inner-city youth: Beyond ethnicity and gender*. New York: Teachers College Press.

———, & McLaughlin, M. (1994). The best of both worlds: Connecting community schools and community youth organizations for all-day, all-year learning. *Educational Administration Quarterly, 30* (3), 278–300.

Hebdige, D. (2002). The meaning of MOD. In S. Duncombe (Ed.), *Cultural resistance reader*. London: Verso.

Helms J. (1990). *Black and white racial identity: Theory and research in counseling*. New York: Greenwood.

Henke, S. (2000). *Representations of secondary urban education: Infusing cultural studies into teacher education*. Unpublished doctoral dissertation, Miami University.

Herrnstein, R., & Murray, C. (1994). *The bell curve: Intelligence and class structure in America*. New York: Free Press.

Hess, A. (2000). Who leads small schools? Teacher leadership in the midst of democratic governance. In W. Akers, M. Klonsky, & G. Lyon (Eds.), *A simple justice: the challenge of small schools*. New York: Teachers College Press.

Hill, D., Sanders, M., & Hankin, T. (2002). Marxism, class analysis and postmodern-ism. In D. Hill, P. McLaren, & G. Rikowski (Eds.), *Marxism against postmodernism in educational theory*. New York: Lexington Books.

Hill, P., & Celio, M. (1998). *Fixing urban schools*. Washington, DC: Brookings Institute.

Hilliard, A., III. (1997). Language, culture, and the assessment of African American children. In L. Goodwin (Ed.), *Assessment for equity and inclusion: Embracing all our children*. New York: Routledge.

Hobsbawm, E. (2002). Primitive rebels. In S. Duncombe (Ed.), *Cultural resistance reader*. London: Verso.

Hodgkinson, H. (2002). Demographics in teacher education: An overview. *Journal of Teacher Education, 53* (2), 102–105.

Hoffman Davis, J. (2003, October 8). In defense of failure. *Education Week, 23* (6), pp. 28, 30.

Hollingshead, A. (1949). *Elmtown's youth: The impact of social classes on adolescents*. New York: John Wiley & Sons.

———. (1975). *Elmtown's youth and Elmtown revisited*. New York: John Wiley & Sons.

Holloway, D., & Krensky, B. (Eds.). (2001). The arts, urban education, and social change [Special issue]. *Education and Urban Society, 33* (4).

hooks, b. (1990). *Black looks*. New York: Routledge.

———. (1990). *Yearning*. New York: Routledge.

———. (1994). *Teaching to transgress: Education as the freedom of practice*. New York: Routledge.

Horn, R. (2000). *Teacher talk: A postformal inquiry into educational change*. New York: Peter Lang.

Horowitz, R. (2004). *Summary of large-scale arts partnership evaluations*. Washington, DC: Arts Education Partnership.

Howard, G. (1999). *We can't teach what we don't know*. New York: Teachers College Press.

Hudis, P. (2000). Can capital be controlled? *The Journal of Marxist-Humanism?* Retrieved April 20, 2001, from http://www.newsandletters.org/Issues/2000/April/4.00_essay.htm.

Hung, D., Bopry, J., Looi, K., & Koh, T. (2005). Situated cognition and beyond: Martin Heidegger on transformations in being and identity. In J. Kincheloe & R. Horn (Eds.), *Educational psychology: An encyclopedia*. Westport, CT: Greenwood.

Hurley, D. (2003). *Developing students as change agents: Urban education and reform*. Retrieved March, 2003, from http://www.eastern.edu/publications/emme/2003spring/hurley.html.

Intrator, S. (2002). *Stories of the courage to teach: Honoring the teacher's heart*. San Francisco: Jossey-Bass.

Irvine, J. (1991). *Black students and school failure*. New York: Praeger.

Itzigohn, J. (2000). *Developing, poverty: The state, labor market deregulation, and the informal economy in Costa Rica and the Dominican Republic*. University Park: University of Pennsylvania Press.

Jacobs, J. (2004). *Dark age ahead*. New York: Random House.

James, J. (1997). *Transcending the talented tenth: Black leaders and American intellectuals*. New York: Routledge.

Jensen, A. (1969). How much can we boost IQ and scholastic achievement? *Harvard Educational Review, 39* (1), 1–23.

Joel, S. (2000). *Deculturation and the struggle for euality.* Burr Ridge, IL: McGraw-Hill High Education Press.

Johnson, J. (2002). Will parents and teachers get on the bandwagon to reduce school size? *Phi Delta Kappan, 83* (5), 353–356.

Jones, R. (2001, January/April). The liberatory education of the talented tenth: Critical consciousness and the continuing black humanization project. *The Negro Educational Review, 52* (1/2) 3–18.

Kabat-Zinn, J. (1994). *Wherever you go there you are: Mindfulness meditation in everyday life* (p. 21). New York: Hyperion.

Karabel, J., & Halsey, A. (1977). *Power and ideology in education.* New York: Oxford University Press.

Karenga, M. (1993). *Introduction to black studies* (2nd ed.). Los Angeles: University of Sankore Press.

Kase-Polisini, J. (Ed.). (1985). *Creative drama in a developmental context.* New York: University Press of America.

Kegan, R. (1994). *In over our heads: The mental demands of modern life.* Cambridge, MA: Harvard University Press.

Kelley, G. (1997). *From Vietnam to America: A chronicle of the Vietnamese immigration of the United States.* Boulder, CO: Westview Press.

Kent, J. (1968). The Coleman report: Opening Pandora's box. *Phi Delta Kappan, 49,* 242–245.

Kessler, R. (n.d.). *The teaching presence.* The PassageWays Institute. Retrieved September 25, 2002, from http://www.mediatorsfoundation.org/isel/articles.html.

———. (2000). *The soul of education: Helping students find connection, compassion, and character at school.* Alexandria, VA: ASCD.

Kincheloe, J. (1995). *Toil and trouble: Good work, smart workers, and the integration of academic and vocational education.* New York: Peter Lang.

———. (2003). Critical ontology: Visions of selfhood and curriculum. *JCT: Journal of Curriculum Theorizing, 19* (1), 47–64.

———. (2005). *Classroom teaching: An introduction.* New York: Peter Lang.

———. (2005). *Critical constructivism.* New York: Peter Lang.

Kincheloe, J., & Steinberg, S. (1993). A tentative description of post-formal thinking: The critical confrontation with cognitive theory. *Harvard Educational Review, 63* (3), 296–320.

———. (1997). *Changing multiculturalism.* Buckingham: Open University Press.

———. (1998). Addressing the crisis of whiteness: Reconfiguring white identity in pedagogy of whiteness. In J. Kinchloe, S. Steinberg, N. Rodriguez, & R. Chennault (Eds.), *White reign: Deploying whiteness in America* (pp. 3–29). New York: St. Martin's Griffin.

———, & Gresson, A. (Eds.). (1996). *Measured lies: The bell curve examined.* New York: St. Martin's Press.

———, & Hinchey, P. (1999). *The postformal reader: Cognition and education.* New York: Falmer Press.

———, & Villaverde, L. (Eds.). (1999). *Rethinking intelligence: Confronting psychological assumptions about teaching and learning.* New York: Routledge.

Kindlon, D., & Thompson, M. (2000). *Raising Cain: Protecting the emotional life of boys.* New York: Ballantine.

King, J. (1994). Dysconscious racism: Ideology, identity, and the miseducation of teachers. In L. Stone (Ed.), *The education feminism reader* (pp. 336–348). New York: Routledge.

———. (2000). *Race.* Mahwah, NJ: Lawrence Erlbaum Associates.

Kinnucan-Welsch, K. (2005). Reconsidering teacher professional development through constructivist principles. In J. Kincheloe & R. Horn (Eds.), *Educational psychology: An encyclopedia.* Westport, CT: Greenwood.

Klonsky, M. (2000). Grounded insights. In W. Akers, M. Klonsky, & G. Lyon (Eds.), *A simple justice: The challenge of small schools.* New York: Teachers College Press.

Klonsky, S. (2000). Art, with algebra, guards the gate. In W. Akers, M. Klonsky, & G. Lyon (Eds.), *A simple justice: The challenge of small schools.* New York: Teachers College Press.

———, & Klonsky, M. (1999). In Chicago: Countering anonymity through small schools. *Educational Leadership, 57* (1), 38–41.

Kozol, J. (1991). *Savage inequalities: Children in America's schools* (1st ed.). New York: Crown.

Krishnamurti, J. (2000). *On education.* Chennai, India: Krishnamurti Foundation India.

Ladson-Billings, G. (1994/1997). *The dreamkeepers: Successful teachers of African-American children* (1st and 2nd eds.). San Francisco: Jossey-Bass.

———, & Tate, W. (1995, Fall). Toward a critical race theory of education. *Teachers College Record, 97* (1), 47–68.

———. (2000). Fighting for our lives: Preparing teachers to teach African American students. *Journal of Teacher Education, 51* (3), 206–214.

Lantieri, L. (2001). A vision of schools with spirit. In L. Lantieri (Ed.), *Schools with spirit: Nurturing the inner lives of children and teachers* (pp. 7–20). Boston: Beacon.

Latham, A., Gitomer, D., & Ziome, R. (1999). What the tests tell us about new teachers. [Electronic version]. *Educational Leadership, 56,* 23–26.

Lavine-Rasky, C. (2000). Framing whiteness: Working through the tensions in introducing whiteness to educators. *Race, Ethnicity and Education, 3* (3), 271–292.

Lee, E., Menkart, D., & Okazawa-Rey, M. (Eds) (1999). Beyond heroes and holidays: A practical guide to K–12 anti-racist, multicultural education and staff development. Washington, DC: Network of Educators on the Americas.

Leonardo, Z. (2004). Race. In J. Kincheloe & D. Weil (Eds.), *Critical thinking and learning: An encyclopedia for parents and teachers.* Westport, CT: Greenwood.

Lepani, B. (1998). *Information literacy: The challenge of the digital age.* Retrieved March, 2003, from http://www.acal. edu.au/lepani.htm.

Lesko, N., & Bloom, L. (1998). Close encounters: Truth, experience and interpretation. *Curriculum Studies, 30* (4), 375–395.

———, & Bloom, N. (2000). The haunting of multicultural epistemology and pedagogy. In R. Mahalingam & C. McCarthy (Eds.), *Multicultural curriculum: New directions for social theory, practice and policy* (pp. 242–260). New York: Routledge.

Lester, J. (1971). *The seventh son: The thought and writings of W.E.B. DuBois* (Vol. II). New York: Vintage Books.

Levant, R. (1995). Toward the reconstruction of masculinity. In R. Levant. & W. Pollack (Eds.), *A new psychology of man* (pp. 229–251). New York: Basic.

Levine, W. (1996). *The opening of the American mind.* Boston: Beacon Press.

Levine-Rasky, C. (2000). Framing whiteness: Working through the tensions in introducing whiteness to educators. *Race, Ethnicity and Education, 3* (3), 271–292.

Levinson, B., & Holland, D. (1996). The cultural production of the educated person: An introduction. In B. Levinson, D. Foley, & D. Holland (Eds.), *The cultural production of the educated person: Critical ethnographies of schooling and local practices* (pp. 1–31). Albany: SUNY Press.

Lewis, A. (1954, May). *Economic development with unlimited supplies of labour, 22* (2), 139–191. The Manchester School of Economics and Social Studies.

———. (1980). The ritual process and community development. *Community Development Journal, 15* (3), 190–199.

Lewis, D. (1993). *W.E.B. DuBois: Biography of a race, 1868–1919.* New York: Henry Holt.

Lindsey L. (2000). *Sociology: Social life and social issues.* Upper Saddle River, NJ: Prentice Hall.

Loevinger, J., & Wessler, R. (1970). *Measuring ego development* (Vols. 1 & 2). San Francisco: Jossey-Bass.

Lomawaima, T. (1993). Domesticity in the federal indian schools: The power of authority over mind and body. *American Ethnologist, 20* (2), 227–240.

London, B., & Smith, D. (1988). Urban bias, dependence, and economic stagnation in non-core nations. *American Sociological Review, 53* (3), 454–463.

Lowe, S. (2001). The art of community transformation. *Education and Urban Society, 33* (4), 457–471.

Lyon, G. (2000). When *jamas* is enough: Creating a school for a community (a conversation with Tamara Witzl). In W. Akers, M. Klonsky, & G. Lyon (Eds.), *A simple justice: The challenge of small schools.* New York: Teachers College Press.

Macedo, D. (2002). The colonialism of the English only movement. *Education Research, 29* (3), 15–24.

MacLeod, J. (1987). *Ain't no makin' it: Leveled aspirations in a low-income neighborhood.* Boulder, CO: Westview Press.

———. (1995). *Ain't no makin' it: Aspirations and attainment in a low-income neighborhood.* Boulder, CO: Westview Press.

Madison, G. (1988). *The hermeneutics of postmodernity: Figures and themes.* Bloomington: Indiana University Press.

Mahiri, J. (1998). *Shooting for excellence: African American and youth culture in new century schools.* Urbana, IL: National Council of Teachers of English.

Malaki, A. (1996). *Development patterns in the commonwealth Caribbean: Jamaica and Trinidad and Tobago.* Institute of Latin American Studies. Stockholm: Almqvist & Wiksell International.

Malewski, E. (2001). Administration–Administrative leadership and public consciousness: Discourse matters in the struggle for new standards. In J. Kincheloe & D. Weil (Eds.), *Standards and schooling in the United States: An encyclopedia* (3 vols.). Santa Barbara, CA: ABC-Clio.

Mahalingham, R., & McCarthy, C. (2000). *Multicultural curriculum: New directions for social theory, practice and policy.* New York: Routledge.

Malott, C., & Peña, M. (2004). *Punk rocker's revolution: Pedagogy of gender, race and class.* New York: Peter Lang.

Marcus, G. (1986). Contemporary problems of ethnography in the modern world system. In J. Clifford & G. Marcus (Eds.), *Writing culture: The poetics and politics of ethnography* (pp. 165–193). Berkeley: University of California Press.

———. (1998). *Ethnography through thick and thin.* Princeton, NJ: Princeton University Press.

Marger, M. (2000). *Race and ethnic relations.* Belmont, CA: Wadsworth.

Marshall G. (1991). *Spirit of '69: A skinhead bible.* London: STP Publishing.

Massey, D. (1994). *Space, place, and gender.* Minneapolis: University of Minneapolis Press.

Mattera, P. (1985). *Off the books.* New York: St. Martin's Press.

May, T. (1993). *Between genealogy and epistemology: Psychology, politics, and knowledge in the thought of Michel Foucault.* University Park: Pennsylvania State University Press.

McCarthy, C. (1998). Living with anxiety: Race and the renarration of public life. In J. Kincheloe, S. Steinberg, N. Rodrigues, & R. Chennault (Eds.), *White reign: Deploying whiteness in America* (pp. 329–341). New York: St. Martin's Press.

McCartney, J. (1971). Effect of financial support on growth of sociological specialties. In E. Tiryakian (Ed.), *The phenomenon of sociology.* (pp. 395–406). New York: Appleton Century-Crofts.

McCoy, K. (1997). White noise—The sound of epidemic: Reading/writing a climate of intelligibility around the "crisis" of difference. *Qualitative Studies in Education, 10* (3), 333–347.

McDermott, P., & Rothenberg, J. (2000). Why urban parents resist involvement in their children's elementary education. *The Qualitative Report, 5* (3/4). Retrieved March, 2003, from http://www.nova.edu/ssss/qr/qr5-3/mcdermott.html.

McIntyre, A. (1997). Making meaning of whiteness: Exploring racial identity with white teachers. Albany: State University of New York Press.

———. (2002). Exploring whiteness and multicultural education with prospective teacher. *Curriculum Inquiry, 32* (1), 31–49.

McLaren, P. (1994). *Life in school: An introduction to critical pedagogy in the foundation of education.* White Plains, NY: Longman.

———. (1997). Decentering whiteness: In search of a revolutionary multiculturalism. In *Multicultural education, 1* (5), 12–15.

———. (1997). *Revolutionary multiculturalism: Pedagogies of dissent for the new millennium.* Boulder, CO: Westview Press.

———. (1997). Unthinking whiteness, rethinking democracy: Or farewell to the blonde beast; toward a revolutionary multiculturalism. *Educational Foundations, 11* (2), 5–39.

———. (2000). *Che Guevara, Paulo Freire, and the pedagogy of revolution.* New York: Rowman & Littlefield.

———. (2002). *Life in schools: An introduction to critical pedagogy in the foundations of education* (4th ed.). Boston: Allyn & Bacon.

———. (2002). Marxist revolutionary praxis: A curriculum of transgression. *Journal of Critical Inquiry into Curriculum and Instruction, 3* (3), 36–41.

———, & Farahmandpur, R. (2005). *Teaching against global capitalism and the new imperialism: A critical pedagogy.* New York: Rowman & Littlefield.

———, & Farahmandpur, R. (2002). Breaking signifying chains: A Marxist position on postmodernism. In D. Hill, P. McLaren, & G. Rikowski (Eds.), *Marxism against postmodernism in educational theory.* New York: Lexington Books.

———, & Giroux, H. (1997). *Writing from the margins: Geographies of identity and power.* Boulder, CO: Westview Press.

McLaughlin, M. (2001). Community counts. *Educational Leadership, 58* (7), 14–18.

———, & Irby, M. (1994). Urban sanctuaries: Neighborhood organizations that keep hope alive. *Phi Delta Kappan, 76* (4), 300–304.

———, Irby, M., & Langman, J. (1994). *Urban sanctuaries: Neighborhood organizations in the lives and futures of inner-city youth.* San Francisco: Jossey-Bass.

MDRC (Manpower Demonstration Research Corporation) for the Council of the Great City Schools. (2002). *Foundations for success: Case studies of how urban school systems improve student achievement.* Retrieved March, 2003, from http://www.cgcs.rg/reports/foundations.html.

Meditation benefits abound for schoolchildren, study finds. (2003, January 21). Medical College of Georgia. Retrieved July 26, 2003, from http://www.mcg.edu/news/2003.

Meier, D. (2002). Just let us be: The genesis of a small public school. *Educational Leadership, 59* (5), 76–79.

———. (2000). The crisis of relationships. In W. Akers, M. Klonsky, & G. Lyon (Eds.), *A simple justice: The challenge of small schools.* New York: Teachers College Press.

———, & Schwartz, P. (1995). Central Park East Secondary School: The hard part is making it happen. In M. Apple & J. Beane (Eds.), *Democratic education.* Alexandria, VA: Association for Supervision and Curriculum Development.

Michie, G. (2005). *See you when we get there: Teaching for change in urban schools.* New York: Teachers College Press.

Miles, R. (1987). *Capitalism and unfree labor: Anomaly or necessity?* New York: Tavistock.

Miller, J. (1994). *The contemplative practitioner: Meditation in education and the professions.* Westport, CT: Bergin & Garvey.

Miller, R. (1997). *What are schools for? Holistic education in American culture.* Brandon, VT: Holistic Education Press.

Milwaukee Symphony. (2004). *Education programs.* Retrieved May 12, 2004, from http://www.milwaukeesymphony.org.

Miron, L. (2004). How do we locate resistance in urban schools. In S. Steinberg & J. Kincheloe (Eds.), *19 urban questions: Teaching in the city.* New York: Peter Lang.

Moll, L., & Diaz, S. (1987). Change as the goal of education research. *Anthropology & _Education Quarterly, 18* (4), 287–299.

Moore, J. (2003). *Booker T. Washington, W.E.B. DuBois, and the struggle for racial uplift.* Wilmington, DE: Scholarly Resources.

Morgan, H. (1995). *Historical perspectives on the education of black children.* Westport, CT: Praeger.

Morrell, E. (2003). Legitimate peripheral participation as professional development: Lessons from a summer research seminar. *Teacher Education Quarterly.* Retrieved March, 2003, from http://www.findarticles.com/p/articles/mi_qa3960/is_200304/ai_ n9166599.

Morrison, T. (1992). *Playing in the dark: Whiteness in the literacy imagination.* Cambridge, MA: Harvard University Press.

Morrow, R., & Torres, C. (1995). *Social theory and education: A critique of theories of social and cultural reproduction.* Albany: State University of New York Press.

National Commission on Excellence in Education. (1983). *A nation at risk: The imperative for educational reform.* Washington, DC: Government Printing Office.

National Council for Accreditation of Teacher Education (NCATE). (2002). *Professional standards for the accreditation of schools, colleges and departments of education,* Washington, DC: NCATE.

Nations, C. (2005). Allowing children to make sense of our world: Accepting and embracing constructivist/engaged learning approaches to teaching and learning. In J. Kincheloe & R. Horn (Eds.), *Educational psychology: An encyclopedia.* Westport, CT: Greenwood.

Neary, M. (2002). Youth, training and the politics of "cool." In D. Hill, P. McLaren, & G. Rikowski (Eds.), *Marxism against postmodernism in educational theory.* New York: Lexington Books.

Nespor, J. (1997). *Tangled up in school.* Mahwah, NJ: Lawrence Erlbaum Associates.

Ng, J. (2003). Multicultural education in teacher training programs and its implications on preparedness for effective work in urban settings. In G. Lopez & L. Parker (Eds.), *Interrogating racism in qualitative research methodology.* New York: Peter Lang.

Nichols, B. (2003). *Demographic characteristics of arts attendance, 2002.* Research division note #82, July 2003. Washington, DC: National Endowment for the Arts.

———, & Charnoski, R. (Producer & Director). (2003). *Northwest* [Film]. New York: Charnoski Productions and Flexifilm.

Nieto, S. (1992). *Affirming diversity: The sociopolitical context of multicultural education.* New York: Longman.

———. (2003). *What keeps teachers going?* New York: Teachers College Press.

Nietzsche, F. (1996). *On the genealogy of morals a polemic: By way of clarification and supplement to my last book, Beyond good and evil.* Oxford: Oxford University Press.

Noddings, N. (2005). *The challenge to care in schools: An alternative approach to education* (2nd ed.). New York: Teachers College Press.

Norris, N. (1998). Curriculum evaluation revisited. *Cambridge Journal of Education, 28* (2), 207–219.

Novick, M. (1995). *White lies/white power: The fight against white supremacy and reactionary violence.* Monroe, ME: Common Courage Press.

Novick, P. (1988). *That noble dream: The "objectivity question" and the American historical profession.* Cambridge, UK: Cambridge University Press.

Ogbu, J. (1978). *Minority education and caste: The American system in cross cultural perspective.* San Diego: Academic Press.

O'Reilley, M. (1998). *Radical presence: Teaching as contemplative practice.* Portsmouth, NH: Boynton-Cook/Heinemann.

O'Sullivan, E. (1999). *Transformative learning: Educational vision for the twenty-first century.* New York: Zed.

Owen, D., & Doerr, M. (1999). *None of the above: The truth behind the SATs.* Lanham, MD: Rowman & Littlefield.

Palmer, P. (1998). *The courage to teach: Exploring the inner landscape of a teacher's life.* San Francisco: Jossey-Bass.

Perkins, D. (1994). *The intelligent eye: Learning to think by looking at art.* Santa Monica, CA: J. Paul Getty Trust.

————. (1995). *Outsmarting IQ: The emerging science of learnable intelligence.* New York: The Free Press.

Peterson, B. (1995). La escuela frantney: A journey toward democracy. In M. Apple & J. Beane (Eds.), *Democratic education.* Alexandria, VA: Association for Supervision and Curriculum Development.

Peterson, K. (1994). *Building collaborative cultures: Seeking ways to reshape urban schools.* Retrieved March, 2003, from http://www.ncrel.org.sdrs/areas/issues/educatrs/leadrship/le0pet. htm.

Pickering, J. (1999). The self is a semiotic process. *Journal of Consciousness Studies, 6* (4), 31–47.

Pipher, M. (1994). *Reviving Ophelia: Saving the selves of adolescent girls.* New York: Grosset/Putnam.

Podlozny, A. (2000). Strengthening verbal skills through the use of classroom drama: A clear link. *The Journal of Aesthetic Education, 34* (3–4): 239–276.

Pojman, L. (2001). *What can we know? An introduction to the theory of knowledge* (2nd ed.). Belmont, CA: Wadsworth.

Portes, A., Castells, M., & Benton, L. (1989). *The informal economy: Studies in advanced and less developed countries.* Baltimore, MD: Johns Hopkins University Press.

Prawat, R. (2000, August). The two faces of Deweyan pragmatism: Inductionism versus social constructivism. *Teachers College Record, 102* (4).

Pulido, L. (2001, Winter). To arrive is to begin: Benjamin Saenz's Carry me like water and the pilgrimage of origin in the borderlands. *Studies in Twentieth Century Literature, 25* (1), Special issue on Literature and Popular Culture of the U.S.-Mexican Border.

Purpel, D. (1989). *The moral and spiritual crisis in education: A curriculum for justice and compassion in education.* Granby, MA: Bergin & Garvey.

Quartz, K., Olsen, B. & Duncan-Andrade, J. (2003). *The fragility of urban teaching: A longitudinal study of career development and activism.* Retrieved March, 2003, from http:// www.idea.gseis.ucla. edu/publications/utec/reports/pdf.

Rakowski, C. (1994). *Contrapunto: The informal sector debate in Latin American perspectives.* New York: State University Press of New York.

Reddock, R. (1994). *Women, labor, and politics in Trinidad and Tobago.* London: Zed Books.

Reed, A., Jr. (1997). *W.E.B. Du Bois and American political thought* (p. 53). New York: Oxford University Press.

Reyhner, J. & Eder, J. (1989). A history of Indian Education. Billings, MT: Eastern Montana College Publication.

Rikowski, G. (2002). Education, capital and the transhuman. In D. Hill, P. McLaren, & G. Rikowski (Eds.), *Marxism against postmodernism in educational theory.* New York: Lexington Books.

Rist, R. (1970). Student social class and teacher expectations: The self-fulfilling prophecy in ghetto education. *Harvard Educational Review, 70* (3), 257–265.

Rockefeller, S. (1994). *Meditation, social change, and undergraduate education* (p. 4). The Contemplative Mind in Society Meeting of the Working Group. Retrieved September 20, 2000, from http://www.contemplativemind.org/Rockefellerpaper.htm.

Roman, L. (1993). White is a color! White defensivenss, postmodernism, and anti-racist pedagogy. In C. McCarthy & W. Crinchlow (Eds.), *Race, identity and representation in education.* New York: Routledge.

Rose, K. (2005). Philosophy matters for teachers. In J. Kincheloe (Ed.), *Classroom teaching: An introduction.* New York: Peter Lang.

———, & Kincheloe, J. (2003). *Art, culture, and education: Artful teaching in a fractured landscape.* New York: Peter Lang.

Ross, W. (2000). Diverting democracy: The curriculum standards movement and social studies education. In D. Hursh & W. Ross (Eds.), *Democratic social education: Social studies for social change* (pp. 43–63). New York: Falmer Press.

Rozman, D. (1994). *Meditating with children: The art of concentration and centering.* Boulder Creek, CA: Planetary.

Safa, H. (1995). Economic restructuring and gender subordination. In M. Smith & J. Feagin. (Eds.), *The capitalist city: Global restructuring and community politics* (pp. 252–274). New York: Basil Blackwell.

Saha, L., & Zubrzycki, J. (1997). Classical sociological theories of education. In L. Saha (Ed.), *International encyclopedia of the sociology of education.* Canberra, Australia: Pergamon.

Sanyal, B. (1991). Organizing the self-employed: The politics of the urban informal sector. *International Labor Review, 130,* 39–56.

Scheler, M. (1961). *Ressentiment* (W.W. Holdheim, Trans.). New York: Schocken Books.

Schick, C. (2000). By "virtue of being white": Resistance in anti-racist pedagogy. *Race, ethnicity and education, 3* (1), 84–102.

Schubert, W. (2000). John Dewey as a philosophical basis for small schools. In W. Akers, M. Klonsky, & G. Lyon (Eds.), *A simple justice: The challenge of small schools.* New York: Teachers College Press.

Schugurensky, D. (2000). *Citizenship learning and democratic engagement: Political capital revisited.* Retrieved November, 2004, from http://www.edst.educ.ubc.ca/aerc/2000/schugurenskyd1-final.PDF.

Sefton-Green, J. (Ed.). (1998). *Digital diversions: Youth culture in the age of multimedia.* New York: Routledge.

———. (1999). *Young people, creativity, and new technologies.* New York: Routledge.

Seidel, K. (1995). *Leaders' theatre: A case study of how high school students develop leadership skills through participation in theatre.* Unpublished doctoral dissertation, University of Cincinnati, Cincinnati, OH.

Shor, I. (1992). *Empowering education: Critical teaching for social change.* Chicago: University of Chicago Press.

Shujaa, M. (Ed.). (2001). *Beyond desegregation: The politics of quality in African-American schooling.* Thousand Oaks, CA: Corwin Press.

Simmer-Brown, J. (1999). Commitment and openness: A contemplative approach to pluralism. In S. Glazer (Ed.), *The heart of learning: Spirituality in education* (pp. 97–112). New York: Tarcher.

Sink, M. (2003, February 8). Yoga in Aspen public schools draws opposition. *New York Times,* p. 36.

Skinhead Reggae. (1999). On a Trojan box set (60768-02892). [CD]. London: Trojan Records.

Sleeter, C. (1993). How white teachers construct race. In C. McCarthy & W. Crinchlow (Eds.), *Race, identity and representation in education.* New York: Routledge.

————. (1996). *Multicultural education as social activism.* Albany: State University of New York Press.

————, & McLaren, P. (Eds.). (1995). *Multicultural education, critical pedagogy, and the politics of difference.* Albany: State University of New York Press.

Smith, D. (1996). *Third world cities in global perspective: The political economy of uneven urbanization.* Boulder, CO: Westview Press.

Smith, L. (1999). *Decolonizing methodologies: Research and indigenous peoples.* Dunedin, NZ: University of Otago Press.

Soja, E. (1989). *Postmodern geographies.* London & New York: Verso.

Soloman, R. (1990). Nietzsche, postmodernism, and resentment. In C. Koelb (Ed.), *Nietzsche as a postmodernist: Essays pro and contra* (pp. 267–293). Albany: State University of New York Press.

Sparks, D. (2003, Spring). Interview with Peter Block: The answer to "when?" is "now." *Journal of Staff Development, 24* (2), pp. 52–55. Retrieved May 30, 2004, from http://www.nsdc.org/library/publications/jsd/block242.cfm.

————. (2003, Summer). Honor the human heart: Schools have a responsibility to nurture those who work in them. Interview with Parker Palmer. *Journal of Staff Development, 24* (3), pp. 49–53. Retrieved October 17, 2003, from http://www.nsdc.org/library/publications/jsd/palmer243.html.

Spindler, G. (Ed.). (2000). *Fifty years of anthropology and education: 1950–2000.* Mahwah, NJ: Lawrence Erlbaum Associates.

Spirituality in leadership. (2002, September). *School Administrator.* Retrieved September 20, 2002, from http://www.aasa.org/publications/sa/2002_09.

Steinberg, S. (2001). *Multi/intercultural conversations: A reader.* New York: Peter Lang.

————, Kincheloe, J., & Hinchey, P. (1999). *The post-formal reader: Cognition and education.* New York: Falmer.

Stern, D. (2000). Practicing social justice in the high school classroom. In W. Akers, M. Klonsky, & G. Lyon (Eds.), *A simple justice: The challenge of small schools.* New York: Teachers College Press.

Sunker, H. (1994). Pedagogy and politics: Heydorn's survival through education and its challenge to contemporary theories of education (bildung). In S. Miedema, G. Bieste, & W. Wardekke (Eds.), *The politics of human science.* Brussels, Belgium: VUB Press.

Sussmann, L. (1967). Educational research programs of the office of education: An interview with Dr. R. Louis Bright, Associate Commissioner for Research. *Sociology of Education, 40* (2), 158–169.

Symarip. (1991). On *Skinhead moonstomp: The Album.* [CD]. London: Trojan Records, 10786-20564.

Takaki, R. (1993). *A different mirror: A history of multicultural America.* Boston: Little, Brown.

Tatum, B. (1997). *Why are all the black kids sitting together in the cafeteria? and other conversations about race.* New York: Basic Books.

Taylor, E. (2005). Transformative learning: Developing a critical worldview. In J. Kincheloe & R. Horn (Eds.), *Educational psychology: An encyclopedia.* Westport, CT: Greenwood.

Terman, M. (1923). *Intelligence tests and school reorganization.* New York. World Book.

Testing teacher candidates: The role of licensure tests in improving teacher quality. (n.d.). Retrieved May 30, 2004, from http://books.nap.edu/catalog/10090.html.

Thayer-Bacon, B. (2000). *Transforming critical thinking: Thinking constructively.* New York: Teachers College Press.

————. (2003). *Relational "(e)pistemologies."* New York: Peter Lang.

Thorndike, L. (1920). *Intelligence and its uses.* New York. Harper.

Timberlake, M., & Kentor, J. (1983). Economic dependence, overurban-ization, and economic growth: A study of less developed countries. *The Sociological Quarterly, 24,* 489–507.

Tobin, J. (2000). *"Good guys don't wear hats": Children's talk about the media.* New York: Teachers College Press.

Tripp, A. (1997). Changing the rules: The politics of liberalization and the urban informal economy in Tanzania. Berkeley, Los Angeles, & London: University of California Press.

Trueba, E. (1999). *Latinos unidos: From cultural diversity to politics of solidarity.* Lanham, MD: Rowman & Littlefield.

Tunks, J. (1997). *The partnership assessment project: Changing the face of American education.* Evaluation report. Dallas, TX: Partnership for Arts, Culture, & Education.

University of Cincinnati Evaluation Services Center. (2000, 2001, 2002, 2003). *Evaluation reports on the art in the market project prepared for the Community Design Center.* Cincinnati, OH: Author.

Urban Teacher Collaborative, The. (2000). *Urban teacher challenge report, council of the great city schools.* Retrieved January 22, 2003, from http://www.cgcs.org.

U.S. Department of Education, National Center for Education Statistics. (1999). *Elementary school arts education survey: Fall 1999.* Fast Response Survey System. FRSS 67. Washington, DC: National Center for Education Statistics.

U.S. Department of Education, National Center for Education Statistics. (1999). *Secondary school arts education survey: Fall 1999.* Fast Response Survey System. FRSS 67. Washington, DC: National Center for Education Statistics.

U.S. Department of Education, Office of Educational Research and Improvement. (1999). *The NAEP 1997 arts report card.* Washington, DC: National Center for Education Statistics.

USSR (Urban Schools Symposium Report). (1998). *Relationship, commun-ity, and positive reframing: Addressing the needs.* Retrieved March, 2003, from http://www. inclusiveschools.org/procsho.htm.

Vaughn, K., & Winner, E. (2000). SAT scores of students who study the arts: What we can and cannot conclude about the association. *The Journal of Aesthetic Education, 34* (3–4), 77–89.

Wallace, C. (1987). *For richer, for poorer.* New York: Tavistock.

Wang, M., & Kovach, J. (1996). Bridging the achievement gap in urban schools: Reducing educational segregation and advancing resilience-promoting strategies. In B. Weil, D. (2001). World class standards? Whose world, which economic classes, and what standards? In J. Kincheloe & D. Weil (Eds.), *Standards and schooling in the United States: An encyclopedia.* (3 vols.). Santa Barbara, CA: ABC-Clio.

Wasley, P., & Lear, R. (2001). Small schools, real gains. *Educational Leadership, 58* (6), 22–27.

Watkins, W. (2001). *The white architects of black education: Ideology and power in America, 1865–1954.* New York: Teachers College Press.

Weiler, J. (2000). *Codes and contradictions: Race, gender identity, and schooling.* Albany: SUNY Press.

Weiner, L. (1993). *Preparing teachers for urban schools: Lessons from thirty years of school reform.* New York: Teacher College Press.

———. (1999). *Urban teaching: The essentials.* New York: Teachers College Press.

Weis, L. (1990). *Working-class without work: High school students in a de-industrializing economy.* New York: Routledge.

———, & Fine, M. (Eds.). (2000). *Construction sites: Excavating race, class, and gender among urban youth.* New York: Teachers College Press.

———, & Fine, M. (2001). Extraordinary conversations in public schools. *International Journal of Qualitative Studies in Education, 14* (4), 497–524.

Weitz, J. (1996). *Coming up taller: Arts and humanities programs for children and youth at risk.* Washington, DC: President's Committee on the Arts and Humanities.

Welch, N. (Ed.). (1995). *Schools, communities, and the arts: A research compendium.* Washington, DC: National Endowment for the Arts.

Werner, C. (1999). *A change is gonna come: Music, race & the soul of America.* New York: Penguin.

Wertsch, J. (1998). *Mind as action.* New York: Oxford.

West, C. (1993). *Race matters.* Boston: Beacon Press.

Wilber, K. (1998). *The marriage of sense and soul: Integrating science and religion.* New York: Broadway.

Wilber, K. (2000). *Integral psychology: Consciousness, spirit, psychology, therapy.* Boston: Shambhala.

Willis, P. (1976). *Learning to labor: How working class kids get working class jobs.* New York: Columbia University Press.

———. (1977). *Learning to labour: How working-class kids get working-class jobs.* Westmead, England: Saxon House.

Winant, H. (1997). Whiteness and contemporary U.S. racial politics. In M. Fine, L. Weis, L. Powell, & L. Wong (Eds.). *Off white: Readings on race, power, and society* (pp. 40–56). New York: Routledge.

Yasin, S. (1999). The supply and demand of elementary and secondary school teachers in the United States. *ERIC Digest.* [Electronic version]. Washington, DC: ERIC Clearinghouse on Teaching and Teacher Education. Retrieved June, 2004, from http://www.ericdigests.org/2000-3/demand.htm.

Yon, D. (2000). *Elusive culture: Schooling, race, and identity in global times.* Albany: SUNY Press.

Young, M., & Rosick, J. (2000). Interrogating whiteness. *Educational Researcher, 29* (2) 39–44.

Zajonc, A. (2003, Winter). Spirituality in higher education: Overcoming the divide. *Liberal Education, 89* (1), 50–58. Retrieved November 21, 2005, from http://www.findarticles.com/p/articles/mi_m0NKR/is_1_89/ai_99907663.

Zeichner, K. (1996). Closing the achievement gap: Opportunity to learn, standards and assessment. In B. Williams (Ed.), *Closing the achievement gap: A vision for changing beliefs and practices.* Alexandria, VA: Association for Supervision and Curriculum Development.

Zellner, W. (1995). *Countercultures: A sociological analysis.* New York: St. Martin's Press.

Index

About the Contributors

CHRISTINE ANDERSON is currently serving as the Executive Director of the Milwaukee Partnership Academy (MPA). The purpose of the MPA is to enhance the quality of teaching and learning in the Milwaukee Public Schools (MPS). The 2003 Wisconsin PK-16 Leadership Council awarded Dr. Anderson and the MPA a "Program of Distinction" award as an urban initiative that clearly represents the best of educational collaboration by bringing together a diverse group of leaders from the area public schools, public and private postsecondary education sectors, the local education association and school board, as well as industry and business. She has worked in MPS since 1974 in various capacities—as a classroom teacher, drug resource coordinator, human relations specialist, and teacher-leader of the Home and Hospital Instruction Program. She has received many teaching awards including a Kohl Fellowship, MPS High School Teacher of the Year in 1990, and most recently, the National High School Association Wisconsin Educator of the Year, 1998–1999. From 1979 to 1982, she served as president of the Milwaukee Teachers' Education Association. Her area of emphasis has always been developing teacher-leaders and embedding professional development at schools. She has chaired professional development teams that include work on teacher emeritus and mentoring programs, developing Goals for 2000, and the development of a teacher center. She has presented at numerous conferences and has been recognized by *Milwaukee Magazine* as an educator who will influence education in Milwaukee. Dr. Anderson received a PhD from the University of Wisconsin-Milwaukee in 1990 in Urban Education with a minor in Industrial and Labor Relations. In 2006, the U.S. Postal Service named Dr. Anderson a "Woman putting a Stamp on Metro Milwaukee in Education."

PHILIP M. ANDERSON is Professor of Urban Education and Executive Officer of the PhD Program in Urban Education at the Graduate Center of the City University of New York and Professor of Secondary Education and Youth Services at Queens College/CUNY. He has produced numerous publications on the teaching of literary reading, the English curriculum, cultural theories and schooling, teacher preparation, and curriculum theory and praxis.

MARY M. ATWATER is a professor in the Science Education Department at the University of Georgia. With her strong physical science background, she has designed and conducted professional development activities for urban elementary and middle school teachers that focused on enhancing both science content knowledge and pedagogical content knowledge. In addition, she has been very active in developing standards for teachers of early adolescents with the National Board of Professional Teaching Standards. Her research focuses on the socio-cultural-political factors that influence science teaching and learning.

DAVID BARONOV is Associate Professor and Chair of the Sociology Department at St. John Fisher College in Rochester, New York. He has recently published *Conceptual Foundations of Social Research Methods* (2004, Paradigm). In addition, he has published numerous chapters and articles in *Radical Pedagogy, Caribbean Studies, Socialism and Democracy,* and *The Discourse of Sociological Practice.*

LINDA B. BENBOW is a PhD candidate (ABD) in the Sociology Department at the Graduate School and University Center, CUNY, and has fulfilled the requirements for the Women's Certificate Program. She teaches as a full-time lecturer in the Sociology and Black Studies Departments at the State University of New York at New Paltz. Her areas of concentration are organizational effectiveness, race and ethnicity, women and work, and stratification. Linda's in-progress dissertation, near completion, is an ethnographic study of diversity in the workplace entitled *Race, Class, and Gender in a Federal Bureaucracy: The Paradoxes of Diversity.* She has developed and taught the following: Introduction to Sociology, Social Inequality, Sociology of Children, Contemporary Social Issues in the Black Community, Black and Latino Leadership, and Social Problems. Linda has cotaught an introduction to women's studies course, Women: Images and Realities.

GRACE BENIGNO is a doctoral student in the Department of Curriculum and Instruction at the University of Maryland at College Park with a research interest in mathematics education.

DONALD BLUMENFELD-JONES is the Lincoln Associate Professor for Ethics and Education at Arizona State University. He specializes in arts-based education research, ethics and classroom discipline, hermeneutics, and critical social theory and curriculum. He has published in such journals as the *Journal of Curriculum Theorizing, Educational Theory, Journal of Thought, Journal of Qualitative Studies in Education,* and *Qualitative Inquiry.* He also has numerous book chapters dealing with dance curriculum, ethics and curriculum, and arts-based education research. Prior to his academic career, he danced professionally for twenty years, studying, performing, and choreographing modern dance in New York City. He has performed, choreographed, and taught throughout the United States and Canada.

THOMAS BRIGNALL III received his PhD in Sociology from Western Michigan University. He currently teaches at Tennessee Technical University in the Department of Sociology and Political Sciences. His research interests are currently in education inequality, race relations, political movements, pop culture, and the social implications of the Internet. His primary teaching interests are in sociological theory, race/class/gender, mass media, technology and society, and music in social movements.

SHORNA BROUSSARD is currently an Assistant Professor in the Department of Forestry and Natural Resources at Purdue University. Dr. Broussard has an extensive background in educational program evaluation, a field of study that focuses on evaluating the process and outcomes of educational strategies. Prior work has included a national program evaluation of Natural Resource Extension programs, environmental education curriculum development and evaluation with urban youth, and innovative program design and development to reach underserved audiences. Dr. Broussard is the Communications and Educations Editor of the *Journal of Forestry* and her published works include papers in the *Journals of Forestry Extension* and several book chapters in *Conserving Biodiversity in Agricultural Landscapes* (2004).

ANTHONY L. BROWN is a doctoral candidate in the Department of Curriculum & Instruction at the University of Wisconsin-Madison. A former elementary school teacher and school administrator, his research interests include teacher pedagogy, multicultural education, and the educational history of African Americans. His current research examines the social and academic interactions between African-American male teachers and African-American male students.

KEFFRELYN D. BROWN is a doctoral candidate in the Department of Curriculum and Instruction at the University of Wisconsin-Madison. She has worked as an elementary and middle school teacher, as well as a school administrator and curriculum consultant/writer. Her current research focuses on how multiple educational sites conceptualize the ideas of risk and academic achievement.

PATRICIA BURDELL is an Associate Professor in the Teacher Education and Professional Department at Central Michigan University in Mount Pleasant Michigan. She taught middle school and high school for twenty years in Lansing, Michigan, prior to obtaining her doctorate in curriculum and instruction from the University of Wisconsin at Madison in 1993. Her interests are in the critical analysis of the curriculum of adolescents and young adults in secondary schools; reflective engagement in teacher education curriculum and practice; and issues related to the use of personal narrative as a methodology in educational literature.

MALCOLM B. BUTLER is a former middle school and high school mathematics and science teacher. Dr. Butler is currently an Assistant Professor in the Science Education Department at the University of Georgia. Prior to the University of Georgia, he spent time on the faculty at Texas A&M University-Corpus Christi. He also spent two years as a Mathematics and Science Program Specialist with the Southeast Eisenhower Regional Consortium for Mathematics and Science Education. In this capacity, Dr. Butler spent part of his time providing technical assistant and professional development to rural and urban communities across the southeastern United States.

SHIRLEY BYNUM is a Program Specialist for Career-Technical Education in Winston-Salem/Forsyth County Schools, Winston-Salem, NC. Dr. Bynum is responsible for curriculum, current research, and safety issues in the program areas of Business and Marketing Education, Career Management, Family and Consumer Sciences, and Health Occupations. Dr. Bynum earned her doctorate in curriculum and teaching with a curriculum specialist license, and a postbaccalaureate certificate from the Women's Studies Program at the University of North Carolina, Greensboro. Her research interests include black spiritual women, outreach ministries, power of relationships, and curriculum.

KAREN CADIERO-KAPLAN is Associate Professor in the Policy Studies in Language and Cross Cultural Department in the College of Education at San Diego State University. She has published articles in the areas of critical literacy, language policy, and critical issues of technology in K–12 classrooms. She recently published a book, *The Literacy Curriculum and Bilingual Education: A Critical Examination*, with a focus on research on literacy curriculum and programming in schools.

JOSEPH CARROLL-MIRANDA was born and raised in San Juan, Puerto Rico. He was and is seriously involved in student movements and student government for more than a decade in Puerto Rico, Latin America, and with Global Youth. Joseph earned his BA from the University of Puerto Rico in 1998. In addition, he earned his MA in Curriculum and Instruction from New Mexico State University. Currently he is a semester short of the ABD designation for a doctorate in Curriculum and Instruction, focusing on Learning Technologies with a minor in Critical Pedagogy.

RONNIE CASELLA is Associate Professor of Educational Foundations and Secondary Education at Central Connecticut State University. His research interests include violence and conflict resolution, urban education, and globalization. He is the author of *"Being Down": Challenging Violence in Urban Schools* and *At Zero Tolerance: Punishment, Prevention, and School Violence* and of articles that have appeared in *The Urban Review*,

Teachers College Record, Urban Education, Anthropology and Education Quarterly, and other journals. He is on the Advisory Committee for the Safe Schools and Communities Coalition of the Governor's Prevention Partnership for Connecticut and has worked closely with various community and peace groups.

IMELDA CASTAÑEDA-EMENAKER earned her doctoral degree in educational foundations from the University of Cincinnati. Dr. Castañeda-Emenaker is a researcher, evaluation specialist, teacher, and experienced administrator. Her areas of interest and research are in multicultural issues, alternative education, and integrated curriculum. As an Asian, Dr. Castañeda-Emenaker brings her multicultural perspectives into her various endeavors. She is currently working as consultant and evaluator for seven alternative schools in different counties of Ohio. In the area of integrated curriculum, Dr. Castañeda-Emenaker had been involved with the evaluation of an arts integrated curriculum program in Greater Cincinnati for six years. She wrote articles, technical reports, and presented papers in professional conferences along the areas of multicultural issues, alternative education, and integrated curriculum. Her administrative experience includes managing a college, directing outreach programs and service learning, and administering a restaurant school for street children in the Philippines. Dr. Castañeda-Emenaker is currently a research associate, evaluation specialist, and adjunct professor at the University of Cincinnati.

LESLEY COIA is an Associate Professor and the Director of Teacher Education Programs at Agnes Scott College. She taught English (7–12) in London and East Anglia, and English as a Foreign Language for Kursverksamheten, the extramural department of Stockholm University in Sweden. She received her PhD in Philosophy of Education from the University of London Institute of Education. Her research interests include self-study practices in teacher education, feminist philosophy, and autoethnography. Her work has been published in *The National Reading Conference Yearbook, Perspectives on Urban Education,* and *The Encyclopaedia of Life Writing.*

WILLIAM CRAIN is Professor of Psychology at The City College of New York and the editor of the journal *Encounter: Education for Meaning and Social Justice.*

MYRON H. DEMBO is the Stephen Crocker Professor in Education in the Rossier School of Education at the University of Southern California. He is a fellow in the American Psychological Association and an associate editor of the *Elementary School Journal* and *Journal of College Reading and Learning.Behavior.* Professor Dembo specializes in the areas of learning and motivation with a focus on teaching students how to become more self-regulated learners. He has written three books and more than 75 research articles on the teaching-learning process. His educational psychology textbook, *Applying Educational Psychology,* is now in its fifth edition. His most recent book is *Motivation and Learning Strategies for College Success: A Self-Management Approach* (2nd ed.).

GENE DIAZ is a visual artist and educational ethnographer who teaches courses in curriculum theory, arts-based research, and critical ethnography at Lesley University. A Fulbright Scholar in Medellin, Colombia, in 2002, she collaborated with Zayda Sierra in teaching and research at the Universidad de Antioquia. In 2004 she coedited, with Martha McKenna, *Teaching for Aesthetic Experience,* based on the work of Maxine Greene, published by Peter Lang.

ANNE DICHELE is an Associate Professor of Reading and Language Arts at Quinnipiac University, Hamden, Connecticut, in the Master of Arts in Teaching Program, Division of Education. Dr. Dichele was previously a Reading Consultant for the Boston School system and an elementary school teacher.

GREG DIMITRIADIS is an Associate Professor in the Department of Educational Leadership and Policy at the University at Buffalo, SUNY.

DANIEL J. DONDER is currently principal of Riverside University High School in the Milwaukee Public Schools. He is former Director of Strategic Planning and Community Outreach for the Milwaukee Public Schools. He served as the district's external point of contact with community groups, businesses, and government entities and serves as the communication link between the superintendent and other administrators, city and county offices, and schools. He provides collaborative leadership with the partners of the Milwaukee Partnership Academy. Dr. Donder received a PhD in 1984 at the University of Illinois at Urbana-Champaign with an emphasis on special education and school administration. He has worked in many educational settings with the Milwaukee Public Schools: as a special education teacher, special education supervisor, middle school principal, and high school principal. A strong advocate for special education needs, he has presented at national conferences and published research-based articles and chapters pertaining to education of students with severe handicaps in regular education settings and articles pertaining to proactive administrative strategies to ensure the success of students with disabilities in regular education classrooms. He has also presented at national conferences pertaining to social justice issues and the critical need for students to enroll and pass algebra as a gatekeeper for high school graduation and opportunities for success in post high school. He is an arts advocate and promoted the arts as principal at Lincoln Middle School of the Arts and Milwaukee High School of the Arts and has also presented at national conferences illustrating the relationship of students' involvement in arts and the positive relationship to academic achievement. Dr. Donder is currently an active participant in professional organizations pertaining to middle level education and numerous boards of directors for local arts organizations. In addition, he has been the recipient of local awards for educational leadership.

JOANNE KILGOUR DOWDY is an Associate Professor at Kent State University, Ohio. A graduate of Juilliard School in the theatre division, Dr. Dowdy continues to use her drama training to prepare teachers for the literacy classroom and as a performer who facilitates writing development through interactive workshops. Her major research interests include documenting the experiences of black women involved in education from adult basic literacy to higher education. Her first book is a volume coedited with Dr. Lisa Delpit, titled The Skin that We Speak: Thoughts on Language and Culture in the Classroom (The New Press). Her second book, GED Stories: Black Women & Their Struggle for Social Equity, is published by Peter Lang.

TIBBI DUBOYS earned a Bachelor's degree in Classics at Brooklyn College, a Master's degree in Counseling and Guidance at Hunter College, and a PhD in Counselor Education at Fordham University. Prior to joining the faculty in the School of Education at Brooklyn College, she taught third, fourth, and sixth grades in public schools in Brooklyn. She found Social Studies least focused upon in elementary schools, and brought to the college her interest in teacher's interpretations of the social science disciplines. She has often spoken publicly about the Holocaust, and has published in this area as well. She is interested in the ways in which oppression has influenced and affected the lives of children. She is completing a book about Holocaust education, and is planning another. She is an Associate Professor in the School of Education at Brooklyn College of the City University of New York.

JEFFREY M. R. DUNCAN-ANDRADE is Assistant Professor of Raza Studies and Education Administration and Interdisciplinary Studies, and Co-Director of the Educational Equity Initiative at San Francisco State University's Cesar Chavez Institute. Duncan-Andrade's research interests and publications span the areas of urban schooling and curriculum change, urban teacher retention and development, critical peda-gogy, and cultural and ethnic studies. He is currently completing a co-authored book on effective uses of critical pedagogy in the secondary classroom and a book on the role of youth culture in the culture of schools and the classroom.

MOSTAFA MOUHIE EDDINE was born and raised in Casa Blanca, Morocco. He received his undergraduate degree in psychology and a master's in education at University of Massachusetts, Amherst. He is currently working on his PhD in curriculum and instruction with a major in critical pedagogy and a minor in teaching English as a second language from New Mexico State University.

GUSTAVO E. FISCHMAN is an assistant professor in the Division of Curriculum and Instruction at Arizona State University. His research interests are in the areas of comparative and international education, gender studies, and qualitative studies in education. Dr. Fischman is the author of two books and several articles on Latin American education, teacher education, cultural studies and education, and gender issues in education. He is associate editor of the online journals Reseñas Educativas/ Education Review and Archivos Analíticos de Políticas Educativas/Education Policy Analysis Archives.

DAVID FORBES teaches school counseling in the School of Education, Brooklyn College/CUNY. He is the author of *Boyz 2 Buddhas: Counseling Urban High School Male Athletes in the Zone* (2004, Peter Lang) and *False Fixes: The Cultural Politics of Drugs, Alcohol, and Addictive Relations* (1994, SUNY Press). He worked in a school-based sub-stance abuse prevention program in Brooklyn and practices meditation and yoga.

LUIS ARMANDO GANDIN earned a PhD at the University of Wisconsin-Madison and is Professor of Sociology of Education in the School of Education of the Federal University of Rio Grande do Sul in Porto Alegre, Brazil. His research interests are in the areas of critical analysis of educational policy, curriculum theory, and education for transformation. Dr. Gandin has published three books, collaborated on chapters in books, and written articles in academic journals in Brazil, Australia, Portugal, the United States, and the United Kingdom. He is editor of the journal Currículo sem Fronteiras (http://www.curriculosemfronteiras.org), a free-access, peer-reviewed academic journal, with many articles available both in Portuguese and in English.

HOLLYCE C. GILES is Associate Professor in the School of Education at Brooklyn College, City University of New York. Dr. Giles has served as Education Advisor with the Industrial Areas Foundation, and is currently a Senior Research Fellow with the Public Education Association, and is currently a Senior Research Fellow at the Institute for Education and Social Policy at New York University. Her research and publications focus on the social and psychological dimensions of community organizing initiatives to reform schools. She holds a Master of Divinity degree from Union Theological Seminary and a PhD in Counseling Psychology from Teachers College, Columbia University, and is a psychologist in private practice.

MARIE GIRONDA is a 31-year-veteran English Honors and Advanced Placement teacher in a magnet high school in the same district where coauthor John Pascarella teaches. She is a PhD candidate in modern history and literature at Drew University in Madison, New Jersey.

MERRYL GOLDBERG is a Professor of Visual and Performing Arts at California State University San Marcos (CSUSM), where she teaches courses on arts and learning, and music. She is also Founder and Director of Center ARTES (Art, Research, Teaching, Education, and Schools) at CSUSM, an organization whose mission is to restore arts education to schools and communities in California. She also oversees the Arts and Lectures Series for the university. Merryl is a professional saxophonist and recording artist. She toured internationally for 13 years with the Klezmer Conservatory Band, and has recorded more than a dozen CDs with Vanguard Records, Rounder Records, and other labels. Her publications include the books *Teaching English Language Learners through the Arts: A SUAVE Experience* (2004, Allyn & Bacon), *Integrating the Arts: An Approach to An Integrated Approach to Teaching and Learning in Multicultural and Multilingual Settings*, 3rd edition (2006, Allyn & Bacon), and *Arts as Education* (1992, Harvard Educational Review), as well as articles and book chapters on learning through the arts. She is the recipient of Spencer, John D. and Catherine T. MacArthur, and Fulbright-Hays Foundations grants relating to her work with arts in the schools. Her program, SUAVE, is the recipient of the U.S. Department of Education Model Arts grant and numerous California Arts Council and California Department of Education grants. Merryl lives in southern California with her daughter, Liana Cai Goldberg.

MORDECHAI GORDON is an Associate Professor of Education in the Division of Education at Quinnipiac University, Hamden, Connecticut. He is the editor of *Hannah Arendt and Education: Renewing our Common World* (2002, Westview Press) and author of numerous articles in journals such as *Educational Theory* and *Encounter: Education for Meaning and Social Justice*.

MERIDITH GOULD has more than 15 years' experience working with inner-city youth. She is a diversity, conflict resolution, violence prevention, leadership, communication, and anger-management trainer. She has worked for many nonprofit and public policy organizations as a program associate, consultant, lobbyist, and researcher. She is an adjunct professor at Spelman College, Emory University, and Southern Polytechnical College in Atlanta, Georgia, while completing her dissertation. She has designed and conducted numerous trainings for youth and educators. Meridith earned a BA in sociology with a concentration in racial and ethnic relations, an MS in dispute resolution, and is ABD with a PhD in conflict analysis and resolution.

ERIC HAAS is a lawyer and Assistant Professor of Education Policy at the University of Connecticut. His research interests include education law and media presentations of education issues.

SILVERIO HARO teaches part-time for California State University at San Marcos and Palomar College. His experience focuses on issues of equity and access, with special attention to attrition and persistence among university students, precollegiate programming for underrepresented groups, and leadership development and capacity-building among minority-based community organizations. His areas of research include campus climate assessment, aspects of institutional quality within higher education, and educational outcomes assessment.

KECIA HAYES is currently a PhD candidate and MAGNET Scholar at the CUNY Graduate Center. Her research focuses on how social policies and practices impact the educational experiences of children and parents of color in urban communities. kecia's dissertation examines the educational experiences of court-involved youth. She has taught graduate courses at the International Center for Cooperation and Conflict Resolution of Teachers College, Columbia University, and was an educational consultant with the NYU School of Education Metropolitan Center, as well as the Center for Social and Emotional Education. She is a founding Trustee of Harlem Episcopal School. kecia has provided research assistance for *The Colors of Excellence: Hiring and Keeping Teachers of Color in Independent Schools* by editors Pearl Rock Kane and Alfonso J. Orsini, coauthored a chapter in *19 Urban Questions: Teaching in the City* by editors Shirley Steinberg and Joe Kincheloe, and is an editor of two forthcoming texts *Metropedagogy: Power, Justice, and the Urban Classroom* from Sense Publishers, and *City Kids: Understanding, Appreciating, and Teaching Them* from Peter Lang Publishing.

FRANCES HELYAR is a doctoral student in Urban Education and Leadership at City University of New York. She is also a broadcaster, an elementary school teacher, and a substitute teacher.

RAYMOND A. HORN, JR., is a retired public school educator and Assistant Professor of Education and Director of the Interdisciplinary Doctor of Education Program for Educational Leaders at Saint Joseph's University. Dr. Horn has numerous publications in the fields of educational leadership, teacher education, and curriculum studies. His most recent books are *Understanding Educational Reform: A Reference Handbook* and *Standards Primer*. Dr. Horn's research interests include critical theory, cultural studies, and educational change and reform.

CLAUDIA HUIZA holds a BA in Spanish and English and American Literature and a Master's degree in Comparative Literature from the University of California at San Diego (UCSD). She is ABD in Literature and Cultural Studies at UCSD. She teaches at National University, American Intercontinental University, and Kaplan University.

CHANNELLE JAMES is a lecturer at the University of North Carolina at Greensboro in the Department of Business Administration. Dr. James teaches undergraduate courses in business administration and works primarily with freshmen business majors. Dr. James earned her doctorate in curriculum and teaching/cultural studies and a postbaccalaureate certificate in Women's Studies at the University of North Carolina at Greenboro. Her research areas include diversity, cultural studies, and ethics and justice in business practices.

GAETANE JEAN-MARIE is an Assistant Professor at Florida International University, Department of Educational Leadership and Policy Studies. Dr. Jean-Marie teaches graduate courses in leadership and education, and school personnel management in the Educational Leadership/Administration program area. Dr. Jean-Marie earned her doctorate in curriculum and teaching/cultural studies with a postbaccalaureate certificate from the Women's Studies Program at the University of North Carolina, Greensboro. Her research interests include women and educational leadership, urban school reform, and issues of equity and social justice.

KAREN EMBRY JENLINK is Dean of the School of Education at St. Edward's University in Austin, Texas. She currently serves as associate editor of *Teacher Education and Practice* and recently published her second book, *Portraits of Teacher Preparation: Learning to Teach in a Changing America*. Her research focuses on teacher preparation, urban education, teacher identity, and leadership.

PATRICK M. JENLINK is a Professor of Doctoral Studies in the Department of Secondary Education and Educational Leadership, as well as the Director of the Educational Research Center at Stephen F. Austin State University in Nacogdoches, Texas. Currently, his teaching emphasis in doctoral studies includes courses in ethics and philosophy of leadership, critical studies in politics and policy, and dynamics of change. Dr. Jenlink's research interests include politics of identity, social systems design and change, cultural-historical activity theory, democratic education and leadership, and postmodern inquiry methods. He has authored numerous articles, guest-edited journals, authored or coauthored numerous chapters in books, and edited or coedited several books. Currently he serves as editor of *Teacher Education & Practice* and as coeditor of *Scholar-Practitioner Quarterly*. His most recent books are *Dialogue as a Collective Means of Communication* (Kluwer Publishing) and *Portraits of Teacher Preparation: Learning to Teach in a Changing America* (Rowman & Littlefield, 2005). Dr. Jenlink's current book projects include the coedited *Scholar-Practitioner Leadership: A Post-formal Inquiry* (forthcoming from Peter Lang) and *Developing Scholar-Practitioner Leaders: The Empowerment of Educators* (forthcoming from Falmer Press).

MARINA KARIDES is an Assistant Professor at Florida Atlantic University. She has conducted research on street vendors in the The Republic of Trinidad and Tobago and The Republic of Cyprus. She is currently working on a book about Port of Spain street vendors, globalization, and the construction of space.

JOE L. KINCHELOE holds the Canada Research Chair in Education at McGill University in Montreal. He is the author of numerous books and articles about pedagogy, research, education and social justice, issues of cognition and cultural context, and educational reform.

TRICIA KRESS is a third-year doctoral student in the Urban Education Department at The Graduate Center of the City University of New York and she is a doctoral fellow sponsored by The Discovery Institute at The College of Staten Island, CUNY. She began working with educational technology in 1994 when she designed *The Magic Rabbit*, an interactive CD-ROM combining silent video with text to help demonstrate English verb tense changes to ASL (American Sign Language) students. In 1998 she began working as an adjunct professor teaching composition and college writing for the English Department at The College of Staten Island and Kean University. Two years later, she returned to her roots and began teaching Computers for Teachers and Computers for Teachers on Sabbatical. Currently, she is involved with The Discovery Institute's Curriculum Writing Workshops for in-service teachers, and has organized a group of teachers to write lessons specifically geared to incorporating computers into the New York City public high school English curriculum.

ROBERT LEHMANN is past president of the Milwaukee Teachers' Education Association, an organization that represents more than 8,000 educators in the Milwaukee Public Schools system. He began his teaching career with MPS in 1972 and has taught English and reading at both the middle and the high school levels. Prior to assuming his duties as MTEA president in 2001, Mr. Lehmann was coordinator of the MPS/MTEA TEAM Program, a nationally acclaimed peer review program that the union and district developed jointly in 1996. He returned to this position in 2005, following his presidency. His leadership vision is founded on the belief that public education unions must be lead partners in shaping educational improvement.

TONDRA L. LODER is currently an Assistant Professor in the Educational Foundations Program in the School of Education at the University of Alabama at Birmingham. Her research examines the influence of social change and public policy on the lives of urban educators and urban education from the theoretical and methodological perspectives of the life course and life history.

MARVIN LYNN is an Assistant Professor of Minority and Urban Education in the Department of Curriculum and Instruction at the University of Maryland at College Park. His research explores race, urban schooling, and the work and lives of black male teachers. His work has been influential in expanding the discourse on critical race theory and education. Among several articles published in this area, his article "Toward a Critical Pedagogy" has been widely used in a number of disciplines to help draw important links between race and teaching. He has published articles in *Urban Education*, *Review of Research in Education*, *Educational Philosophy and Theory*, and others. This year, his articles will appear in such journals as *Teachers College Record*, *Qualitative Studies in Education*, and *Educational Theory*. He is cofounder and director of the Minority and Urban Education program in the Department of Curriculum and Instruction at the University of Maryland.

CURRY MALOTT is professor of education in a number of colleges and universities throughout New York City and the state. His research interests include the social studies, Marxism, and the counterhegemonic reality and potential of countercultural formations as spaces of resistance. Included in his list of publications is the recently published book, *Punk Rocker's Revolution: A Pedagogy of Race, Class, and Gender* (2004). Malott continues to ride his skateboard and produce music under the banner of what he calls "the Punk Army."

TIM MAY earned degrees at the London School of Economics and Political Science (1985) and Universities of Surrey (1986) and Plymouth (1990). Tim has authored, co-authored, and edited books on social theory, methodology, methods and philosophy of social science, organizational transformation, and thinking sociologically. He is series editor of *Issues in Society* (McGraw-Hill/Open University Press) and Director of the Centre for Sustainable Urban and Regional Futures (www.surf.salford.ac.uk), where he conducts research into urban policy, universities and regionalization, science policy, knowledge production and transfer, and economic and social development.

COLLEEN MITCHELL is an MA student in the Department of Urban Planning at the University of Maryland at College Park.

RONALD L. MIZE is currently Assistant Professor of Latino Studies and Development Sociology at Cornell University. He was the main Principal Investigator, from 2000 to 2004, for the CSU-San Marcos-San Diego Head Start Higher Education Partnership, funded by the DHHS-Administration on Children Youth and Families. He previously taught sociology, ethnic studies, and history at the University of Saint Francis-Fort Wayne, CSU-San Marcos, University of California–San Diego, Southwestern College, Colorado State University, and University of Wisconsin–Rock County. His research focuses on the historical and contemporary lived experiences of Chicano/a and Mexican immigrant communities. He has published in *Latino Studies Journal, Cleveland State Law Review, Ambulatory Pediatrics, Contemporary Sociology, Rural Sociology*, and several encyclopedias.

CAROL A. MULLEN is Associate Professor of leadership studies at the University of South Florida. Her fields of research include mentorship and diversity, and she supervises the Writers in Training (WITs), a thriving doctoral cohort. Dr. Mullen has published more than 130 journal articles and book chapters and, as guest editor, 11 special issues of academic journals. This award-winning qualitative researcher has also published nine books, most recently *A Graduate Student Guide* (2006, Rowman & Littlefield), as well as *Climbing the Himalayas of School Leadership* (2004, ScarecrowEducation), as well as *Fire and Ice* and *The Mentorship Primer* (2005, Peter Lang). Dr. Mullen is editor of the refereed international journal *Mentoring & Tutoring* (Carfax Publishing/Taylor & Francis Group).

ANTHONY NAVARRETE is a doctoral candidate in Literature at the University of California at San Diego (UCSD). He was program manager for the California State University–San Marcos Head Start program between 2000 and 2004. He currently teaches in the writing program at UCSD.

ALBERTO M. OCHOA is Professor and Chair of the Department of Policy Studies in Language and Cross-Cultural Education in the College of Education at San Diego State University. Since 1975, he has worked with more than sixty school districts, providing technical assistance in the areas of language policy and assessment, bilingual instructional programs, curriculum programming, staff development, community development, organizational development and school climate, program management, and monitoring and evaluation. His research interests include public equity, school desegregation, language policy, critical pedagogy, student achievement, and parental leadership.

EDWARD M. OLIVOS is an Assistant Professor in the Division of Teacher Education at California State University–Dominguez Hills. He has published in the areas of critical literacy, parent participation, critical pedagogy, and biliteracy issues of K–12 classrooms. He taught elementary school in bicultural communities for more than ten years in San Diego.

CYNTHIA ONORE is a Professor in the Department of Curriculum and Teaching at Montclair State University in New Jersey. During her tenure as Director of the Center of Pedagogy at Montclair State, Dr. Onore created the Urban Teaching Academy, a program designed to recruit, prepare, and support teachers for New Jersey's urban schools. A former high school English teacher in Newark and New York City, Dr. Onore was founding director of teacher education at The New School University. She has also been a faculty member in English Education at The City College of New York and Teachers College. Her research interests include urban teacher education, professional development for school leadership and change, and collaboration in teacher education.

GLORIA PARK is a doctoral student in the Department of Curriculum and Instruction at the University of Maryland at College Park, with a research interest in teaching English as a second language.

PRIYA PARMAR is an Assistant Professor of Adolescence Education at Brooklyn College-CUNY. Professor Parmar's scholarly interests include critical and multiple literacies, multicultural education, youth and hip-hop culture, and other contemporary issues in the field of cultural studies in which economic, political, and social justice issues are addressed. Professor Parmar's published scholarly works include "Critical Thinking and Rap Music: The Critical Pedagogy of KRS-One" in *The Encyclopedia of Critical Thinking* (2004, Greenwood) and *Encyclopedia of Contemporary Youth Culture*, coedited with Shirley Steinberg and Birgit Richard (Greenwood Publishing, 2005). Her forthcoming book, *Rapping Against the Grain: The Pedagogy of an Urban Griot: KRS-One*, will be published by Sense Publishers in 2006.

JOHN PASCARELLA is a first-year English teacher at a magnet high school in an inner-city community in northern New Jersey and a part-time PhD candidate in Urban Education at The City University of New York Graduate Center. He is also a published writer and assistant editor of *Taboo: The Journal of Culture and Education*.

MICHAEL A. PETERS is Professor of Education at the University of Illinois at Urbana-Champaign and Adjunct Professor at the Faculty of Education, the University of Auckland (New Zealand), and School of Communication Studies at the Auckland University of Technology. He has research interests in educational theory and policy and in contemporary philosophy. He has published more than thirty books in these fields, including *Poststructuralism and Educational Research* (2004); *Critical Theory and the Human Condition* (2003); *Futures of Critical Theory* (2004); *Poststructuralism, Marxism and Neoliberalism: Between Theory and Politics* (2001); *Nietzsche's Legacy for Education: Past and Present Values*, (2001); *Wittgenstein: Philosophy, Postmodernism, Pedagogy* (1999) with James Marshall; *Poststructuralism, Politics and Education* (1996); *Curriculum in the Postmodern Condition* (2000), and *Education and the Postmodern Condition* (1995).

LINDA POST is Chairperson and Associate Professor in the Department of Curriculum and Instruction at the University of Wisconsin-Milwaukee. As such, she provides leadership in all teacher education programs and has worked extensively in the area of selection and retention of teachers for children in urban poverty. Over the past six years, Dr. Post has been in a leadership role in the development of alternative certification programs nationally. Her Metropolitan Multicultural Teacher Education Program is regarded as a model of excellence by the National Association for Alternative Certification. She has been a resource in the development and implementation of the Milwaukee Teacher Education Center. Dr. Post is currently the Director of the Urban

Network to Improve Teacher Education (UNITE) and also serves as the Great Cities Universities (GCU) team leader for the Milwaukee Partnership Academy (MPA) at UW-Milwaukee.

MARLEEN C. PUGACH is Professor of Teacher Education in the Department of Curriculum and Instruction at the University of Wisconsin-Milwaukee and Director of the Collaborative Teacher Education Program for Urban Communities. She earned her PhD at the University of Illinois at Urbana-Champaign in 1983. Her scholarly interests include the preparation of teachers for urban schools, school-university partnerships, and building collaborative relationships between the preparation of special and general education teachers. Dr. Pugach has authored and coauthored numerous articles and book chapters on special education and teacher education. She is coauthor of *Collaborative Practitioners, Collaborative Schools,* and coeditor of *Teacher Education in Transition* and *Curriculum Trends, Special Education, and Reform.* She is a member of the American Educational Research Association (AERA) and is chapter author for AERA's Panel on Research in Teacher Education. Dr. Pugach was the principal investigator of the PT3 *Technology and Urban Teaching Grant* and is currently coprincipal investigator of the Carnegie Corporation Teachers for a New Era project, both at the University of Wisconsin-Milwaukee. In February, 1998, she received the Margaret Lindsey Award from the American Association of Colleges for Teacher Education for her contributions to research in teacher education.

VICTORIA RAMIREZ is the School Programs Manager at the Museum of Fine Arts, Houston, where she manages museum and school collaborations including the development of teacher programming and curriculum materials. She is also pursuing her doctoral degree in social education at the University of Houston. She has a master of arts in museum education from the George Washington University and a bachelor's degree in art history from the University of Maryland.

DAVID REED is an Administrator of Distance Learning, Saturday School Programs, and Secondary Summer School for the Gilbert Public School District in Gilbert, Arizona. He earned his Bachelor of Science degree in Occupational Education from Southern Illinois University, a Master of Education degree in Curriculum and Instruction from Arizona State University, and is currently a PhD student in Educational Leadership and Policy Studies in the College of Education at Arizona State University.

PATRICIA RIVAS-McCRAE studied Latin American Studies at San Diego State University. Inspired by her work with Head Start, she is working toward a degree in Early Education. Upon completion of the CSU-San Marcos Head Start grant, she returned to San Diego Hospice and Palliative Care, where she worked with the HIV/AIDS Case Management Program.

ALFONSO RODRIGUEZ is In-Kind Co-Principal Investigator and Director of Training, Research, and Evaluation for Neighborhood House Association Head Start Program of San Diego County. Dr. Rodriguez has been involved with research and training in Head Start for the past 24 years.

JILL ROGERS graduated from a dual degree program at Columbia University's Law School and Teachers College in May 2004. During 2003, she was a coordinator of Legal Outreach's Summer Law Institute where she taught eighth-graders about the law and being a lawyer. Before moving to New York she became a certified teacher while at Northwestern University, and taught high school English briefly at the Latin School of Chicago. She thanks L'Tanya Evans, Daniel Rubin, Sara Schwebel, Julia Heaton, Jane Spinak, Douglas Rogers, and Nancy Rogers for their help with this book's chapter, "Tolerance with Children: A Critique of Zero Tolerance in School Discipline."

KAREL ROSE is Professor of Education and Women's Studies at the City University of New York. (CUNY) (Brooklyn College) and is a member of the doctoral faculty at the CUNY Graduate Center. She has worked with teachers at all levels in the United States and abroad, and lectures widely on women's issues. Dr. Rose's publications include books on literacy and African-American literature, and articles on feminism, writing, the arts, and teacher education. Her most recent book, the coauthored publication *Arts, Culture and Education: Artful Teaching in a Fractured Landscape*, was published in 2003. Dr. Rose's primary research interests are the arts and social issues and university faculty development. She was honored by Brooklyn College with the Teacher of Excellence Award and in 2005 received the Tow Award for Distinguished Teaching.

WOLFF-MICHAEL ROTH is Lansdowne Professor of Applied Cognitive Science at the University of Victoria, Canada. His research interests are broad and focus on knowing and learning across contexts of human social life (formal education, workplace, mundane life) and across the lifespan. Together with Ken Tobin, he has conducted extensive research on teaching in urban schools in Philadelphia. Roth has published 16 books and more than 300 articles and chapters. His recent publications include *Rethinking Scientific Literacy* (2004), *Toward an Anthropology of Graphing* (2003), *Being and Becoming in the Classroom* (2002), and *Talking Science: Language and Learning in Science Classrooms* (2005).

AMANDA M. RUDOLPH earned her PhD in Curriculum and Instruction with an emphasis in arts education from the University of Arkansas. She is currently an Assistant Professor at Stephen F. Austin State University in Nacogdoches, Texas.

ROBERT RUEDA is a Professor in the area of Educational Psychology at the Rossier School of Education at the University of Southern California. His research has focused on the sociocultural basis of learning as mediated by instruction, with a focus on reading and literacy in English learners, students in at-risk conditions, and students with mild learning handicaps. He has most recently been affiliated with two major national research centers, CREDE (Center for Excellence, Diversity, and Education at the University of California at Santa Cruz) and CIERA (Center for the Improvement of Early Reading Achievement at the University of Michigan), and serves on the Advisory Board of CRESST (Center for Research on Evaluation, Standards, and Student Testing at the University of California at Los Angeles). His most recent work has focused on how paraeducators mediate instruction and provide cultural scaffolding to English learners and on issues of reading engagement among inner-city immigrant students in a central city community. He has consulted with a variety of professional, educational, and government organizations, has spoken at a wide range of professional meetings, and has published widely in the previously mentioned areas. He served as a panel member on the National Academy of Science Report on the Overrepresentation of Minority Students in Special Education and is currently serving as a member of the National Literacy Panel (SRI International and Center for Applied Linguistics) looking at issues in early reading with English language learners.

REBECCA SÁNCHEZ is a doctoral student in the Department of Curriculum and Instruction at New Mexico State University. Her specialization area is critical pedagogy and her minor area is linguistics. Her research interests are in critical teacher development, democratic education, and critical theory. Rebecca is the coordinator of a project that aims to recruit, retain, and fund teachers returning to the university for MA-level degrees in bilingual education and as Teachers of English to Speakers of Other Languages (TESOL).

RUPAM SARAN is an elementary school teacher with the New York City Department of Education. Ms. Saran is a migrant from India and a doctoral student at The Graduate Center, City University of New York. Her research is on Asian-Indian students and

the complexities of positive stereotyping. She is on the math committee for professional development of early childhood teachers. Rupam Saran is a recipient of the
CUNY Writing Fellowship dissertation award for the 2005–06 academic year.

ROSLYN ABT SCHINDLER is Associate Professor and deputized Chair in the Department of Interdisciplinary Studies in the College of Liberal Arts and Sciences at Wayne
State University (Detroit, Michigan). She publishes in the fields of interdisciplinary
studies, adult learning, and Holocaust Studies, and is past president of the Association
for Integrative Studies. She is coeditor, with Joachim Dyck, Martin Herman, and Marvin
Schindler, of the two-volume *Festschrift, University Governance and Humanistic Scholarship:
Studies in Honor of Diether Haenicke* (2002).

KENT SEIDEL is Assistant Professor with the Educational Administration and Urban
Education Leadership graduate programs at the University of Cincinnati (Ohio) and
serves as Executive Director for the Alliance for Curriculum Reform, a collaborative
project of more than 20 national education organizations. He holds a PhD in Education Research and Theatre Education. Dr. Seidel was editor and contributing author
for *Assessing Student Learning: A Practical Guide* (2000). He has also written on program
evaluation and student assessment for the National Association of Secondary School
Principals and the Association for Supervision and Curriculum Development, and has
a book in publication on the use of student achievement data in school improvement.
He has written on performing arts research for the *New Handbook of Research on Music
Teaching & Learning* and contributed articles to *Arts Education Policy Review* and the
national journal *Teaching Theatre*. Dr. Seidel has consulted on development of arts education standards and assessments for six states and several urban districts, as well as
numerous schools and community arts organizations. He was one of 25 National
Steering Committee members overseeing the development of the National Assessment of Educational Progress exams for the arts and one of six authors of the *National
Standards for Arts Education* in theatre.

JUDITH J. SLATER is Professor of Education at Florida International University
where she teaches courses in curriculum theory, evaluation, and organizational culture. She is the author of Anatomy of a Collaboration and Acts of Alignment, and is
coeditor of The Freirean Legacy: Educating for Social Justice, Pedagogy of Place and
the forthcoming Teen Life in Asia.

ANTHONY TADDUNI served as an AmeriCorps member in Atlanta Public Schools
for two years, where he trained inner-city students in peer mediation and engaged
students in enrichment programming focusing on human rights, diversity, leadership,
and community service. He is a member of the Atlanta chapter of the National Coalition
Building Institute (NCBI). Anthony also serves on the steering committee for Southern
Truth and Reconciliation (STAR), a nonprofit agency that aims to aid communities in
addressing histories of racial and ethnic violence through community education and
community-building events. He is a graduate of Emory University.

MONICA TAYLOR is currently an Assistant Professor in the Department of Curriculum and Teaching in the College of Education and Human Services at Montclair State
University in Montclair, New Jersey. She received her doctorate at the University of
Arizona in Language, Reading, and Culture. Her research interests include autobiography as a reflective tool for teachers, self study, feminist pedagogy, teaching for social
justice, new literacies and adolescent culture, and professional development school
partnerships.

DEIDRE ANN TYLER is an Associate Professor of Sociology at Salt Lake Community
College and an Adjunct Assistant Professor of Sociology at the University of Utah. Her

areas of interest include education, black families, and gender. She is a motivational speaker and the author of *A Woman's Guide to Setting Boundaries.*

LYNNE A. WEIKART entered academia as an Associate Professor of Public Administration at Baruch College School of Public Affairs after a dintinguished career in New York State and City government. Specializing in urban budgeting and finance, Dr. Weikart has delivered lectures and presentations on urban issues at New York's Nonprofit Connection, Progressive Urban Agenda for the New Millennium, and International Center for Advanced Studies and at numerous conferences. Dr. Weikart was also Executive Director of City Project, a nonprofit fiscal think tank that advocates equity and social justice in the allocation of government resources. She is the author of several articles on urban budgeting and finance issues.

LOIS WEIS is Distinguished Professor of Sociology of Education at the University at Buffalo, State University of New York. She is author or coauthor of numerous books pertaining to race, social class, gender, and schooling in the United States. Her most recent books include *Class Reunion: The Remaking of an American White Working Middle Class* (Routledge, 2004); *Working Method: Research and Social Justice* (with Michelle Fine, Routledge, 2004); *Silenced Voices and Extraordinary Conversations: Re-Imagining Schools* (Teachers College Press, 2003), and *Beyond Black and White: New Faces and Voices in U.S. Schools* (State University of New York Press, 1997, with Maxine Seller). Her newest collection, *Beyond Silenced Voices: Class, Race, and Gender in United States Schools,* was released by SUNY Press in 2005. Dr. Weis sits on numerous editorial boards and is editor of the *Power, Social Identity, and Education* book series with SUNY Press.

JEN WEISS is a doctoral candidate in Urban Education at the City University of New York Graduate Center. She is Founder of Urban Word NYC, an afterschool program for teenagers based in New York City, and the coauthor of *Brave New Voices: Teaching Spoken Word Poetry* (2001, Heinemann). Recipient of the Graduate Center Dissertation Research Grant (2006–2007), she researches urban youth, literacy, and surveillance.

GREG WIGGAN is an Assistant Professor of Sociology at Salem College in North Carolina. His research interests include student achievement and educational policy studies in urban communities or in an urban sociological context. He is also interested in racial and ethnic relations and the racialization of the social class system. An additional principal concern is imperialism and globalization in developing countries. He is interested in the role of the World Trade Organization, the International Monetary Fund, and the World Bank in creating public policies in developing countries.

A. DEE WILLIAMS is a doctoral student in the Department of Curriculum and Instruction at the University of Maryland at College Park, with a research interest in urban teacher education.